The Impact of the Haitian Revolution
in the Atlantic World

THE CAROLINA LOWCOUNTRY AND THE ATLANTIC WORLD
Sponsored by the Lowcountry and
Atlantic Studies Program of the College of Charleston

Money, Trade, and Power
Edited by Jack P. Greene, Rosemary Brana-Shute, and Randy J. Sparks

The Impact of the Haitian Revolution in the Atlantic World
Edited by David P. Geggus

The Impact of the
HAITIAN REVOLUTION
in the Atlantic World

EDITED BY
DAVID P. GEGGUS

UNIVERSITY OF SOUTH CAROLINA PRESS

© 2001 University of South Carolina

Published in Columbia, South Carolina, by the
University of South Carolina Press

Manufactured in the United States of America

05   04   03   5   4   3   2

Library of Congress Cataloging-in-Publication Data

The impact of the Haitian Revolution in the Atlantic world / edited by
David P. Geggus.
    p. cm. — (The Carolina lowcountry and the Atlantic world)
    Includes bibliographical references and index.
    ISBN 1-57003-416-8 (cloth : alk. paper)
    1. Haiti—History—Revolution, 1791-1804—Influence. 2. France—
History—Revolution, 1789-1799—Influence. 3. America—History—
19th century. 4. Political culture—History—19th century. 5. Antislavery
movements—History—19th century. 6. Slave insurrections—History—
19th century. 7. Political refugees—United States—History—19th century.
8. Political refugees—Haiti—History—19th century. 9. America—Race
relations. I. Geggus, David Patrick. II. Series.
F1923 .I53 2001
973.5—dc21   2001003349

CONTENTS

PART FOUR: REFUGEES

TABLES, FIGURES, AND MAPS

PREFACE

Compared to the Russian or Chinese Revolution, or the French Revolution with which it was intertwined, the revolution that two hundred years ago created Haiti was a small-scale affair. Played out in a population of some 600,000 people, it was confined to an area of less than twelve thousand square miles, a speck of land compared to the swathes of North and South America freed from colonial rule in the preceding and succeeding decades. Despite these demographic and geographic limitations, the Haitian, or Saint-Domingue, Revolution of 1789–1804 has several major claims to a prominent place in world history.

The French colony of Saint-Domingue was a powerhouse of the Atlantic economy, and had been the leading exporter of tropical staple crops for most of the eighteenth century. The slave uprising that began in August 1791 and transformed the immensely wealthy colony was probably the largest and most dramatically successful one there has ever been. It produced the world's first examples of wholesale emancipation in a major slaveowning society (1793), and of full racial equality in an American colony (1792).[1] Of all American struggles for colonial independence it surely involved the greatest degree of mass mobilization, and brought the greatest degree of social and economic change. Twelve years of desolating warfare—much of it guerrilla warfare, a decade before the term was coined—left the most productive colony of the day in ruins, its ruling class entirely eliminated. Haiti became Latin America's first independent country, the first modern state in the Tropics.[2]

On 1 January 1804, the former slave Jean-Jacques Dessalines declared Saint-Domingue independent and gave it the aboriginal Amerindian name of "Haiti" to emphasize the break with Europe and anchor the new state to the American past. Having defeated armies of the three main colonial powers, France, Spain, and Britain, the former slaves and free persons of color turned to making laws for themselves and building a state apparatus. A symbol of black freedom and anti-imperialism, Haiti's first constitution defiantly prohibited landownership by whites and soon was amended to offer citizenship to anyone of African or Indian descent who took up residence in the country.[3] All this occurred in a world dominated by Europeans, where slavery and the slave trade were at their apogee, and where ideas about racial hierarchy were gaining in legitimacy.

It is easy to list the reasons why the Haitian Revolution is important but it is much more difficult to define how it affected the wider world. To date there has been no attempt to fully explore its multifarious and complex influence. Specialist studies have shed light on different aspects of Haiti's impact, but without achieving any sort of scholarly consensus. Two general works of fairly limited scope have addressed its impact on, respectively, Hispanic America and the United States.[4] Yves Bénot and Robin Blackburn have weighed its contribution to the contemporaneous revolution in France. José Luciano Franco and, more recently, the essays in Gaspar and Geggus, *A Turbulent Time* (1997) have gone some way in charting the interaction between the two revolutions in the Greater Caribbean region.[5] This volume is intended to continue that enterprise focusing particularly on the repercussions of the black revolution in different parts of the Atlantic world.

From the beginning of the great slave uprising in Saint-Domingue's northern plain, the black insurgents seem to have felt they were acting on a world stage. "The world has groaned at our fate," they told Saint-Domingue's governor in the first month of the insurrection.[6] Two years later, the slave leader Georges Biassou looked back to those days as "a period that will be forever memorable among the great deeds of the universe." He informed the governor of Spanish Santo Domingo, "All Europe and the entire world have their eyes turned toward us, watching what course of action we are going to take."[7] And finally, at the revolution's end in 1804, Louis Boisrond-Tonnerre, author of the declaration of independence, finished his memoirs by addressing the "slaves of all countries" with an incendiary message that encapsulated the Haitian experience: "you will learn from this great man [Dessalines] that mankind by its nature carries freedom in its heart and the keys to freedom in its hands."[8]

To assess the international repercussions of this tremendous upheaval, it is helpful to consider five or six broad questions. In what ways did the enslaved, free colored, and white sectors of New World society respond to news of the Haitian Revolution? How did the governments of the colonial powers react? How important was the revolution in stimulating resistance among slaves and free people of color, either by example or by direct intervention? What economic and cultural impact did migrants from revolutionary Saint-Domingue have in the different parts of the Americas they settled? And was the revolution's overall impact on the antislavery movement, and on the debate about race, positive or negative?

News of the revolution spread widely and rapidly. Within one month of the 1791 uprising, slaves in Jamaica were singing songs about it.[9] Within a few years, slaveowners from Virginia and Louisiana to Cuba and Brazil were complaining of a new "insolence" on the part of their slaves, which they often attributed to awareness of the successful black revolution.[10] Late in 1795, the governor of Cuba lamented that the name of the revolt's leader, Jean-François, "resounded in the ears of the populace like an invincible hero and savior of the slaves." In 1800, when the ex-slave Toussaint Louverture became the unchallenged ruler of Saint-Domingue, slaves sang on the streets of Kingston, "Black, white, brown, all the same."[11] The year after Haitian independence, slaves in Trinidad parodied the Catholic mass: "The bread we eat is white man's flesh. The wine we drink is white man's blood. Remember St. Domingo."[12] Even in distant Rio de Janeiro some free black and mulatto militiamen were found in 1805 to be wearing round their necks medallion portraits of the emperor Dessalines, who had been crowned only months before.[13]

A more subtle example comes from long after the revolution, when in 1836 Cuban officials in Bayamo discovered that the local Carabalí *cabildo* (or Biafran associa-tion) had replaced the royal crown on its flag, symbolic of the Spanish monarchy, with a plumed cocked-hat, representative of Haitian heads of state.[14] Some doubts remain as to how much news penetrated rural regions. But the basic facts of the Haitian Revolution appear to have been rapidly disseminated along maritime trade routes by sailors, refugees, and proselytizing privateers of diverse origins.[15]

Even if the revolution was not quite, in my view, an "unthinkable event," as Rolph Trouillot has called it, nothing like it had happened before.[16] In an age of tumultuous events, the deeds of Saint-Domingue's slaves and former slaves seized international attention. This was true, as Karin Schüller (chapter 4) shows, even in countries so little connected with the Caribbean as the German states. Though lacking colonial linkages, Germans wanted to read about the black revolution, not only because of their interest in race and slavery, but also because of its relevance to their own political concerns.[17] For the colonial powers and their slaveowning sub-jects, interests were far more direct; fear and greed, as David Davis puts it (chapter 1), were dominant reactions. When news of the 1791 slave revolt reached England, *The Times* suggested it brought a profitable opportunity for British intervention, although stocks on the London exchange fell immediately by 1 percent.[18] More concerned with aggrandizement than defense, Britain and Spain soon tried to seize the strife-torn colony from France, but all three imperial powers suffered costly and humiliating defeats at the hands of the black population. These took the lives of more than seventy thousand European soldiers and seamen. The policy of Britain, Spain and the United States toward the revolution fluctuated according to each government's relations with France. Although they sought at certain moments to crush the black insurgents, all three states proved willing to assist them commercially or militarily, when they considered France a greater threat. None favored the emergence of an independent black state but, with the exception of the Jeffersonian embargo of 1806–1810, none cut off trade relations.[19]

For slaveowners, the Haitian Revolution must have seemed like the realiza-tion of their worst nightmare. Yet for many it was also an opportunity to profit from the high prices for tropical staples caused by the destruction in Saint-Domingue. As the revolution went from strength to strength, planters across the Americas worried how their slaves would react. On occasion, they feared direct intervention from Haiti, or voiced concern that their own society might become "another St. Domingo." Opinions diverged as to how much to assist the French colony, whether to legislate improved treatment of slaves, or to restrict the inflow of enslaved Africans. Even in normal times, a mixture of paranoia, complacency, and prudent calculation seems to have been typical of slaveowning classes. Olwyn Blouet (chapter 5) charts the reactions of Bryan Edwards, spokesman of the Jamaican plantocracy, who witnessed firsthand the early days of the slave insurrec-tion. His eagerness to help his French rivals was not shared by all Jamaican planters, and did not extend to supporting Britain's attempted occupation of Saint-Domingue, which gave Domingan colonists access to the British market. Though progressive by planter standards, Edwards campaigned to keep the slave trade open.

In Cuba and Puerto Rico, where the slave population remained relatively small, the elite still had the choice whether to develop a full-fledged plantation complex with its attendant dangers. In chapter 6, Juan González Mendoza examines the hesitations of the Puerto Rican elite at a critical conjuncture, as it debated the attractions of the world market and the risks of expanding slave-based agriculture. Despite such fears, and although restrictions on immigration from French colonies were widespread, only Spanish Louisiana suspended the import of slaves from Africa as a security measure, and for only a few years.[20] During the Haitian Revolution the slave trade to the Spanish West Indies took off at an unprecedented rate, while in the United States and much of the British Caribbean it reached an all-time peak.

As the slave economy of the United States expanded during the 1790s, the idealism of the American Revolutionary period faded, and racial divisions sharpened. Simon Newman (chapter 7) argues that a growing conservatism in American political culture can be linked to the Haitian Revolution. He emphasizes how quickly not just Federalists but certain Republicans turned against the French Revolution, especially because of its impact on Saint-Domingue. Events in Saint-Domingue redefined the meaning of revolution and encouraged Jeffersonians to substitute in their rhetoric "patriotism" for "the rights of man." Support for antislavery, as for the black revolution, became ironically confined to the conservative Federalists, and politics became increasingly sectional. It is in the context of these political divisions that Robert Alderson (chapter 8) sets the rumors of a widespread slave conspiracy that troubled Virginians and South Carolinians in 1793. The burning of Cap-Français that summer, which precipitated the abolition of slavery in Saint-Domingue by republican officials, sent perhaps ten thousand refugees including slaves to the United States and increased conservative opposition to the French Revolution. Alderson pursues two hypotheses: that the rumors either reflected a genuine multiracial conspiracy or that they were fabricated by Domingan refugees and their Federalist allies.

The frequency of slave revolts and conspiracies in the Americas reached a peak in the 1790s and the largest insurrections all occurred during the forty years following the 1791 uprising. There were many causal influences at work in the rebellions of the period, both local and external, but among them historians have identified several types of connection to the Haitian Revolution. Transplanted, so-called "French" slaves or free coloreds show up in numerous rebellions in English, Dutch-, and Spanish-speaking territories from the 1790s to 1820s and beyond. In Louisiana in 1811, Charles Deslondes from Saint-Domingue led the largest slave revolt in North American history. Francophone slaves also led a large rebellion on Curaçao in 1795, along with a local slave who took the name of Domingan revolutionary André Rigaud. The leader of Venezuela's bloody Coro rebellion, who the same year demanded "the law of the French," was a local sharecropper who had earlier visited Saint-Domingue.[21] The example of Haiti was more explicitly invoked by slave conspirators in Barbados in 1816 who planned "to set fire . . . the way they did in St. Domingo." Denmark Vesey, who had briefly lived in Saint-Domingue, went even further when, in 1822, he promised his followers the help of Haitian soldiers once they had taken over the city of Charleston. It is also probable

Vesey planned to escape to the black republic, which was then advertising for black immigrants in U.S. newspapers.[22]

Laurent Dubois (chapter 9) has uncovered further evidence of resistance inspired by events in Saint-Domingue on Guadeloupe during the revolutionary regime of 1794–1802. Since Guadeloupe was the only other French colony where slavery was successfully abolished, these cases are unusual since they involve former slaves under a forced labor regime and the black army that was meant both to guarantee their freedom and compel their obedience. With assistance from Guadeloupe, multi-class uprisings ravaged much of the Windward Islands in the mid-1790s. Though these insurgencies were more directly the product of French Revolutionary influence, the struggle in Saint-Domingue that revolutionized France's colonial policy can be claimed as their root cause. However, the most striking example of Haiti's influence on slave resistance is the 1812 conspiracy organized in Havana by José Antonio Aponte. As Matt Childs shows in chapter 10, Aponte was, like Denmark Vesey, a free black carpenter who also promised his followers assistance from Haiti. Besides seeking out the support of visiting Haitians who had fought in the revolution, he inspired recruits using images of Toussaint Louverture, Jean-Jacques Dessalines, and Henry Christophe, who had recently been crowned king of Haiti.

The Haitian help promised by Vesey and Aponte, and later in Cuba's Escalera conspiracy in 1843, was almost certainly a fiction. Fear of a retaliatory maritime blockade prevented Haitian heads of state from seeking to export slave insurrection in the manner of Guadeloupe's republican regime in the mid-1790s. However, black and mixed-race privateers from Saint-Domingue did organize a revolutionary plot in Maracaibo, Venezuela, in 1799. Aline Helg (chapter 11) sheds light on this little-known conspiracy and another that occurred shortly before in Cartagena, involving Francophone slaves and local inhabitants. She then analyzes why the Caribbean coast of New Granada proved inhospitable to local emulation of the Haitian Revolution. Marixa Lasso (chapter 12) takes the study of Cartagena province into the early national period in search of the political culture of the lower classes that fought in the wars of independence. After noting the active engagement of Haitian sailors and soldiers in the short-lived Republic of Cartagena, she examines several incidents of racial conflict in which images of Haiti were invoked by people of color. These hint at the importance of the Haitian Revolution in shaping a popular republicanism among people of African descent that until recently historians have neglected. In the nineteenth century, Haitian independence day would become a celebration among blacks in certain U.S. cities.[23] Afro-Jamaicans of the post-emancipation era would occasionally suggest their own island needed a Haitian-style revolution to end "injustice and oppression"; and in Cuba in the 1890s small-town residents were known to sing the praises of Haiti and the Dominican Republic as countries where "citizens were respected" and which had "defeated the invincible."[24]

The Haitian Revolution's economic impact was exerted in two ways. It created a dramatic shortfall in the world supply of tropical products, and a diaspora of colonists and slaves whose skills and capital stimulated production elsewhere in the Americas. Saint-Domingue in the 1780s had been the world's main importer of slave labor and the major producer of sugar and coffee. Because the revolution damaged the colony's sugar estates far more than its coffee plantations, its international impact was most pronounced in the market for sugar, whose price skyrocketed and remained high through the 1790s. Spurred by this opportunity, as well as by population growth and urbanization in the Atlantic world, new frontiers opened in the Spanish islands, Louisiana, and the south Caribbean, while production revived in Jamaica and Brazil.[25] Employed as refiners, boilermen, and millwrights, Domingan refugees made important contributions in Cuba and Louisiana, but their impact was most visible in coffee cultivation. Almost a French monopoly before the revolution, coffee was a crop refugees with few resources could grow. French pioneer activity in the decade after 1791 helped increase output eleven-fold in the mountains of Jamaica. In Cuba's Oriente province, Domingan migrants established more than 200 coffee farms by 1810. [26]

Whites and blacks driven from Saint-Domingue also had a cultural impact of varying longevity. In Jamaica and the eastern seaboard of the United States, they reinforced existing Catholic communities, impressing their hosts as cultivated and worldly, but generally they moved on or were absorbed within a generation or two.[27] In Trinidad, they were far fewer but helped strengthen the island's French and creole cultures that lasted through the nineteenth century. It remains unclear to what extent Domingan refugees, or later migrants, are responsible for the Gallic and French creole traces that have persisted in the culture (festivals, religion, dance) of eastern Cuba.[28] However, the ten thousand who were deported from there to New Orleans in 1809 obviously did play a major role in shaping Louisiana's francophone cultures, which thrived until the Civil War.[29]

Two-thirds of those deportees were people of color, equally divided between slave and free, whereas people of African descent made up about one-tenth of the five thousand or so Domingans who arrived in Philadelphia. The experiences of the latter group are examined in chapter 13 by Susan Branson and Leslie Patrick. Moving beyond popular images of the colored courtesan, they explore the hardships encountered by former slaves, especially women, who, though freed in accordance with Pennsylvania's manumission law, were condemned to labor as indentured servants. Excluded from the charity offered to white refugees, migrants of African descent appear to have been further ignored by the local black community, notwithstanding rare cases of upward mobility and integration. Paul Lachance's comprehensive overview of the Haitian Revolution's repercussions in Louisiana (chapter 14) shows how the massive influx of 1809–1810 altered New Orleans's population structure and enracinated there the three-tier pattern of race relations typical of the Caribbean. He also points to the revolution's central role in transferring the Louisiana Territory from French to United States rule, as well as the part played by Domingan refugees in the battle of New Orleans and in strengthening the state's commitment to slavery in the nineteenth century. Chapter 15 focuses on the case of a famous family of refugees that settled in South Carolina. It examines their experience of exile, and contrasts memories of their role in the revolution and of the world it destroyed that were kept alive through the nineteenth century in Haiti and South Carolina, among the family's white and black descendants, and in the historiography of the revolution.

The Haitian Revolution occurred at a time when the antislavery movement, libertarian ideology, and humanitarianism were gaining ground but when scientific enquiry was undermining concepts of the oneness of mankind, so preparing the way for the "scientific racism" of the mid-nineteenth century. The revolution's overall impact on ideas about race and abolition remains in dispute, because it fueled both sides of both debates. While the spectacle of a people rising from slavery inspired some commentators, a selective reading of the revolution's numerous atrocities provided easy propaganda to their opponents. The sharply divergent death rates of white and black soldiers in the tropics probably also encouraged people to think in terms of immutable racial differences.[30] Seymour Drescher has suggested that scientific racism developed earlier in France than in England, because of the positive influence of abolitionism in Britain, and the negative response in France to the Haitian Revolution.[31] Karin Schüller's survey of opinion in Germany (chapter 4), which had no abolition movement but seems to have resembled the British case, makes the revolution's negative impact on French ideas look even stronger.

In the 1790s, however, the epic struggle for Saint-Domingue evidently caused the temporary triumph of abolitionism in France, while it helped set back the movement in Britain. The revolution's influence on antislavery thereafter is more controversial. At the Cortes of Cádiz in 1811, and more generally in the Hispanic world, the dangers of the Haitian example were commonly cited as reasons both to end the slave trade and not to end slavery.[32] The refuge and assistance President Pétion provided to Simón Bolívar in 1816 made a vital contribution to the winning of national independence in northern South America, and the payment Pétion stipulated was slavery's abolition in the liberated regions. Some scholars suggest that Bolívar's belated and piecemeal emancipation owed less to Haiti than to the military and political pressures he faced in Venezuela, though if so, it was still Pétion's help that enabled Bolívar's return.[33]

Robin Blackburn has stressed the antislavery struggle's cumulative character and the Haitian Revolution's chronological primacy as the first major breakthrough in that struggle. Besides enhancing metropolitan opinion of blacks, and inspiring abolitionists, the revolution contributed to a progressive discrediting of slaveowners and politicians' weariness with defending slavery.[34] Some consider the Haitian Revolution's role in weakening French commercial competition a prerequisite of British politicians' finally responding to abolitionist pressure. Seymour Drescher, on the other hand, argues that Haiti's significance was more symbolic than substantive; providing propaganda to both pro- and antislavery forces, it contributed unequivocally to neither. He asserts there is no evidence it was a decisive issue in the key debates in the British parliament; fear of "another Haiti" did not translate into abolitionist action.[35] David Brion Davis adopts a position intermediate between these two. He has pointed to the revolution's contribution to tarnishing the slaveowners' image and to weakening Franco-British rivalry, but also to the revolution's negative effects on the antislavery movement.[36] Doubtful about Haiti's impact on the decisions that ended the British slave trade, he argues (chapter 1) for a Haitian influence on the closing of the United States slave trade and on British action in 1797 and 1805 to limit slavery's expansion in Trinidad and the Guianas.

He further notes how ex-slave and abolitionist Frederick Douglass eagerly sought out news of Haiti as a young man and brandished it as a symbol in old age, but made little reference to the country in his antislavery campaigns. These three pre-eminent authorities on slave emancipation, Davis, Drescher, and Blackburn, open this volume with concise and contrasting assessments of the Haitian Revolution's international impact.

From Philadelphia to Rio de Janeiro, from the imagination of poets to the world commodity markets, the violent birth of Haiti caused a variety of repercussions. Accounts of apocalyptic destruction and of a new world in the making were a source of alarm and inspiration for slaves, slaveowners, and many others. Great power politics, slave resistance, movements of migration, and attitudes to race and the future of slavery were all affected. The essays that follow explore a diverse range of topics that shed light on these and other issues, taking us further toward a full understanding of the Haitian Revolution's place in world history.

NOTES

1. The French *Code Noir* of 1685 did not recognize any distinctions between free persons based on phenotype, but it was not enforced in the Caribbean and soon was contradicted by local legislation. The French Legislative Assembly voted an end to white supremacy in the colonies on 28 Mar. 1792 to encourage free men of color in Saint-Domingue to help suppress the slave uprising that began the preceding August.

2. The most comprehensive general works on the subject remain Thomas Madiou, *Histoire d'Haiti,* 3 vols. (Port-au-Prince: J. Courtois, 1847–1848), vols. 1–2; Beaubrun Ardouin, *Études sur l'histoire d'Haïti* (Port-au-Prince: Dalencour, 1958 [1853]), vols. 1–6; and Horace Pauléus Sannon, *Histoire de Toussaint-Louverture,* 3 vols. (Port-au-Prince: A.A. Héraux, 1920–33). Still the most exciting introduction is the Marxist classic by C. L. R. James, *The Black Jacobins: Toussaint L'Ouverture and the San Domingo Revolution* (New York: Vintage Books, 1963 [1938]). The outstanding study written from a right-wing perspective is Pierre Pluchon, *Toussaint Louverture: un révolutionnaire noir d'Ancien Régime* (Paris: Fayard, 1989).

3. David Nicholls, *From Dessalines to Duvalier* (Cambridge: Cambridge University Press, 1979); David Geggus, "The Naming of Haiti," *New West-Indian Guide* 71 (1997): 43–68.

4. Eleázar Córdova-Bello, *La independencia de Haití y su influencia en Hispanoamérica* (Caracas: Instituto Panamericano de la Geografía y Historia, 1967); Alfred Hunt, *Haiti's Influence on Antebellum America: Slumbering Volcano in the Caribbean* (Baton Rouge: Louisiana University Press, 1988).

5. Yves Bénot, *La Révolution française et la fin des colonies* (Paris: La Découverte, 1988); Robin Blackburn, *The Overthrow of Colonial Slavery* (London: Verso, 1988); José Luciano Franco, *La batalla por el dominio del Caribe y el Golfo de México,* 3 vols. (Havana: Instituto de Historia, 1965), vol. 2; David Barry Gaspar, David Patrick Geggus, eds., *A Turbulent Time: The French Revolution and the Greater Caribbean* (Bloomington: Indiana University Press, 1997).

6. Pamphile de Lacroix, *Mémoires pour servir à l'histoire de la Révolution de Saint-Domingue,* 2 vols. (Paris: Pillet, 1819–20), 1: 102.

7. Biassou to García, 24 Aug. 1793, in García to Acuña, 23 Nov. 1793, Archivo General de Simancas, Guerra Moderna, 7157. Another copy exists in Audiencia de Santo Domingo 956, Archivo General de Indias, Seville.

8. Louis Félix Boisrond-Tonnerre, *Mémoires pour servir à l'histoire d'Haïti* (Port-au-Prince: Editions des Antilles, 1991 [1804]), 119.

9. David Patrick Geggus, *Slavery, War and Revolution: The British Occupation of Saint Domingue, 1793–1798* (Oxford: Clarendon Press, 1982), 90.

10. Douglas R. Egerton, "The Tricolor in Black and White: The French Revolution in Gabriel's Virginia," in *Slavery in the Caribbean Francophone World: Distant Voices, Forgotten Acts, Forged Identities,* ed. Doris Y. Kadish (Athens, Ga.: University of Georgia Press, 2000), 96; David Geggus, "The French and Haitian Revolutions and Resistance to Slavery in the Americas," *Revue Française d'Histoire d'Outre-Mer* 282–83 (1989): 107–124, and "The Influence of the Haitian Revolution on Blacks in Latin America and the Caribbean," forthcoming in *Blacks and National Identity in Nineteenth-Century Latin America,* ed. Nancy Naro (London: University of London).

11. Las Casas to Príncipe de la Paz, 16 Dec. 95, Archivo General de Indias, Seville, Estado 5, exp.176; Michael Craton, James Walvin, David Wright, eds., *Slavery, Abolition and Emancipation: Black Slaves and the British Empire* (London: Longman, 1976), 138.

12. Michael Craton, *Testing the Chains: Resistance to Slavery in the British West Indies* (Ithaca, N.Y.: Cornell University Press, 1982), 236.

13. Luiz Mott, "A revolução dos negros do Haiti e o Brasil," *Mensario do Arquivo Nacional* (Rio de Janeiro) 13 (1982): 3–10. These men are, apparently wrongly, described as slaves in João José Reis, *Slave Rebellion in Brazil: The Muslim Uprising of 1835 in Bahia* (Baltimore: Johns Hopkins University Press, 1993), 48.

14. José Luciano Franco, *Ensayos históricos* (Havana: Editorial de Ciencias Sociales, 1974), 185.

15. Julius S. Scott III, "The Common Wind: Currents of Afro-American Communication in the Era of the Haitian Revolution" (Ph.D. dissertation, Duke University, 1986).

16. Michel-Rolph Trouillot, *Silencing the Past: Power and the Production of History* (Boston: Beacon, 1995), 70–107. Many people since the 1770s had predicted or warned of a major upheaval in the colony—rather more, I suspect, than ever predicted the coming of the French Revolution. If they did not imagine the emergence of a modern black state, the same might be said of the abolition of the French aristocracy and monarchy, which was the more remarkable in view of the popularity of egalitarian and republican ideas in the 1780s.

17. Karin Schüller, *Die deutsche Rezeption haitianischer Geschichte in der ersten Hälfte des 19. Jahrhunderts* (Cologne: Böhlau,1992).

18. David Geggus, "British Opinion and the Haitian Revolution, 1791–1805," in *Slavery and British Society, 1776–1848,* ed. James Walvin (London: Macmillan, 1982), 123–24.

19. David Geggus, "The Great Powers and the Haitian Revolution," in *Tordesillas y sus consecuencias,* ed. Bernd Schröter, Karin Schüller (Madrid: Iberoamericana, 1995), 113–25. Certain members of the John Adams administration favored independence but Adams maintained neutrality on the question. Ironically, though Jefferson was far more hostile to the black revolution, he was the only president (briefly, in October 1801) to propose recognizing independence. See Rayford Logan, *The Diplomatic Relations of the United States with Haiti, 1776–1891* (Chapel Hill: University of North Carolina Press, 1941), 85–89, 125.

20. Beginning in 1810, revolutionaries in South America abolished the slave trade after it was already defunct.

21. Above, note 10; David Geggus, "Slavery, War, and Revolution in the Greater Caribbean, 1789–1815," in Gaspar and Geggus, eds., *Turbulent Time,* 5–18.

22. Michael Craton, *Testing the Chains: Resistance to Slavery in the British West Indies* (Ithaca, N.Y.: Cornell University Press, 1982), 231; Edward A. Peterson, ed., *Designs Against Charleston: The Trial Record of the Denmark Vesey Slave Conspiracy of 1822* (Chapel Hill: University of North Carolina Press, 1999), 118.

23. David Brion Davis, *Revolutions: Reflections on American Equality and Foreign Liberations* (Cambridge: Harvard University Press, 1990), 53.

24. Mimi B. Sheller, "Democracy After Slavery: Black Publics and Peasant Rebellion in Postemancipation Haiti and Jamaica" (Ph.D. diss., New School of Social Research, 1996), 59–60; Ada Ferrer, *Insurgent Cuba: Race, Nation, and Revolution, 1868–1898* (Chapel Hill: University of North Carolina Press, 1999), 107.

25. David Eltis, *Economic Growth and the Ending of the Transatlantic Slave Trade* (New York: Oxford University Press, 1987), 37–39.

26. Patrick Bryan, "Emigrés, conflict and reconciliation: The French emigrés in 19th century Jamaica," *Jamaica Journal* 7 (1973): 13–19; Orlando Patterson, *The Sociology of Slavery* (London: MacGibbon & Kee, 1967), appendix 3; Alain Yacou, "Esclaves et libres français à Cuba au lendemain de la Révolution de Saint-Domingue," *Jahrbuch für Geschichte von Staat, Wirtschaft und Gesellschaft Lateinamerikas* 28 (1991): 163–97.

27. Jacques de Cauna, "La diaspora des colons de Saint-Domingue et le monde créole: le cas de la Jamaïque, *Revue Francaise d'Histoire d'Outre-Mer* 81 (1994): 333–59; Winston Babb, "French Refugees from Saint Domingue to the Southern United States: 1790–1810" (Ph.D. diss., University of Virginia, 1954); Frances Childs, *French Refugee Life in the United States, 1790–1800* (Baltimore: Johns Hopkins University Press, 1940).

28. Jean Lamore, ed., *Les Français dans l'Oriente cubain* (Bordeaux: Maison des Pays Ibériques, 1993); Judith Bettelheim, ed., *Cuban Festivals: An Illustrated Anthology* (New York: Garland, 1993); Carlos Padrón, *Franceses en el suroriente de Cuba* (Havana: Ediciones Unión, 1997).

29. Hunt, *Haiti's Influence,* ch.2; Paul Lachance, "The Formation of a Three-Caste Society: Evidence From Wills in Antebellum New Orleans," *Social Science History* 18 (1994): 211–42.

30. Geggus, *Slavery, War and Revolution,* 287; Geggus, "British Opinion," 127–30, 137–38, 142–45.

31. Seymour Drescher "The Ending of the Slave Trade and Evolution of European Scientific Racism," *Social Science History* 14 (1990): 415–50. On Germany, see above, note 17.

32. Hubert H.S. Aimes, *The History of Slavery in Cuba, 1511–1868* (New York: Octagon Books, 1967 [1907]), 64, 73.

33. Paul Verna, *Petión y Bolívar: Cuarenta años de relaciones haitiano-venezolanas* (Caracas: 1969), 87–298; John Lombardi, *The Decline and Abolition of Negro Slavery in Venezuela, 1820–1854* (Westport, Conn.: Greenwood, 1961), 13, 41.

34. Blackburn, *Overthrow,* 526–29.

35. Seymour Drescher, *Capitalism and Antislavery* (New York: Oxford University Press, 1987), 96–99, 105–6.

36. David Brion Davis, *The Problem of Slavery in the Age of Revolution, 1770–1823* (Ithaca, N.Y.: Cornell University Press, 1975), 81, 117, 329, 440.

ACKNOWLEDGMENTS

All but two of the following essays were presented at a conference held in October 1998 at the College of Charleston under the auspices of the Carolina Lowcountry and Atlantic Studies Program directed by Jack Greene. Organized by Rosemary Brana Shute, Randy Sparks, and myself, the conference received major funding from the National Endowment for the Humanities, which is gratefully acknowledged. Other participants included Edward Cox, Stan Deaton, Sylvia Frey, Jane Landers, Lester Langley, Karen Racine, James Sidbury, and James Walvin. Jim Sloan of the University of Florida Geography Department drew the maps. To all who collaborated in the project, I wish to express my gratitude for making it such a rewarding and enjoyable experience.

Parts of the preface and epilogue are drawn from my 1999 Elsa Goveia Memorial Lecture, "International Repercussions of the Haitian Revolution," delivered at the University of the West Indies, Jamaica, and published by the university's Department of History.

Part One

Overview

Chapter 1

Impact of the French and Haitian Revolutions

DAVID BRION DAVIS

ON 2 JANUARY 1893 FREDERICK DOUGLASS delivered a speech dedicating the Haitian pavilion at the Chicago World's Fair. As a recent United States minister and consul general to Haiti, and as an exposition commissioner of the Haitian government, Douglass had helped to plan the exhibits of the pavilion, which he called "a city set upon a hill." After replying to the common stereotype that Haitians were lazy barbarians who devoted their time to voodooism and child sacrifice, Douglass looked back on the previous century of slave emancipation. Born a slave himself in 1818, he had won international fame as an abolitionist orator and writer and had become the most prominent black spokesman and statesman in the New World. Speaking, as he said, for the Negro, Douglass had no difficulty in identifying the central event in the history of emancipation: "We should not forget that the freedom you and I enjoy to-day; that the freedom that eight hundred thousand colored people enjoy in the British West Indies; the freedom that has come to the colored race the world over, is largely due to the brave stand taken by the black sons of Haiti ninety years ago. When they struck for freedom . . . they struck for the freedom of every black man in the world."[1]

Douglass said the blacks owed much to the American and British abolitionists and to the antislavery societies in various countries of the world, "but we owe incomparably more to Haiti than to them all." For Haiti was "the original pioneer emancipator of the nineteenth century." It had been Haiti's mission to teach the world the dangers of slavery and the latent powers and capabilities of the black race. After the former slaves of Saint-Domingue had defeated fifty thousand of Napoleon's veteran troops and had established their own independent nation, the white world could never be the same. Until Haiti spoke, Douglass pointed out, "no Christian nation had abolished Negro slavery. . . . Until she spoke, the slave trade was sanctioned by all the Christian nations of the world, and our land of liberty and light included. . . . Until Haiti spoke, the church was silent, and the pulpit dumb."[2]

Douglass knew that history was more complex than that; he knew that if whites had seen Haiti as "a very hell of horrors" whose "very name was pronounced with a shudder," as he noted at the beginning of his speech, the revolution had inevitably had contradictory effects. As an abolitionist from 1841 to 1863 Douglass had hardly mentioned the Haitian Revolution in his public speeches, debates, and interviews. For numerous whites the Haitian Revolution reinforced the conviction that emancipation in any form would lead to economic ruin and to the indiscriminate massacre of white populations. But Douglass's address of 1893 contained a profound truth. The Haitian Revolution was indeed a turning point in history. Like the Hiroshima bomb, its meaning could be rationalized or repressed but never really forgotten, since it demonstrated the possible fate of every slaveholding society in the New World. The Haitian Revolution impinged in one way or another on the entire emancipation debate from the British parliamentary move in 1792 to outlaw the African slave trade to Brazil's final abolition of slavery ninety-six years later. Like the Exodus narrative in the Bible, the Haitian Revolution showed blacks that liberation was a possibility in historical time. Their condition was not an inescapable fate. A brief discussion of the significance of Haiti's birth will help us see some of the ways in which New World slavery was being transformed in the Age of Revolution.

In the 1780s the French colony of Saint-Domingue was the centerpiece of the Atlantic slave system. It produced over half the world's coffee, mainly with slaves and land owned by free colored people, and in 1787 exported almost as much sugar as Jamaica, Cuba, and Brazil combined. But between 1791 and 1804 this "pearl of the Antilles" was destroyed by revolution and civil war, ignited by the French Revolution. The slaves and free descendants of slaves defeated not only their masters but the most formidable armies of Spain, Britain, and France. As Douglass put it, Haiti's freedom "was not given as a boon, but conquered as a right! Her people fought for it. They suffered for it, and thousands of them endured the most horrible tortures, and perished for it."[3] Whereas the American Revolution had been led by "the ruling race of the world," who "had the knowledge and character naturally inherited from long years of personal and political freedom," the Haitian rebels represented a race that "stood before the world as the most abject, helpless, and degraded of mankind."[4]

This heroic achievement evoked little applause from whites, even those who rejoiced over the European and Latin American movements of national liberation. Two notable exceptions, young recent graduates of Yale, Abraham Bishop, a Jeffersonian, and Theodore Dwight, a Federalist brother of Timothy, both affirmed the black slaves were fighting for the same cause and principles that Americans fought for in their own revolution, and urged American aid for the black rebels.[5] But in general, the Haitian Revolution reinforced the conviction that slave emancipation in any form would lead to economic ruin and to the indiscriminate massacre of white populations. The waves of fear traveled even faster than the Dominguan refugees who streamed westward to Cuba and Jamaica and northward to Spanish Louisiana and the port cities and towns of the United States.

Throughout the Americas planters and government officials learned to live in a state of alert. The very words "Santo Domingo," which English-speakers used to refer to the doomed French colony Saint-Domingue, evoked at least a moment of alarm and terror in the minds of slaveholders throughout the Americas. Sometimes this example of self-liberation was dismissed as the freakish result of French legislative and military blunders exacerbated by the subversive ideology of abolitionism and the tropical diseases that decimated British and French armies. Abolitionists, both contemporary and in later decades, vacillated between a policy of ignoring the explosive subject and warning that insurrections and racial war would be inevitable unless the slaves were peacefully emancipated and converted into grateful free peasants.

But whether the Haitian Revolution hastened or delayed the numerous emancipations of the following century, imagery of the great upheaval hovered over the antislavery debates like a bloodstained ghost. No internet was required to distribute Bryan Edwards's unforgettable descriptions of a white infant impaled on a stake, of white women being repeatedly raped on the corpses of their husbands and fathers, and of the fate of Madame Séjourné: "This unfortunate woman (my hand trembles while I write) was far advanced in her pregnancy. The monsters, whose prisoner she was, having first murdered her husband in her presence, ripped her up alive, and threw the infant to the hogs. —They then (how shall I relate it) sewed up the head of her murdered husband in ——-!!! ——Such are thy triumphs, Philanthropy!"[6]

But in human life, fear seldom overcomes greed. Planters in Cuba, Brazil, Jamaica, and Trinidad clamored for more African slaves who could help make up the deficit in world sugar and coffee production left by the devastation of Saint-Domingue. The destruction of slavery in Saint-Domingue gave an immense stimulus to plantation slavery from neighboring Cuba to far-off Brazil. In December 1803, just after the disease-ridden French army had finally capitulated to Jean-Jacques Dessalines's former slaves, South Carolina reopened the slave trade and in the next four years imported some forty thousand Africans. As Charleston's merchants well knew, the defeat of Napoleon's New World ambitions had opened the way for the Louisiana Purchase, which along with the new cotton gin, ensured that American slavery could expand westward without foreign interference into the Lower Mississippi Valley.

On the other hand, even Cuba, South Carolina, and other slave-importing regions sought to exclude bondsmen from colonies in which blacks had been exposed to revolutionary ideas. Although slave insurrections had usually been associated with a labor force containing a high proportion of recently imported Africans, white leaders were now far more fearful of blacks who had been contaminated by French or abolitionist conceptions of liberty.

In Britain and the United States abolitionists argued that slavery itself was the obvious cause of slave revolts. Early in 1792 abolitionist leader Thomas Clarkson insisted that while the French Revolution had presented the slaves with an opportunity to vindicate their humanity, the insurrection in Saint-Domingue could be attributed only to the slave trade and the oppressive system it produced. Far from being an argument against Britain's anti-slave trade petitions, the events in Saint-Domingue showed that it was sheer madness for the British to continue transporting Africans who, having "the passions of men," would sooner or later avenge their wrongs.[7] Such reasoning was clearly influential in the United States, where planters could rely on a rapid natural increase in the slave population and where opposition to further slave importation had won sanction from the War of Independence. The nation as a whole was outraged and alarmed by South Carolina's reopening of the slave trade in 1803; the Haitian Revolution strengthened the political argument for outlawing the American slave trade in 1808, the earliest date allowed by the Constitution. The Haitian example, reinforced in 1800 and 1802 by major slave conspiracies in Virginia, also led to laws restricting manumission and nourished interest in deporting free blacks to some distant colony.

Haiti's effects on British policy were more ambiguous. British planters lived as small white minorities surrounded by vast slave majorities. But they were accustomed to risk and were convinced that their fortunes depended on a labor force that would soon die off unless replenished by continuous imports from Africa. The catastrophe in Saint-Domingue, they claimed, showed the dangers of abolitionist agitation, not of a labor supply on which the Caribbean colonies had always depended. Even in 1795–1796, when the British colonies were most seriously threatened by racial warfare and by French armies that included large numbers of emancipated slaves, Parliament deferred to the West India planters and merchants and failed to renew a 1792 resolution calling for an end to the slave trade in four years. Indeed, the British successfully defended their slave colonies only by enlisting black troops directly from the slave ships. It would be difficult to show that fear of another Haitian Revolution motivated Parliament's crucial votes in 1806 abolishing the slave trade to rival foreign markets, which prepared the way in 1807 for abolishing the British slave trade altogether.

Yet it cannot be denied that both the government and British public had learned a lesson from William Pitt's disastrous attempt to conquer Saint-Domingue, restore slavery, and subdue Toussaint Louverture. In 1796, nearly three years after the first British forces landed in Saint-Domingue, the Pitt administration sent off to the West Indies one of the greatest expeditionary forces in British history. Before the end of the year Edmund Burke received the news that ten thousand men had died in less than two months! It was reported in the House of Commons that almost every Briton had a personal acquaintance that had perished in the Caribbean campaigns. Burke wrote caustically of "recruits to the West Indian grave" and of fighting to conquer a cemetery.[8] Although the mortality figures were somewhat exaggerated and British casualties were much heavier in the Windward Islands than in Saint-Domingue, there were good grounds for public outrage and for opposition party attacks on the conduct of the war. The loss in the Caribbean of nearly fifty thousand British soldiers and seamen, to say nothing of the expenditure of over £16 million, (almost as much as the later compensation for freeing 800,000 colonial slaves), underscored the cost of defending colonies that might at any moment become replicas of Saint-Domingue. The West Indian "image," already tarnished by years of antislavery literature and iconography, never recovered from Britain's defeat in Saint-Domingue.

In this broad sense the Haitian Revolution surely contributed to the British government's decisions, beginning in 1797, to limit the expansion of plantation agriculture in Trinidad, an undeveloped frontier which Britain had just seized from Spain. While there were many competing interests, shrewd politicians and reformers were able to dramatize the extreme danger of any policy that would encourage the unlimited importation of slaves into newly ceded colonies like Trinidad and Guiana. The failure of British and French armies to subjugate Saint-Domingue fostered discussion of alternative forms of labor and made it easier for government leaders to restrict the flow of slaves to Trinidad and Guiana, despite the pressure from planters and investors who were eager to profit from the rising world demand for cotton, sugar, coffee, and other plantation staples.

Despite the radical principles of the French Revolution, there was much awareness that the French government, whose bankruptcy ignited the revolutionary crisis, drew crucial revenues from slave colonies; and that millions of French jobs in port cities like Bordeaux depended on the slave trade and the stability of the slave system. Thus the French *slave trade* continued to receive an official subsidy until 1793, i.e. even after the abolition of the monarchy and the execution of Louis XVI, and two years after the start of the massive slave insurrection in Saint-Domingue. Moreover, in the West Indies, free blacks and coloreds generally supported the slave regime; in North Province many people of color had become indispensable as managers of sugar estates. As members of the militia and especially the rural police, they provided security forces that captured runaway slaves, kept the maroons at bay, and preserved the colony's peace.

But the French coloreds deeply resented the indignities and discriminations designed to reduce them to an under-caste. And in actuality, it was this issue of rights and representation for free coloreds that opened the way for slaves to free themselves. I cannot here describe the complex interplay and convergence of events. Suffice it to say that by April 1792, when beleaguered whites in South Province had armed their slaves to fight the mulattoes, the new Legislative Assembly in Paris decreed full equal rights for all free blacks and mulattoes in French colonies. This was one of the truly *great* achievements of the French Revolution, full racial equality as a matter of law; but it is seldom noticed in history texts. In 1794 the French National Convention outlawed slavery in all French colonies and granted the rights of citizenship to all men regardless of color. Such actions would have been inconceivable during the first four years of the Revolution—and Napoleon later, in 1802, rescinded this action and restored slavery wherever he could.

Yet the French emancipation decree of 1794 was a crucial precedent, successfully defended by the blacks of Saint-Domingue against Spanish, English, and then Napoleon's best French troops; this abolition of slavery was embodied in constitution of Haiti. News spread everywhere, especially carried by thousands of refugees and their slaves, that some half million slaves had not only risen in revolt in Saint-Domingue but that their freedom had been validated by France, and that the blacks had then proclaimed their own independence. This information inspired black rebels in neighboring Cuba as well as Virginia, South Carolina, and South America.

It is not generally known that Toussaint's crucial defeat of André Rigaud, the mulatto leader of the French forces, depended in part on secret aid from the U.S.; President Adams's secretary of state, Timothy Pickering, wishing above all to end the French presence in what was to become Haiti, sent arms and supplies to Toussaint. American ships even ferried Toussaint's troops to a strategic point behind Rigaud's lines (America's first venture in CIA-Contra-like intervention). Shortly before, in 1798, Great Britain concluded a secret treaty with Toussaint, granting special commercial privileges.

But the fate of Haiti hung by a thread in 1802–1803. Toussaint was captured by a ruse and shipped off to die in a freezing fortress high in the Jura Mountains. The black leaders Henry Christophe and Jean-Jacques Dessalines both surrendered, with amnesty, after Christophe had been given assurances from General Leclerc that all blacks would be free under a new code for liberty and equality. Christophe even entrusted his nine- year-old son to the French, and provided funds for his education, but the boy was thrown into an orphan asylum in Paris, and died in neglect and want.

Saint-Domingue burst into flames when news arrived of the restoration of slavery in Guadeloupe, the revival of old discriminations against mulattoes, and the reopening of the French slave trade. Although Napoleon now sent ten thousand more troops, twenty thousand in all after General Leclerc's death, the response of the black masses in Saint-Domingue marked a turning point in the history of New World slavery. General Rochambeau began a war of true extermination, marked by the slaughter of children and whole populations. After the French defeat and withdrawal, on 1 January 1804, Dessalines declared the independence of the Republic of Haiti. Before being crowned emperor in October, Dessalines ordered early in 1804 the massacre of whites remaining on the island. This spirit of revenge was clearly detrimental to Haiti's image and reputation, just as the new nation needed friendly relations with the wider world.

Yet even the vaguest awareness that blacks had somehow cast off their chains and founded the new republic of Haiti brought a glimmer of hope to thousands of slaves and free blacks who were the common victims of a remarkably unified Atlantic slave system. In Philadelphia, the site of the largest concentration of free blacks in the United States and a refuge for many whites and blacks from the French colonies, there was a deep concern over the welfare of Haiti. James Forten, the rich sailmaker and black leader, explained his community's deep interest in the future of Haiti in 1817: Haiti, he said, was an example of what blacks could achieve; proof that blacks in America "would become a great nation" and they "could not always be detained in their present bondage."[9]

Or as a black orator put it in 1825, at a meeting at the house of an African Methodist minister in Baltimore, Haiti presented "an irrefutable argument to prove . . . that the descendants of Africa never were designed by their Creator to sustain an inferiority, or even a mediocrity, in the chain of being; but they are as capable of intellectual improvement as Europeans, or any other nation upon the face of the earth."[10] Later celebrations of Haitian independence spread to other American cities. Thus in 1893 Frederick Douglass gave voice to convictions that had long been deeply embedded in African American culture, though the whole subject would long be suppressed or marginalized by white historians.

NOTES

1. "Lecture on Haiti," in Frederick Douglass, *The Life and Writings of Frederick Douglass,* 5 vols., ed. Philip S. Foner, (New York: International Publishers, 1950–75), 4:484.

2. Ibid., 4:485–86.

3. Ibid., 4:486.

4. *The Chicago Tribune,* 3 Jan. 1893.

5. Tim Matthewson, "Abraham Bishop, 'The Rights of Man of Black Men,' and the American Reaction to the Haitian Revolution," *Journal of Negro History* 67 (1982): 148–53; Theodore Dwight, *An Oration Spoken Before "The Connecticut Society for the Promotion of Freedom and the Relief of Persons Unlawfully Holden in Bondage"* (Hartford, 1794), 12, 18–21.

6. Bryan Edwards, *An Historical Survey of the French Colony in the Island of St. Domingo* (London: J. Stockdale, 1797), 97.

7. Katherine Plymley Diaries, 1066/1, Book 5:10–15, County Record Office, Shrewsbury, England.

8. David P. Geggus, *Slavery, War and Revolution: The British Occupation of Saint Domingue, 1793–1798* (Oxford: Clarendon Press, 1982), 212.

9. Julie Winch, *Philadelphia's Black Elite: Activism, Accommodation, and the Struggle for Autonomy, 1787–1848* (Philadelphia: Temple University Press, 1988), 50.

10. Ira Berlin, *Slaves Without Masters: The Free Negro in the Antebellum South* (New York: Pantheon, 1975), 314–15.

Chapter 2

The Limits of Example

SEYMOUR DRESCHER

IS IT POSSIBLE TO IMAGINE a history of slavery, without designating the Haitian Revolution as its pivotal event? David Brion Davis takes Frederick Douglass's affirmative response as a profound truth and his own point of departure: "Like Hiroshima . . . the Haitian revolution of the black masses impinged, in one way or another, on the entire emancipation debate from the British parliamentary move in 1792 . . . to Brazil's final abolition of slavery ninety-six years later" as " a turning point in the history of New World slavery." I enthusiastically second Davis's characteristically wide-ranging view of the revolution.

Regarding Haiti itself, two hundred years of historiography agree that the slave revolution beginning in 1791 represents the biggest, and most influential, moment in its history. In 1791 the largest slave colony in the Caribbean became the site of the most violent and most successful uprising in the history of slavery. Forty years ago, in his *The Age of the Democratic Revolution,* R. R. Palmer measured the relative intensity of the American and French Revolutions on the basis of the number of émigrés per thousand inhabitants fleeing each society. He estimated that, during their respective revolutions, there were five émigrés per thousand from France, and twenty-four per thousand from the Thirteen Colonies. The slave revolution in Saint-Domingue did not appear in his account. On my own early conservative estimate the Haitian figure was at least twenty émigrés per thousand. The true intensity of the Caribbean revolution is more fully revealed by another statistic. Its toll of violent deaths was probably closer to two hundred per thousand.[1] Moreover, all of the white and much of the old colored planter class simply vanished by 1804. The armies of the world's three most powerful Atlantic empires were shattered in the course of a decade. No wonder that both the means and the end of this event caught the attention of peoples thousands of miles from the scene, becoming a powerful mythos for tens of thousands of slaves and their descendants in the Americas.

But how much of a turning point for Atlantic slavery was the revolution, beyond the boundaries of Hispaniola? Much of the answer to this question depends upon the geographical and temporal scope of one's analysis, as well as upon the variables selected for measurement. I will for the most part follow the parameters and the time-period delineated by Davis—the Atlantic world in the age of the democratic revolution.

I would suggest that there is heuristic value in reversing one of Davis's formulations, and moving from symbolic discourse to reality. Whether the Haitian Revolution hastened or delayed slave emancipations in the Americas, assessing its impact affords an opportunity for comparative analysis. The initial success of the Saint-Domingue revolution was clearly of critical importance in the timing, and probably the scope, of the French emancipation decree of February 1794. For at least two more years the reverberations of that decision imperiled slavery in the eastern Caribbean. By 1798, however, the initial offensive had receded. Well before the end of the Napoleonic Wars, the slave population of the Caribbean had virtually regained its pre-revolutionary peak, at a level which would not again decline before British colonial slave emancipation.[2] Within the Americas as a whole, the slave population continued to increase steadily for another half-century. If one wishes to describe the situation, as of 1814, as a balance sheet between greed and fear, greed had won hands down. Of all the areas of the Caribbean in which slaves had gained de facto or de jure freedom between 1791 and 1796 all but one area had been restored to slavery by 1802.

Beyond the Caribbean islands, the Haitian revolution seems to have played its most significant, if delayed, role in Gran Colombia.[3] Its impact on Brazil, as a stimulus to emancipation or to slave trade abolition seems meager at best. Haiti's impact upon African slavery was smaller still.

Even restricting our focus to the slave trade, a decisive impact of the Haitian Revolution is difficult to detect. In North America many of the United States had outlawed their slave trade before the uprising in Saint-Domingue. The Federal Constitution of 1787 had also previously forecast a time limit upon the slave trade. The abolitionist process in the United States would appear to have been more firmly rooted in the dynamic of mainland American politics than in the tumultuous events in the French Caribbean.

North America's major exception is interesting in this respect. South Carolina's reopening of the trade, at the very climax of the Haitian revolution, seems to point to an inverse relationship between the number of slaves already in a society, and its planters' fears of allowing more to enter. The link between importation and fear of revolution also paradoxically increased with a society's distance from the epicenter of the revolution. Any historian invoking "revolutionary trauma" or "the great fear," as a psychologically significant cause of abolition must come to grips with this profile of comparative reaction. Why did the chief European loser, in terms of population, pride and prosperity, persist in attempting to recover and to re-enslave Saint-Domingue? Two separate French regimes relaunched the slave trade before 1815. Europe's most traumatized rulers, the Bourbons, are classically said to have learned nothing and forgotten nothing from the Revolution in France. They were remarkably consistent overseas, too. Far from giving up their old slave colonies, they dreamt in 1814 of recovering and re-developing them all, including Saint-Domingue.[4]

The British therefore seem to offer the best scenario for a Haitian-impacted slave trade abolition. Why the British should have been more fearful of the outcome of Saint-Domingue's revolution than the French, or the Iberians, is mystifying. As Davis notes, British planters on the spot did not clamor to be saved from African "seeds of destruction." Even at the depths of the West Indian Great Fear in 1795–1796, Parliament deferred to the slave interest against abolition. On the eve of British slave trade abolition in 1807 it was uncommonly difficult to find parliamentary abolitionists emphasizing the threat from Haiti, either in terms of physical force or by infectious example. The motion for abolition was grounded on an explicitly non-insurrectionary premise about the prior behavior of British slaves. Haiti's new rulers seemed to be far too preoccupied with internal struggles to pose a threat of force in 1806–1807.[5]

Viewing the entire decade before British abolition hardly alters this assessment. Davis maintains that "the Haitian Revolution surely contributed to the British government's decisions to limit the expansion of plantation agriculture, beginning in 1797," and culminating in slave trade abolition. In 1797, at the very moment the British government held up land sales in Trinidad, slaving capital was allowed to flow in the millions of pounds to Demerara.[6] During the following decade the British government did not hesitate to collect new slave colonies at the fastest rate in imperial history. Of course, the British had learned some important strategic and financial lessons from Saint-Domingue—not to overextend their forces, and to minimize epidemiological risks to their armies. With black regiments, the British began to call in the Old World's slaves to redress the balance of ex-slave armies in the New.

In terms of slavery's value to the imperial government, we must not overlook the fact that sugar revenues to the Crown more than quadrupled between the outbreak of the French Revolution and the cessation of African imports into the British Caribbean. As P. J. Marshall concludes in the new *Oxford History of the British Empire,* a swing away from "slavery" was not manifest before Waterloo. Neither as military threat, nor as threatening example, did Haiti loom large in British policy after 1805.[7]

All this is not to deny that the Haitian revolution dramatically affected the culture and politics of Atlantic slavery. As Davis emphasizes, European images and black self-images of Africans were powerfully altered. In an age of nationalist romanticism, Toussaint Louverture became the most widely known and sympathetic black hero in the West. Until the 1790s it was a commonplace in British commentary that European settler societies posed a greater risk to empire than those peopled by descendants of Africans. Such easy generalizations vanished after the 1790s, along with the presumption, of some early abolitionists and racists alike, that blacks were too broken in spirit, or too inferior in capacities, to undertake sustained large scale uprisings.

At the end of the Napoleonic wars, New World slavery was economically as dynamic as it had been on the eve of the Saint-Domingue Revolution. It was poised to participate, and successfully so, in the further expansion of the industrialized world. Politically, however, slavery was on the defensive. It no longer had a virtually unquestioned status in the imagined futures of Atlantic empires and nations. The range of destabilizing possibilities had expanded enormously for those who held, who protected, or who were, slaves. Was it the British or the Haitians who loomed larger in the political calculations of slaving powers after 1808? Was the Haitian tail really wagging the British Lion?[8]

That the Haitian Revolution remained a powerful image in the minds of slaves is indisputable. That Haiti was itself a direct catalyst in most subsequent slave mobilizations in the Caribbean is questionable. As David Geggus suggests, the one successful slave revolution was the outcome of a unique combination of circumstances. Haiti was both unforgettable and unrepeatable.[9]

Contemporary assessments of Haiti were also not quite as racially polarized as Davis's selection of African American quotes implies. Napoleon's threat to Britain's survival made it possible for Britons to openly proffer congratulations to black leaders for attaining independence against the armies of France. In Britain, and elsewhere outside France, the end of the European war stimulated almost-utopian hopes for the future even beyond the abolitionist ranks. Sir Joseph Banks, deeply pessimistic in 1792 about the possibility of freeing British West Indian slaves, imagined a different role for Haiti in 1815: "Was I Five and Twenty, as I was when I embarked with Capt Cooke, I am very sure I should not Lose a day in Embarking for Haiti. [T]o see a sort of Human beings emerging from Slavery and making most Rapid Strides towards the perfection of Civilization, must, I think be the most delightful of all Food for Contemplation."[10] Such effusions, of course, eventually became part of Haiti's burden. Three decades later, Victor Schoelcher, the first major abolitionist to visit the republic, excoriated Haiti's political oppression as a betrayal of Africa's first civilized nation in the West. Haiti's emblematic designation as the guarantor of black progress is clearly evident in Davis's summary of Douglass's defensive speech of 1893.

It is only a decade since the bicentennial of the French Revolution. In that late twentieth-century retrospective, the age of the democratic revolution was also recognized as an age of racial and genocidal conflict. In that respect, too, the Haitian Revolution anticipated more of the world's future than Frederick Douglass could have imagined a century ago.

NOTES

1. Compare R. R. Palmer, *The Age of the Democratic Revolution,* 2 vols. (Princeton University Press, 1959), 1:188; and Seymour Drescher, *Dilemmas of Democracy: Tocqueville and Modernization* (Pittsburgh: University of Pittsburgh Press, 1968), 155 n.

2. Stanley L. Engerman and H. B. Higman, "The Demographic Structure of the Caribbean Slave Societies in the Eighteenth and Nineteenth Centuries," in *General History of the Caribbean,* vol. 3, *The Slave Societies of the Caribbean,* ed. Franklin W. Knight (London/Basingstroke: UNESCO Publishing/Macmillan Education Ltd., 1997), 45–104; Figure 1, 47, Caribbean populations, 1700–1900: total and slave.

3. See Robin Blackburn, *The Overthrow of Colonial Slavery 1776–1846* (London: Verso, 1988), 331–79.

4. Seymour Drescher, *Econocide: British Slavery in the Era of Abolition* (Pittsburgh: University of Pittsburgh Press, 1977), 152–57.

5. Ibid., 168–69; Roger Anstey, *The Atlantic Slave Trade and British Abolition, 1760–1810* (Atlantic Highlands, N.J.: Humanities Press, 1975), 286–320.

6. Drescher, *Econocide,* 99–103; 169–70; Roger Norman Buckley, *Slaves in Red Coats: The British West India Regiment 1795–1815* (New Haven, Conn.: Yale University Press, 1979), 82–105.

7. Peter J. Marshall, "Conclusion," in *Oxford History of the British Empire,* Vol 2, *The Eighteenth Century,* ed. P. J. Marshall (Oxford: Oxford University Press, 1998).

8. Seymour Drescher, "Whose Abolition? Popular Pressure and the Ending of the British Slave Trade," *Past and Present* 143 (1994): 136–66.

9. David Geggus, "Slavery, War, and Revolution in the Greater Caribbean, 1789–1815," in *A Turbulent Time: The French Revolution and the Greater Caribbean,* ed. David Barry Gaspar, David Patrick Geggus (Bloomington: Indiana University Press, 1997), 31.

10. John Gascoigne, *Joseph Banks and the Enlightenment* (Cambridge: Cambridge University Press, 1994), 41.

Chapter 3

The Force of Example

ROBIN BLACKBURN

DAVID BRION DAVIS OFFERS A commanding strategic assessment of the impact of the Haitian revolution on the Americas and on prospects for slave emancipation. He rightly insists on the fact that the revolution in Saint-Domingue/Haiti represented the first really major blow to the slave systems. Previous antislavery moves have their own significance, including the Emancipation Law in Pennsylvania in 1780 and the rise of a mass abolitionist movement in Britain in the late 1780s. But Pennsylvania had very few slaves and the law was very moderate, in principle only conferring freedom on those born to slave mothers after they reached their majority. The British movement aimed at ending the Atlantic slave trade, not slavery, and was anyway unsuccessful in this first phase. As Davis rightly reminds us, the French Revolution itself did not immediately emancipate the slaves, notwithstanding the Declaration of the Rights of Man, though it did give rise to a historic antiracist battle to establish the equal rights of free people of color, many of them themselves the owners of slaves.

In fact the late eighteenth and early nineteenth century present us with a sharp paradox. On the one hand slavery was deprecated by many; on the other it was hard to make any headway against the planter stake in slavery, because it was buttressed by (1) widely accepted conceptions of the sacredness of private property, (2) racial perceptions of Africans and blacks as lacking in the qualities needed for, or entitling them to, freedom, and (3) a view of national interest in a rivalrous international system that identified it with plantation wealth and the commerce based on it. For the established order in the Atlantic world, and the elites prevailing over it, these were all very potent considerations. They could only be neutralized or overcome in the most extreme conditions, conditions in which (1) property was under suspicion and assault, (2) racial perceptions of Africans and blacks were being challenged, notably as a consequence of their own actions, and (3) the national interest was being redefined to meet a potent threat.

David Brion Davis rightly observes that it took the French Revolution, a mighty social and political upheaval reaching across the Atlantic, to furnish the conditions in which the former slaves of Saint-Domingue could entrench the first forms of an antislavery power. This achievement itself reacted back on the metropolitan revolutionary process in 1793–4. By this time popular anger against the rich was a strong force in the revolutionary centers. Merchants were deeply unpopular and there were attempts to control prices that were even more radical than those witnessed in Philadelphia in 1779–80. The free people of color had already been identified as potential allies of the metropolitan power when it confronted treacherous white colonists. Indeed by the time of the historic decree of 16 Pluviôse An II (4 February 1794) many of the planters of the French Antilles had been revealed as shameless collaborators with the national enemy, having entered a compact with the British monarchy and facilitated British occupation of their islands. This permitted a patriotic reconstruction of the national interest that undertook emancipation partly to punish the traitors and partly to cement an alliance with the new black power in Saint-Domingue.[1]

Thus the first impact of the Saint-Domingue revolution was its impact on the French revolution, which it signally radicalized on the slavery question. At this point, however, we should also register the impact of French revolutionary ideas on the struggle in Saint-Domingue, for initially the great slave uprising of August 1791 encompassed freedom for those directly involved but not a general assault on slavery. The black generals, understandably enough, were prepared to fight for the king of Spain, since he helped to arm them; but the price of this alliance was a willingness to ignore the antislavery theme. It was only in the year 1793 that Toussaint Louverture, on the one hand, and Sonthonax, on the other, began to vie with each other in declarations against slavery, and only in the following year that the forces they represented were united to make a reality of those declarations. The dispatch of a delegation from Saint-Domingue famously allowed the perspective of the "Black Jacobins" of the colony to impinge on the outlook of the metropolitan Revolutionary Convention. As the title of the classic work by C. L. R. James suggests, the eventual adoption of revolutionary emancipationism reflected a congruence of universalizing impulses within Jacobinism and of the specific impetus of slave revolt. At this juncture the black general issued decrees in French while the metropolitan emissaries knew that Jacobin declarations would be vain unless couched in Kréyol. And in the years 1794–1798 the French Republic allied itself with the slave rebels and sent large quantities of war materiel to reinforce and extend emancipation in the Caribbean. The French expedition in the Eastern Caribbean drew off major British forces and inflicted heavy losses upon them, as Davis reminds us. At different times Spain and Portugal had used black troops, and Britain was soon to do so, but, unlike Republican France, they drew the line at any general antislavery appeal.

Indeed if there is one criticism that could be directed at the title of this collection it is the choice of the abbreviated term 'Haitian Revolution' for a process that began over a decade before the establishment of Haiti in the struggles 'ignited' – as Davis felicitously puts it – by the French Revolution. In debating the impact of the Haitian Revolution we must not forget either the impact of the French Revolution on the Americas or the impact of the revolt in Saint-Domingue on revolutionary France. We can be quite certain that without the pressure of the Saint-Domingue revolt, and of the black power that issued from it, the French Revolution would not have embraced emancipationism. On the other hand the revolutionary emancipationist offensive of 1794–1798 in the Caribbean gave the new black power in Saint-Domingue the time and resources it needed to consolidate itself; if the British and their counterrevolutionary allies had been able to concentrate all their forces on Saint-Domingue they might well have succeeded in capturing the colony. Moreover, a number of the revolutionary conspiracies of the 1790s and early 1800s in the wider circum-Caribbean region were inspired as much or more by revolutionary France as by the new authorities in Saint-Domingue. Free people of color were particularly impressed by the fact that one of the great European powers had opted for a New World strategy that granted them recognition and rights.[2]

Of course the revolution in Saint Domingue/Haiti eventually had to confront France itself but this was a France that, with encouragement from the United States and Britain, had turned its back on emancipationism. Napoleon's defeat in Haiti was in fact a defeat for all the slave powers of the New World. Inescapably it put all pro-slavery forces into a state of exceptional mobilization and brought down upon Haiti itself a Cold War that was to last until at least the 1860s, with the effect of fostering militarization and commercial isolation. Nevertheless, Haiti remained a major supplier of peasant-grown coffee but could only find an outlet in France for its produce after agreeing to indemnify the former plantation owners and saddling itself with a loan to this end.

Outside the slave zone the first response of metropolitan public opinion to slave revolt, with its attendant bloodshed and episodes of race war, did not help the antislavery cause, though after a while, as Davis also observes, the institution of slavery could be seen as making such excesses almost inevitable. It is worth stressing, however, that it was the new post-slavery order, born out of revolution, not the bloodshed of revolt as such, which eventually won over significant sectors of metropolitan opinion to the antislavery cause. The figure of Toussaint Louverture served as a hugely influential symbol of responsible black power throughout the nineteenth century and beyond. Innumerable poems, essays, and biographies were dedicated to him by figures as disparate as William Wordsworth, Victor Schoelcher, Lamartine, and Wendell Phillips. And so far as African Americans, Jamaicans, Afro-Cubans or Afro-Brazilians are concerned, what they found impressive about Haiti was that it displayed the trappings of properly constituted authority. Black conspirators would often cherish the official insignia of the black republic or kingdom and would hold out the prospect of Haitian support to their followers.[3] Haiti was a symbol of black power and authority, not of desperate rebellion, and that is why it could inspire or terrify.

The Haitian Revolution, and prior triumph of revolutionary emancipationism in Saint-Domingue, may have helped to remobilize the slave regime where the slaveholders were strongest and conditions for slavery expansion most propitious—above all in Cuba, Brazil, and the U.S. South—but in other parts of the Atlantic world it helped to supply a context where significant further advances could be made. It is interesting that moderate emancipation laws were passed in New York in 1799 and New Jersey in 1804, when similar legislation had failed in both states in the 1780s.

In the case of the British Act for the abolition of the Atlantic slave trade in 1807, there was, of course, a complex conjuncture, dominated by the Hanoverian oligarchy's need to rally a widespread popular coalition in the war with Napoleon's France. The influential arguments used by James Stephen and Lord Brougham to urge the cause of abolition both made reference to Haiti, with Stephen pointing up the significance of resistance to Napoleon in the island and Brougham using it to underscore the wisdom of a prudent colonial policy.[4] Even a conservative abolitionist such as William Wilberforce was happy to engage in a long correspondence with Henry Christophe, when he ruled the kingdom of Haiti. The republican President Boyer was to court Wilberforce by naming one of his ships of war after him, a vessel which impressed British opinion by successfully intercepting a slave trading clipper in 1819, at a time when the Royal Navy was having little impact.[5]

If we contrast the Spanish American revolutions of the early nineteenth century with the revolution in North America, then it is striking that emancipation laws, albeit mainly of the Pennsylvania 'free womb' type, made greater inroads, including in areas like Venezuela and Peru where slaveowning was quite widespread amongst the elite. The well-known assistance extended to Bolívar by President Pétion was certainly a factor in the injection of an emancipationist theme into the Spanish American independence struggle, though of course Bolívar certainly grasped the military significance of emancipation laws as an aid to black recruitment.

The impact of the Haitian Revolution hastened and accentuated a process of differentiation within the Atlantic world, dividing it more neatly into slave and non-slave zones. It helped to weaken slavery in areas where it was already weak, vulnerable or marginal, while it alerted and galvanized planters who were more advantageously placed. The destruction of the sugar industry in Saint-Domingue furnished a huge commercial opportunity to producers in Cuba, Louisiana, and Brazil which they exploited with the help of refugees from the former French colony.[6] The slave and race codes were tightened in Cuba, the United States, and Brazil in the early decades of the nineteenth century, with slave revolts and conspiracies, and rumors of Haitian involvement, often furnishing the pretext. The planters felt able to count on slave labor for two reasons: (1) the slaves did not comprise the great majority of the population in these lands, as they had or did in the smaller Caribbean islands, (2) the slaveholders were not weakened by absenteeism, and had confidence in their preponderant influence over the state. The planters rightly felt that the slave order could regroup and flourish, using Haiti as a caution and an opportunity. But their counterparts in the British and remaining French Caribbean were not so favorably situated and were to be caught between metropolitan abolitionism and the episodic unrest of slaves and free people of color, so that any real crisis could precipitate the speedy and comparatively pacific winding up of slavery. Undoubtedly memories of Saint-Domingue helped to promote such denouements in the 1830s and 1840s in the British and French slave colonies.

Toussaint Louverture is supposed to have earned his name by gaining a dramatic opening in a decisive early engagement. The revolution in Saint-Domingue and Haiti opened a dramatic breach in the slave systems of the Americas. There are limits to the force of example, and antislavery only made its way in the century to come because of a succession of antislavery alliances and revolutionary or near-revolutionary conjunctures. However, within most of them it is possible to identify black or white abolitionists who took inspiration from the revolution that had established Haiti. The task faced by antislavery activists in the antebellum United States and in the Brazilian empire was more forbidding than that which confronted the English or French abolitionists. After all, they confronted a slaveholding class on its own territory and used to ruling. The example of Haiti did not furnish an exact parallel and even the most resolute abolitionists would wish to encompass their objective without the terrible bloodshed and strife that had been witnessed in the former French colony. But some had a presentiment that revolutionary methods might after all be required and for them the knowledge that victory had been gained in Haiti was a source of great encouragement.

One can fittingly conclude by quoting some lines from a book that sold hugely in the antebellum United States and to which Frederick Douglass attributed a major role in his own development, *The Columbian Orator,* first published in 1797. The lines are taken from Everett's Commencement Day poem, "General Description of America," spoken at Dartmouth College in 1795:

> The fertile isles their rich luxuriance pour,
> And western dainties crowd the eastern shore.
> But weep, humanity, the black disgrace,
> And spread thy blushes o'er oppression's face!
> Ye sons of mirth, your bowls, your richest food,
> Is mingled with fraternal tears and blood.
> Still groans the slave beneath his master's rod,
> But nature, wrong'd, appeals to nature's GOD.
> The sun frowns angry at th' inhuman sight;
> The stars offended, redden in the night:
> In western skies, drear horror gathers round
> And waking vengeance murmurs under ground;
> O'er all the gulph the dark'ning vapours rise,
> And the black clouds sail awful round the skies.
> From heaven to earth swift thunder bolts are hurl'd,
> And storm's dread demon shakes th' astonished world.
> The rich plantation lies a barren waste,
> And all the works of slavery are defac'd.
> Ye tyrants own the devastation just;
> 'Tis for your wrongs the fertile earth is curs'd.[7]

NOTES

1. The best general account remains C. L. R. James, *The Black Jacobins: Toussaint L'Ouverture and the San Domingo Revolution,* first published in 1938 but subsequently much reprinted (e.g. London 1980, revised edition). Carolyn Fick, *The Making of the Haitian Revolution* (Knoxville: University of Tennessee Press, 1990), has much valuable material on the 'revolution from below,' while David Geggus, *Slavery, War and Revolution: The British Occu-*

pation of Saint Domingue, 1793–1798 (Oxford: Oxford University Press, 1982), greatly illuminates the wartime disintegration of the slave system. In *The Overthrow of Colonial Slavery* (London: Verso, 1988), 161–264, I seek to trace the interaction of the struggles in metropolis and colony upon one another. See also *Révolutions aux Colonies* (Paris: Annales Historiques de la Révolution Française, 1993), with contributions by Michel Vovelle, Yves Bénot, Sabine Manigat, and Léo Elisabeth.

2. See the various contributions to Michel L. Martin and Alain Yacou, eds., *De la Révolution française aux révolutions créoles et nègres* (Paris: Eds. Caribéennes, 1989) and to David P. Geggus and D. Barry Gaspar, eds., *A Turbulent Time: The French Revolution and the Greater Caribbean* (Bloomington: Indiana University Press, 1997).

3. For example, José Luciano Franco, "La conspiración de Aponte," in his *Ensayos Históricos,* (Havana: Editorial de Ciencias Sociales, 1974), 125–90.

4. Henry Brougham, *Inquiry into the Colonial Policy of the European Powers* (London: E. Balfour, 1803) and James Stephen, *The Opportunity, or Reasons for an Immediate Alliance with St. Domingo* (London: 1804). See also David Geggus, "British Opinion and the Emergence of Haiti," in James Walvin, ed., *Slavery and British Society* (London: Macmillan, 1982), 123–49, 241–46.

5. David Murray, *Odious Commerce: Britain, Spain and the Abolition of the Cuban Slave Trade* (Cambridge: Cambridge University Press, 1980), 78.

6. Fernando Novais, *Portugal e Brasil na crise do antigo sistema colonial (1777–1808)* (2nd ed., São Paulo: Editora Hucitec, 1983), 287–94, 306–90, and Gloria García, "El Auge de la sociedad esclavista en Cuba," in *Historia de Cuba,* I, *La Colonia, evolución socioeconómica y formación nacional de los origines hasta 1867* (Havana: Instituto de Historia, 1994), 225–64.

7. Caleb Bingham, *The Columbian Orator,* edited and introduced by David Blight, (New York: New York University Press, 1998), 207–8.

PART TWO

POLITICS

Chapter 4

From Liberalism to Racism

German Historians, Journalists, and the Haitian Revolution from
the Late Eighteenth to the Early Twentieth Centuries

KARIN SCHÜLLER

IN "GERMANY"[1] FROM THE END of the eighteenth to the beginning of the
twentieth century, it was mostly intellectuals — historians, journalists and writers
of fiction — who were interested in the history of Haiti. This interest was closely
related to developments in Germany and Europe that used Haiti time and again as
a reference point, as a mirror through which to look back at events at home. The
Haitian Revolution was the starting as well as the focal point of this preoccupation,
but with the passing of time the result of the revolution, the independent state of
Haiti, increasingly became the center of attention, too.[2]

In the beginning the connection between the Haitian and French revolutions
was the main reason for this German interest in a slave revolt in the Caribbean.
After 1804, another aspect was the role of Haiti as the second independent state of
the Americas. At the same time, Germany saw the beginnings of political movements which were defined in part by the attitude of their members toward the
United States and the French Revolution. The contemporary debate was very
much characterized by a discussion of the republican form of government, which
meant that from the beginning there was a strong interest in the Haitian constitu-
tions, together with their French and American counterparts, as the first examples
of this form of government. In addition, ideas about race, slavery and the slave
trade had become important topics starting in the Enlightenment. The abolitionist
debate took place almost exclusively in Europe, with Germany — on the one hand
a country without slaves; on the other, center of the European *Gelehrtenrepublik*
(republic of scholars) — as a very important scene of this discussion. Later generations of German journalists and historians would continue this interest in the
Caribbean island, even while in the background Germany and Europe were
changing. But the corresponding conditions in Haiti were important, too. Haiti
and its history were judged differently, depending on whether it was the reign of

President Boyer or of Soulouque. Therefore I would like to sketch first that part of Haitian history that was interpreted by German intellectuals.

In 1791, in the course of the French Revolution, a great slave revolt erupted in the western part of Hispaniola, leading to the foundation of the first independent Latin American state in 1804.[3] The events of this Haitian Revolution caused the French Jacobin commissioners in 1793 to gradually abolish slavery in Saint-Domingue. Only one year later, in 1794, the mother country abolished slavery in all French colonies. These events constituted the context that allowed for the rise of the former slave Toussaint Louverture to the rank of governor of Saint-Domingue. Toussaint tried to stabilize the country politically and economically by inducing the white plantation owners who had fled, to return, and by giving everybody the same rights, regardless of skin color. After Napoleon had taken over the French government, a military expedition attempted in 1802 to reestablish the prerevolutionary conditions and hence to reintroduce slavery. A war of independence broke out. In its course Toussaint Louverture was arrested and deported to France, where he died in April 1803. Nevertheless, the blacks succeeded in their struggle for freedom, putting a victorious end to the fighting.

In 1804 Jean-Jacques Dessalines, the new leader of the struggle for independence, became the first ruler of an independent Haiti. Dessalines represented the stratum of black field-slaves within the slaveholder society. He not only countenanced the massacre of the remaining French inhabitants of the island in 1804, but also decreed in the constitution of 1805 that all Haitians were "blacks," whatever their skin color. However, the so-called *anciens libres,* who in colonial times had formed a free class of mixed racial descent, did not approve of his power. In 1806 Dessalines was assassinated and the country split into two states of different character. The southern republic under the rule of the mulatto president Alexandre Pétion was confronted with the northern kingdom of the black Henry Christophe. The economy of the kingdom continued to rely on the profitable system of plantations and compulsory labor, while the republic carried out the first land reform in Latin America, with the result that small holdings predominated in the countryside. "Two avenues were opened up during the next dozen years, one by Christophe, the other by his southern and mulatto rival, Pétion. The former was the road of discipline, hard work, and feudal control; the latter was one of persuasion, *laissez faire,* and small properties. Haiti ultimately chose the second."[4]

In 1820 Christophe was overthrown and the successor of Pétion, Jean-Pierre Boyer, also assumed rule over the northern part of Haiti. This was the first of three events of far-reaching importance that occurred during the administration of President Boyer. In 1822, two years after the reunification of north and south, the previously Spanish eastern section was occupied. The French could have used this part of the island to land in an attempt to reconquer Haiti, and it would have facilitated the building of a land-based army reserve. This danger was ruled out while the whole island was governed for more than twenty years by Port-au-Prince. The third critical event of the Boyer administration was the de facto and de jure recognition of Haiti by France, which brought far more economic advantages to the former metropole than to Haiti itself.[5] Yet the state was now secure in terms of foreign policy; it had obtained diplomatic status. President Boyer's administration provided the country with more than two decades of peace and political stability between 1820 and 1843, decades when Hispanic America was already riven by civil wars and anarchy. Only in the last years of Boyer's reign an opposition movement developed and ultimately led to his overthrow in 1843. In 1847 the black former slave Faustin Soulouque became president. The Haitian upper classes were not successful in their plan to use him as a puppet ruler. After a brutal purge among their ranks in April 1848, Soulouque governed from August 1849 as Emperor Faustin I. Just as Dessalines, the first head of state, had erected an empire in Haiti parallel to Napoleon I's, Soulouque governed during the same time as Napoleon III, until he was toppled from his throne in January 1859.[6]

The Haitian Revolution and the development of an independent Haiti were thoroughly covered by the German press of the first half of the nineteenth century.[7] First reports about the slave uprising of 1791 were published in 1792. There followed a regular flow of news throughout the period up to the late 1830s. In quantitative terms a first peak was reached in 1802, when Napoleon sent his army to Saint-Domingue. Haiti's declaration of independence in 1804 was an event that Europeans found hard to believe and journals took up the topic with great interest. Another peak in press coverage was reached in 1818 reflecting the news of president Pétion's death and the negotiations between France and Haiti regarding recognition of Haitian independence. Finally, in 1825 a number of articles reported the *de jure* recognition of independence of that year.

I quantified the reporting on Haiti in comparison with reporting on all the Americas using a representative example. I chose a magazine that covers the whole of the first half of the nineteenth century, *Minerva,* which was published from 1792 until 1858 and can be considered careful in its evaluations.[8] I compared the reporting on the United States and on Latin America, while at the same time considering articles on Haiti separately. Only articles which clearly focused on these topics

FIGURE 4.1 Articles in the German Press on Haiti

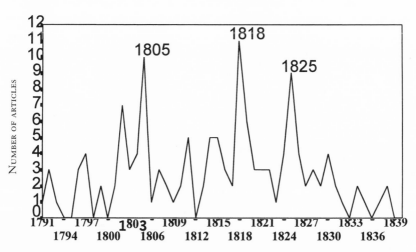

Source: List of articles in Schüller, *Die deutsche Rezeption,* 284–95.

were taken into account, while more general essays which contained only brief references were not included.

Between 1792 and 1858 *Minerva* published ninety-nine articles on the United States and ninety-four on Latin America. It is thus possible to speak of a certain balance of interest regarding North and South America. Of the ninety-four articles on Latin America twenty-four dealt with Haiti, accounting for more than a quarter of the published articles, far more on this small insular nation than on any other Latin American state. Furthermore, if one divides the period under study according to landmarks of Latin American history, Haiti is the topic in eleven of seventeen articles published on Latin America between 1792 and 1807. These years correspond with the time of the Haitian Revolution and its early beginnings as an independent nation. The second period, that of the Iberian American independence movements, lasted from 1808 until about 1830, a period offering far more pieces on Latin America than on the United States. There are forty-four articles on the United States compared with sixty-nine on Latin America, of which twelve deal with Haiti. Finally, the last period encompasses the years between 1831 and 1858, the latter being the last year of publication for *Minerva*. During these years coverage of the United States and its increasing importance dominated, while the interest in Latin America clearly waned. There are twenty-nine articles on the United States as against eight reports on the Latin American states of which only one focuses on Haiti.[9] After the 1830s Haiti figured only rarely as a topic in the German press.

But German reporting is not only remarkable with respect to its quantity but also regarding its contents. As it is impossible to present here the whole range of opinions, I would like to concentrate on general tendencies to show a representative image of Haiti for every period. In the first half of the nineteenth century the accounts of events differ, which is remarkable because the Germans had to rely

FIGURE 4.2: Articles in the Journal *Minerva,* 1792–1858

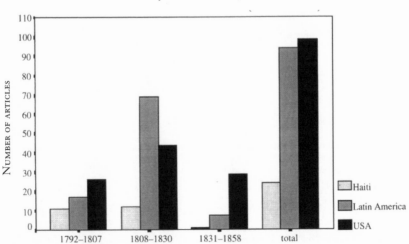

Source: Minerva, 1–263 (1792–1858).

largely on French and English sources. Most of them, but especially the French, evoked a more or less negative image. The German states were not colonial powers, as were England and France, and as a result there was hardly any direct contact with people of color. With respect to America, the terms "black" and "slave" were regarded as synonymous. Furthermore, the economic interests that in France or England were related to slavery were also missing in Germany. Therefore, the Haitian Revolution's significance for Germany was very different than for either the United States or those European countries which continued to have American colonies.[10] As Robin Blackburn notes in chapter 3, "plantation wealth and the commerce based on it" were "very potent considerations" for the elites of the Atlantic world. It is true that there existed in Prussia and the Hanseatic towns an interest in trade with Haiti, and that this commerce started soon after independence,[11] but these commercial links had scarcely any influence on the dominant intellectual considerations. This ultimately means that we are here faced with prejudices against blacks and opinions about them that were exclusively motivated by what is best described as a *Weltanschauung,* that is a complex and comprehensive personal philosophy of human life and the universe.

One prerequisite for Germans' assessment of the Haitian Revolution was the existing conception of race that had been developed at the end of the eighteenth century by the newly established disciplines of anthropology and ethnology, and connected to this the question of slavery. At that time, there was a widespread consensus regarding the inhumane treatment of slaves in the European colonies in the Americas. The cruelties of slavery were condemned by every author dealing with this topic.[12] Regarding racial concepts hardly anyone (with one or two exceptions)[13] tried to justify slavery by assuming the inferiority of blacks. What existed was a feeling of cultural superiority, but not of a racial, i.e. biologically determined superiority. These findings for Germany have been confirmed for all of eighteenth-century Europe as well.[14] But this assumption of the cultural inferiority of blacks also meant that, in the beginning, a state led by former slaves had to appear unthinkable to Europeans.

At the turn of the eighteenth century, the differentiation of public opinion in terms of its political orientation and its underlying *Weltanschauung* was also defined by the attitude toward the French Revolution. In Germany the development of political trends was closely related to the revolution of 1789, which at the same time sparked the revolution in Haiti. The great slave revolt erupted in 1791. At the turn of the century, the conservative opponents of the revolution condemned both the French Revolution and the revolution in Haiti, while its advocates looked with benevolence upon the island. Still, during the early years the frightening image of the insurgent slave dominated German reports. As David Brion Davis remarks in chapter 1, for many whites the Haitian Revolution reinforced the belief that emancipation in any guise would bring economic ruin and the indiscriminate massacre of white populations.

Opponents of the revolution in Germany used reports of the atrocities committed by slaves to confirm what they considered to be the altogether disastrous effects of the French Revolution. In this respect Gottlob Benedikt Schirach, the editor of the important German magazine *Politisches Journal,* was in line with other

European enemies of the revolution such as the French author Pierre-Victor Malouet and the British author Bryan Edwards.[15] With a few exceptions,[16] this negative image prevailed in Germany during the first years of Haitian independence. Napoleonic propaganda hostile to blacks and meant to justify the single, unsuccessful attempt to reconquer Haiti in 1802-1803, is also of importance in this context.

The revision of the European and hence the German image of Haiti in the nineteenth century received an important impetus from the publication of a book in London in 1805, of which a German translation followed in 1806. It was the work of the British author Marcus Rainsford entitled *An Historical Account of the Black Empire of Hayti*. The author had been to Saint-Domingue in 1799 and met with Toussaint Louverture, at that time governor. Rainsford had intended his book as a correction of the misinterpretations of facts contained in reports on the revolution. He was well aware of the deeply rooted prejudices he was questioning with his account and, indeed, he seems to have received little praise for his work: "In many instances the writer has heard reasoning, and witnessed manners of acuteness and elegance, the relation of which would appear incredible, from those who were remembered in a state of servitude, or whose parents were in situations of abject penjury; while sallies of wit, not frequently surpassed, have enlivened many an hour. It would ill become him, notwithstanding the tide of prejudice, which has always pervaded his assertions, to suppose his readers capable of gratification from the chit-chat of a St. Domingo table . . . he therefore contents himself with stating, that the enjoyments of life were to be found in a high degree in the capital of St. Domingo, and that their alloy did not exceed, nor perhaps always equal, that of ancient European cities."[17]

In Germany Rainsford's work brought about a drastic change in the evaluation of Haiti. Its instant translation into German and its wide echo in the historical and political magazines illustrate the willingness to abandon the French line of propaganda as much as the enormous dependency of German judgment on foreign reports. The editor of one of the most important magazines of the time, *Minerva,* commented on Rainsford's book: "These reports which are presented with many a pleasant detail and great expertise in a pleasant style by an eye-witness draw back the curtain on this Negro-theatre and provide us with a view of the matter which differs completely from the one we have obtained from biased reports. The friends of contemporary history believed their ideas to be correct but after reading this work they will find that until now they have had only very incorrect concepts and opinions on this strange event and its causes. The Negroes whom we have, by all means, considered to be monsters do now appear in an entirely new light, and their first leader, Toussaint Louverture, emerges as a highly admirable, truly great man whose sad fate one wants to mourn."[18] These words clearly state the change of perception regarding the young state that Rainsford had brought about. This change was also supported by Alexander von Humboldt, who was an outspoken and uncompromising opponent of slavery and had just returned from his American journey. In 1803 Humboldt noted in his travel diary that nowhere else in the world did a European have to be more ashamed of himself than in the West Indies, for nowhere else in the world could you find more black slaves and nowhere else did they receive so horrible a treatment. "To fight over the question of which nation treats the blacks with more humanity is to mock the concept of humanity itself . . ."[19] Still, this Prussian, who was enthusiastic about reform, abhorred revolutionary changes at the cost of human lives. This applies also to the Haitian Revolution. Yet he advocated Haiti's independence, as one can deduce from the version of his *Ensayo político sobre la isla de Cuba* published in 1825. There he says: "Let us entertain the hope that the power of public opinion, the progress of enlightenment, the customs which have become milder, the legislation of the new republics of the continent and the recognition of Haiti by the French government — an event which can be called happy and important at the same time — have a fortunate influence on the improvement of the conditions of the Negroes in the rest of the West Indies, as well as of those in North and South Carolina (USA) and the various Guianas and Brazil."[20]

There were still other European opponents of slavery who influenced the German image of Haiti. The Abbé Grégoire, whose works emphasized the equality of blacks and whites, had exchanged letters with Toussaint Louverture. Part of their correspondence was published in a German magazine in 1808.[21] The English abolitionists whose works were put into circulation by committed German journalists were equally important.[22]

The question of the abolition of slavery was also discussed during the Congress of Vienna (1814–1815), so that it gained more and more attention in Europe. This topic touched Haiti, too, as it included the problem of race. German publications of the time argued more frequently in favor of the abolition of slavery. A detailed description of the slave trade written by Albert Hüne was published in 1820. The author ranks among those contemporaries who held that slavery, apart from the abuses of the trade and regardless of the level of treatment of the slaves, had to be resisted first and foremost by the slaves themselves. To him, blacks were in every respect on a par with whites. He justified his point of view with reference to the talents and abilities of the Haitian independence fighters: "The young Negro state of Haiti proves that a flat nose and thick lips do not prevent the adoption of certain follies and weaknesses as well as the better customs of the Europeans; men like Toussaint Louverture, Dessalines and Christophe have well shown that the black and frizzy head of a Negro can shelter as great a mind as any other."[23] This judgment is reinforced by a short survey of the history of Haiti based on Haitian publications. These impressive descriptions and justifications had been published in translation in German historical and political magazines. In both of the Haitian states, in the republic as well as in the kingdom, writings intended especially to justify Haitian independence and emphasizing the equality of races were published. The two counselors of king Christophe, the Baron de Vastey and the Duke de Limonade, who were responsible for the kingdom's foreign policy, need to be mentioned in this context. Vastey wrote various papers dealing with colonization and slavery. Above all, he was an ardent critic of using European racial theories to justify them.[24] "The intellectual products of the Haitians clearly prove what has long been doubted: that the blacks are not in the least inferior to the whites with respect to their mental faculties."[25] To Hüne Haiti is an example which proved the equality of blacks and whites, and thus an important argument for the abolition of the slave trade.

In the second quarter of the nineteenth century, the German liberals of the so-called *Vormärz*[26] were full of admiration for Haiti. The enlightened bourgeoisie of the late eighteenth century had admired the revolution in North America. The liberal bourgeoisie which had emerged in the early nineteenth century looked expectantly to the Latin American republics which were consolidating themselves at that time.[27] The Latin American states which had just achieved independence seemed to establish what a liberal bourgeoisie longed to see come true in Germany: "the codification of fundamental and liberal rights, the division of power, representation of the people and administration of the state on the grounds of a written constitution."[28] We are thus faced with the phenomenon of the projection of German wishes onto conditions which were actually quite remote. It is remarkable that this projection should occur with respect to Haiti, peopled and governed by blacks and half-castes.

Probably the most interesting work expressing the liberal German attitude to American history and policy is Alexander Lips' *Statistik von Amerika,* published in 1828, near the end of the Hispanic American struggle for independence. "There has not been any other time, not even at the time of its discovery, that America has held the attention of a surprised Europe more than since its southern half began its fight for freedom and independence and thus broke away from its mother country."[29] Lips begins his work with this statement. He approves of the independence movement, which he does not see as a loss for Europe but considers as positive since America has thus attained its freedom. The colonial period, in turn, appeared as a cruel time of oppression. The liberal historian is so obsessed with his wishful thinking that he writes in a dreamy fashion about the regions of South America: "They are paradises which do not require anything else to be heaven on earth but freedom and the effort of Man."[30] To him the independence of the American states was a turning point in the history of the world and the end of European colonial rule. Lips depicts the future of America in the brightest colors. America would be at once the happiest and the most powerful continent. As a liberal, he shows special interest in the new forms of politics and state formation, which he also sees as the essential American influence on Europe: "No matter how much the old and decaying building of European institutions is propped up — there is no power in the world that can keep it upright or away from the influence of this wind that blows across the Atlantic Ocean."[31] To him America had opened up new political pathways. In his opinion the "constitutional power" was more important than anything else that until then had been discovered by humankind, in fact, even more important than the discovery of the continent itself. But the author was mistaken when he believed that America was a *tabula rasa* on which any form of state could be established. This seemed to be more difficult in Europe due to conditions that had evolved over the centuries.

His work begins with a general section dealing with the history, geography, anthropology and politics of both North and South America. He continues with the description of the corresponding states, starting off with the United States. Lips calls slavery the cancer of America, especially attacking the United States where, according to him, the prejudices against blacks were even greater and more cruel than in Hispanic America.

The author starts his chapter on Haiti with a statement that an uncivilized mass, by taking the step from slavery to freedom, had suddenly ascended to the heights of civilization. A multitude of blacks had thus formed a republic and a people, a sight that in his opinion was new and unique in world history and could serve as an example to the African continent. The existence of Haiti as a nation particularly touched the question of slavery, disproving previous arguments for its necessity. "This proves," Lips writes, "that black people, too, can be sufficient unto themselves and become free citizens."[32] Yet his summary of Haitian history is short and given in broad outlines, and therefore full of mistakes, whereas the contents of the republican constitution of 1816 are presented in detail. This constitution was liberal and established the presidential system in Haiti following the example of the United States. Yet in fact the country was ruled in a dictatorial way both by Pétion, whose administration had designed the constitution, and by Boyer who retained it. Like many other liberals of his time, Lips judges Haiti by its constitution and pays less attention to the political reality: "It is a highly interesting and strange phenomenon to see a people which only recently had borne the yoke of slavery and is now, as the constitution shows, taking great strides on the road toward civilization, improving its laws and conditions so much that in many respects it can already set an example for the old European nations and serve as a mirror."[33] Because of its political stability during the Boyer administration, which was in sharp contrast with the civil wars of South America, several German liberals held Haiti up as a shining example to the rest of the continent. Yet Lips goes even further than his contemporaries by holding Haiti up as an example even to Europe: "Haiti, a Negro state, has a civil code appropriate to the conditions of the nation and its people whereas Germany, a highly cultured country, has to toil under old statutes from the times of the Romans or the Reich!!!"[34] On the whole, Alexander Lips' description of Haiti is positive, yet not very sound and basically shaped by his liberal wishful thinking.

In the first decades of the nineteenth century, the emergence and development of an independent Haiti on the whole enhanced the status of blacks in Germany; cases to the contrary remained rare. The Germans continued to perceive progress in the development of the Caribbean island nation well into the time of the Boyer administration, and it was not least because of Haiti's generally quiet development during the 1820s and 30s that the public interest diminished. In 1830 a liberal German journalist wrote about Haiti: "The republic is safe outside and quiet inside; nowhere else in the West Indies are individuals and personal property safer, while the black people are slowly prospering in refinement, thus embarrassing many a white nation. May Negro republics arise everywhere in the West Indies and bloody seeds bring such harvest."[35]

For the first half of the nineteenth century, three central aspects have to be emphasized regarding German attitudes to Haitian history: First of all, no other Latin American state was covered as often in the German press. Secondly, the German image of Haiti was very heterogeneous until the middle of the century. Yet thirdly, views on Haitian history and its interpretation generally tended to become more benevolent and idealized.

This German image of Haiti changed during the second half of the nineteenth century, when advocates of a more anthropological way of historic reflection "discovered," so to speak, the role of race in history. Furthermore, with the Industrial Revolution the problems of the proletariat and of the ideology of class conflict emerged in Europe. Thus the German and European background for the debate on Haiti became profoundly different around the middle of the century.

Wilhelm Jordan, in his two-volume *Geschichte der Insel Hayti und ihres Negerstaates* (published 1846–1849), was the first German author to reflect these changes.[36] The two decisive arguments he uses to explain his interest in the history of Haiti are the categories of race and class as historical forces.[37] The pressing questions of the Industrial Revolution in Europe preoccupy the Old World. Like the French abolitionist Victor Schoelcher, who wrote on slavery at around the same time,[38] Jordan compares American slaves to European workers. Just as social inequalities had led to the Haitian Revolution, in the same way the unsolved "social question" of the European societies might end in the proletarian revolution predicted by Marx: "Well now, take a look at Haiti! Its recent past is a miniaturized mirror of Europe's future, which has to happen and will happen if the agonized cries of the oppressed and emaciated pillars of the whole society are not heard and the slaves are forced **to free themselves!**"[39]

On the topic of race relations, Jordan assumed the superiority of whites over blacks. He expounded his views in an article from 1845, "On the Natural History of the Human Races," in which he equates the history of nations with the history of races. Within this historical system whites (and among them the Jews and the Germans) rank highest, blacks lowest.[40] Jordan does regard the revolution in Haiti as the Caribbean counterpart to the French Revolution, but, in accordance with his historical viewpoint, emphasizes racial conflict as the most important difference. Not only their interests separated the warring parties, but "first and foremost their obvious natural difference," i.e. race. The Haitian Revolution therefore became one of the main chapters in his "natural history of races." For blacks, according to Jordan, the whites and the *affranchis* had to be their natural enemies whose existence could not be reconciled with their own, and against whom they had to wage a war of annihilation if they wanted to survive.[41]

Around the middle of the century, Wilhelm Jordan was the first German who integrated the Haitian Revolution extensively as an example into a historical system that was determined by race. From then on, this tendency dominated the assessment of Haitian history in German publications. This phenomenon coincided with a growing tendency in all of Europe during the second half of the century to accord special importance to race as an historical influence. Joseph Arthur, comte de Gobineau's *L'essai sur l'inégalité des races humaines* (1853–1855) is the prime example of the views of those Europeans who interpreted human history as a history of races. He was the first to develop a comprehensive theory regarding the assumed connection between race and history.[42] Gobineau found recognition among German intellectuals fairly soon, and his theories were introduced into general reference works during the course of the second half of the nineteenth century.[43]

Heinrich Handelmann (1827–1891) was the first professional historian in Germany who, as part of an extensive study of the whole of the Americas, also turned to the history of Haiti,[44] while at the same time being guided by contemporary views on race. He made the meeting of the different human races on the American continents the defining element of a comprehensive history of America. For Handelmann, the United States, Haiti, and Brazil were the "states of the black and white race."[45] In 1856 he published a *Geschichte der Vereinigten Staaten* and a *Geschichte der Insel Hayti*. Four years later, he followed this up with a *Geschichte von Brasilien,* thereby finishing the first half of the all-encompassing history of the Americas he had planned. To him the Hispanic American states, whose history he also intended to write, were characterized by the "white and red races." But he was unable to carry out this second part of his ambitious project.[46]

Handelmann had studied with the most important German historians of the nineteenth century, Johann Gustav Droysen, Georg Waitz, and Leopold von Ranke.[47] Therefore, we can expect from him the rigorous criteria in dealing with sources so characteristic of German historicism. Handelmann not only cites the material he actually used but also other works deemed important yet unavailable to him. On the other hand he disregarded several voluminous foreign monographs even though they were available in translation.[48] He completely ignored the detailed treatment of Haitian history in German magazines of the first half of the nineteenth century. The works of Lepelletier de Saint-Rémy and Gustave d'Alaux (both French) were his main sources,[49] and he also took over their judgment of events. In addition, he did not cite references, a practice still fairly common at that time even among professional university historians.

Handelmann clearly was an opponent of slavery and the slave trade.[50] Yet his history of the island is mainly a political one and excludes any opinions of his own, in deference to the claims of the "non-judgmental" historicism. Therefore the reader cannot easily tell what he thinks of the revolution and subsequent formation of an independent Haitian state. But he often calls the various armed conflicts during and after the revolution "race wars."[51] Although he thereby simplifies the complexity of the military developments, at least he does not blame the atrocities only on the rebellious slaves, but also on the French.[52] During the last stage of the revolution, that is the war for independence against the Napoleonic forces, Handelmann even saw more cruelty on the side of the French troops. He writes ironically: "Unfortunately, it cannot be denied that this time, in such ignoble competition, French "civilisation"'was victorious over the African barbarism."[53] Handelmann contrasts the "French (or European) civilization" several times with "African barbarism,"[54] but without giving any clear definition of either. However, we can deduce his concept of "African barbarian" from his characterizations of the different protagonists. The description of Toussaint Louverture is especially revealing: "Not only did he possess a keen intelligence and the art of the most profound pretense, but also a talent for military leadership and governing that was unusual in these regions and even more so among members of his race."[55] Handelmann attributes certain characteristics to Toussaint — and denotes them as positive — while at the same time making it clear that they are not typical for blacks. On the other hand, Toussaint's petty vanity, his one character trait that Handelmann rates negative, is described as typical for blacks.[56] All in all, Handelmann approves of Toussaint's measures to consolidate Saint-Domingue, significantly enough because "under all circumstances, European culture, not African roughness, was the crucial standard."[57] But Handelmann also appreciates Toussaint's ability to steer clear of all the different interests and factions in the colony during the revolutionary war, and to free himself of racial prejudices: and therefore, "it is worthy of recognition that an uneducated slave who as the leader of his tribe first vanquished the whites and the coloreds, did not then turn around and made black skin color the prerequisite for aristocracy. He was able to utterly renounce all racial prejudice and instead to apply only the measure of general humanity."[58] The author expresses his own ideals in this kind of judgment,[59] but it was overshadowed by his prejudice toward blacks. While granting Toussaint a lack of prejudice concerning racial difference, he himself judges the *anciens libres,* the mulatto freedmen, as the "higher-ranking race" in Haiti.[60] Handelmann concurs here with the observations of Lepelletier de Saint-Rémy.

Handelmann's basic racism becomes especially apparent at the end of the book, in his treatment of Soulouque. His "African race" is being blamed for his negative features: his vanity[61] as well as his "innate Negro wildness."[62] Handelmann's treatment of Soulouque was based mainly on the work of Gustave d'Alaux, whose negative views and racist clichés he adopted together with the juxtaposition of civilization and barbarity. Handelmann's obvious sympathy for Haiti's neighbor, the Dominican Republic, without doubt also goes back to d'Alaux. During France's Second Empire (1852–1870) Soulouque became an important means to caricature Napoleon III.[63] The disparagement of Soulouque's empire was so widespread that his name became a contemporary object of derision and invective all over Europe. Karl Marx and Friedrich Engels, for example, called various politicians of the nineteenth century "Soulouque" as a way to denigrate them. Apart from Napoleon III, in whose case the contemporaneous existence of the second French and Haitian empires made the comparison easy,[64] they used this name for Simón Bolívar (the substantial time interval notwithstanding),[65] and even Bismarck.[66] Handelmann's description of Soulouque corresponds entirely to the Zeitgeist.

Heinrich Handelmann represents the first instance of racist tendencies in German professional historical writing on Haiti. However, it has to be noted that he was not without sympathy for blacks, which led him to a number of contradictions, and the racist passages of his book, essentially limited to his treatment of Soulouque, are easily traced back to Handelmann's French sources. One cannot yet discern a fully developed pattern of racist thought in his description of Haitian history. This would only happen in the work of one other German author at the beginning of the twentieth century.

Until well into this century, Handelmann's remained the only German history of Haiti written by a professional historian, and thus stayed an important source of information for those (although there were few) interested in Haiti. One result, for example, was that Leopold Contzen (1836–1918), a Prussian gymnasium teacher who taught several generations of students during the German empire and also published several works on Latin American history, described Haitian history as characterized by racial conflict only.[67] Contzen was a typical intellectual representative of the newly founded Germany of 1871 with strong patriotic feelings. The German *Kaiserreich* became a colonial power (in Africa and Asia) and around the turn of the century economically and strategically the most important rival of the

United States in the Caribbean.[68] But with World War I, Germany dropped out of competition in the Caribbean area.

In the second half of the nineteenth century, in the intellectual field, Social Darwinism had been added to race as a historical force.[69] But both factors were recognized more widely in European thought only with the turn of the century. There is a quantifiable rise in racist writings especially after 1900, and an intrusion of this kind of thinking into academic disciplines. These tendencies were not limited to Europe but could be found in the United States as well, where Madison Grant and Lothrop Stoddard were the most important ideologues of race.[70] In Germany, it was Oswald Spengler who was mainly responsible for the transfer of naturalist and biological laws onto history.[71] Two works published at the beginning of the twentieth century demonstrate the fact that Haiti, and especially the revolution, could be interesting subjects for this kind of history: Stoddard's *The French Revolution in San Domingo,* published in 1912, and Erwin Rüsch's *Die Revolution von Saint Domingue,* published in 1930. I do not want to review Rüsch's book extensively here, but I would like to take two typical examples and briefly analyze them.

German historians of the interwar years were mainly members of the bourgeoisie and as such not only afraid of the revolutionary masses but opposed to any fundamental social change and the modernization of society.[72] Foreign policy became one of the areas where Social Darwinism found its way into historical thinking. "There was a tendency to transpose the laws of nature onto history. As in nature, the law of the strongest governed international politics, too, the law of the strong state and strong nation....."[73] But Germany had lost the last war, and, much to the regret of the bourgeoisie, its Kaiser as well. The Weimar Republic did not measure up to the challenges of the time, whether in domestic or foreign policy, and only a consummate statesman, a true leader, seemed to promise a solution. "Politics was interpreted as the 'art' of the individual genius, whose powers were more irrational than rational in nature, more artistic than intellectual."[74]

Erwin Rüsch was rooted in this Zeitgeist, without any doubt, and he transferred these general tendencies of German thought onto his interpretation of the Haitian Revolution. He saw the different groups of inhabitants during the colonial era as antagonistic races, and the whites as feeling threatened by blacks simply because of their minority status. In his view, the legal discrimination against the *affranchis* was necessary for the physical survival of the whites: "We have already seen how the masses of Negroes have uprooted the white population by their simple existence; and the mixed race of the Creoles provided daily examples of the superior power of assimilation of black blood. Something like a *pénétration pacifique* threatened, a gradual and imperceptible absorption of the Aryan element; from this vantage point the dividing wall between the races was not high enough by far."[75] Rüsch does not view the beginnings of the slave revolt as a conscious effort on the part of the blacks to fight for their freedom; instead he calls this first phase "an orgy of destruction" and a "Vaudoux dance of gigantic proportions."[76] "The Negroes had not yet awakened to a racial consciousness and racial pride; they are still very far from an awareness of their equality among nations."[77] One aspect of Rüsch's view of history that was typical of the times becomes very clear here: nations and races have to fight for their position against each other. During the initial phase of the Haitian Revolution, which in Rüsch's periodization ended around the middle of 1794, he cannot yet discern a constructive struggle of the slaves; it was rather a complete "process of disintegration,"[78] and accordingly he calls the first part of his book "The Fall of Saint-Domingue."

In Rüsch's opinion, an element of revolution was added only in the second phase, and he calls it a "psychological revolution." If the first phase was wholly determined by its "African nature" and therefore neither conscious nor purposeful, then exactly these missing elements appeared in the second phase.[79] This was possible — another typical observation for Rüsch's time — because of a born leader, Toussaint Louverture. Therefore, the second part of his book is titled "The Dictator." Before turning to Rüsch's characterization of Toussaint, I would first like to discuss his interpretation of the course of the revolution, as the first important aspect of his ideology is revealed here. The "genius of the leader" and success of the army during the second phase of the revolution enabled the blacks to develop their self-consciousness. "His person became the symbol of their equality among the races, even to the point of stirring up a feeling of superiority here and there."[80] But the community that Toussaint had built did not yet have a "people," because whites, blacks, and *affranchis* still possessed equal rights.[81] A first glimpse of a "racial consciousness" was offered by the uprising headed by Toussaint's nephew Moïse, which was motivated in part by Toussaint's alleged preferential treatment of whites. "And even more so than this revolt, the embodiment of the slowly growing racial consciousness of the Negroes, developing in reaction to Toussaint Louverture's state, was Dessalines, still strictly obedient in appearance but secretly griping."[82]

Rüsch calls this third part "The Nation," describing the struggle of the blacks against the invading forces of Napoleon. Now in charge was Dessalines, for Rüsch the typical African who, after a transitional period of a growing sense of liberty and independence under Toussaint, brought a black, African consciousness into the last phase of the revolution and thus made the independent state of Haiti possible. For Dessalines, unlike Toussaint, the "African nature" is no longer a reason for shame and disgust, something to be overcome; instead he emphasizes it on purpose, as his possession and that of his nation and therefore special. He hates European culture and everything touched by it, because he regards it as alien."[83] In this interpretation of the course of the revolution, the first aspect of Rüsch's ideology becomes apparent: the formation and self-assertion of a nation needs a homogeneous people. Typically enough, he then accuses Dessalines and the emerging Haitian state of not fighting the "racial conflict" to the utmost degree, in the sense of carrying it beyond the borders of Haiti. Haiti had developed into a nation that had thrown off the French yoke, but with unassuageable enmity only against the French and not against all whites. For Rüsch, it seemed to be a violation of "natural law" that Haiti "does not view itself as representative of a large racial community and champion of a fundamental divide between black and white."[84] But after fifteen years of struggle, with a desolate economy and the constant threat of French invasion (which finally ended only in 1825), a policy of non-intervention in the affairs of its neighbors had to be one of the foundations of Haitian politics. Here, Rüsch's interpretation displays an irrationality that is far removed from historical reality, and which is the result of the interpretive restrictions of his racial ideology.

Apart from the "racial" element, the other dominant factor in Rüsch's interpretation of the Haitian Revolution is the figure of the leader. With Toussaint, this element reaches critical importance during the second phase of the revolution, by guiding events for the first time in a way that consciously defined "black" against "white" interests. Toussaint is successful because of his two characteristic attributes, his will to power and his ability to reflect. His "inquisitive, discerning mind" allowed him to give order to a revolution that had been "moved by blind desire" and to direct it according to his intentions.[85] "This leads me to an observation which I deem the most important of the present work, its main thesis, which is the foundation of my view of the Saint-Domingue Revolution in its form as well as its content and, if proven wrong, would discredit this view. It is the realization that Toussaint was not African but, being in his will related to the Occident, belonged to its sphere."[86] Now Rüsch gets caught up in the contradictions of his ideology. He assigns certain immutable qualities, determined by biology, to the different races. This becomes clear from the "racial" concepts already mentioned above. But Toussaint does not fit into these ideas on Africans, on blacks—he acts like a European, a white person: "The untrammelled energy, purposeful and steady, guided by clearly defined values, this is European, not African."[87] But if Rüsch transforms Toussaint from black/African to white/European,[88] then this contradicts the biological invariability of races that is central to his views. If Toussaint follows "European or white patterns of behavior," these must be cultural and therefore variable differences, in violation of his racist ideology. His argumentation remains inconclusive, his premise regarding Toussaint untenable within his own line of reasoning, and we are allowed— following his own standards—"to disregard his whole view of the Revolution." But Erwin Rüsch's interpretation remains the only available German monograph on the Haitian Revolution, and it represents an almost perfect example of an important part of German historiography during the interwar years, when nation, race, and leader were stylized as central elements of historical process.[89] Rüsch's Latin American topic was also representative, as the charismatic fighter for independence seemed to be the perfect choice to illustrate the figure of the leader and its role in history that were so popular in Germany during the 1920s and '30s.[90]

German attitudes toward Haitian history changed in two ways between the end of the eighteenth and the beginning of the twentieth century. Into the second quarter of the nineteenth century, the German press reported extensively on Haiti. No other Latin American state was covered as often. The German image of Haiti was very heterogeneous, and thinking on Haitian history and its interpretation generally tended to become more benevolent and idealized during that period. From the middle of the nineteenth century, German historians and journalists chose Haitian topics only rarely, thus drastically reducing their quantitative importance. Subsequent discussion was now characterized by its reflection of contemporary German and European problems. By the second quarter of the nineteenth century, German liberals projected their wishes onto the Haitian state. Around the middle of the century, fears of the industrial proletariat and a proletarian revolution were reflected back onto the revolution against the slaveholders of Saint Domingue. During the second half of the nineteenth century, the emerging ideologies of race made Haiti a renewed object of interest for historians. In the interwar years, the racial viewpoint gained new ground, and the longing for a leader was added. The result was the first extensive discussion of the Haitian Revolution by a German writer, one who projected onto the Caribbean island the central elements of the new ideologies: race and the *Führerprinzip* (leadership principle). The extensive and differentiated discussion of the early 1800s diminished toward the end of the century into an increasingly one-sided view of Haitian history. Haiti instead became the mirror for contemporary German political topics, the canvas upon which these questions and problems were projected. To judge this development in a European context, it would be important to know more about the reception of Haitian history in England and France, topics that are yet largely unexplored.

NOTES

1. Until the early nineteenth century Germany consisted of numerous states of different size connected only loosely in the Holy Roman Empire, which was dissolved in 1806. An attempt to unite the states into one nation in the 1848 revolutions failed and this was achieved only in 1871 with the founding of the second *Reich* that was succeeded in 1918 by the Weimar Republic, and in 1933, by the third *Reich*.

2. The perception of the Haitian Revolution in Germany partially contradicts the very interesting consideration of Michel-Ralph Trouillot's "An Unthinkable History: The Haitian Revolution as a Non-Event," in Trouillot, *Silencing the Past: Power and the Production of History* (Boston: Beacon Press, 1995), 70–107. For an extensive treatment of the reception of Haitian history in Germany during the first half of the nineteenth century see my *Die deutsche Rezeption haitianischer Geschichte in der ersten Hälfte des 19. Jahrhunderts. Ein Beitrag zum deutschen Bild vom Schwarzen* (Cologne: Böhlau,1992). For the role of Haiti in German fiction, see Herbert Uerlings, *Poetiken der Interkulturalität. Haiti bei Kleist, Seghers, Müller, Buch und Fichte* (Tübingen: Niemeyer, 1997).

3. For the role of the slave uprising in connection with the revolution see the detailed analysis in Carolyn E. Fick, *The Making of Haiti: The Saint Domingue Revolution from Below* (Knoxville: University of Tennessee Press, 1990). A general overview of the political history of the revolution can be found in T. Ott, *The Haitian Revolution 1789–1804* (Knoxville: University of Tennessee Press, 1973).

4. James G. Leyburn, *The Haitian People* (New Haven: Yale University Press, 1941), 42.

5. Benoit Joachim, "La reconnaissance d'Haïti par la France (1825): Naissance d'un nouveau type de rapports internationaux," *Revue d'histoire moderne et contemporaine* 22 (1975): 369–96.

6. For the history of independent Haiti up to 1859 see David Nicholls, *From Dessalines to Duvalier. Race, Colour and National Independence in Haiti* (Cambridge: Cambridge University Press, 1979), 33–102; Leyburn, *Haitian People,* 32–93. For the conflicting views on the regime of Soulouque see John E. Baur, "Faustin Soulouque, Emperor of Haiti. His Character and his Reign," *The Americas* 6 (1949): 131–66, and Murdo J. MacLeod, "The Soulouque Regime in Haiti, 1847–1859: A Reevaluation," *Caribbean Studies* 10 (1970): 35–48. The latter

tries to break out of the stereotypical and polemical debate about Soulouque that had been the norm since the nineteenth century.

7. See Schüller, *Die deutsche Rezeption,* 167–261.

8. *Minerva. Ein Journal historischen und politischen Inhalts* (Berlin, ed. J. W. Archenholz), 263 vols. (1792–1858).

9. Schüller, *Die deutsche Rezeption,* 260–61.

10. See David P. Geggus, "Slavery, War, and Revolution in the Greater Caribbean, 1789–1815," in *A Turbulent Time: The French Revolution and the Greater Caribbean,* ed. D. B. Gaspar, D. P. Geggus (Bloomington: Indiana University Press, 1997), 1–50; John E. Baur, "International Repercussions of the Haitian Revolution," *The Americas* 26 (1970): 394–418.

11. Most German commerce with Haiti was through the port of Bremen. See Hermann Kellenbenz, "Eisenwaren gegen Zucker. Rheinischer Handel mit der Karibischen Welt um 1834," *Jahrbuch für Geschichte von Staat, Wirtschaft und Gesellschaft Lateinamerikas* (hereafter *JbLA*) 8 (1971): 250–74; Michael Zeuske, "Die vergessene Revolution: Haiti und Deutschland in der ersten Hälfte des 19. Jahrhunderts. Aspekte deutscher Politik und Ökonomie in Westindien," *JbLA* 28 (1991):285–325.

12. I studied in detail the classic texts of Johann Friedrich Blumenbach, Immanuel Kant, Eberhard August Wilhelm von Zimmermann, Samuel Thomas Sömmering, Christoph Meiners, Johann Jacob Sell, and Christian Georg Andreas Oldendorp; see Schüller, *Die deutsche Rezeption,* 56–73.

13. Christoph Meiners and maybe also Samuel Thomas Sömmering.

14. Urs Bitterli, *Die "Wilden" und die "Zivilisierten": Grundzüge einer Geistes- und Kulturgeschichte der europäisch-überseeischen Begegnung* (Munich: Beck,1991 [1976]), 323.

15. *Politisches Journal nebst Anzeige von gelehrten und andern Sachen,* published annually in Hamburg from 1781 to 1840. Victor P. Malouet, *Beschreibung der westindischen Insel San-Domingo* (Weimar: Landes-Industrie-Comptoir, 1808); B. Edwards, *Geschichte des Revolutionskriegs in Sanct Domingo,* 2 vols. (Leipzig: Dyk, 1798).

16. For example, the journal *Frankreich im Jahr [1795–1805]. Aus den Briefen deutscher Männer in Paris,* published annually from 1795 to 1805 in Altona.

17. Marcus Rainsford, *An Historical Account of the Black Empire of Hayti: Comprehending a View of the Principal Transactions in the Revolution of Saint Domingo; with its Ancient and Modern State* (London: James Cundee, 1805), 221. German translation: *Geschichte der Insel Hayti oder St. Domingo besonders des auf derselben errichteten Negerreichs* (Hamburg: Adolph Schmidt, 1806), 258–59.

18. "Toussaint Louverture. Eine historische Schilderung für die Nachwelt," *Minerva* 4 (1805): 277–78.

19. Alexander von Humboldt, *Lateinamerika am Vorabend der Unabhängigkeitsrevolution: Eine Anthologie von Impressionen und Urteilen ,* ed. M. Faak (Berlin: Akademie-Verlag, 1982), 66.

20. Alexander von Humboldt, *Cuba-Werk,* vol. 3, *Alexander von Humboldt. Studienausgabe,* ed. by Hanno Beck (Darmstadt: Wissenschaftliche Buchgesellschaft: 1992), 116.

21. "Briefe des General Toussaint Louverture an den Bischoff und Senator Gregoire (Aus der französischen Handschrift übersetzt)," *Europäische Annalen* (Tübingen, 1795–1820; ed. by E. L. Posselt), 3 (1808): 173–86. Gregoire mentions his correspondence with Toussaint in one of his works: Henri Gregoire, *Die Neger. Ein Beitrag zur Staats- und Menschenkunde: Aus dem Französischen übersetzt* (Berlin: Braunes, 1809), 117.

22. The most important one was Matthias Christian Sprengel: see Schüller, *Die deutsche Rezeption,* 68–69.

23. Albert Hüne, *Vollständige historisch-philosophische Darstellung aller Veränderungen*

des Negersclavenhandels von dessen Ursprunge an bis zu seiner gänzlichen Aufhebung, 2 vols. (Göttingen: J. F. Römer, 1820), 1:512.

24. David Nicholls, "Pompée Valentin Vastey: Royalist and Revolutionary," *JbLA* 28 (1991): 107–23. Vastey had published an apologia on the revolution and the formation of an independent Haitian state, which had appeared in two German journals, first as excerpts in 1820 and the full text in 1825: "Die haytischen Staaten. I. Das Königreich. Aus des Baron de Vastey, Kanzler des Königs von Hayti, Essai sur les causes de la Revolution et des Guerres civiles d'Hayti, übersetzt von Dr. Pfeilschifter," *Europäische Annalen* 8 (1820): 161–98; "Ueber die Ursachen der Revolution und der Bürgerkriege in Hayti. Vom Baron de Vastey," *Der Staatsmann* 7 (1825): 1–66, 99–164, 199–230, 305–25.

25. Hüne, *Negersclavenhandel,* vol. 2, 368.

26. The German "Vormärz" comprises the era between the Congress of Vienna and the Revolution of 1848, which began in March of that year.

27. Karin Schüller, "Das Urteil der deutschen Liberalen des Vormärz über Lateinamerika. Eine historische Skizze," *JbLA* 31 (1994): 189–207. Spanish version: "La actitud de los liberales alemanes de la primera mitad del siglo XIX hacia América Latina. Un bosquejo histórico," in *Ciencia e independencia política,* ed. by A. Gil Novales (Madrid: Ediciones del Orto, 1996), 129–46.

28. Hans-Otto Kleinmann, "Die politische und soziale Verfassung des unabhängigen Mexiko im Bild und Urteil liberaler deutscher Zeitgenossen": *JbLA* 8 (1971): 221–22.

29. Alexander Lips, *Statistik von Amerika oder Versuch einer historisch-pragmatischen und raisonirenden Darstellung des politischen und bürgerlichen Zustandes der neuen Staaten-Körper von Amerika* (Frankfurt a.M.: Wilmanns, 1828), 1.

30. Ibid., 3.

31. Ibid., 5.

32. Ibid., 398.

33. Ibid., 406.

34. Ibid., 411.

35. "Die amerikanischen Staaten und Colonien am Ende des Jahrs 1829," *Columbus. Amerikanische Miszellen* (ed. C. N. Röding), 1 (1830): 9.

36. See Schüller, *Die deutsche Rezeption,* 150–66.

37. Wilhelm Jordan, *Geschichte der Insel Hayti und ihres Negerstaats,* 2 vols. (Leipzig: Jorany, 1846–1849), 1:3–5.

38. See Schüller, *Die deutsche Rezeption,* 112–13.

39. Jordan, *Geschichte der Insel Hayti,* 1:4–5. Emphasis in the original.

40. Wilhelm Jordan, "Zur Naturgeschichte der Menschenracen," *Wigands Vierteljahresschrift* (Leipzig) 2 (1845): 273– 75.

41. Jordan, *Geschichte der Insel Hayti,* 1:96–97.

42. See Patrick von zur Mühlen, *Rassenideologien. Geschichte und Hintergründe* (Berlin: Droste, 1977), 52–73; also Imanuel Geiss, *Geschichte des Rassismus* (Frankfurt a.M.: Suhrkamp, 1988), 167–69 and George L. Mosse, *Toward the Final Solution. A History of European Racism* (London: H. Fertig, 1978), 51–57.

43. The changing viewpoints on race at that time can be traced in two of the most important encyclopedias of the nineteenth century. The *Staatslexikon,* published by liberals of the Vormärz, explained the assumed differences in the development levels of races as being caused by the environment. In other words, the differences were cultural (and could thus be changed) instead of being biologically determined. See G. F. Kolb, "Racen der Menschen," *Das Staatslexikon: Encyklopädie der sämtlichen Staatswissenschaften für alle Stände,* ed. by Carl von Rotteck and Carl Welcker, 12 vols. (Altona: Hamerick, 1845–1848), 11:277–90. The Haitian revolutionaries were seen as fighting for human rights: Schüller, *Die deutsche*

Rezeption, 270–71. The tendencies at the beginning of the second half of the nineteenth century differed markedly, see Johann Bluntschli, "Arische Völker und arische Rechte," *Deutsches Staats-Wörterbuch,* 11 vols. (Stuttgart: J. Bluntschli u. K. Brater, 1857–1870), 1:319–31. Here Gobineau, whose influence is very apparent in the article, is included in the list of secondary works (p. 331). See also Bluntschli, "Rasse und Individuum," *Deutsches Staats-Wörterbuch* (1864), 8:474–80.

44. As a professional historian, his only predecessor worth mentioning is Carl Eduard Meinicke, *Versuch einer Geschichte der europäischen Colonien in Westindien* (Weimar: Landes-Industrie, 1831). Cf. Schüller, *Die deutsche Rezeption,* 263–67.

45. Heinrich Handelmann, *Geschichte der Vereinigten Staaten* (Kiel: Schwerssche Buchhandlung, 1856), 11.

46. The author is working on an article about Handelmann's writings on America.

47. *Allgemeine Deutsche Biographie,* 56 vols., supplement Fri-Han (Berlin: Duncker & Humblot, 1981 [1875–1912]), 49:748.

48. For example, Handelmann mentioned Lacroix's two-volume history of the revolution (published in Paris in 1819) as important, but failed to use it (Heinrich Handelmann, *Geschichte der Insel Hayti* [Kiel: Schwerssche Buchhandlung,1860], vi). The German journal *Minerva* had published a partial translation already in 1819, Schüller, *Die deutsche Rezeption,* 256.

49. Handelmann, *Hayti,* vii.

50. Ibid., 79n.

51. Ibid., 50, 53, 72, 86, 89.

52. Ibid., 47, 50–51.

53. Ibid., 94.

54. Ibid., 89, 164.

55. Ibid., 63–64.

56. Ibid., 77. The imagined "African" characteristics are even more prominent in the description of Dessalines, as he was "equipped with all the childish vanity and flighty moodiness of the African race" (ibid., 99).

57. Ibid., 81. The contradiction between the European (white) and African (black) character that Handelmann saw reflected in Haitian history found its expression also in his judgment on the two regimes of Christophe and Pétion: "So you can observe on Haiti the miraculous — and yet only seemingly so — contradiction that the state of the pure Negro, with African despotism underneath its feudal structures, happily copies the old European colonial system, whereas the one governed by the educated mulatto, with its European-style political freedom, threatens to sink into the careless indolence of Africa" (ibid., 114).

58. Ibid., 77.

59. Handelmann gives such a critical description of Napoleon's attitudes toward blacks and his measures to reintroduce slavery that we have to assume humanitarian standards on his part: ibid., 83, 86.

60. Ibid., 155.

61. Ibid., 153, 157, and 161. Even the modern depiction of Soulouque in Baur, "Faustin Soulouque," still attributes "vanity" to him several times.

62. Handelmann, *Hayti,* 156; in another instance, it is called "African wildness" (ibid., 158).

63. See Carl H. Middelanis, *Imperiale Gegenwelten: Haiti in den französischen Text- und Bildmedien (1848–1870)* (Frankfurt a.M.: Vervuert, 1996), 156–70, especially for Gustave d Alaux.

64. Karl Marx, "Die Klassenkämpfe in Frankreich 1848 bis 1850" [1850], in *Karl Marx, Friedrich Engels: Werke* (hereafter *MEW*) (Berlin: Dietz, 1956–1967), 7:47, 86, 90; idem, "Der

achtzehnte Brumaire des Louis Bonaparte," in *MEW,* 8:206; idem, "Urquhart —Bem—Die türkische Frage im Oberhaus," in *MEW,* 9:269; letter from Marx to Engels, 22 Apr. 1859, in *MEW,* 29:426; letter from Marx to Ferdinand Lassalle, 16 Mar.1859, in ibid., 29:584.

65. Letter from Marx to Engels, 14 Feb. 1858, in *MEW,* 29:280. Bolívar was generally judged negatively by Marx. See Günter Kahle, *Simón Bolívar und die Deutschen* (Berlin: Reimer, 1980), 27–29. (Spanish version: *Simón Bolívar y los alemanes* [Berlin: Inter Nationes, 1980]).

66. Letter from Engels to Marx, 20 Apr. 1864, in *MEW* (1964), 30:393.

67. Leopold Contzen, *Haiti und seine Racenkämpfe: Historisch entwickelt* (Cologne: Bachem, 1863). Cf. Karin Schüller, "Leopold Contzen. Ein Bürger der Kaiserzeit und Lateinamerika," in *Iberische Welten. Festschrift zum 65. Geburtstag von Günter Kahle,* ed. Felix Becker, et al. (Cologne: Böhlau, 1994), 849–64.

68. Brenda Gayle Plummer, *Haiti and the Great Powers, 1902–1915* (Baton Rouge: Louisiana State University Press, 1988).

69. von zur Mühlen, *Rassenideologien,* 74–100.

70. Ibid., 204: "What Grant, Stoddard, and Spengler had in common was their fear of the dark-skinned peoples which were threatening whites." For theories of race and racial politics in the United States as compared to Germany see also Hans-Jürgen Lutzhöft, *Der Nordische Gedanke in Deutschland 1920–1940* (Stuttgart: Klett, 1971), 276–81. Lutzhöft writes on p. 280, n. 450: "It seems that Stoddard was the first to defame certain groups as subhumans." Stoddard's *The Revolt against Civilisation: The Menace of Underman* was published in 1922.

71. Bernd Faulenbach, *Ideologie des deutschen Weges: Die deutsche Geschichte in der Historiographie zwischen Kaiserreich und Nationalsozialismus* (Munich: Beck, 1980), 16.

72. Bernd Faulenbach, "Deutsche Geschichtswissenschaft zwischen Kaiserreich und NS-Diktatur," in *Geschichtswissenschaft in Deutschland: Traditionelle Positionen und gegenwärtige Aufgaben,* ed. B. Faulenbach (Munich: Beck, 1974), 67.

73. Faulenbach, *Ideologie des deutschen Weges,* 16.

74. Ibid., 289–90

75. Erwin Rüsch, *Die Revolution von Saint Domingue* (Hamburg: Friederichsen, 1930), 18.

76. Ibid., 51.

77. Ibid., 56.

78. Ibid., 82.

79. Ibid., 85.

80. Ibid., 160.

81. Ibid., 161.

82. Ibid., 171.

83. Ibid., 197.

84. Ibid., 205–6.

85. Ibid., 152–53.

86. Ibid., 153. Rüsch deals here with Stoddard's interpretation of Toussaint's personality. Stoddard had written that Toussaint could not be compared with whites, but if compared to other blacks, he stood out (ibid., 153–54).

87. Ibid., 154.

88. Ibid., 86: "As the future will show, this man will not be a truly integrating force for his people; he is a stranger because he reaches beyond its natural boundaries."

89. Rüsch's work was reviewed in the only German journal devoted to Latin American studies at that time, as well as in the most important general historical journal. In both cases, the book was praised as an important contribution, without any criticism of the theo-

retical approach: *Ibero-Amerikanisches Archiv* 5 (1931): 209–10 and *Historische Zeitschrift* 144 (1931): 433–34.

90. See for example Wolfram Dietrich, *Simon Bolivar und die lateinamerikanischen Unabhängigkeitskriege* (Hamburg: Hartung, 1934), where he writes in the preface: "Especially today, when the principle of the leader has had its breakthrough in Germany, a leader's course of fate, the knowledge won by the liberator and savior of a whole continent in the course of his eventful life, deserve our special interest." Cf. Kahle, *Simón Bolívar,* 31–33.

Chapter 5

Bryan Edwards and the
Haitian Revolution

OLWYN M. BLOUET

WHEN NEWS OF THE SLAVE revolt in Saint-Domingue reached neighboring Jamaica in September 1791, Bryan Edwards was an influential Jamaican planter, master of thousands of acres and hundreds of slaves. Governor Effingham, responding to requests for assistance, immediately sent warships and aid to the French colony, and Bryan Edwards was included in the mission.[1] Edwards saw horrific scenes, and in the following year, he went to Britain, published two books about the Caribbean, became a member of Parliament, and tried to convince M.P.s that too much talk about the abolition of the slave trade would encourage revolts in the British islands and the destruction of the sugar colonies.

Bryan Edwards is best known as the author of two major works, *The History of the British Colonies in the West Indies,*[2] and *An Historical Survey of the French Colony in the Island of St. Domingo.*[3] In the former he articulated the planter viewpoint concerning the value of West Indian colonies to Great Britain. In his survey of Saint-Domingue he told how an idyllic island environment was transformed into a savage wasteland. As author he was a leading interpreter of the Haitian Revolution and helped to construct an image of that revolution for a British audience. His objective was to prevent similar devastation in the British West Indian islands.

Bryan Edwards was born on 12 May 1743 in Westbury, Wiltshire, England.[4] His father died in 1756, leaving a wife and six children. A wealthy uncle, Zachary Bayly, brought Edwards to Jamaica in 1759 to help manage his sugar plantations.[5] No sooner had Edwards landed in Jamaica than a slave revolt erupted at a plantation in St. Mary Parish, and quickly spread to Uncle Zachary's adjoining "Trinity" estate.[6] The revolt, led by Tacky, a "Koromantyn" (Gold Coast) leader, had a lasting impact on Edwards: between thirty and forty whites were butchered, Tacky was killed by Maroons, and, other leaders were punished brutally. Tacky's Rebellion was instigated by newly arrived Africans, and until the Haitian Revolution, Edwards considered Africans a more dangerous threat than Creole slaves.[7]

After the 1760 rebellion Edwards learned the sugar business from Uncle Zachary, took an interest in science and horticulture, and was elected a Fellow of the American Philosophical Society.[8] On the death of his uncle in 1769, Edwards inherited several plantations, and by the mid-1770s was one of the richest men in Jamaica, holding numerous properties and approximately 1,500 slaves.[9]

Bryan Edwards's political career began in 1765, with election to the Jamaica Assembly. As conflict with the American mainland colonies developed, he supported the thirteen colonies against Great Britain. Edwards believed that colonial assemblies were equivalent to the British Parliament, and "must necessarily be sovereign and supreme within their own jurisdiction, unobstructed by, and independent of, all control from without."[10] He blamed the British government for provoking the American colonists to revolt. Colonists should govern themselves.

In 1774, Bryan Edwards visited England. He appeared before the Board of Trade and tried unsuccessfully to gain acceptance of Jamaican legislation to regulate the slave trade.[11] In London he became involved with the West India Committee, an influential lobby made up of planters and merchants. Towards the end of the American Revolution, in 1782, Bryan Edwards was again in England. Heavily critical of the war, and wishing to have an impact on the peace, he tried unsuccessfully to win a seat in Parliament.[12] Edwards appeared before the Board of Trade to protest the Orders-in-Council of 2 July 1783, that virtually prohibited West Indian trade with the independent United States. In 1784, he published a pamphlet, arguing that West Indian trade with the United States was essential for food, staples and lumber.[13] His arguments had no impact, but these excursions into colonial policy made Edwards realize that London did not understand the needs of distant colonies.

Edwards returned from Britain to his Jamaican sugar estates in 1787 and re-entered the Assembly. The planters now faced a new threat from Britain: the humanitarian revolution to abolish the slave trade.[14] Bryan Edwards was sympathetic, believing that African slaves were more of a security threat than Creoles. He wrote in 1784, that, "As a man, and a Christian, I hope I shall live to see the day . . . when this abominable traffic will be prohibited."[15] But Edwards saw the difficulties of Britain stopping the trade, while other nations continued. He favored regulation of the slave trade, particularly the sex and age of slaves, by the West Indian colonies in hopes of encouraging a natural increase that would make the trade from Africa redundant.[16]

Edwards took the lead in responding to the abolitionist proposals of William Wilberforce. In November 1789 Edwards delivered an anti-abolitionist speech before the Jamaican Assembly and Council, that was published in Jamaica and London.[17] He was careful to admit respect for Wilberforce but pointed out his lack of experience in the sugar islands. Edwards was the spokesman for the planter view that abolition of the trade would hurt merchants, planters, the sugar industry and the empire. Unilateral ending of the British slave trade would not promote humanitarianism in Africa or the West Indies. The "amputation of a single limb will only aggravate the symptoms and heighten the malady," he claimed.[18] Slave numbers would decrease, leading to a shortage of labor on existing plantations and for the development of new land. He knew that thousands of acres in the West Indies had been patented on the assumption that the slave trade would continue. Planters, Edwards asserted, would need compensation.

Less than two years after his slave trade speech news of the Saint-Domingue revolt reached Jamaica.[19] The governor, the Earl of Effingham, viewing the revolution as a concern for all West Indian whites, sent arms, ammunition and provisions, but no troops. Bryan Edwards went on the Jamaican mission that arrived in le Cap on 26 September 1791, to "a dreadful scene of devastation by fire . . . to scenes of anarchy, desolation, and carnage."[20]

After seeing and hearing of bloody atrocities, Edwards sailed back to Jamaica in October 1791. He carried documents, including a letter from Paul Cadusch, president of the Saint-Domingue Assembly, appealing to the prime minister, William Pitt for British intervention.[21] Fear of slave revolt had already spread to Jamaica. The militia was called out, committees of security were established in each parish, and the Assembly requested more troops from Britain. Martial law was declared in December 1791, for Jamaica was on the brink of its own slave revolt,[22] and the threat was real. For example, Thomas Barritt noted that for several weeks, "a body of negroes in Spanish Town who called themselves the Cat Club, had assembled drinking King Wilberforce's health out of a cat's skull by way of a cup, and swearing secrecy to each other. . . ."[23] Negroes had been found with cartridges and firearms. As it turned out, 1791 passed without a revolt, but fear was heightened during the Maroon War of 1795, and continued. In 1800, for example, a letter in *The Times* noted that Mr. Smart, a printer in Jamaica, had detected a slave conspiracy.[24] It involved a plot by Jamaican slaves, plus slaves recently arrived from Saint-Domingue, who planned to set fire to Kingston, Spanish Town, and Port Royal. The conspirators had flags printed representing a black and mulatto, mounting a tricolored cockade, and whipping a white man. Two French accomplices confessed to the plot, and the conspiracy was thwarted. But the impact of the Haitian Revolution in Jamaica was widespread and long-lasting.

Toward the end of 1791, Edwards chaired an Assembly committee that recommended a 100,000-pound loan to the planters of Saint-Domingue. Rejected by the Jamaican Assembly, 10,000 pounds worth of supplies was eventually voted.[25] Edwards was disgusted with the attitudes of some of his fellow Jamaicans, who failed to see that their security might be linked to the fate of Saint-Domingue. Jamaican planters were worried about increased taxes[26] and were not sorry to see competition from Saint-Domingue eliminated.

As a result of the situation in Saint-Domingue, the price of sugar rose steeply in Britain. Many people boycotted sugar, and abolitionist groups were strengthened.[27] At Westminster, in April 1792, William Wilberforce, believing that the slave revolution in Saint-Domingue bolstered the abolitionist argument on security grounds, introduced a successful motion to abolish the slave trade by 1796.[28] Until the Saint-Domingue Revolution, Edwards had called for the amelioration of slavery and the gradual phasing out of the slave trade. He was prepared to debate Wilberforce in a measured way. But the Haitian Revolution was initially used in Britain as an argument to speed up the abolition of the slave trade and slavery. It encouraged abolitionists. Edwards believed the Haitian Revolution was brought on by French abolitionists, and, to prevent British humanitarians sparking a slave revolt in Jamaica, Edwards returned to Britain with the intention of publicizing the planter view. Bryan Edwards first published his two-volume *History, Civil and Commercial, of the British Colonies in the West Indies* in 1793. Much of the scholarly book had been written in Jamaica at his plantation, Bryan Castle.[29]

Historians have scoured his work for information about West Indian affairs but, with the notable exceptions of Elsa Goveia and David Brion Davis, few scholars have discussed Edwards's objectives and perspectives.[30] Goveia presented Edwards as a Creole writer, a foundation figure in West Indian historiography. Davis compared Edwards to fellow slaveholders and philosophes Thomas Jefferson and M.-L.-E. Moreau de Saint-Méry. Edwards had much in common with Jefferson. As Davis pointed out, they were men of the Enlightenment (versed in French), interested in scientific exploration and observation, that wrote works about their "new world" environments. Politicians, who moved from local to national affairs, they defended colonial rights against imperial authority. Jefferson and Edwards were planters, who relied on slave labor, but had qualms with the system, and wished to ameliorate the slaves' condition. Although sharing a humanitarian sensibility, they ultimately protected the institution of slavery, especially as they aged. They hoped slavery would wither away.

The similarities between Edwards and Jefferson can be extended. Born in the same year of 1743, they disputed the Comte de Buffon, who postulated environmental inferiority of the Americas, both using the London publisher John Stockwell. Edwards and Jefferson resented the way British authorities disallowed colonial attempts to restrict the slave trade, and, of course, were equally horror-struck by the Haitian Revolution. We do not know if Edwards read Thomas Jefferson's Notes on the State of Virginia, but we can be fairly sure that Jefferson read Edwards's *History* because who should head the list of subscribers to the American edition of the *History* (Philadelphia, 1806), but President Thomas Jefferson. If Jefferson can be considered a son of the Enlightenment, Edwards also qualifies.

Why did Edwards publish his *History* in 1793, two years after the Haitian Revolution began? He had two major objectives: one scientific, the other political. On the scientific side, he presented information to counter the theories of European scientists, such as Buffon, who thought "new world" environments and peoples inferior.[31] Edwards took issue with the view that plants, animals, and people of the Americas were degenerate. He believed that Creole societies were viable. On the political front, he offered first-hand experience of the institution of slavery and the African trade, to contest abolitionist proposals. In both instances, he delivered a white West Indian perspective in opposition to theoretical, metropolitan models.

To counteract the abolitionists, Edwards reviewed the history and size of the slave trade.[32] He suggested it was in the economic interests of planters to have good conditions on the Middle Passage. He wrote of slaves whom he knew, and suggested that many West Indian slaves had previously lived in slavery in Africa.[33] Slave trade abolition would lead to a shortage of slaves, and an annual decrease of slave numbers of 2.5 percent. More labor would be extracted from the existing slaves resulting in hardship.[34] Presenting himself as "no friend to slavery," he urged West Indian legislatures to reform the system of slavery.[35] In his *History* he included a copy of the new Jamaican Consolidated Slave Act of 1792, which, on paper, banned many cruelties.[36] He hoped amelioration would lead to natural population increase, and an end to the Atlantic slave trade. Edwards cautioned that hasty measures, encouraged by humanitarians, might lead to a *bellum servile* (slave war) "which will probably never end but in the extermination of either the whites or the blacks."[37]

Edwards hardly referred directly to the Haitian Revolution in the *History,* except to suggest that the revolution offered a chance for coffee growing to expand in Jamaica. He included a paper about coffee cultivation in Saint-Domingue, by Samuel Vaughan, who argued that with Saint-Domingue consumed in slave revolt, Jamaica could increase coffee acreage, provided the slave trade continued.[38] In the 1790s the Jamaican economy did profit from less competition, the slave trade was buoyant, and coffee production increased markedly. In fact, Edwards offered an alternative to the chaos and carnage of Saint-Domingue. He envisaged the development of Jamaican society based on the increase of European whites for coffee production, the continuing strength of Creole whites, the inclusion in society of free coloreds and free blacks, and the increase of Creole slaves.[39] He projected a natural movement from slavery to serfdom, with ex-slaves functioning as a peasantry. This was his emancipation plan.

In his pragmatic way, Edwards demonstrated the significance of West Indian property and trade to Great Britain. The West Indies offered markets for British manufactures, produced tropical commodities, and provided ships and seamen for war. The total value of West Indian property he estimated at 70 million pounds, which he called British capital.[40] Edwards turned a humanitarian issue regarding the slave trade into an economic issue concerned with the economy, and security of Great Britain. Abolitionists, who lacked firsthand knowledge, Edwards politely suggested, should stay out of West Indian affairs. Edwards presented himself as a well-informed, moderate commentator, who was not blind to the abuses of the system. He humanized and rationalized the West Indian planter position.[41] This was in contrast to an earlier planter historian, Edward Long, who had published a *History of Jamaica* in 1774. Although Edwards used material from Long's work, he avoided the overt racism of Long.[42] Edwards's tone was more enlightened, and he was elected a Fellow of the Royal Society in 1794, as a result of his book.[43]

Having written a best-seller (the second edition appeared in 1794), Edwards ran unsuccessfully for Parliament in 1795, but the next year was elected to the Cornish seat of Grampound.[44] He joined the West India interest in Parliament that included Sir William Young and Charles Rose Ellis. According to Roger Anstey, Bryan Edwards was "the most distinguished of all the West Indians of his time,"[45] and a notable addition to Parliament, where Wilberforce continued to introduce motions to abolish the slave trade.

As the Haitian Revolution continued, however, popular abolitionist fervor in Britain subsided.[46] In 1793, France and Britain went to war, leading to a more conservative approach by all reform movements in Britain. Reform became associated with Jacobinism. The Haitian Revolution presented an opportunity for Britain to expand her Caribbean empire, and in 1793, British troops began an unsuccessful, costly campaign to take over the French colony. The Haitian Revolution also posed a great problem because of the fear that slave revolt would spread.[47] Slaves in Saint-Domingue were freed in 1794 by Revolutionary edict, adding to the incendiary climate.

The situation in Jamaica was chaotic. Planters dreaded slave rebellion and a French attack. Large numbers of white refugees from Saint-Domingue fled to Jamaica to escape massacre.[48] In this tense atmosphere, the Maroon War of 1795 erupted in Jamaica.[49] Although direct intervention in Jamaica from Haiti has not been proven, contemporary white opinion suspected as much. Thomas Barritt wrote from Jamaica, "Things every day wearing a worse appearance, and some slaves running away from three or four estates . . . and supposed to have joined the said Maroons . . . besides it being imagined that some of the French brigands had got among them. . . ."[50] In Parliament, Edwards was questioned about the Maroon War. William Wilberforce blamed the planters for failing to Christianize and civilize the Maroons.[51] Edwards justified the punishment (banishment to Nova Scotia) meted out to the Maroons, by the Jamaica Assembly, saying the Maroons were unassimilable, since they spoke a Spanish patois, and practiced polygamy and cannibalism. The House seemed satisfied with Edwards's statements, and even the liberal Charles James Fox commented that, from the facts presented, he would not accuse the Jamaican Assembly of keeping bad faith with the Maroons.

After his remarks in Parliament, Edwards published a pamphlet about the Maroon War.[52] He presented the Maroons as barbaric and treacherous. According to Edwards, after the 83rd Regiment left Jamaica in 1795 to sail to Saint-Domingue, the Maroons began to raise the slaves against the whites. Only after the 83rd was recalled, with over a thousand soldiers landing at Montego Bay, did the threat of slave revolution recede.[53] Edwards did not specifically implicate French interference in the Maroon War. Rather he blamed abolitionists for distributing pamphlets and medals to incite rebellion.[54] Slaves received the message that it was acceptable to massacre masters.

Early in 1797 the slave trade issue surfaced again in Parliament.[55] During a debate on Charles Ellis's motion for the "Amelioration of the Condition of the Negroes in the West Indies," Wilberforce reminded the M.P.s that in 1792 the House had resolved to abolish the slave trade within four years.[56] That time had now passed. Edwards supported amelioration, disputed the practicality of abolishing the trade, and maintained that the planters ought to be treated differently. Echoing the American Revolution, he suggested that planters had to be made partners in reform, "or they will unite against you."[57] The motion for amelioration of slave conditions, presented as a step toward gradual abolition of the slave trade, passed by a vote of 99 to 63. Debate on Wilberforce's motion for immediate abolition of the slave trade ensued on 15 May 1797.[58] During the short debate, Edwards cautioned that agitation by *Les Amis des Noirs* (French abolitionists) had stimulated the revolution in Saint-Domingue. When the vote was taken the motion for abolition was defeated by 82 votes to 74.

Three days later (18 May 1797), Edwards spoke in favor of withdrawal of British troops from Saint-Domingue. He confirmed that the planters of Saint-Domingue had wanted Britain to take over the colony in 1791, on the eve of the revolt, but the British government had ignored them. Now, Edwards believed, "all

Europe could not prevent St. Domingo from being a Negro colony."[59] Edwards introduced his own amelioration policy. On 13 June 1797, he gained passage of a bill that made it easier for West Indian assemblies to prevent slaves being sold as chattels to pay masters' debts, which had resulted in families being split apart and worked against the natural increase of slaves.[60] Here was an attempt to tie slaves to the land as a first step on the road to serfdom.

In 1797, Edwards published *An Historical Survey of the French Colony in the Island of St. Domingo.*[61] It was a combative book. A major objective was to explain the Haitian Revolution, including the mulatto insurrection and the slave rebellion. He blamed two French metropolitan institutions for the Revolution: the *Amis des Noirs* and the Revolutionary Parisian Assembly,[62] just as he had blamed the British Parliament for instigating the American Revolution. The Revolutionary Assembly had passed a decree on 15 May 1791, giving privileges of French citizenship, including political rights, to free people of color in French colonies born to free parents. That set people of color against whites and vice versa. In Edwards's opinion, free coloreds in Saint-Domingue were treated badly, being liable for three years' military service and then forced to serve in the militia without pay.[63] But, that was an internal colonial affair. Edwards warned that if Parliament were to pass a law declaring free coloreds of Jamaica eligible to sit in the Assembly, it would be a declaration of civil war.[64]

The decree of 15 May 1791 had also stirred the slaves of Saint-Domingue to revolt. "Upwards of 100,000 savage people, habituated to the barbarities of Africa" attacked "the peaceful and unsuspicious planters, like so many famished tygers [sic] thirsting for human blood."[65] Edwards also blamed the *Amis des Noirs* for lighting fires that "nothing but human blood can extinguish."[66] He littered his text with bloody and sensational atrocities, recording stories of rape and unspeakable cruelty that must have rocked the reading public, in the way that the horrors of the Indian Mutiny would later affect Victorian society.[67]

Slaves were not driven by oppression but "by the vile machinations of men calling themselves philosophers," who were imitators of British abolitionists.[68] Bryan Edwards maintained that, until the revolt in Saint-Domingue, slave rebellions had originated among newly imported African slaves, as occurred in 1760 in Jamaica. But, in Saint-Domingue, some of the leaders were Creoles and favored domestics; some had been taught to read and had acquired subversive ideas from reformers.[69] Edwards's message was clear. Metropolitan abolitionists and legislators should stay out of West Indian affairs. He urged British West Indian colonial assemblies to regulate the slave trade themselves. The example of Saint-Domingue, and "the dictates of self-preservation, like the hand-writing against the wall,"[70] warned the legislatures not to delay.

In his *Survey,* Edwards criticized the belated British policy to win Saint-Domingue. The effort had been expensive and loss of life high. Edwards estimated that between 1791 and 1796 upwards of 300,000 humans perished in the death trap of Saint-Domingue.[71] Venault de Charmilly, a Saint-Domingue planter, who had been courting British assistance since at least 1791, disputed Edwards's pessimistic depiction of events and opposed British withdrawal.[72] He claimed Edwards was against annexation of Saint-Domingue because it would compete with colonies like

Jamaica. Edwards was indeed against the war, and wondered what Britain would do with French West Indian islands, since the inhabitants would never be loyal. He mused that Britain might as well acquire "territories in the moon."[73]

Edwards's *Survey of Saint-Domingue* was reviewed favorably. He had already won a sound reputation for his earlier *History of the West Indies*. He was well respected as a rational planter, a scientist, and member of Parliament, with first hand experience of events in Jamaica and Saint-Domingue. *The Gentleman's Magazine* called Edwards's *Survey* "candid, impartial, well-written."[74] Of course, it was not impartial, for Edwards spoke out strongly against abolitionists, as "hot-brained fanaticks [sic]" who "preach up rebellion and murder."[75]

In April 1798, Wilberforce again introduced into Parliament a motion for the abolition of the slave trade.[76] Edwards spoke extensively against abolition, indicating that planters suspected Wilberforce of wanting to abolish slavery itself. They feared Wilberforce was advocating dangerous French ideas about liberty. Edwards warned that, if abolitionist talk continued, slave revolution would spread "which will not be extinguished until both classes are exterminated."[77] He reminded Parliament that the West India interests would not give up without a struggle. When the abolition motion was put to the vote, it was lost by a majority of only four: 83 yeas, 87 noes. It is surprising how close the vote was, given that abolitionist strength was supposed to be sapped.[78] The close vote of 1798 has been ignored by historians.

Edwards did not speak in the abolitionist debates of 1799, but the West India interest was represented by his friend, Sir William Young, who reminded the House of the Haitian Revolution, and the precarious circumstances in the Caribbean, where "French principles [were] struggling to find their way into the very heart of our colonies."[79] The Haitian Revolution was a powerful antidote to abolitionist pressure, and men like Bryan Edwards and Sir William Young effectively used fear of slave rebellion in their campaign. The anti-abolitionist vote in Parliament in 1799 was 84, versus 54.[80] Wilberforce did not introduce another abolition bill until a change of ministry in 1804 and improvement in the war against France. However, this time it was the abolitionists who played the Haiti card, arguing that the achievement of Haitian independence that year mandated cutting off the flow of slaves into the British colonies.

In 1799, Edwards's health was deteriorating. Since returning to England, he had published two books, been active in Parliament, and followed his scientific interests. In 1797, he succeeded Sir Joseph Banks as secretary of the African Association, a group, largely made up of abolitionists, that sponsored African exploration.[81] He edited Mungo Park's African travel journals for publication.[82] This helped to convince Edwards that the interior states of Africa were perpetually at war and that the slave trade did not promote warfare.[83] In 1799, Edwards feared he was dying and he wrote to Banks, "I sometimes think that my time is nearly come and that I have soon a much longer journey to undertake than poor Park's."[84] He died in 1800 at age fifty-seven.

Bryan Edwards's life spanned the "Age of Revolution." In his youth, he witnessed the Jamaican Slave Revolt of 1760. He lived through the American Revolution, and believed that colonial assemblies should handle internal affairs, just as the Jamaican Assembly dealt with the Maroons after the Maroon War. As the Humanitarian Revolution developed, Edwards was conflicted. Like Thomas Jefferson, he understood the evils of slavery, but in a practical way, thought immediate imperial abolition of the slave trade was ill-advised. Rather, he believed colonial legislatures were in the best position to regulate the trade and ameliorate the condition of slaves. Eventually, the trade would be unnecessary. Unlike Jefferson, Edwards did not suspect the racial inferiority of all Africans, because he understood their cultural diversity. Edwards (having little choice in the case of Jamaica), could envisage an interracial society, whereas Jefferson found the prospect troubling. Ironically, Edwards appears relatively progressive on the issue of race because he imagined the development of a Creole, class-based, hierarchical society. Jefferson projected the image of republican agrarianism, geared to a white society.

The French Revolution stirred up discord in Saint-Domingue and the wider Caribbean. In Edwards's view, the *Amis des Noirs* were revolutionaries. They whipped up prejudice against the French planters, inciting the mulattoes, then the slaves, to rebel. He was convinced that the Revolutionary Assembly in Paris and the *Amis* were instrumental in provoking the horrific death and destruction he witnessed in the Haitian Revolution.

Bryan Edwards was not sure whether the example of slave revolution in Haiti or abolitionist fanaticism in England most threatened the British West Indies. But he realized he had the best chance of influencing events if resident in England. So, in 1792, he moved to the imperial center where he tried to reverse the political trends. He became an M.P., and an authoritative writer, and credible commentator, on West Indian affairs. Against the backdrop of the Haitian Revolution, he attacked the abolitionist position in Parliament and in print. It can be argued he was a crucial voice in countering the abolitionists. Edwards was a creditable opponent of abolitionists, such as Wilberforce, because he refused to defend slavery. Moderate abolitionists and Edwards had similar ends regarding the abolition of the slave trade. Only the means differed. Abolitionists wanted to first stop the trade, giving planters no option but to treat slaves more humanely. Edwards and progressive planters preferred to ameliorate slavery first, leading to the natural end of the slave trade. Edwards's opinions combined humanitarian principles with practical imperialism, and had much appeal.

He felt revolution, whether in the American case, or that of Saint-Domingue, was caused by external forces seeking to change internal affairs. Did the British authorities want to lose the West Indies, as they had the mainland American colonies, and as the French had lost their most valuable colony of Saint-Domingue? To Edwards, evolutionary change, from within the colonial sphere, was preferable to revolutionary change instigated from outside. His *History of the West Indies* demonstrated the significance of the Caribbean islands to Britain, and earned him a reputation as a scientist and thinker. His *Survey of St. Domingo* warned that humanitarian propaganda made slave revolts, especially of Creole slaves, more likely. By studying these two books — one largely written before the Haitian Revolution and the other wholly afterwards — we can judge the impact of the Haitian Revolution on Edwards. Before the Revolution he was prepared to respectfully debate with Wilberforce about the details of the slave trade. He presented research findings, setting out his views of how a Creole society could work. As the Haitian

Revolution dragged on, he vehemently opposed the abolitionists, because they stirred up Creole slaves to rebel. They destroyed his vision of the future that, realistically or not, relied on the successful creolization of society. For Edwards the dreaded alternative was Haiti.

The Parliamentary abolition of the slave trade came in 1807. The impact of the Haitian Revolution on this decision is difficult to assess. By 1807 Haiti was lost to the French empire, effectively ending French competition in the market for tropical commodities, and making Britain the dominant Caribbean power. Michael Duffy has argued that the 1807 abolition was linked to British naval superiority (after Trafalgar), and the perceived strength of the West Indian economy.[85] He pointed out that the slave trade was at its peak in the 1790s as British investment in West Indian properties rose in order to take advantage of the collapse of Saint-Domingue. What is more, the British government purchased slaves for the black West India Regiments. Given these circumstances, and the importance of West Indian financial backing for the war effort, it is difficult to see how the slave trade could realistically have been abolished in the 1790s. Nevertheless, the West Indian interest, represented by men like Bryan Edwards, consistently had to mobilize a defense against abolitionist arguments throughout the 1790s. Both sides could, and did, cite the Haitian Revolution in support of their case. Abolitionists used Haiti as an example of what might happen if the trade continued. The West India lobby used Haiti to warn of the dangers of abolitionist rhetoric.

After the abolition of the slave trade, planter fears of slave revolution continued, and were fulfilled. Large-scale revolts, inspired by Creole leadership, erupted in Barbados (1816), British Guiana (1823), and Jamaica (1831). As humanitarians marshaled their arguments that it was safe to emancipate slaves, the 1831 Jamaican revolt demonstrated that it was too dangerous not to end slavery. Parliament passed the Emancipation Act in 1833. It seems reasonable to assume that Bryan Edwards would not have approved of British legislation to end slavery for the colonies, but he would have approved of the orderly transition from slavery to controlled freedom. The specter of Haiti, that he helped to define, was avoided.

NOTES

The author thanks Brian Blouet, Bob Gross, Howard Johnson, Clarissa Kimber and Richard Sheridan for encouragement with this project. Thanks also to Shelia Lassiter for assistance with production. The National Endowment for the Humanities awarded the author a summer institute fellowship where work on Bryan Edwards began.

1. David Patrick Geggus, *Slavery, War and Revolution* (Oxford: Clarendon Press, 1982), 52.

2. Bryan Edwards, *The History, Civil and Commercial, of the British Colonies in the West Indies,* 2 vols. (London: John Stockdale, 1793). Unless otherwise stated, references are to the 1794 edition, published by John Stockdale.

3. Bryan Edwards, *An Historical Survey of the French Colony in the Island of St. Domingo* (London: John Stockdale, 1797). References are from this edition.

4. Biographical information is taken from "Sketch of the Life of the Author, written

by himself a short time before his Death," in Bryan Edwards, *History* (London: John Stockdale, 1801), ix-xiv; H. E. Vendryes, "Bryan Edwards," *Jamaican Historical Review* 1 (1945): 76–82, and *Dictionary of National Biography.*

5. Another uncle, Nathaniel, was a member of Parliament.

6. Edwards, *History,* 2: 63–67

7. Jamaican planters attempted to put a prohibitive duty on imports of "Koromantyn" slaves after the 1760 slave rebellion.

8. *Proceedings of the American Philosophical Society* (Philadelphia: McCalla & Stavely, 1884), 1:87.

9. Richard Sheridan, "Bryan Edwards" to appear in the *New Dictionary of National Biography* (Oxford: Oxford University Press, forthcoming). See also K. E. Ingram, *Sources of Jamaican History, 1655–1838* (Zug: Inker Documentation, 1976), 2: 708–16.

10. Edwards, *History,* 2: 421.

11. Elizabeth L. Saxe, "The Political Career of Bryan Edwards, 1765–1800" (M.A. thesis, City University of New York, 1971), 24.

12. Saxe, "The Political Career of Bryan Edwards," 42.

13. Bryan Edwards, *Thoughts on the Late Proceedings of Government Respecting the Trade of the West India Islands with the United States of America* (London: T. Cadell, 1784).

14. For a recent study of the popular roots of abolition see, J. R. Oldfield, *Popular Politics and British Anti-Slavery: The Mobilisation of Public Opinion Against the Slave Trade, 1787–1807* (London: Frank Cass, 1998). Planters knew about popular agitation and petitions in Britain. See, for example letters to Nathaniel Phillips, 6 Feb. and 1 July 1788, Slebech Papers, National Library of Wales, Aberystwyth, Mss. 9105, and 11555.

15. Edwards, *Thoughts on the Late Proceedings,* 37.

16. Edwards blamed the uneven sex ratio, and polygamy, for the lack of natural increase in slave numbers. *History,* 2: 147–48. See also, Bryan Edwards to Henry Dundas, 5 Mar. 1796, Melville Papers, Ms. 1075, f. 20, National Library of Scotland. Edwards suggested women slave imports should be under the age of twenty or twenty-five, and young boys under sixteen.

17. Bryan Edwards, *Speech delivered at a free Conference between the Council and Assembly of Jamaica, held on 19 Nov. 1789, on the subject of Mr. Wilberforce's Propositions in the House of Commons, concerning the Slave Trade* (London: 1790).

18. Ibid., 11.

19. Bryan Edwards, *Historical Survey of St. Domingo,* iii-iv.

20. Ibid., v. It was rumored that Edwards was a British agent sent to gauge the response of French colonists to the idea of a British takeover. Edwards denied this.

21. Ibid., xv, and Geggus, *Slavery, War and Revolution,* 52–53.

22. David Patrick Geggus, "Jamaica and the Saint-Domingue Slave Revolt, 1791–93," *The Americas* 38 (1981): 219–33.

23. Thomas Barritt to Nathaniel Phillips, 8 Dec. 1791, Slebech Paper, Ms. 8386. Geggus quotes this also in "The Enigma of Jamaica in the 1790s: New Light on the Causes of Slave Rebellions," *William and Mary Quarterly* 44 (1987): 277–78. He notes there was trouble at Edwards's estate of Brampton Bryan in 1791-1792. For planter fear see Clare Taylor, "Planter Comment on Slave Revolts in Eighteenth Century Jamaica," *Slavery and Abolition* 3 (1982): 245–53.

24. *The Times,* 6 Feb. 1800, 3c.

25. Geggus, "Jamaica," *The Americas,* 227. The planters of Saint-Domingue did not accept the offer.

26. Kean Osborn to Nathaniel Phillips, 8 Feb. 1792, Slebech Papers, Ms. 9234. Osborn wrote, "You will doubtless be astonished when we are complaining of the intolerable bur-

den of our taxes, to learn that our patriots Edwards and Shirley had the, I was going to say ordacity [*sic*], to propose a loan from this island to the French colony at St. Domingo at 100,000 pounds."

27. David Patrick Geggus, "British Opinion and the Emergence of Haiti, 1791–1805," in *Slavery and British Society, 1776–1846,* ed. J. Walvin (Baton Rouge: Louisiana State University Press, 1982). See also Geggus, "The British Government and the Saint-Domingue Slave Revolt," *English Historical Review* 96 (1981): 285–305.

28. Roger Anstey, *The Atlantic Slave Trade and British Abolition, 1760–1810* (Atlantic Highlands, N.J.: Humanities Press, 1975), 275.

29. Frank Cundall, *Historic Jamaica* (London: West India Committee, 1915), 307.

30. The exception is Elsa Goveia, *A Study of the Historiography of the British West Indies to the End of the Nineteenth Century* (Mexico: Instituto Pan Americano de Geografia e Historia, 1956). See also David Brion Davis, *The Problem of Slavery in the Age of Revolution* (Ithaca, N.Y.: Cornell University Press, 1975), 185–95.

31. Antonello Gerbi, *The Dispute of the New World: The History of a Polemic, 1750–1900,* trans. Jeremy Moyle, (Pittsburgh: University of Pittsburgh Press, 1973).

32. Edwards, *History,* 2: 55–58. Much of this material was in his 1789 *Speech.*

33. Edwards, *History,* 2: 104–6. Of twenty-five newly arrived slaves interviewed by Edwards, fifteen were reportedly born to slavery, five were kidnapped, and five were captured in war.

34. Edwards, *History,* 2: 112–15.

35. Ibid., 150.

36. Ibid., 157. Note that the 1792 Act came on the heels of the Haitian Revolution. Other colonies followed suite with reform. See David Barry Gaspar, "Ameliorating Slavery: The Leeward Islands Slave Act of 1798," in *The Lesser Antilles in the Age of European Expansion,* ed. Robert L. Paquette and Stanley L. Engerman (Gainesville: University Press of Florida, 1996), 241–58.

37. Edwards, *History,* 2: 151. His own ideas on amelioration included task work, property rights for slaves, and no work on the Sabbath.

38. Edwards, *History,* 2: 299–302, "Observations on the Cultivation of Coffee in Saint-Domingue and its Probable Increase in Jamaica if the Slave Trade is not Abolished."

39. Edwards, *History,* 2: 1–22. He defended Creole whites against charges of weakness, and wanted to liberalize laws against free coloreds and free blacks.

40. Edwards, *History,* 2: 192–95 and 390–91.

41. Edwards's *History* received good reviews. See *Annual Register* (London, 1793) 417–27, and *Gentleman's Magazine* (London, 1793), 63, pt. 2, 1017 and 64, pt. 1, 50. The review in the *Gentleman's Magazine* placed *The History of the West Indies* "in the highest rank of the annals of the historic literature of Great Britain."

42. See Bryan Edwards, "Notes on Edward Long's *History of Jamaica,*" John Carter Brown Library. These are marginal manuscript notes. Edwards took issue with some of Long's remarks regarding the inferiority of all Africans. For example, Edwards pointed out that he knew several Negroes from Senegal who could read and write in Arabic (2: 353), and he praised cotton cloths from Akim (2: 355).

43. "Certificate of Election," Records of the Royal Society, 5:299, elected 22 May 1794.

44. R.G. Thorne, *History of Parliament: The House of Commons, 1790–1820,* 3 vols. (London, 1986), 1:325–26, 3:670–73.

45. Roger Anstey, *The Atlantic Slave Trade,* 321.

46. For details of the changing circumstances see Geggus, "The British Government and the Saint-Domingue Slave Revolt," and Geggus "British Opinion."

47. Michael Duffy, "The French Revolution and British Attitudes to the West Indian

Colonies" in *A Turbulent Time: The French Revolution in the Greater Caribbean,* eds. Gaspar and Geggus, (Bloomington: Indiana University Press, 1997), 78–101. Duffy noted, "Within barely a year (1794–1795) Britain passed from being on the verge of replacing its lost North American colonies with a massive new Caribbean empire to being on the verge of losing to another revolution its old West Indian colonies" 85.

48. For example see, Thomas Barritt to Nathaniel Phillips, 27 May 1793, Slebech Papers, Ms. 9204, Barritt to Phillips, 13 May 1795, Ms. 9202 and Barritt to Phillips, 27 May 1795, Ms. 9204.

49. A. E. Furness, "The Maroon War of 1795," *Jamaican Historical Review* 5 (1965): 30–50, and Mavis Campbell, *The Maroons of Jamaica, 1655–1796: A History of Resistance, Collaboration and Betrayal* (Granby, Mass.: Bergin & Garvey, 1988). Clare Taylor suggested French insurgents were stirring up the Maroons. See "Planter Comment," 249.

50. Thomas Barritt to Nathaniel Phillips, 15 Aug. 1795, Slebech Papers, Ms. 9207.

51. *Parliamentary History* (London: T. C. Hansard, 1818), 32:1225–28. According to Edwards, the 1795 War was caused by two Maroons, who after stealing pigs, were found guilty of a felony, and whipped as if slaves. Maroons reacted by taking up arms and burning plantations. The Maroons surrendered in 1796, believing they were immune from exile by treaty.

52. Bryan Edwards, *The Proceedings of the Governor and Assembly of Jamaica in regard to the Maroon Negroes, published by Order of the Assembly* (London: John Stockdale, 1796). This was published on 7 Nov. 1796, although it was written before the discussion in the House of Commons.

53. Ibid., xlv-xlvii. Geggus has shown a relationship between slave revolts and troop reductions in "The Enigma of Jamaica."

54. Ibid., l-li.

55. *Parliamentary History,* 33:251–90. (Also, see Anstey, *Slave Trade,* 326–28. Motions for abolition had been defeated in 1795 (78 to 61) and in 1796 (74 to 70), Anstey, *Slave Trade,* 280–315). The West India interest was very concerned about the close 1796 vote. It appears that Dundas, minister of war, was responsible for the defeat of abolition, in 1796, since he controlled eleven of the anti-abolition votes. In 1792, before war broke out, Dundas had supported gradual abolition. But in 1796 he thought abolition would throw the West Indian colonies into the hands of France. Wilberforce thought he could have carried abolition if his supporters had not been in the country or at the opera.

56. Anstey, *Slave Trade,* 276. This had passed the House of Commons but been voted down in the House of Lords. For details see, Robin Blackburn, *The Overthrow of Colonial Slavery, 1776–1848* (London: Verso, 1988), 148–50.

57. *Parliamentary History,* 33:283. Edwards went into details about how the Jamaican Assembly had earlier tried to regulate the slave trade, but to no avail.

58. Ibid., 569–76.

59. Ibid., 587.

60. Ibid., 831. "Bill to repeal the Act for making Negroes real Assets," 13 June 1797.

61. Bryan Edwards, *An Historical Survey of St. Domingo,* (London: John Stockdale, 1797). In 1801, the third edition of Edwards's *History of the West Indies* was published. *An Historical Survey of St. Domingo* became volume 3 of that edition. A fourth edition appeared in 1807, and a fifth in 1819.

62. Ibid., xx, 15, and 57–63.

63. Ibid., 6–12. Mulattoes in Saint-Domingue could not use the surname of their white fathers, and distinction of color did not end, as in Jamaica, with the third generation. Edwards was in favor of more civil rights for free coloreds.

64. Ibid., 58–62.

65. Ibid., 63.

66. Ibid., xix.

67. Ibid., 74–75 and 92.

68. Ibid., 83–85. Edwards called the British anti-slavery group the Old Jewry Associates because they held meetings in the Old Jewry, London.

69. Ibid., xx–xxii.

70. Ibid., 194.

71. Ibid., 241. Edwards presented information about the impact of diseases, such as yellow fever, on the troops "who dropt [*sic*] like the leaves in autumn." (163).

72. Venault de Charmilly, *Answer by Way of Letters to Bryan Edwards, Esq., Containing a Refutation of his Historical Survey of the French Colony of St. Domingo,* London, 1797.

73. *The Times,* 3 Nov. 1797, 3c. British troops evacuated Saint-Domingue in September 1798. Basically, Edwards thought that no matter what forces Britain had sent to Saint-Domingue, she could never have taken the colony.

74. *Gentleman's Magazine* (London, 1797), 67, pt. 1, 409.

75. Edwards, *Survey,* 193.

76. *Parliamentary History,* 33:1376–1415, and *The Times,* 4 Apr. 1798, 2c.

77. Ibid., 1392.

78. It is usually suggested that, even if abolition had passed in the Commons, it would still have been defeated in the Lords. In addition, George III opposed abolition. See Blackburn, *Overthrow of Colonial Slavery,* 150.

79. *Parliamentary History,* 34:529.

80. Anstey, *Slave Trade,* 322.

81. *Records of the African Association, 1788–1831,* ed., Robin Hallett (London: Thomas Nelson,1964), and Robin Hallett, *The Penetration of Africa* (New York: Praeger, 1965).

82. Bryan Edwards, *Proceedings of the Association for Promoting the Discovery of the Interior Parts of Africa, containing an Abstract of Mr. Park's Account of his Travels and Discoveries, abridged from his own Minutes by Bryan Edwards* (London: W. Bulmer, 1798). A version appeared the following year as Mungo Park, *Travels in the Interior Districts of Africa in 1795 and 1796* (London, 1799).

83. *The Times,* 4 Apr. 1798, 2c. Discussions about the Haitian Revolution and abolition appear to have encouraged interest in Africa and African exploration.

84. Hallett, *Records,* 165.

85. Michael Duffy, in *Turbulent Time,* ed. Gaspar and Geggus, 94–95. The British government could not have foreseen that other areas, such as Brazil and Cuba, would expand their sugar industries, leading to increased demand for slave imports from Africa. See J. R. Ward, "The British West Indies in the Age of Abolition, 1748–1815," in *the Eighteenth Century,* ed. P.J. Marshall, vol. 2 in *Oxford History of the British Empire* (Oxford: Oxford University Press, 1998), 428.

Chapter 6

Puerto Rico's Creole Patriots and the Slave Trade after the Haitian Revolution

JUAN R. GONZÁLEZ MENDOZA

BETWEEN 1810 AND 1813 PUERTO RICO'S Creole patriots faced a conjuncture both threatening and pregnant with opportunities. On the one hand, they faced the collapse of metropolitan power due to the Napoleonic occupation of Spain and increasing discontent in Spanish America. On the other hand, the moment presented an opening in the international markets for sugar and coffee brought about by the collapse of Saint-Domingue's plantation economy as a result of the Haitian revolution.

The prostration of the metropolis and the measures taken to counteract it, first by the beleaguered *Junta Suprema* in Seville and later by its successor, the *Consejo de Regencia,* allowed Puerto Rico's elite a unique opportunity to present their vision of how best to "construct" a *patria.* It also allowed them to emphasize their position as natural representatives of their homeland's interests. The convocation of the *Cortes Generales y Extraordinarias de Cádiz* in 1810 had increased their participation in metropolitan and colonial affairs, so that Puerto Rico's Creole patriots enjoyed a freedom of expression unheard of in more stable times.[1]

At the same time, Puerto Rico's elite regarded the destruction of Haiti's plantation economy as a golden opportunity to accelerate the economic transition from cattle ranching and subsistence agriculture to intensive production of commodities such as sugar and coffee. This transformation had been envisaged by eighteenth-century reformers, such as Field Marshal O'Reilly and Fray Iñigo Abbad y Lasierra, but the development of plantations remained haphazard.[2] Events in Haiti promised to change all that, and a sector of Puerto Rico's elite could exclaim with Arango y Parreño, the champion of Cuba's emerging sacharocracy, that the "hour of our happiness has arrived."[3]

But the reality in 1810 was very different than the rosy picture presented by the enlightened observers. Haiti's ex-slaves had seen to it that Saint-Domingue's path to wealth could no longer serve as an untroublesome model for colonial development. For Puerto Rico's and Cuba's emerging planter class, basing progress on slavery became not just an issue regarding labor and the speed of development but a matter of safety, and even survival.

The impressive growth of Cuba's slave population that occurred during the British occupation of Havana in 1762 and was spurred on by subsequent royal decrees aimed at fostering the acquisition of slaves, soon presented the Cuban planters with the danger of *Africanización*. Planter uneasiness intensified as the perils of holding a large number of slaves relative to the white population became evident in Saint-Domingue; and they were not comforted by the realization that Cuba's free *pardo* and *moreno* (mulatto and black) population was increasing rapidly. As with other issues dealing with the island's development, Arango y Parreño cogently expressed the sacharocracy's point of view in his *Discurso sobre la Agricultura de La Habana y medios de fomentarla* (1792) where he suggests, among other things, that white migration should be stimulated to counterbalance the threat represented by a rapidly growing slave population.[4]

Although Puerto Rico's slave population did not achieve as impressive a rate of growth as Cuba's, the island's slaves were more numerous during the first years of the nineteenth century than they had been in the mid-eighteenth century. In fact, between 1765 and 1800, the slave population of regions like San Germán in the southwest had a faster rate of increase than the free population. During those thirty-five years, slaves in San Germán increased at a yearly rate of 5.9 percent, while the free population grew at a rate of 2.9 percent.[5] Like their Cuban counterparts, a sector of the Puerto Rican patriciate would look upon this difference with apprehension and consequently clamor for the cessation of the slave trade. It was also wary about the effects that rapid plantation development could have on existing social relations. As will be seen below, some Creoles feared that a powerful planter class would eclipse the until-then predominant *hatero* and *estanciero* elite of ranchers.

Puerto Rico's patricians had come to a crossroads. They could follow the path already staked out by the older plantation economies of the Caribbean with its attendant risks, or they could encourage a more diversified economy based on small and medium proprietors producing for export and for the internal market that some of them envisioned. The first path implied continuing and protecting the slave trade. The second road implied facilitating white migration to serve as an example of agriculture's virtue to the island's inhabitants. It also meant molding the island's landless population, or *agregados,* into a disciplined labor force.[6]

Regardless of the alternative chosen, the new political language— promoted by discussions in the Cortes and the Constitution of 1812— meant that Puerto Rico's Creole patriots had to grapple with the issue of citizenship. In other words, they had to consider which sectors of the population would be included within the patria and which would be excluded. The *agregados*—who in a sense were recognized as compatriots—were grudgingly granted the potential to become citizens, while the slaves, particularly the *bozales,* were to be excluded from the patria and citizenship altogether. At this juncture, neither the opponents of the slave trade nor its promoters visualized incorporation of slaves into the body politic, not even in a distant future. Viewed as a foreign body in the patria's landscape, Africans and their descendants were thus particularly problematic.

OPPOSITION TO THE SLAVE TRADE: THE SPECTER OF HAITI

Puerto Rico's patricians linked the colony's "state of abandonment" and backwardness to the land tenure system, the dearth of labor to work the land, the primitive state of communications, the lack of markets due to colonial restrictions on trade, and excessive taxes. All these factors conspired to retard the establishment of prosperous plantations.[7] In reality, the question of labor scarcity was not merely a question of numbers. As table 1 shows, the island's population had increased significantly between 1765 and 1809, when don Pedro Irisarri wrote the *Informe* that would serve as a draft of San Juan's instructions to the island's representative in Cádiz. Between 1765 and 1800, Puerto Rico's population had an impressive rate of growth of 3.6 percent per year, while the slave population's annual growth had been even more pronounced at 4.3 percent.[8]

The latter was the result of Bourbon measures to liberalize the slave trade, but there were still not enough slaves to satisfy the demand of aspiring planters. The growing number of *agregados* also managed to elude the authorities' and the planters' efforts to exploit their labor. The population was too dispersed, land was readily available, and existing social relations often assured these shifting cultivators the protection of better-off relatives or landowners eager to hold on to some labor.[9]

Men like San Juan's mayor were aware that some of their compatriots envisioned slavery as a quick solution to the labor question. For them, however, the Haitian revolution was a patent demonstration of the dangers of this course; therefore, a large part of don Pedro's *Informe* was devoted to this thorny issue "that ha[d] to be handled with a firm grasp after a serious, profound, and scrupulous discussion."[10]

Since the search for an alternative to slave labor was foremost in his mind, Iris-

TABLE 1: Puerto Rico: Population, 1765–1812

YEAR	POPULATION	SLAVE POPULATION
1765	44,883	5,037
1776	70,260	6,537
1780	75,343	9,881
1784	91,845	9,627
1788	101,396	11,018
1792	115,557	14,712
1796	132,982	18,742
1800	155,426	21,931
1803	174,902	24,223
1812	183,014	17,536

Sources: (1765) O'Reilly, "Memoria," 538; (1776), Abbad, *Historia,* 153; (1780–1792 and 1800), AGPR, Colección Particular Francisco Scarano; (1796) AGI, Sto. Domingo, 2378; (1803) AGI, Sto. Domingo, 2322; (1812) AGPR, FGEPR, Censo y Riqueza, caja 13. I must thank Dr. Salvador Padilla Escabí for the photocopies of the *padrones* for 1796 and 1803.

arri began his analysis with a description of the miracle of Saint-Domingue and how it had dazzled some of his compatriots: "It has always been considered that black slaves are very useful and even necessary for tilling the soil. . . . *for during all seasons they can withstand the excessive heat of the climate while laboring in the fields.* For this same reason cultivators have procured them, sparing no cost and with increasing eagerness and zeal, having seen the flourishing state that the French part of the island of Santo Domingo achieved in a few years."[11] But this fabulous emporium came crashing down, in a fraction of the time that it had taken to construct it: "the French colony, so rich and opulent, has been destroyed and ruined by the very same people who had cultivated and beautified it. . . . In a moment, everything was dealt a mortal blow by the disorder of a daring and well-conceived insurrection. The mulattoes and black slaves rose en masse and, resisting all legitimate authority, executed on their masters and magistrates the most bloody and horrible massacre, and leaving no stone unturned, they have remained content in their perfect anarchy, without God, without law and without conscience."[12]

Irisarri's depiction of Saint-Domingue as a theater of horrors reveals the racial attitude of the elite and also the sources of its fear. Elsewhere in his report, Irisarri had reproached *agregados* (landless laborers) for their love of an ill-conceived liberty and their ability to withdraw their services, but at least they did so in a peaceful manner. For Saint-Domingue's rebels liberty was "the only object to which all their ideas conspire"; but their warped sense of freedom has manifested itself in "the most bloody and horrendous massacre." This barbaric freedom was the negation of civil society. It represented a denial of legitimate authority as well as the destruction of property and wealth. In his diatribe, the mayor also dismisses the idea that slavery is the only means to Christianize and civilize Africans. He concludes that the discipline of slavery can only produce a superficial domestication, since Saint-Domingue's rebels have returned to their true nature and remain "content in their perfect anarchy, without God, without law and without conscience." If that were not sufficient cause for alarm, they had also defeated the best European armies sent to suppress this return to savagery.[13]

Don Pedro's view of Africans is, then, a mixture of grudging admiration and fear. He recognizes that African labor built the opulence of the French colony. He also grants blacks and mulattoes a measure of rationality and valor, since he recognizes their capacity to execute "a daring and well-planned insurrection." But the Africans are unredeemable, and since their domestication is only skin deep: " they will never cease to be bad citizens, wretched and treacherous, invisible domestic enemies of their masters, of the Patria, and the State." To this catalogue of failings Irisarri adds the sin of ingratitude; after all, the French monarchy had provided for their needs and protection through enlightened legislation and they responded with bloodshed.

In case this gloomy picture failed to convince his opponents, don Pedro attempted to demolish the notion that only Africans were suited to labor in the tropics. To this end he cites the example of those European settlers who "without any other principal or any other protection than their labor have in the course of ten years acquired the status of hacendados." According to him "all the Island [would] be planted by now," if they had only been more numerous.[14]

San Juan's mayor then turns against those who wished to protect slaves. He complains that, despite the fateful example before their eyes, "there is no lack of men in our nation and *las Españas* who are thoroughly enlightened and who encourage and protect [ideas of liberty among the slaves] with conclusive arguments in favor of liberty and detestation of slavery, as if nature had always looked upon it with horror. And if we follow the maxims by which our neighbors the French became powerful, will we not be also . . . in the end poor wretches like they are, and victims of the insatiable fury of black barbarians? . . . And those who escaped their fierce claws, are they not paupers wandering the globe?"[15] In his characteristic jumbled style, Irisarri first lambastes those who argue that nature abhors slavery, and may thus light the tinder that will start a raging fire, and immediately turns on those who, heedless of the Haitian example, wanted to promote the same economic model on the island. Deluded and self-congratulatory, these people think that "we have a finer and more discerning palate, capable of tasting the honey but not bitterness." To those who thought like Irisarri, slave-produced sugar had definitively lost its sweetness and could only leave behind it bitterness and ruin.

One wonders if Irisarri's rhetorical outbursts were not only motivated by a legitimate fear of slave insurrection, but also by the bad example that refugees from Saint-Domingue were giving his compatriots. For in reality not all the refugees from the French colony were wretches "wandering like beggars on the globe." A number of them had managed to develop some of Puerto Rico's finest coffee and sugar haciendas, particularly in the western region closest to Hispaniola. They obviously had not learned the lesson that the mayor wanted to impress on his fellows, and instead joined the chorus that petitioned for increased freedom of the slave trade.

Because he was a member of the traditional elite, don Pedro remarked on the advantages foreigners with capital, technical know-how, and market connections could have over aspiring Creole planters. He feared that the social fabric—and, by extension, the elite's political networks—were about to be rewoven to the detriment of his class. In his view, the old patriciate could be swept from the stage as a major economic and political actor: "Ten or twenty *hacendados* with a superb capital will surely become powerful in every town with the use of slaves, but will all the soil be tilled? Certainly not. Thus it does not seem to me that the system to be promoted is that some cultivate part of the land, but that many cultivate all of it." Irisarri's fears of Creole displacement would be confirmed by later developments. The dislodging of the island's traditional elites from the apex of the colonial hierarchy was one of the noticeable results of the economic changes wrought during the first half of the nineteenth century. The eclipse of Creole influence did not occur with the same intensity everywhere, but by the 1850s there had been a general transformation of the colonial elite in most of the areas of rapid economic expansion.[16]

The advent of a plantation economy based on slave labor was not just a threat to the existing political and economic hierarchies. Its gravest danger, as had already been seen, was the large number of "savages" that now lived among the whites. To underscore his representation of Africans as unredeemable barbarians, Irisarri considered the regulations dealing with the welfare and management of the slave population. He argued that Spanish laws thoroughly dealt with "the control and subjection of these captives." But, he insists, Haiti had demonstrated that no amount of benign legislation could tame the slaves' savage breasts. "Thus, just as it would be impossible to change their color from black to white it would be less possible that their corrupt and vicious hearts be innocent during their captivity. It is true they will submit to force while their number does not exceed or keeps a balance with that of free men, but when that terrible moment [of numerical superiority] arrives, that is the moment when the last misfortune, the destruction of the whole Island, will ensue."

However, the racial equilibrium is not the only question that worries Irisarri. Haiti's example was also dangerous because it might embolden Puerto Rico's slaves, who would find "in Saint-Domingue's insurgent Negroes, an aid in force, quick, immediate and certain, [and] is it not easier to undertake the enterprise of revolution dictated and directed by those that have armed and led another?" To which he added, "The horrible, effective and scandalous homicides that the few [slaves] we possess frequently carry out with the greatest cruelty against their masters, even if they be most innocent priests, are they not live rehearsals in which they practice playing out a tragic scene in the theater of posterity?"[17] The murders committed by slaves were contrary to the script that confined them to the role of submissive servants; they were a rehearsal for a counter-drama that would not be written by the legitimate wielders of power. Thus, their struggle for liberty could never be legitimate, since it was an attack on rightfully held property and against the social order that placed the Creole elite among its highest ranks.

The mayor was also concerned about the possibility of an alliance between Africans and free *morenos* and *pardos*. This issue was still alive some years after Irisarri's report to San Juan's (town council). This time, however, it was the *cabildo* of San Germán that protested against the introduction of slave cargoes after the abolition treaty signed with England in 1817 had taken effect:

> the . . . same Señor Presidente stated: that a ship had arrived . . . loaded with Negroes from the Coast of Africa, the sale of whom according to . . . the Superior Government had been abolished, . . . that for this reason, and by virtue of the great harm that their introduction might bring given what is currently happening in Santo Domingo [following the Haitian invasion of 1822], understanding also that in all these past times an innumerable number of them have been introduced, so that perhaps their number may exceed that of whites, adding also the multitude of *pardos* that can be found everywhere, and also realizing the apathy and rancor that the former and the latter of low birth have always manifested toward those of the Superior sphere, just because of the great inequality [between them]. . . and the fatal state of servitude to which their introducers have subjected them ab inicio: it would seem convenient . . . that steps be taken to abolish an abuse of such nature, . . . that someday may result in evil consequences.[18]

Like Cuban abolitionism, early Puerto Rican abolitionism was partly based on the intertwined fears of Haiti's proximity and that the racial equilibrium be upset in favor of the people of color.[19]

Having erected his "theater of horrors," Irisarri launched an attack on the "partisans of the black party" (*el partido negro*). The latter were not precisely *amis des noirs*, but rather those Creoles that clamored for increased importation of Africans. Irisarri accuses them of sophistry and false patriotism, for "they only heed (as true egoists) their particular interests and not those of their compatriots, and will want to deny and hide with sophistic arguments such imminent risks [that is, of slave rebellion]."[20] The mayor goes on to propose immigration "of a proportionate number of free men, day-laborers (*jornaleros*) from the Canary Islands, the kingdom of New Spain, and from any other place" as a safer alternative to the slave trade. This provision would produce the hoped-for changes, since it would increase the labor force, lower wages, and promote agriculture's virtues among "the multitude of patrician free men who do not want to engage in agricultural occupations, which are done by slaves, and which they judge unworthy of their esteem." Moreover, even if the patricians remained idle, the effects of this measure would be appreciable, because Europeans were more productive than "negro slaves, since the unlimited slothfulness and carelessness of the latter is greatly exceeded by the agility, liveliness, talent, and diligence of the former."[21] Furthermore, although Irisarri concedes that his opponents' arguments may hold some truth, that is, that slave and free labor could be equally productive, political considerations should outweigh mere economic interest when considering the benefits of the slave trade and slave labor. From the perspective of patriotic welfare, the answer to the labor question should still be "to discard those who could remotely be prejudicial to the State and Patria," and this implied the cessation of the slave trade, the only measure that would insure the natural and peaceful extinction of slavery.[22]

THE "PARTIDO NEGRO":
THE SLAVE TRADE AS ESSENTIAL TO THE PATRIA'S PROGRESS

The Diputación Provincial (provincial council) was one of the salient political spaces opened by the Spanish constitution of 1812.[23] During its short life (1813–1814) it was one of the forums where debates on the slave trade occurred. On 14 December 1813 the Diputación considered the matter, and don Antonio Sánchez eloquently argued against those who proposed the cessation of the slave trade.[24]

Sánchez began his address by admitting "the dangers of an internal hostility, due to the daily progressive increase of the people of color above the number of whites." However, he asked, "through what other means can the lack of Negroes be made up, if the commerce in them ceases?" Whatever basis the fears of others might have, one had to place in the balance the benefits that could accrue for agriculture an "art [that] has been unknown in Puerto Rico."

Having said this, he claimed that European labor arrangements could not solve Puerto Rico's labor shortage. "[Unfortunately] the *hacendado* cannot procure the work of wage laborers that can be continuously applied to labor in the fields [as he does in Spain]." In the first place, the *jornalero* "is difficult to find." Secondly, he "always works for short periods at a time" and for very high wages, "costing six or eight pesos a month, that should be reckoned as twelve or fourteen if account is taken of the food that must also be provided them." In short, free workers did not provide constant and disciplined labor at low cost. Simple arithmetic should suffice to discard wage labor as a viable alternative for planters seeking increased productivity and wealth. "If a farmer needed, for example, twenty-five men to perform all his plantings or other work, he would have to disburse three hundred and fifty pesos every month, and this exceeds the revenue of any hacienda, even one with a larger number of slaves. Even though it is true that slaves cost their masters twice as much as a day-laborer would in two years, it is also true that they keep their worth and can be counted as part of capital, and the owner is not subject to suffering the type of loss that would be caused by an equal number of contracted workers, since they are wont to take the day off as they please, leaving the landowner at the most critical moment of his harvest or other work."[25]

Like his Cuban counterparts, Sánchez suggests ". . . not only that the introduction of Negroes should continue for now, but that it seems a necessity." He also thinks "the situation merits, if the island is to prosper, that this commerce be protected, by whatever just means are within the powers and faculties of this Diputación Provincial. . . ." The defense of the slave trade was, of course, particularly important, because of the rumblings coming from Britain regarding the "odious commerce." Four years after don Antonio spoke these words, England would impose on Spain the first of a series of ineffectual treaties regarding the slave trade to her colonies.[26]

Having established the economic basis for his argument, the spokesman for the *partido negro* tried to dispel the specter of Haiti that San Juan's mayor had conjured up in 1809. His reasoning would deploy geographical, demographic, and racial arguments for rejecting the idea that a slave insurrection on Haiti's scale was possible in Puerto Rico. Furthermore, his perception of racial relations and his confidence in patrician abilities would form part of his arsenal. To this end, he fashioned a heroic past which was not so distant, given the proximity in time of Abercomby's failed siege of San Juan (1797) and the reconquest of Spanish Santo Domingo (1808). In both these incidents Creoles, like Ramón Power, Puerto Rico's deputy to the Cortes of 1810, and Sánchez himself, had played a prominent role.[27]

Don Antonio first discounted the possibility that the black population would surpass the white inhabitants, and added, "[even if in] future centuries they were to exceed [whites] by four or six times," he was not convinced that "they should become terrible in the fields." The reasons were very simple, according to Sánchez. Geography was one: "the island is not large enough and lacks a lair where they could take refuge to harass the whites."[28] The other reason was African inferiority. Sánchez argued that it would be difficult for the island's slaves to attempt an insurrection or expect aid from Haiti, because "they could never have arms, money, nor resources for such [an insurrection], since even if all the brigands that Saint-Domingue hides in its forests and lairs tried to come to their aid, they could never manage it, because they would have to launch maritime expeditions, *and these savage beasts are incapable of such endeavors*" (my emphasis).

Even if the Haitians secured the aid of a capable power, there was little to fear, since Puerto Rico's inhabitants had given ample proof they could handle such enemies, as was shown by their glorious feats of arms:

> and if [those from Saint-Domingue], protected by a more capable enemy, attempt such a thing, they will be greeted by its inhabitants, as were the French and Dutch pirates who assembled on the beaches of Loiza in the year of 1557; or General Estrén in Arecibo, who was thoroughly defeated by a small picket of Urban Militia under the command of Captain Correa; not to mention the glorious actions that have taken place in the capital, for it is well known, how much the sally that captain don Juan de Amézquita made from el Morro castle cost the Dutch, who already occupied the plaza in the year of 1615 (sic). . . . and when during the year of '97 the British dared lay siege to the plaza with a large squadron and 7,000 men in their landing party, they found themselves besieged, without knowing how to extricate themselves from Cangrejo's sands, where they finally left behind a large number of dead, all their campaign gear, and more than two hundred prisoners.

This sector of the patriciate was, therefore, self-confident almost to the point of smugness.

Don Antonio continued in this patriotic vein, arguing that Puerto Rican society was naturally suspicious of troublesome elements and "would within moments finish off the authors of the conspiracy, and if necessary all the rabble that followed them." He added that the elite was united in purpose and not divided; thus, by implication, they would not commit the blunders of Saint-Domingue's whites "who, having ruined themselves, [allowed] the Negroes [to] become the larger party." Sánchez further claimed that the island's population had always been renowned for its fidelity and patriotism, so that "the head of any seducer that would attempt to [cause a slave insurrection], would not be secure either, since the fidelity, union, and patriotism of its inhabitants has nothing to envy the most renowned provinces of all of America, and even of the Peninsula itself to which we have always given our greatest respect."

The deputy's confidence was also reinforced by the demographic particularities of the island. Given the small number of plantations, Puerto Rico's slave population had different characteristics than those of the sugar islands. For the moment, the danger of a slave uprising was annulled by a simple fact "almost half of the Negroes are women, children, old and cripples, of which there is a great number in the few haciendas that today are considered well endowed because they have sixty or seventy Negroes of all classes."

Furthermore, Puerto Rican society exhibited patterns of racial relations unlike those of the non-Hispanic Caribbean. In the long period that had elapsed since the collapse of the sixteenth-century "sugar experiment," the colony had evolved as a settler rather than as an exploitation colony.[29] Though this was a society organized around notions of nobility and racial purity (*pureza de sangre*), it must be stressed that the lines of demarcation between the Creole elite, that considered itself white, and the rest of the free population were not as rigid as in full-fledged plantation societies. Puerto Rican society was characterized by racial relations similar to the "color continuum" Hoetink suggests for Santo Domingo.[30]

This prompted Sánchez's reasoning that people of mixed racial descent would side with the patricians in the eventuality of a slave uprising. After all, *pardos* and *morenos* had distinguished themselves as militiamen in the defense of their homeland, so they could also be granted a place in that heroic past that the deputy had outlined. One wonders if Sánchez was indulging in wishful thinking or whether his perception points to a certain commonality of interests between the elite and the free colored.[31] Far from constituting a menace, these plebeians were regarded by Sánchez as trustworthy allies, "because the mulattoes that are not obviously dark-skinned will never join such a class of people, even though they may have their remote origin in Africa, because they all aspire to improve their quality and, of course, will form a single body with the whites, since it is from them that they can expect satisfaction." Sánchez is alluding to those *pardos* and mulattoes that strived to improve their social position by whitening, of which there are abundant examples in other parts of the Spanish Empire; but there is some evidence that suggests poorer *pardos* and mulattoes were also distancing themselves from recently arrived African slaves.[32]

Moreover, the Haitian Revolution had not only displaced white planters, it had also resulted in the exile of a good number of mulattoes. Western Puerto Rico had become home for a large number of refugees from both halves of Hispaniola; it was also one of the regions experiencing rapid plantation development. One can only wonder if Sánchez was also thinking of these Saint-Domingue mulattoes as potential pillars of a regime that had aided and welcomed them.[33]

Sánchez concludes by revisiting the demographic issues, first addressing the fears of *Africanización,* then considering the political issues involved in the extension of citizenship to the free coloreds. On the first matter he suggested that "improvement of the island will be proportionate only to the number of Negroes introduced, and this will consequently increase the number of whites, who—attracted by the island's advantages, agriculture, and commerce—shall come to settle, procreating more abundantly than blacks." According to don Antonio, this was a principle of sound political economy, and "experience showed . . . that once the island barely began to leave the extreme poverty and state of almost complete abandon it had been buried in for many years, its population doubled in less than thirty years." Finally, he thought that the benefits of the new political system could be amplified if citizenship were granted to the free coloreds. From the third or so blacks and mulattoes, "*there could result a sufficient number of citizens* to elect two deputies to the Cortes and a replacement, since it is a discredit and almost a dishonor that an island as populous as Puerto Rico should elect only one deputy."[34]

Thus, the new language of citizenship that emanated from the Constitution of 1812 presented Creole patriots with interesting possibilities. On the one hand, it could induce the acquiescence of the free people of color in the elite's hegemonic project, and thus assure the necessary counterweight to the dangers implicit in the rapid expansion of the servile population. On the other, the patriots could represent themselves as the true spokesmen of colonial interests.[35] An additional deputy in the Cortes would increase *criollo* leverage in "national," that is, metropolitan politics, while colonial institutions like the *cabildos* and the Diputación Provincial would be dominated by *criollos,* since it was obviously hoped that Puerto Ricans would back Puerto Ricans in colonial political contests.[36]

CONCLUSION

In the end, as is well known, the *partido negro* won the debate in both Cuba and Puerto Rico. By the 1840s, the slave population of both Antilles surpassed all previous levels, a clear demonstration that the abolition treaties of 1817 and 1835 were flagrantly ignored, as the San Germán *cabildo* had protested in 1823. But this victory carried a heavy price. The spectacular growth of Cuba's slave population was a factor in the development of La Escalera, one of the most dangerous and widespread conspiracies in Cuban history.[37] In Puerto Rico, don Pedro Irisarri's warnings soon came true. Between 1815 and 1845, as sugar plantations came to dominate the economy, a new elite of planters and merchants became powerful in the towns. By the time plantation building was complete, however, this new class had largely displaced the old patrician elite from its former preeminence.

In the end, neither colony could lay the specter of racial war to rest. The continuation of slavery was one factor that stifled the Cuban and Puerto Rican patriciates' attempts to reform an increasingly arbitrary colonial regime for fear that any open confrontation with the metropolis would conjure up the ghost of slave rebellion. The victors in the debate over the slave trade confirmed don Pedro's perception: they had seduced and fooled themselves into thinking that their finer and more discerning palate was capable of tasting honey but not bitterness. And slavery was bitter fruit indeed.

NOTES

I must thank the Universidad Interamericana de Puerto Rico for the sabbatical leave that allowed me time for research and writing as well the National Endowment for the Humanities, for accepting me in the Summer Seminar for College Teachers, "Freedom and Slavery in Caribbean History," directed by Francisco A. Scarano and held at the University of Wisconsin, Madison, in 1996. I wish to thank Joseph Dorsey, John Garrigus, Steve Meyer, Francisco Scarano, and the other *seminaristas* for their encouragement and helpful comments, and Rosemary Brana-Shute and David Geggus for inviting me to Charleston and commenting on the paper. I also wish to exonerate them from any faults that may still plague this work.

    1. This essay is based on the *Informe* (1809) that don Pedro Irisarri prepared for San Juan's town council as a draft of the *Instrucciones* (similar to *cahiers de doléances*) that were written as a guide to don Ramón Power y Giralt, the island's elected deputy to the Cortes (1810–1812); and the extant minutes of some of the sessions of the first Diputación Provincial (1813–1814). The "Informe dado por el alcalde don Pedro Yrisarri al Ayuntamiento de la Capital. 1809" is in *Ramón Power y Giralt Diputado puertorriqueño a las Cortes Generales y Extraordinarias de España 1810–1812 (Compilación de documentos),* ed. Aida Caro de Delgado (San Juan: 1969), 45–69. The minutes for the Diputación Provincial can be consulted in the

Archivo General de Puerto Rico (hereafter AGPR), Fondo de Gobernadores Españoles de Puerto Rico (hereafter FGEPR), Diputación Provincial (hereafter DP), Sesiones, caja 312.

2. O'Reilly, had suggested the Danish island of St. Croix as a model for Puerto Rico in his *Memoria* of 1765, while Fray Iñigo Abbad y Lasierra presented Saint-Domingue and Martinique as examples of model and profitable colonies in his *Historia geográfica, civil y natural de la Isla de San Juan Bautista de Puerto Rico* (Río Piedras: Editorial Universitaria, 1970 [1786]). O'Reilly's "Memoria de D. Alejandro O'Reylly sobre la Isla de Puerto Rico" is in *Biblioteca Histórica de Puerto Rico,* ed. Alejandro Tapia y Rivera (San Juan: Instituto de Literatura Puertorriqueña, 1945), 526–45.

3. See Francisco de Arango y Parreño, "Representación hecha a S. M. con motivo de la sublevación de esclavos en los dominios franceses de la isla de Santo Domingo" and "Discurso sobre la Agricultura de la Habana y medios de fomentarla" in *Obras,* 2 vols. (La Habana: Dirección de Cultura-Ministerio de Educación, 1952), 1:109–33, 114–61. The quote is from "Discurso," 134.

4. Arango y Parreño, "Discurso," 151–52, 158. Naranjo and González argue that Arango "presents white colonization only as an alternative to contain possible rebellions among the black population, and stimulate whites to work in agricultural tasks, particularly those who were then wandering the countryside [without known occupation]." Consuelo Naranjo Orovio and Armando García González, *Racismo e Inmigración en Cuba en el siglo XIX* (Madrid: Ediciones Doce Calles, 1996), 48.

5. Juan R. González-Mendoza, "The Parish of San Germán de Auxerre in Puerto Rico, 1765–1850: Patterns of Settlement and Development" (Ph. D. diss., SUNY at Stony Brook, 1989), 159, Table 2:9.

6. See Juan R. González Mendoza, "*Hombres incultos, desagradecidos, inconstantes y desaplicados autores particulares de la destrucción de su Patria:* los agregados puretorriqueños como cimiento endeble de la patria," *Colonial Latin American Review* 7 (1998): 225–50.

7. See the description that San Juan's mayor wrote of the island's "best" plantations in Caro de Delgado, 50.

8. See González Mendoza, "The Parish of San Germán," 142, 157.

9. Francisco A. Scarano, "Congregate and Control: The Peasantry and Labor Coercion in Puerto Rico before the Age of Sugar, 1750–1820," *Nieuwe West-Indische Gids / New West Indian Guide* 63 (1989): 23–40. Scarano argues that by the early nineteenth century efforts to extract labor from the shifting cultivators had waned. At the local level, town councils also promulgated measures to curb vagrancy. San Germán's *cabildo* debated the issue of vagrants and unemployed at least six times between 1799 and 1806. See Archivo Histórico Municipal de San Germán (hereafter AHMSG), *Actas 1;* also Fernando Picó, *Libertad y servidumbre en el Puerto Rico del siglo XIX,* 3rd ed. (Río Piedras: Ediciones Huracán, 1983), and Andrés Ramos Mattei, "Technical Innovations and Social Change in the Sugar Industry of Puerto Rico, 1870–1880" in *Between Slavery and Free Labor: The Spanish Speaking Caribbean in the Nineteenth Century,* ed. Manuel Moreno Fraginals, Frank Moya Pons and Stanley L. Engerman (Baltimore: Johns Hopkins University Press, 1985), 162.

10. Caro de Delgado, 50.

11. Ibid., 51.

12. Ibid., 51.

13. Irisarri's discourse uses stereotypes that were familiar to the French. See William B. Cohen, *The French Encounter with Africans: White Response to Blacks, 1530–1880* (Bloomington: Indiana University Press, 1980), 1–34, 59 and 60–99; also Michèle Duchet, *Antropología e historia en el siglo de las luces: Buffon, Voltaire, Rousseau, Helvecio, Diderot,* trad. Francisco González Aramburo, 2nd ed. (México: Siglo XXI, 1984), 33–34, 44–50 and 121–68.

14. Caro de Delgado, 53–54.

15. Ibid., 52.

16. See Francisco A. Scarano, *Sugar and Slavery in Puerto Rico: The Plantation Economy of Ponce, 1800–1850* (Madison: University of Wisconsin Press, 1984), 83, 85; Scarano "Inmigración y estructura de clases: Los hacendados de Ponce, 1815–1845," in *Inmigración y clases sociales en el Puerto Rico del siglo XIX,* ed. Francisco A. Scarano (Río Piedras: Ediciones Huracán, 1981), 21–66; Laird W. Bergad, *Coffee and the Growth of Agrarian Capitalism in Nineteenth Century Puerto Rico* (Princeton: Princeton University Press, 1983), 26; and Pedro San Miguel, *El mundo que creó el azúcar: Las haciendas de Vega Baja, 1800–1873* (Río Piedras: Ediciones Huracán, 1989), 78–79.

17. Caro de Delgado, 52.

18. Copy of the minutes of the cabildo meeting of 20 Feb. 1823, AGPR, FGEPR, Municipios, caja 554. For the treaty see, Arturo Morales Carrión, *Auge y decadencia de la trata negrera en Puerto Rico (1820–1860)* (San Juan: Centro de Estudios Avanzados de Puerto Rico y el Caribe-Instutito de Cultura Puertorriqueña, 1978), 22–25.

19. See Raúl Cepero Bonilla, *Azúcar y abolición* (Barcelona: Editorial Crítica, 1976), particularly 37–40, and Naranjo y García, *Racismo e inmigración*. In Puerto Rico a Haitian-inspired conspiracy was denounced in the western port of Aguadilla in 1795, while Haitian agents were suspected of fomenting anarchy. See Guillermo Baralt, *Esclavos rebeldes: Conspiraciones y sublevaciones de esclavos en Puerto Rico (1795–1873)* (Río Piedras: Ediciones Huracán, 1981), 16.

20. Caro de Delgado, 52–53.

21. Ibid., 53.

22. Ibid., 53.

23. This institution was one of the modifications introduced by the new constitutional system. Although it was not a true colonial legislative assembly, it gave some representation to the colonial elite in the administrative affairs of the island. For more details see Jesús Lalinde Abadía, *La administración española en el siglo XIX Puertorriqueño (Pervivencia de la variante indiana del decisionismo castellano en Puerto Rico)* (Seville: Escuela de Estudios Hispano-Americanos de Sevilla, 1980): 126, 147–50; Luis E. González Vales, *Alejandro Ramírez y su tiempo* (Río Piedras: UPRED, 1978): 145–251; and Delma Arrigoitia, "La segunda Diputación Provincial de Puerto Rico (1820–1823)," *Caribe* 4–5 (1983–84): 91–103.

24. Antonio Sánchez had been active in the process that resulted in Power's election as deputy to the Supreme Junta in Spain. On 4 May 1809, he was named as one of the candidates for deputy, and received two votes. See "Asuntos relacionados con la elección de Power," in Caro de Delgado, 25. The minutes of the 14 Dec. 1813 session of the Dipuatación from which I will quote are in manuscript form without folio numbers, in AGPR, FGEPR, DP, Sesiones, caja 312.

25. Sánchez's argument is similar to Arango y Parreño's defense of the Cuban slave trade in 1805. Arango estimated the cost of slave labor at 200 pesos a year, and the cost of free labor at 400 pesos annually. Included in the cost of slave labor was "the price of the slaves' upkeep and the average annual amortization of the invested capital." See Manuel Moreno Fraginals, *El ingenio: Complejo económico social cubano del azúcar,* 3 vols. (Havana: Editorial de Ciencias Sociales, 1978), 1:260.

26. See Morales Carrión, *Auge y decadencia*.

27. For a scholarly treatment of Abercomby's expedition, see Arturo Morales Carrión, *Puerto Rico and the Non Hispanic Caribbean: A Study in the Decline of Spanish Exclusivism,* 2nd ed. (Río Piedras: University of Puerto Rico, 1971), 113–17, and María M. Alonso y Milagros Flores, *The Eighteenth Century Caribbean and the British Attack on Puerto Rico in 1797* (San Juan: The National Park Service-Publicaciones Puertorriqueñas, 1997). For the reconquest

of Santo Domingo, see Frank Moya Pons, *Historia Colonial de Santo Domingo* (Santiago, Santo Domingo: Universidad Católica Madre y Maestra, 1974), 394–400.

28. He conveniently forgets the slave insurrection on St. John (1733) that was crushed only after French troops were sent from Martinique. However, Puerto Rico's military establishment was far superior to the scanty force that the Danes had kept on that island. See Neville A. T. Hall, *Slave Society in the Danish West Indies: St.Thomas, St. John and St. Croix,* ed. B. W. Higman (Jamaica: University of the West Indies Press, 1992), 11.

29. See Franklin W. Knight, *The Caribbean: The Genesis of a Fragmented Nationalism,* 2nd ed. (New York: Oxford University Press, 1990), 70–80.

30. H. Hoetink, "Race and Class in the Caribbean," *Caribbean Contours,* eds. Sidney Mintz, Sally Price (Baltimore: Johns Hopkins University Press, 1985), 61. See also Picó, *Al filo del poder: Subalternos y dominantes en Puerto Rico, 1739–1910* (Río Piedras: Editorial de la Universidad de Puerto Rico, 1993).

31. Schwartz suggests that Brazil's *mestiço* and mulatto populations developed a "precocious" sense of colonial identity. See Stuart B. Schwartz, "The Formation of a Colonial Identity in Brazil" in *Colonial Identity in the Atlantic World,* eds. Nicholas Canny, Anthony Padgen (Princeton: Princeton University Press, 1987), 16. López Cantos cites examples of concerted action against the colonial authorities by Puerto Rico's free of all classes. See Angel López Cantos, "Aproximación al hombre de color puertorriqueño. Siglo XVIII" in *Puerto Rico Negro,* ed. Jalil Sued Badillo, Angel López Cantos (Río Piedras: Editorial Cultural, 1986), 264.

32. Picó, *Al filo del poder,* 111, 135–36.

33. In San Germán, *pardos* from Guarico (Haiti) were a substantial proportion (36.3 percent) of the foreigners registered in Montoso, a sparsely settled highland ward. See González Mendoza, "The Parish of San Germán," 184, n. 65, and "Matrícula de extranjeros [1838]," AGPR, FGEPR, Censo y Riqueza, caja 14.

34. See Article 5, Chapter II, Title I and Article 22, Chapter IV, Title II of the Constitution in José Trías Monge, *Historia Constitucional de Puerto Rico,* 4 vols. (Río Piedras: Editorial de la Universidad de Puerto Rico, 1980–83), 4:255–56.

35. The Creole elite adopted a popular mask when presenting its political demands. See Francisco A. Scarano, "The Jíbaro Masquerade and the Subaltern Politics of Creole Identity Formation in Puerto Rico, 1745–1823," *American Historical Review* 101 (1996): 1398–1431.

36. The first elections under the Constitution of 1812 were heavily contested. One of the major divisions was precisely that between the "sons of the land" and foreigners (meaning émigrés and European-born Spaniards). See Lidio Cruz Monclova, *Historia de Puerto Rico (siglo XIX),* 6 vols. (Río Piedras: Editorial de la Universidad de Puerto Rico, 1970), 1: 52–53. Elections for the Junta de Provincia (the body in charge of electing the island's representative to the Cortes) were particularly contested in San Germán. See AHMSG, *Act. 2,* [1812], "Elecciones parroquiales," fols. 4v, 5–6, 10–30v.

37. See Robert L. Paquette, *Sugar Is Made with Blood: The Conspiracy of La Escalera and the Conflict between Empires over Slavery in Cuba* (Middletown, Conn.: Wesleyan University Press, 1988).

38. Sources for the table are: (1765) O'Reilly, "Memoria," 538; (1776), Abbad, *Historia,* 153; (1780–1792 and 1800), AGPR, Colección Particular Francisco Scarano; (1796) AGI, Sto. Domingo, 2378; (1803) AGI, Sto. Domingo, 2322; (1812) AGPR, FGEPR, Censo y Riqueza, caja 13. I must thank Dr. Salvador Padilla Escabí for the photocopies of the *padrones* for 1796 and 1803.

Chapter 7

American Political Culture and the French and Haitian Revolutions

Nathaniel Cutting and the Jeffersonian Republicans

SIMON P. NEWMAN

IT WAS A MORE PROPHETIC moment than most who witnessed it could ever have imagined. While Americans celebrated the victorious conclusion of their war for independence, the bands of the defeated British army at Yorktown lamented their government's loss of thirteen North American colonies by playing "The World Turned Upside Down." After years of warfare and social, economic and political upheaval, most Americans and Europeans looked forward to peace and stability, yet the age of revolution was beginning rather than ending, and soon the French Revolution would engulf Europe as the Haitian Revolution erupted in the Caribbean.

No sooner had Americans finished fighting their revolutionary war for independence, and constructing a new national government, than they were confronted by radical revolutions elsewhere in the world. As David Brion Davis and Robin Blackburn point out earlier in this volume, the Haitian Revolution racialized the age of revolution, raising the possibility that liberty, equality, and fraternity could overturn slavery and extend republican liberty to all. The contemporary and subsequent effects of this revolution are addressed by Davis, Blackburn and Seymour Drescher: while Davis and Blackburn believe that the French and Haitian Revolutions speeded emancipation in parts of the United States and in the British Empire, Drescher cautions that slavery was to remain a vibrant part of the European and American economies for decades to come.

For citizens of the early national United States, revolution was more than a vague and abstract concept. Twenty years of resistance and war against Britain had educated them in the ideas and language of revolutionary republicanism, and each year they gathered together on the Fourth of July to reaffirm their commitment to the values enshrined in the Declaration of Independence. As political parties began developing during the presidency of George Washington, the Federalists in government and the Jeffersonian Republicans in opposition had to define themselves in relation both to their own revolutionary heritage and to the ongoing revolutions in Europe and the Caribbean. The Federalists styled themselves the "friends of order," and were happy to regard their own revolution as a completed event and to distance themselves from radical social revolution elsewhere.

In contrast, the Jeffersonian Republicans defined themselves as the party that would defend the ideals of the American Revolution against domestic and foreign enemies alike, and their parades, festivals, toasts and the whole range of their political culture revolved around this central mission. It was in the language and rituals of their popular political culture, in their toasts and their parades, and especially in their annual celebrations of the anniversary of American independence that the Jeffersonian Republicans constantly reaffirmed their self-anointed status as the defenders of the "spirit of '76." Thus, the party was quick to welcome the French Revolution and to glory in the spread of republican ideals. However, as a party whose strongest base lay in the slave-holding South, the Republicans grew increasingly troubled by the reality of radical social revolution in France and racial revolution in Saint-Domingue.

Just how the Jeffersonian Republicans dealt with the resulting quandary is the subject of this essay. Their strategy is worthy of the praise of today's most accomplished political "spin doctors," for the Republicans managed to continue to present themselves as the party of the American Revolution in particular, and of republican revolutionary values in general, while distancing themselves from revolutions outside the United States and the implications of those revolutions for Americans. Such was their success that the Republicans would win control of the national government and hold it for a generation, the longest period of one-party rule in the nation's history.

This essay will examine the ways in which the Republicans sought to continue to project themselves as *the* party of republican revolution, while yet distancing themselves from foreign social and racial revolutions that threatened the American status quo, by examining the changes in meaning and interpretation that underlay their political culture in conjunction with the writings of Nathaniel Cutting — a Republican on hand to witness and write about the American, French and Haitian Revolutions. In certain respects Cutting was an unusual Jeffersonian: a New Englander deeply immersed in the Atlantic commercial world, his background appears quite Federalist in character. Yet in his deep and abiding pride in the ideology of Jefferson's Declaration of Independence, and in his vehement opposition to what he interpreted as the elitist and counter-revolutionary nature and policies of the Federalist administrations of Washington and Adams, his political beliefs and ideals suggest that Cutting was typical of the Northern men of seaport cities who forged the Republican alliance with Southern yeoman and planters that won control of the national government in the elections of 1800.

Nathaniel Cutting allows us a unique insight into this inherently counter-revolutionary process, for he witnessed the three great revolutions of the late-eighteenth century, and like the political party he aligned himself with, Cutting was forced by the troubling implications of what he had seen to reformulate his most basic political beliefs. Born and raised in revolutionary Massachusetts, he had for some years worked as the master of a ship based in Newburyport.[1] From there Cutting moved on to Europe, and between 1786 and 1789 he lived and worked in the French port of Le Havre, buying goods brought in by British and American ships for resale in France. By the late summer of 1789, however, Cutting had decided that it was "impolitic" to remain in revolutionary France, and after borrowing money from a friend he departed for the western coast of Africa.[2] Cutting became a slave trader, residing in the French colony of Saint-Domingue between November 1791 and June 1792, where he observed the early stages of the Haitian Revolution.

Almost all Americans had greeted the early stages of the French Revolution with enormous enthusiasm, for they were enraptured by the idea that Europe might follow in the republican footsteps of the United States. Americans of all political complexions welcomed the news from France, and George Washington spoke for many of his countrymen and women when he observed that "the peculiar light of the age seems to have opened the eyes of almost every nation in Europe," and he rejoiced that "the American Revolution has been productive of happy consequences on both sides of the Atlantic."[3] Nathaniel Cutting, too, was typical in the way he gloried in the thought that the French Revolution "may date its *conception*" from "the late glorious struggle for Liberty" in America.[4] Newspapers from New Hampshire to Georgia sustained popular enthusiasm for the French Revolution by filling their pages with enthusiastic accounts of events in France, often supplanting domestic politics.[5]

However, as the French Revolution became ever more radical and violent, it quickly became more controversial within the United States, and the debate between Thomas Paine and Edmund Burke was replayed in American politics during the 1790s. In *The Rights of Man* (1791) and *The Age of Reason* (1794) Paine celebrated social and political revolution and the Enlightenment ideals that fueled it, while in *Reflections on the Revolution in France* (1790) Burke had observed that if partisan political executions and social revolution were based upon an appeal to abstract Enlightenment ideals, the ethical norms and all of the institutions of civilized society would fall. Americans echoed these sentiments: John Adams's *Discourses on Davila* (1805), for example, echoed Burke's distrust of human nature and his fear of radical revolution, while in "The Key of Liberty" (1799) William Manning demonstrated that democratic concepts of human progress and perfectibility were alive and well in the new American republic.[6]

Since the earliest stages of the American Revolution, there had been Americans who were uncomfortable with the episodes of social and political radicalism that had punctuated resistance and rebellion against British authority, and they had railed against such alleged excesses as those of Boston's Stamp Act crowds in 1765, and Philadelphia's Fort Wilson rioters in 1779. As historians from Charles Beard on have noted, the Federal Constitution marked a step back from the radical revolutionary spirit of the 1770s. Under the new frame of government the Federalists, styling themselves the Friends of Order, condemned "Revolutionary principles" that threatened the "security of life, liberty and property, which is the end and design of all Legitimate Governments."[7] The Federalists were opposed by Jeffersonian Republicans who sought to nurture revolutionary Enlightenment ideology and radical republicanism as the foundation of their opposition to the Federalists. To their supporters and to many historians since, the Republicans were defenders of the Enlightenment ideals of the American Revolution, and the party whose principles would take the United States on toward Jacksonian democracy.

However, by 1793 the French Revolution had become far more controversial in America, deepening the divide between the Federalists and their Republican opponents. The increasing radicalism of events in France, particularly the executions of Louis XVI and Marie Antoinette and then the attacks on organized Christianity, shocked and frightened those Americans who were identifying themselves with the emerging Federalist party. For these men, the Federal Constitution represented the successful institutionalization of a politically and socially conservative reaction to the more radical ideology of the American Revolution, and they interpreted events in France as a threat to the very fabric of their own society. Horrified Federalists accused deist or even atheist American "Jacobins" of joining subversive Democratic-Republican societies: the Whiskey Rebellion of 1794 appeared to prove that these Francophilic societies posed a very real threat to social order, property, and legitimate political authority in the United States.[8] As early as the beginning of 1793, Federalists had begun to distance themselves from the French Revolution and all that it symbolized in the United States.[9] The Federalist lawyer Joseph Dennie, for example, wrote to his parents that he had always admired the "old whigs of 1775," until, that is, they had mounted a French Revolutionary festival in Boston "and taught the rabble that they were viceroys."[10] William Bentley described the people who participated in this festival as no better than a "rabble," while John Quincy Adams dismissed the entire affair as "anarchical."[11]

Although the French Revolution's violent attacks on people and property worried the Federalists, it was their fear that such violent radicalism might destroy Great Britain and then spread to America that truly terrified them. Fear of social and political disorder permeated Federalist thought, and the Friends of Order conjured up images of Republican "highfliers [who] use every means to make the people abhor the laws, the constitution, Congress, and the executive officers."[12] "A Farmer" worried that America had a "corps of officers to lead" the rabble, and "bring about a state of what the Jacobins term *sovereign insurrection* and *permanent revolution*."[13] Two decades later John Adams wrote to Thomas Jefferson recalling "the terrorism excited by [French ambassador Edmond] Genet, in 1793, when ten thousand people in the streets of Philadelphia, day after day, threatened to drag Washington out of his house, and effect a revolution in the government."[14]

In loud and colorful opposition to the Federalists stood many of the residents of the port cities of the northern states, whose Anglophobia and radical republicanism led them to laud the French Republic in elaborate festivals in celebration of French military victories, Bastille Day, and a variety of other French events and anniversaries. In the hundreds and even thousands they took to the streets of Boston, New York, Philadelphia and other smaller northern towns, singing French revolutionary songs and wearing tri-colored cockades, badges that identified them both as supporters of the French and as opponents of what they interpreted as the Anglophilic and Francophobic policies of Washington's administration. The symbolic language of these rites and festivals illustrate that many Republicans interpreted events in France as a vindication of the radicalism of the American revolution, and an indictment of what they interpreted as the counter-revolutionary policies of the Federalists. The French Revolution politicized the American nation, and the young mechanic Benjamin Tappan was one of many for whom the French Revolution provided a defining political experience, for he first took "his stand on the democratic side" at a festival honoring "the recapture of Toulon from the British & Spanish."[15]

The French Revolution, the "greatest event in the annals of time," thus provided many Republicans with a powerful symbol of all that the American Revolution had represented, along with a millennial promise of greater things to come.[16] Reveling in revolutionary ideology, Philadelphians who had participated in a Feast of Reason drank toasts to "The Eighteenth Century," hoping that "the revolutions which it has given birth to, [may] know no limit but the utmost boundaries of the earth."[17] Domestic politics were a vital core within these enthusiastic celebrations of the progress of "LIBERTY and EQUALITY" in France, for they provided Republicans with opportunities to gather together and acclaim such sentiments as the "rights of man" – Liberty and Equality," and the "republicans" in both France and America who defended them.[18] In Rutland, Vermont, citizens celebrating the recapture of Toulon toasted the sentiment, "May the American Congress ever continue the true guardians of the people's liberty," while in Charleston, South Carolina, those celebrating the anniversary of the Franco-American alliance drank to "Citizen Madison, and the Republican party in Congress."[19]

The Republican leadership at first rejoiced in these popular outpourings of support for revolution and opposition to the Federalists, interpreting support for France as proof of loyalty to liberty, equality, democracy, and republicanism, the ideals of the American Revolution as articulated and defended by their own party. Watching Philadelphians celebrate the French Revolution, Jefferson enthused that "All the old spirit of 1776 is rekindling."[20] From 1789 until the summer of 1793, Jefferson and other leading Republicans interpreted Federalist opposition to the French Revolution as the counter-revolutionary efforts of aristocratic "monarchists" or "monocrats." Members of the Democratic Society in New York City were quite clear on this point, asserting "that he who is an enemy to the French Revolution, cannot be a firm republican; and, therefore, though he may be a good citizen in every other respect, ought not to be entrusted with the guidance of any part of the machine of government."[21]

However, for all their enthusiastic support for the French Revolution and their unhesitating employment of it in partisan politics, the increasing radicalism of the revolutions in France and then Saint-Domingue ultimately proved far more troubling to the Jeffersonian Republicans than to their Federalist opponents. As revolution became bloodier and more radical in Europe and the Caribbean, American Republicans who were struggling to win control of state and national governments were forced to reevaluate their commitment to revolution, both as an abstract idea and as a contemporary reality. Issues of race and class were of vital import, and it is in the Republicans' attempts to maintain the illusion of commitment to revolutionary ideals while distancing themselves from the reality of radi cal social and racial revolution in France and Saint-Domingue that one may see the paradox at the heart of the party that governed the United States for the first quarter of the nineteenth century.

Increasing violence and social dislocation in France, but more particularly the violent and racial hue of revolution in Saint-Domingue gave Republican leaders grave cause for concern. This process began early for Nathaniel Cutting, on the scene in France as he was, and his disapproval and even fear of the violence of the lower sorts in France encouraged him to articulate fears that sounded almost Federalist. At first he had looked forward with eager anticipation to a French "revolution in Politicks," and in his accounts of the constitutional changes going on in Paris, Cutting enthusiastically championed "a very total Revolution . . . in the Government of this Country," achieved with remarkably "little opposition or Bloodshed."[22]

However, as the lower sorts began to take a more active and violent part in the revolution, and as constitutional reformation gave way to radical social and political revolution, Cutting grew increasingly uncomfortable. In describing local struggles over food and grain in July 1789, he dismissed the protagonists as a "mob" of "lawless Banditts [sic]," and he was more than a little concerned "that People of all Ranks & Denominations, both Male & Female," were standing around discussing revolutionary politics.[23] As the violence increased, both in Paris and in Le Havre, Cutting grew ever more distressed. He castigated "the Mob passions" and "the impending Fury of the Multitude," and by the end of July 1789, Cutting was telling friends that "no news is good news."[24]

Complaining that French "Citizens have all at once become so excessively enamour'd up with Liberty" that people and property were no longer secure, Cutting described how "the enraged Populace" of Le Havre had murdered an army officer and torn his body apart.[25] Within a week he had decided to leave a country whose revolution had barely begun, but which already terrified him. It would be another five years before the majority of Republicans in the United States followed Cutting's lead. Perhaps the Atlantic Ocean lessened the reality of violent social revolution, and perhaps events in France were less important in and of themselves than they were as symbols within American politics. Republican leaders were the first to follow Cutting's lead and distance themselves from radical revolution. The wars of the French Revolution appeared a potent and menacing force, which threatened to upset the balance of power in Europe. Disenchantment was quickened by the disastrous embassy of citizen Edmond Genêt, who attempted to ride over Washington's neutrality by making use of popular support for France and commissioning French privateers in American ports.[26] Then, following the Directory's March 1797 decision to invalidate the Franco-American alliance of 1778 and begin seizing American ships carrying British goods, diplomatic relations between the French and American republics began quickly to degenerate, and the party of Jefferson quietly abandoned their French cause célèbre.[27] A few radicals continued to celebrate the ideals and reality of the French Revolution, from the Boston sailors who celebrated Bastille Day in 1796, to the Philadelphians who celebrated French victories in Italy in 1797, to the Kentucky farmers who commemorated the French Revolution in early 1800.[28] By and large, however, although the French Revolution had during the early 1790s inspired more public celebrations in the United States than any other person or event, by the close of the decade it had been abandoned by the Republicans.[29]

However, while changes in Franco-American relations help explain this dramatic shift, the Republicans' movement away from the revolutionary ideology encapsulated by the French Revolution had deeper roots. What terrified Cutting, the power of the crowd to destroy life and property, assumed a new significance for Republicans during the latter half of the 1790s and the opening years of the nineteenth century. When the French Revolution spread to Saint-Domingue, when the contagion of liberty reached the colony's enslaved population, and when France's revolutionaries abolished slavery first in Saint-Domingue and then throughout their colonies, the party of Jefferson outdid the Federalists in slamming the door shut on true revolution in their own sort of Thermidorian reaction.[30]

At first, the dangers were far from apparent. As French authority eroded in the most valuable colony in the Caribbean, planters who objected to commercial restrictions and free men of mixed race who were unhappy with their second-class status sent delegates to the meeting of the Estates General in Paris.[31] Nathaniel Cutting, once again on the scene, applauded their actions, inspired as they were by "the patriotic motive of securing the blessings to the Inhabitants of this Colony and their Posterity the blessings of a liberal constitution, calculated to promote the happiness of all who dwell beneath its salutary influence!"[32] As an American, Cutting could not "help feeling interested in behalf of the persecuted Colonists. Indeed I think that every Free American who indulges Political Reflections must feel himself peculiarly interested in the Fate of the valuable and flourishing Colony of Saint Domingue, which at some future period may possibly fall within the Jurisdiction of the Thirteen United States! At least one may venture to predict that such an intimate intercourse will one day be established between them as will mutually invigorate those principles of Constitutional Freedom which have apparently taken such deep root in both Countries and will be productive of that Reciprocal advantage which is the most durable cement of Political Union." [33]

However, as infighting within the French colony grew, and with little help from Paris where the revolution was entering a new phase, the Haitian Revolution took an unexpected and, for Cutting, Jefferson and other Republicans, a most unwelcome turn. During the late summer of 1791, revolutionary fervor spread to the colony's 500,000 slaves, who began fighting to regain the freedom that a majority of them had known in Africa. Over the following decade the violence worsened, exacerbated by the presence of both British and French armies, and by the time that Jean-Jacques Dessalines proclaimed the Republic of Haiti in 1804, more than 300,000 people had died.[34]

To Cutting, there were enormous differences between the constitutional protests of the "good patriots" amongst the white population and the "crimes" and "consequent devastation" of the "Revolted Slaves."[35] The thousands of refugees who fled Saint-Domingue for the safe havens of the United States shared Cutting's opinions, and their stories and very presence spread the specter of black insurrection throughout the southern United States. That both the slaves and the "good patriots" sought the same republican freedom and equality never occurred to Cutting, or perhaps it was too horrifying a thought to record on paper. The actions of the former slaves were not, at least as far as Cutting was concerned, the actions of revolutionaries, but rather were no more than the "indiscriminate fury" of "Brigands."[36] As more and more slaves joined the revolution, the infighting between the French colonists intensified, leading Cutting to adopt Federalist rhetoric to condemn the "many-headed monster" of "the Populace with out doors." [37] With slaves controlling more and more of the interior, Cutting went so far as to propose "that it will be most prudent for Government to enter into a Treaty with them similar to that which the Government of Jamaica formerly made with the Maroon Negroes in that Island." [38] He quickly concluded that "the desolation" of Saint-Domingue was inevitable, and he abandoned another revolution, convinced that the United States was "the only Asylum from Anarchy and Tyranny."[39]

Republicans perceived there to be a direct causal link between French radicalism and events in Saint-Domingue. Cutting wrote with disgust of those revolutionaries "in France & elsewhere," who sought to destroy "the finest colony on earth" with "their leveling principles."[40] Indeed, the French decision to abolish slavery in Saint-Domingue in August 1793, and then throughout the French colonies in February 1794, horrified Republican leaders throughout the slaveholding South and beyond. Jefferson predicted that all of the Caribbean islands "will remain in the hands of the people of colour, & a total expulsion of the whites sooner or later will take place."[41] Even before the outbreak of the French and Haitian Revolutions, Jefferson had found it all but impossible to comprehend a society where former white slaveowners and former black slaves could peacefully live together: "Deep rooted prejudices entertained by the whites; ten thousand recollections, by the blacks, of the injuries they have sustained; new provocations; the real distinctions which nature has made; and many other circumstances. will divide us into parties, and produce convulsions which will probably never end but in the extermination of the one or other race."[42] The extension of revolutionary ideology to black slaves made such a bloodbath all the more inevitable, and Jefferson gloomily warned that "the revolutionary storm, now sweeping the globe, will [soon] be upon us."[43]

Before the outbreak of the French Revolution, some five hundred American ships had been engaged in trade with Saint-Domingue, and the small colony that produced such enormous quantities of sugar and coffee and consumed large amounts of plantation supplies was the second largest trading partner of the United States. For a variety of reasons, the Federalist administrations of both Washington and Adams were willing to work hard to keep this trade alive, even after the island's former slaves began to dominate the troubled island. The Federalists sought smooth relations and open trading with Great Britain, while opposing the French at every turn. As Franco-American relations began deteriorating in the mid-1790s, Saint-Domingue presented the Federalists with an opportunity to expand American commerce while striking at French economic, political and military power in the New World. With American merchant and naval ships battling the ships of the French Republic in 1798 and 1799, Adams and Secretary of State Timothy Pickering posted Edward Stevens to the island as American consul general, authorizing him to establish relations with Toussaint Louverture and the black rebels.[44]

American trade was vital to the success of the Haitian Revolution, providing the rebels with their only reliable source of food and arms, and a market for their crops. On one occasion American warships blockaded and fired upon several ports in Saint-Domingue, in support of Toussaint Louverture's forces.[45] In the United States the Republicans were criticizing the Federalists as counterrevolutionaries bent on consolidating the power of a socio-economic elite, while in Saint-Domingue these same Federalists were actively aiding the most radical revolution of their age.

But not all Americans agreed with this policy. While every July 4 the Republicans commemorated the Spirit of '76, they were appalled by events in Saint-Domingue. Thousands of white planters fled from Saint-Domingue to the comforting shores of the southern United States, bringing with them tales of black rebellion and atrocities.[46] Some brought a few slaves with them, much to the consternation of local whites. In 1792 the South Carolina legislature took action against this influx by passing a law that prohibited the importation of any slaves, and other southern states soon followed suit.[47] More significantly, the small yet significant waves of manumission that had swept through the upper South in the years following the American Revolution began to ebb, as state after state made it harder for planters to free their slaves, and even harder for those slaves who were freed to remain in the state. At the same time southern legislatures moved to curtail the few privileges enjoyed by blacks, whether free or enslaved.[48]

American blacks inspired by the Haitians were to be feared above all else. During the 1790s and well into the nineteenth century, white Americans were terrified that black revolutionaries would destroy liberty, property and society itself, bringing race war into the communities of the United States. Nor was this a uniquely Southern phenomenon, for after a slave began a fire in Albany, New York, in 1793, rumors of similar fires spread through such communities as Philadelphia, Schenectady, Waterford, Boston, Hartford, New London, and Elizabethtown.[49]

Republican fears of the Haitian Revolution coalesced within both a domestic and an international context of insurrection on a scale never before seen. Not only had the American republic been born of its own revolution, but its society and polity assumed shape within a fiery crucible of almost constant rebellion and revolution. The Federal Constitution that was intended to bring order to the nascent republic was in no small part a response to Shays' Rebellion in Massachusetts in 1787. Two years later, with the new Constitution in place, Washington was inaugurated as the first president against the backdrop of the outbreak of the French Revolution. As revolutionary fervor began spreading out from France, Washington's presidency was tested by the Whiskey Rebellion, a domestic insurrection stretching from North Carolina to New Jersey, which represented a serious threat to the power and legitimacy of the new national government. As the eighteenth century drew to a close, French-inspired republican revolution swept Europe's *ancien regime* aside, with even the British Royal Navy briefly paralyzed by a Painite mutiny. On the western side of the Atlantic the Haitian Revolution took an unassailable hold in the Caribbean, while in the United States Fries' Rebellion in Pennsylvania and Gabriel's Rebellion in Virginia showed citizens of the American republic that their own recent revolution did not render them immune from revolutionary insurrection by both whites and blacks.[50]

Although distancing themselves from the reality of the radical and racialized revolutions of France and Saint-Domingue, the Jeffersonian Republicans continued to employ the rhetoric of the American Revolution in their partisan struggle against the Federalists. Presenting themselves as the party of Thomas Paine and Thomas Jefferson, the heirs of the Patriots of 1776 and the defenders of what they characterized as the legitimate ideals of the American Revolution, the Republicans employed a political culture defined by a passionate attachment to vaguely defined yet vehemently defended revolutionary values, and whenever Republicans gathered together their toasts and ritual activities revolved around their defense of the American Revolution against both foreign and domestic threats. The Republican opposition coalesced around "the principles of the Revolution," contrasting themselves with the deference and hierarchy of the Federalist Friends of Order who argued that the "Whiggism of 1776, was to rally round the *Venerable Statesmen and Patriots* of our country."[51] While Republicans opposed the policies and personnel of the Washington and Adams administrations in the name of "the true principles of liberty, equality, and [the] sovereignty of the people," the Federalists reasoned that the American "people have made a government" and "He who would support the government of the people, may be supposed to be the friend of their power and their rights."[52]

Nathaniel Cutting was typical of Republicans in the ways in which he viewed the "late glorious" American Revolution.[53] While in Le Havre he commemorated the fourteenth anniversary of the Battle of Lexington and the beginning of the "immortal Revolution," and he even went so far as to think of the Fourth of July as his own birthday, musing in his journal "indeed I was Born again on this day, — that is, politically born."[54] In their celebrations of the anniversary of independence, Republicans articulated their opposition to deferential ritual and conservative policies, and their allegiance to the revolutionary ideals of 1776. In 1794, for example, one group of Philadelphia militia men raised their glasses to the hope that "principles and not men [will] ever be the object of republican attachment," while others toasted "American Independence – May the principles that dictated the act, ever be supported by the people."[55] Citizens in Elizabethtown, New Jersey, wished for "Perpetuity to the principles" of the American Revolution, while residents of Lynchburg, Virginia, toasted the "spirit of 1776."[56]

Ritual celebration of the American Revolution constituted a vital part of the process whereby elite party leaders, white yeoman farmers and planters, and urban craftsmen and workers bound themselves together in the Republican coalition. By the time they won control of the national government, the Republicans had so completely molded Independence Day into a partisan event that some Federalists refused to participate in these festive rites. Republicans interpreted this as unpatriotic, and were quick to call their enemies to account: they were infuriated, for example, by an 1804 article in the Federalist *New York Evening Post* that attacked "the practice of reading the *declaration*" of Independence on the grounds that Britain and the United States were now allies, and they deplored the "federalists of Boston" who had refused to participate in any Independence day celebrations.[57]

The Fourth of July, then, provided Republicans with an opportunity to celebrate their vision of the nature and the heritage of the American Revolution, all within the context of their partisan battles with the Federalist administrations of Washington and Adams. Every Independence Day they worked hard to present themselves as the legitimate defenders of the liberty and equality fought for in 1776, and they incorporated the Declaration of Independence into their festive rites. Thomas Jefferson, as the author of the Declaration, was both leader and hero to the party faithful: when he became president they enthused that the "election of a Republican President is a new Declaration of Independence," and raised their glasses to sentiments like "The principles of the 4th July, 1776, confirmed the 4th March, 1801," and "The reign of Genuine Liberty."[58] Such language was vital to the rites of the Republican party that had taken shape during the preceding decade. Indeed Republican political culture had dominated and even defined the 1790s, with partisan celebrations of Independence Day and French Revolutionary battles and constitutional anniversaries far outnumbering the Federalists' preferred festivals in honor of George Washington.

To those who created it, and to historians ever since, the American Revolution signified nothing less than that "America [had] become the Enlightenment fulfilled."[59] The Jeffersonian Republicans believed that their revolution had created an opportunity to move civilization forward, and in their popular political culture the Republicans presented themselves as the true defenders of the promise of the American Revolution. In Augusta, Georgia, militiamen celebrated Independence Day in 1801 by pledging their "attachment for Liberty, Equality, and the Rights of Man," while citizens in Hartford, Connecticut, toasted "Republicanism. – Repentance to enemies – perseverance to its friends – and a glorious triumph of its principles throughout the world."[60]

The radicalism of the early American Revolution had been enshrined in such texts as Thomas Paine's *Common Sense,* the Pennsylvania state constitution of 1776, and the opening paragraphs of Jefferson's Declaration of Independence. In the debate over the ratification of the federal Constitution, and then in the emergence of an ideologically driven opposition to the policies and the very style of the Federalist administrations of Washington and Adams, we can trace the persistence of this radicalism. Moreover, in their enthusiasm for and encouragement of the spread of revolution, the Republicans at first appeared somewhat like those twentieth-century nations that sought to encourage either Marxist or Islamic revolution beyond their own borders. It was the Haitian Revolution, more than anything else, that tempered this enthusiasm, and won the Republicans over to a positively Washingtonian view of the desirability of isolationism and an avoidance of entangling alliances.

These white men's attachment to their hard won rights and liberties remained very real, and the American Revolution continued to inspire the fervent allegiance of Republicans. But when the French Revolution spread to the propertyless, and then in Saint-Domingue to property itself, Republican leaders renounced real revolution: the rhetoric remained, but the ideological substance was gone. In order to protect the property rights and constitutional liberties secured in the American Revolution, and celebrated and commemorated every July 4, the party of Jefferson struggled to retain the Enlightenment ideology of republican revolution while draining it of its radical essence.

Behind the Jeffersonian Republican rhetoric of revolution, then, lay an increasing fear of both the revolutionary ideology and the social reality of France and Saint-Domingue in the late 1790s and early 1800s. Thus, while still championing themselves as the party of '76, by the time that Jefferson entered the White House in 1801 the Republicans had all but renounced basic tenets of their faith in human progress and the promise of radical revolution. Revolutions abroad, most especially in Saint-Domingue, played a crucial role in changing Republican political ideology and culture, shattering optimistic convictions about human progress and perfectibility by demonstrating the full and awesome potential of revolution by those without power and property, including enslaved African Americans.

It is profoundly ironic that it was during the 1790s that Jefferson's Republicans appeared to be at their most radical. While Jefferson enthused to James Madison about the need for frequent revolution, the party that began coalescing around him championed freedom of speech, a steady expansion of the franchise, and the right of legitimate dissent against a democratically elected Federalist government. Moreover in the symbols and rituals of their political culture, in their songs, their cockades, their toasts, their French Revolutionary festivals and their Independence Day celebrations, the Republicans championed radical republican revolution. Yet this radicalism was of a profoundly eighteenth-century Enlightenment character, for it was based upon a classical republican vision of the rights of an educated elite to rule over a polity comprised of adult white male citizens, who were by definition men of property, men with a vested interest in the stability of an inherently unequal and undemocratic society. From France and Saint-Domingue a far more modern sense of revolution was beginning to emerge, one premised upon the basic human and political rights of all people, regardless of race and class. It was this vision that so horrified the party of Jefferson, which managed to win power as the champions of the radical American revolution while simultaneously mounting a fierce assault on the extension of freedom and political liberty to those excluded from the American revolutionary settlement.

The threat of revolution as slave rebellion seemed all the more real in the plantation South.[61] Virginia Governor James Monroe was typical in his worry that the "scenes which are acted in Saint Domingo, must produce an effect in all the people of color in this and the States south of us, more especially our slaves, and it is our duty to be on our guard to prevent any mischief resulting from it."[62] Jefferson agreed, dismissing Saint-Domingue's black revolutionaries as "cannibals" and worrying that if their "combustion can be introduced among us under any veil whatever, we have to fear it."[63] When Gabriel's Rebellion erupted in Richmond at the turn of the century, the worst fears of Republican planters appeared to be confirmed: revolution had spread from Saint-Domingue to the American South. Typical was the reaction of one Richmond newspaper editor who denounced other newspapers for publishing any news from Saint-Domingue, and especially the new Haitian constitution.[64]

It is possible to see the early radical promise of the American Revolution surviving into the nineteenth century, informing the gradual development of universal white male suffrage, the development of abolitionism, and even the rise of the women's rights movement. But during the 1790s the ideology of the Revolution had been transformed, and through the first quarter of the nineteenth century the Republicans had renounced a modern view of revolution as a linear movement informed by human progress. When confronted by the bloody violence and attacks on property of the French Revolution, and its fostering of the slave revolution in Saint-Domingue, Republicans appeared to be reverting to a pre-Enlightenment view of revolution as a cyclical motion. Horrified by the implications of real social and political revolutions, the Republicans withdrew to their fortress and drew up the drawbridge in an attempt to protect their own society, with its constitutional liberties and property rights intact. As Burkean as any Federalists, they continued to celebrate the form of their own revolution every Independence Day, but it was a sanitized shell drained of radical content. No longer did they celebrate radical revolution elsewhere, especially when it was – in their eyes – contaminated by race.

Republicans throughout the northern states began violently excluding black Americans from their celebrations of the American Revolution every Independence Day, celebrations in which enslaved black southerners had never enjoyed an active role. Writing in the early nineteenth century, James Forten complained "that black people, upon certain days of public jubilee, dare not be seen after twelve o'clock in the day." Angrily he concluded, "I allude particularly to the *Fourth of July*!"[65] On one Independence Day free blacks assembled alongside white Philadelphians outside Independence Hall, only to be beaten away under a stream of abuse. Bitter resentment at their exclusion from the commemoration of the revolution encouraged other black Philadelphians to take to the streets in unofficial militia units, parodying the white militia parades seen earlier in the day, and beating white citizens who crossed their path.[66] As David Brion Davis has argued earlier in this volume, it would be almost a century before black Americans were able to begin publicly to articulate what the Haitian Revolution had meant to them, and the ways in which it had shown them that the age of revolution could transcend the color line.

* * *

While Nathaniel Cutting was unusual in that he was one of the only Americans to record his first-hand experiences of the three great revolutions of the late eighteenth century, his profound pride in the American Revolution, his initial enthusiasm for the French Revolution and then his growing antipathy towards both the French and Haitian Revolutions were in line with the reactions of his fellow Jeffersonians. Cutting shared with other Republicans an abiding faith in the spirit of '76 and a deep loyalty to Thomas Jefferson, the man whose words had given some coherence to that spirit. He shared, too, a growing horror of the events and ideals of the revolutions in France and Saint-Domingue. In their celebrations of Jefferson's election and inauguration they may well have paid homage to the radical spirit of their own revolution, but by the turn of the nineteenth century many sought to ensure that the age of enlightened revolution was over. The real achievement of Republican political culture was that it allowed the leaders and supporters of the party to keep alive the spirit and ideology of radical republican revolution, while all the time distancing themselves from its ever more threatening reality. Celebrations of revolutionary anniversaries defined Republican political culture during the 1790s, but the French and Haitian Revolutions transformed these events, draining them of any real ideological commitment and substance. Despite their vilification of the Federalists the Republicans joined the ranks of the counterrevolutionaries, a process most poignantly illustrated by Thomas Paine's funeral in New York in the summer of 1809, which was attended by less than a dozen people. An embarrassment to those who celebrated the American Revolution every Independence Day, the greatest revolutionary of his age was buried and forgotten on his farm in "a scene to affect and wound any sensible heart."[67] By the early nineteenth century, with the Republican party firmly in control of the national government, toasts to Thomas Paine, to liberty, equality and fraternity, and to the rights of man were all but forgotten, replaced by sentiments such as "Consistent Patriotism," which translated into the belief that "the revolutionary whig on the 4th of July, 1776" had evolved into "a Republican on the 4th of July, 1801."[68]

Celebrating their revolutionary heritage each Fourth of July, and continuing to employ revolutionary rhetoric and ritual in their partisan festive culture, the Jeffersonians abandoned the most radical revolutions of their day. Jefferson's administration ended diplomatic relations and banned trade with the new Haitian republic. In the years that followed, as the Jeffersonian Republicans evolved into the Democratic party that eventually would wage the counterrevolutionary struggle of the American Civil War, talk of gradual emancipation in the party's southern base was replaced first by the idea of perpetual slavery as a necessary evil, and then as a positive good, while in the northern states free blacks were segregated and excluded from such public institutions as skilled labor, churches, the militia and festive parades.[69] When Jefferson became president, supporters hailed the "spirit of '76," and they honored this and subsequent election victories as representing "the completion of the revolution of 1776, and the commencement of the happy æra of true liberty."[70] Years later Jefferson would recall "the revolution of 1800" with considerable pride.[71] Thermidor had come.

NOTES

1. Biographical material is drawn from *Proceedings of the Massachusetts Historical Society, 1871–1873,* 1 (1873): 60.

2. Nathaniel Cutting, Journal, 22 Aug. 1789, Nathaniel Cutting Papers, Massachusetts Historical Society. Hereafter cited as NCP.

3. George Washington to Hector Saint John De Crèvecoeur, Mount Vernon, 10 Apr. 1789, *The Writings of Washington,* ed. John C. Fitzpatrick (Washington: United States Government Printing Office, 1939), 30:281; Washington to Catherine Macaulay Graham, 9 Jan. 1790, *The Writings of Washington,* 30:497.

4. Nathaniel Cutting to Harrison Gray Otis, Aug. 1789, Letterbook, 1:71, NCP.

5. Beatrice F. Hyslop, "The American Press and the French Revolution of 1789," *Proceedings of the American Philosophical Society* 104 (1960): 54–85.

6. Adams's essays first appeared in the *Gazette of the United States* in 1790, but were then reprinted, anonymously, as *Discourses on Davila: A Series of Papers on Political History*

(New York: Da Capo Press, 1973 [1805]). Manning wrote the first draft of "The Key of Liberty" in 1797, but it was not published during his lifetime. See Michael Merrill and Sean Wilentz, *The Key of Liberty: The Life and Democratic Writings of William Manning, "A Laborer,"* 1747–1814 (Cambridge: Harvard University Press, 1993).

7. Francis Dana, Grand Jury Charge, Plymouth, Massachusetts, May 1796, Dana Family Papers, Massachusetts Historical Society. See also Charles A. Beard, *An Economic Interpretation of the Constitution of the United States* (New York: Macmillan, 1913), and Gordon S. Wood, *The Creation of the American Republic, 1767–1787* (Chapel Hill: University of North Carolina Press, 1984), 519–64.

8. For the Republican Societies and the Whiskey Rebellion, and the Federalist response, see Thomas P. Slaughter, *The Whiskey Rebellion: Frontier Epilogue to the American Revolution* (New York: Oxford University Press, 1988), [1986] 156–65, 190–221.

9. Most historians have found little evidence of Federalist opposition to the French Revolution before 1795. See, for example, Gary B. Nash, "The American Clergy and the French Revolution," *The William and Mary Quarterly,* 3d. ser., 22 (1965): 392–412. My own research suggests that while the enormous popularity of the French Revolution made it all but impossible for Federalists to openly condemn it, they made their feelings clear by refusing to participate in the enthusiastic Republican parades, feasts and festivals in honor of the French. While the supporters of the Republicans and the Federalists struggled for control over celebrations of Washington's birthday and the Fourth of July, French Revolutionary festivals remained the exclusive terrain of the Republicans. See Newman, *Parades and the Politics of the Street: Festive Culture in the Early American Republic* (Philadelphia: University of Pennsylvania Press, 1997).

10. Joseph Dennie to Joseph Dennie Sr. and Mary Green Dennie, 25 Apr. 1793, Joseph Dennie Papers, Houghton Library, Harvard University.

11. William Bentley, *The Diary of William Bentley, D.D. Pastor of the East Church, Salem, Massachusetts* (Gloucester, Mass.: P. Smith, 1962 [1905]), 2:3; John Quincy Adams to John Adams, 10 Feb. 1793, *Writings of John Quincy Adams,* ed. Worthington Chauncey Ford (New York: Macmillan, 1913), 1:134.

12. *Gazette of the United States* (Philadelphia), 31 Oct. 1792.

13. A Farmer, "For the Gazette of the United States," *Gazette of the United States* (Philadelphia), 11 Feb. 1794.

14. John Adams to Thomas Jefferson, 30 June 1813, in *The Adams-Jefferson Letters: The Complete Correspondence Between Thomas Jefferson and Abigail and John Adams,* ed. Lester J. Cappon (Chapel Hill: University of North Carolina Press, 1959), 2:346–47.

15. "The Autobiography of Benjamin Tappan," ed. Donald J. Ratcliffe, *Ohio History,* 85 (1976): 115.

16. On the political millennialism of the French Revolution in the United States, see Ruth Bloch, *Visionary Republic: Millennial Themes in American Thought, 1756–1800* (New York: Cambridge University Press, 1988), 150–86.

17. "CIVIC FESTIVAL," *Aurora* (Philadelphia), 20 Apr. 1795.

18. "Celebration of the FEAST of LIBERTY and EQUALITY," *The Independent Chronicle and the Universal Advertiser* (Boston), 31 Jan. 1793; "NEWARK, APRIL 8," *Aurora,* 10 Apr. 1795; "BALTIMORE CIVIC FESTIVAL," *Aurora,* (Philadelphia), 22 Apr. 1795.

19. "RUTLAND, FEBRUARY 3," *The Farmer's Library. Or, Vermont Political & Historical Register* (Rutland), 3 Feb. 1794; "Charleston, Feb. 17," *Columbian Herald, Or The Southern Star* (Charleston), 17 Feb. 1794.

20. Thomas Jefferson to James Monroe, 5 May 1793, *The Papers of Thomas Jefferson,* ed. John Catanzariti (Princeton, N.J.: Princeton University Press, 1992), 661.

21. "Address to the Republican Citizens of the United States, May 28, 1794," *The New-York Journal, Or General Advertiser* (New York), 31 May 1794.

22. Cutting to Andrew Hall, Jan. 1789, Letterbook, 1:8; Cutting to Harrison Gray Otis, 18 July 1789, Letterbook, 1:50, 54, NCP.

23. Cutting, Journal, 15 July 1789; Cutting to Harrison Gray Otis, Aug. 1789, Letterbook, 1:108, NCP.

24. Cutting to Harrison Gray Otis, Aug. 1789, Letterbook, 1:102, NCP.

25. Cutting, Journal, 31 July 1789, 13 Aug. 1789, NCP.

26. Harry Ammon, *The Genet Mission* (New York: W. W. Norton, 1973), 44–131.

27. Alexander DeConde, *The Quasi-War: The Politics and Diplomacy of the Undeclared War with France, 1797–1801* (New York: Scribner, 1966), 16–17.

28. "FRENCH REVOLUTION," *Aurora* (Philadelphia), 21 July 1796; "CELEBRATION OF THE VICTORIES OF THE FRENCH REPUBLIC IN ITALY," *Aurora* (Philadelphia), 14 Apr. 1797; *The Kentucky Gazette* (Lexington), 30 Jan. 1800.

29. For a survey of the celebrations of the French Revolution, Independence Day, and Washington's Birthday during the 1790s, see Newman, *Parades and the Politics of the Street*. Between 1792 and 1796, American celebrations of the French Revolution outnumbered celebrations of Washington's birthday and even Independence Day.

30. See David Brion Davis, *Revolutions: Reflections on American Equality and Foreign Liberations* (Cambridge: Harvard University Press, 1990), 29–54, for an insightful overview of changing American reactions to foreign revolutions. Davis argues that a combination of millennial beliefs and traditional fears of unchecked power informed the evolution of American reactions against both the French and Haitian Revolutions.

31. Alfred N. Hunt, *Haiti's Influence on Antebellum America: Slumbering Volcano in the Caribbean* (Baton Rouge: Louisiana State University Press, 1988), 16. See also Donald R. Hickey, "America's Response to the Slave Revolt in Haiti, 1791–1806," *Journal of the Early Republic* 2 (1982): 361–79. While Hunt is interested in the impact of the Haitian Revolution on pro- and anti-slavery thought in nineteenth-century America, Hickey is somewhat more concerned with its effects on the first political party system. Michael Zuckerman has explored how Thomas Jefferson reacted to Saint-Domingue, concluding that Jefferson's racism overcame all other concerns. See Zuckerman, "The Power of Blackness: Thomas Jefferson and the Revolution in Saint-Domingue," in *Almost Chosen People: Oblique Biographies in the American Grain* (Berkeley: University of California Press, 1993), 175–218.

32. Cutting to Thomas Jefferson, 9 Aug. 1790, *Papers of Thomas Jefferson,* 17:329.

33. Cutting to Thomas Jefferson, 19 Apr. 1791, *Papers of Thomas Jefferson,* 17:240.

34. Hickey, "America's Response," 362; Hunt, *Haiti's Influence,* 20; Hickey, "America's Response," 364.

35. Cutting, Journal, 26 Mar. 1792, 9 Nov. 1791, NCP; Cutting to Thomas Jefferson, 21 Feb. 1792, *Papers of Thomas Jefferson,* 23: 127; Cutting, Journal, 11 Nov. 1791, NCP.

36. Cutting, Journal, 17 Apr.1792, NCP.

37. Cutting to Thomas Jefferson, 13 Apr.1792, *Papers of Thomas Jefferson,* 23: 415.

38. Cutting to Thomas Jefferson, 1 Mar. 1792, *Papers of Thomas Jefferson,* 23:179.

39. Cutting to Thomas Jefferson, 1 Mar. 1792, *Papers of Thomas Jefferson,* 23:178; Cutting, "Journal," 12 Nov. 1791, NCP.

40. Cutting, Journal, 1 Dec. 1791, NCP.

41. Thomas Jefferson to James Monroe, 14 July 1793, as quoted in Herbert Aptheker, *American Negro Slave Revolts* (New York, 1963), 42.

42. Thomas Jefferson, "Notes On the State of Virginia" (1786), in *The Portable Thomas Jefferson,* ed. Merrill D. Peterson (New York: Viking Press, 1975), 186.

43. Jefferson to Saint George Tucker, 28 Aug. 1797, as quoted in Winthrop D. Jordan, *White Over Black: American Attitudes Toward the Negro, 1550–1812* (Chapel Hill: University of North Carolina Press, 1968), 386.

44. Linda K. Kerber, *Federalists in Dissent: Imagery and Ideology in Jeffersonian America* (Ithaca, N.Y.: Cornell University Press, 1970), 45–46; Hickey, "America's Response," 366–67. See also Zuckerman, "The Power of Blackness."

45. Hickey, "America's Response," 367.

46. See, for example the account of the murder of forty-four white men, women and children reprinted in the *Virginia Gazette and General Advertiser* (Williamsburg), 11 Dec. 1802.

47. Hunt, *Haiti's Influence,* 108–110.

48. Jordan, *White Over Black,* 406–9.

49. Gary B. Nash, *Forging Freedom: The Formation of Philadelphia's Black Community, 1720–1840* (Cambridge: Harvard University Press, 1988), 174–75.

50. Simon Newman, "The World Turned Upside Down: Revolutionary Politics, Fries' and Gabriel's Rebellions, and the Fears of the Federalists," *Pennsylvania History: A Journal of MidAtlantic Studies,* 67 (2000): 5–20.

51. Alexander Graydon, *Memoirs of a Life, Chiefly Passed in Pennsylvania, Within the Last Sixty Years* (Edinburgh: George Ramsay and Company, 1822 [1811]), 348; "New-York, July 31," *American Minerva, And The New-York (Evening) Advertiser* (New York), 31 July 1795.

52. "FOR THE BEE," *The Bee* (New London, Conn.), 11 Sept. 1799; *Gazette of the United States* (Philadelphia),16 Mar. 1793.

53. Cutting to Harrison Gray Otis, Aug. 1789, Letterbook, 1:71, NCP.

54. Cutting, Journal, 19 Apr. 1789, 4 July 1789, NCP.

55. *Aurora* (Philadelphia), 9 July 1794, 8 July 1794.

56. "ELIZABETH-TOWN, July 10," *Aurora* (Philadelphia), 15 July 1793; "LYNCH-BURG, Vir. July 19," *Gazette of the United States* (Philadelphia), 30 July 1794.

57. This article was reprinted and commented on in the *Aurora,* 11 July 1804; "FROM THE BOSTON DEMOCRAT," *Aurora* (Philadelphia), 18 July 1808. For the partisan politics of July Fourth celebrations, see Newman, *Parades and the Politics of the Street.*

58. *The Guardian of Liberty* (Newport, R.I.), 3 Jan. 1801; "LANCASTER REPUBLICAN FESTIVAL," *Aurora. General Advertiser* (Philadelphia), 11 Mar. 1801; "Carlisle, December 31," *Kline's Carlisle Weekly Gazette* (Carlisle, Pa.), 31 Dec. 1800.

59. Gordon S. Wood, *The Radicalism of the American Revolution* (New York: Knopf, 1992), 191.

60. "INDEPENDENCE OF THE UNITED STATES OF AMERICA," *The Augusta Chronicle and Gazette of the State,* 4 July 1801; "TOASTS, ON THE GREAT ANNIVERSARY," *Aurora* (Philadelphia), 14 July 1801.

61. Hunt, *Haiti's Influence,* 115–17.

62. Monroe to Brigadier General Mathews, 17 Mar. 1802, as quoted in Douglas R. Egerton, *Gabriel's Rebellion: The Virginia Slave Conspiracies of 1800 & 1802* (Chapel Hill: University of North Carolina Press, 1993), 47.

63. Jefferson to John Page, 24 Jan. 1799, in *The Works of Thomas Jefferson,* ed. Paul L. Ford (New York: Knickerbocker Press, 1896), 7:323; Jefferson to James Madison, 12 Feb. 1799, ibid., 7:349.

64. Jordan, *White Over Black,* 384.

65. James Forten, *A Series of Letters by a Man of Color* (1813), as excerpted in *A Documentary History of the Negro People in the United States,* ed. Herbert Aptheker (New York: Citadel Press, 1951), 64.

66. Gary B. Nash, *Forging Freedom,* 177; *New York Evening Post,* 12 July 1804.

67. Margaret de Boneville, cited in Alfred Owen Aldridge, *Man of Reason: The Life of Thomas Paine* (Philadelphia: Lippincott, 1959), 316.

68. "TWENTY-SIXTH ANNIVERSARY OF EMANCIPATION FROM THE BRITISH YOKE," *Aurora* (Philadelphia), 7 July 1801.

69. John Taylor provides, in his writings, a good example of the transition from ideas of emancipation to new defenses of slavery. See Hunt, *Haiti's Influence,* 123–24. For a discussion of the impact of the Haitian Revolution on the status of blacks in the northern states, see Jordan, *White Over Black,* 406–418.

70. "East Windsor, 9 March 1801," *The Bee* (New London, Conn.), 3 Apr. 1801; "TOASTS," *Aurora* (Philadelphia), 9 Mar. 1801.

71. Jefferson to Spencer Roane, 6 Sept. 1819, *Writings of Jefferson,* 10:140.

PART THREE

RESISTANCE

Chapter 8

Charleston's Rumored Slave Revolt of 1793

ROBERT ALDERSON

DURING THE LATTER HALF OF 1793, various sources reported that a slave insurrection was being prepared in Charleston, South Carolina. If the rumors were true, this slave revolt would be unusual because it would be an interstate affair, supposedly involving most of the southeastern seaboard. It also would be unusual in that the revolt would have international links to the French and Haitian Revolutions. Through these links could be found a connection to both an international and a black version of republicanism. On the other hand, if the rumors were not true, they would show an interesting pattern in the domestic and foreign politics of the United States. This pattern indicates that a coalition of Americans and Frenchmen manipulated the fear of slave insurrections for political gain. In any case, the revolt reports show a deepening rift in the ranks of the French in Charleston. At issue was the French Revolution and its effects in Haiti.

On 24 August 1793, an official and troubling warning reached South Carolina Governor William Moultrie from Lieutenant Governor James Wood of Virginia. Enclosed in the packet were letters that Wood had recently received from officials in Norfolk and York County. Of this group of letters, the most alarming for the governor of South Carolina was dated 8 August 1793. Magistrate William Nelson of York County nervously reported that a letter addressed to the "Secret Keeper, Norfolk," from the "Secret Keeper, Richmond" had been found in the streets of Yorktown. The magistrate did not know who the secret keepers were, but believed that the messenger was an itinerant black preacher named Garvin, who had disappeared. The Richmond Secret Keeper wrote his counterpart in Norfolk that "the great secret that has been so long in being with our colour has come nearly to a hed [*sic*]." He went on to report that the insurrectionists had about five hundred firearms and plenty of shot, but lacked powder. Most alarming for the governor of South Carolina was the statement that, "since I wrote you last I got a letter from our friend in Charleston he tells me he has listed near six thousand men & there is a gentleman that says he will give us as much powder as we want and when we begin he will help us all he can."[1] According to some reports, the insurrection was already planned for 13 or 15 October. Wood included another letter in the packet, which was addressed to Wood from the commander of Norfolk's militia, Colonel Thomas Newton. Newton implicated black immigrants from the French colony of Saint-Domingue—modern-day Haiti—in the plans: "I suppose there may be two hundred or more Negroes brought from Cape Francois [in Saint-Domingue] by the unfortunate French people. These I have no doubt would be ready to operate against us with the others."[2]

The governor had even more reason for concern when he received a letter in early October. This letter was purportedly from a free black in Charleston who was in on "the secret." The freeman warned Moultrie not to "let your attention be directed to frenchmen alone, you & I believe in our situation we also have enemies to the Northward." "A Black" advised the governor to keep patrols working until "after the 10th January next at least."[3]

Moultrie quickly placed the militia on alert and ordered them to "mount Guards at such Places as I conceived, would secure the Peace of the Citizens and the Safety of the State. . . & keep up constant Patrols."[4] The troubling question of who in Charleston was involved in the plot remained unanswered. Rumors, however, already suggested that people who adhered to the revolutionary government in France held principles which "tend visibly to the subversion of the political existence of the four southern states of America and to the destruction of the lives and property of their inhabitants." Such men, the author of the letter continued, "swore the ruin of it [Saint-Domingue], and they have very near accomplished their designs."[5] The leader of these revolutionary Frenchmen in Charleston was Consul Michel-Ange-Bernard de Mangourit. Since his arrival in South Carolina in September 1792, the consul had been on good terms with Governor Moultrie.[6] Moultrie had supplied Mangourit with information to aid with the planned invasions of Spanish Florida and Louisiana. These invasions were part of a plan for international republican revolution on the part of the Girondin government in France. In August and September 1792, the Girondins had been responsible for the abolition of the French monarchy and the proclamation of the French Republic. Mangourit was retained by the French Republic, even though he had received his credentials from the royal government. He was recognized as a true republican, one who had supported the French Revolution since the storming of the Bastille. The consul remained loyal to the Republic and enthusiastically executed the Republic's plans to export the French Revolution. Although the Girondins aimed at introducing the forces of revolution into the holdings of Spain and Great Britain, the international ramifications of the French Revolution had already made themselves felt in France's Caribbean colonies, especially in Saint-Domingue, the "Pearl of the Antilles."

Soon after the onset of the French Revolution, the white planters of Saint-Domingue demanded more independence within the colonial relationship, while the colony's free blacks also sought a share of political power. While the planters and free blacks vied for control of the colony, the thirst for liberty percolated down to the colony's slaves. In August 1791, a major slave revolt broke out and refugees, many of whom were white planters, began pouring into the major port cities of the United States. In April 1792, the National Convention passed a law giving equal political rights to all free people in French colonies. In September 1792, a three-man commission, led by *Commissaire Civil* Sonthonax, arrived in the troubled colony. His attempts to bring equal rights to all inhabitants merely polarized the colony. After the proclamation of the French Republic in September 1792 and Louis XVI's execution in January 1793, the revolution in Saint-Domingue and the exodus of French planters intensified. In June 1793, the city of Cap-Français was sacked by Sonthonax's supporters, including large numbers of rebel slaves. Yet another wave of émigrés sailed for the United States. On 29 August 1793 Sonthonax, attempting to solidify his base of support among the black population of the colony, issued a proclamation that gave general liberty to blacks in the northern province of Saint-Domingue. It was not until February 1794 that the French government endorsed Sonthonax's actions by emancipating all slaves in French colonies.[7]

As one of the closest American ports to Saint-Domingue, Charleston received a large number of refugees from the island. Relations between the refugee white planters of Saint-Domingue and the French consulate in Charleston were contentious. Mangourit's problems with the planters, "colonial aristocrats" as he called them, began shortly after he arrived in Charleston. Mangourit's use of the term "colonial aristocrats" to describe the émigrés is somewhat misleading. A majority of the new arrivals were not aristocrats in the traditional sense. Nevertheless, the consul identified many of the refugees as overt royalists and counterrevolutionaries. Like many revolutionaries, Mangourit labeled those who opposed the French Revolution as aristocrats. For the purposes of this essay, the term "colonial aristocrats" will serve as convenient shorthand for the émigrés who opposed French colonial policy in Saint-Domingue. Mangourit pledged to keep an eye on the ever-increasing number of colonial aristocrats.[8] Sniping between the consular staff and the French Patriotic Society,[9] made up largely of these Domingan émigrés, even predated Mangourit's arrival in Charleston. Against a good deal of opposition, Mangourit sought and gained membership in the French society because he felt that joining was necessary to preserve "the harmony of the French in Charleston," although he also felt that it was as important to keep an eye on the émigrés as it was to create goodwill.[10]

Jacques Delaire was one of the Domingans in the club who especially concerned Mangourit.[11] Delaire and many other Domingans joined the French Patriotic Society as an organ of opposition to the consul. The émigrés attacked French colonial policy, making the most of the French government's decision of April 1792 to grant equal political rights to all races in French colonies.[12] One of their favorite targets was the Girondin leader, Jacques-Pierre Brissot de Warville, who was also one of the founders of the abolitionist *Société des Amis des Noirs*. By linking Brissot with French diplomats in the United States, the colonial aristocrats implicated French officials like Mangourit as agents of international black revolution. Mangourit rapidly lost his patience with the French society, arguing that the society was "in the hands of the colonial aristocrats, [such as] . . . Delaire."[13]

The French Patriotic Society was not the only organization that aided the émigrés. Leading South Carolinians formed the Benevolent Society to oversee relief efforts. Apparently, the society was not interested solely in relief. Among the members was Edward Penman, who was probably the leading "secret and dangerous agent of England" in Charleston.[14] The British were a powerful group in Charleston; many Charleston merchants were either indebted to or worked for British concerns.[15] Mangourit claimed that most of the money for the relief operations came from British sources, with Penman often giving dinners for the émigrés. Providing meals to men like Jacques Delaire was the easiest way to gain information, because, as the consul wrote, "during dessert one lifts up the veil of reserve."[16] The majority of the members of the society can be divided into three groups: those with British connections or anti-French convictions; those with connections to the planters of Saint-Domingue; and Federalists.[17]

There were other societies in Charleston as well, many of which reflected the schism in national politics. On the national level, the Federalists, who were pro-British and were under the leadership of Secretary of the Treasury Alexander Hamilton, were one of these groups. The group that supported France became known as the Republicans. In President Washington's cabinet, Secretary of State Thomas Jefferson represented the Republicans. The division between the Republicans and Federalists on the national level divided the leaders of South Carolina as well. The Federalists were clearly in charge of South Carolina's government. Although the governor himself was a Republican, the state legislature, especially the Senate, was in the hands of the Federalists.[18]

Nevertheless, South Carolina's Republicans did support France. A majority of the people probably backed the French cause, especially veterans of the American Revolution and nearly all the rural population. Pro-French South Carolinians came from a discontented class of citizens who had been put off by the government and overlooked in the years following the American Revolution.[19] They organized the Republican Society of South Carolina.[20] Many of its 109 members were openly involved in Mangourit's schemes to export the French Revolution, including the president of the society, Stephen Drayton, who was also the personal secretary of Governor William Moultrie.

Mangourit's relationships with Moultrie and Drayton, upon which the success of his mission depended, were placed in jeopardy in October 1793. The atmosphere in Charleston in the months leading up to the date of the rumored slave revolt became increasingly tense. Word of the revolution in Saint-Domingue led local authorities to consider tightening regulations on the importation of slaves, and to establish a night guard in Charleston. Meanwhile, the escape of French slaves, acts of arson, and murders by slaves were increasing. In mid-April, Dr. Stephen St. John was murdered by a group of five slaves. An overseer at a plantation on the Cooper River was also found murdered, apparently by the same slaves. At the same time, Charleston intendant (mayor) John Huger offered a reward for an arsonist who had set a fire on 12 April. On 8 June, an "alarming fire" broke out on Third Street that caused "a considerable loss of property." Word of the sack of Cap-Français reached Charleston by 6 July. The fact that freed slaves were integral to Commissioner Sonthonax's attack on the city received no mention; the papers only referred to the activities of "insurgents." Shortly thereafter, Governor Moultrie ordered buildings on Sullivan's Island prepared to receive and quarantine refugees from "the massacre at Cape Francois." It seemed that events in the French islands were only getting worse: "the accounts [which] daily arrive . . . fill every one with horror—burning estates, and putting all prisoners to death, fill up the measure of every day's calamity."[21]

In mid-August, Delaire publicly accused Mangourit of fomenting a slave revolt: "You are really, as you say yourself, citizen consul, a *public spy,* and as your friends, Polverel and Sonthonax, have sent you a private one, I, and I dare say all the French now on the continent, would be very much obliged to you to send him back from whence he came." Delaire added that the citizens of "Charleston will not see, with a tranquil eye, such a fierce execution of a certain law, and of the despotic and sanguinary orders of your friends." Delaire, without directly citing the various decrees extending rights to people of color, nevertheless made his point very clear to South Carolina's planters. It was a point that Delaire drove home when he reported that the National Convention decree of April 1792 precluded planters from holding office. This provision, Delaire wrote, "was proposed by the modest Brissot, for the purpose of divesting the guilty colonists of their national rights." In meetings of refugees from the French colony, "the words—Brissot—gold—hypocrisy—treason—revenge—malevolence and barbarity, occurred very often, and not without the best foundation." "A Native American" echoed Delaire's thoughts: he asked South Carolinians to "recollect the unprepared situation of the southern states, in case of internal commotion—depending upon militia alone, who are only useful when time is given to bring them into the field: recollect the fate of St. Domingo—I need not speak plainer; be prudent—be grateful to France, but remember that self-preservation is the first law of nature."[22]

Fear gripped Charleston as search parties fanned out. One such party searched the home and papers of a free black named Peter Mathews, who reported that he was happy to cooperate in the search of his papers, "as none of them are criminal." Only "an old pistol without a flint, a broken sword, and an old cutlass, of such little value that they were stuck up in the shingles of my house" were found.[23]

Charleston was gripped by fear and suspicion when a vessel from Saint-Domingue sailed into the harbor. Around the beginning of October, the brig *Maria* arrived bearing French soldiers and civilians from Cap-Français. Pursuant to the governor's orders, *Maria* was placed in quarantine under the guns of Fort Johnson. The leader of the new arrivals, Lieutenant Colonel G. Josnez, wrote Mangourit requesting supplies and permission to land in Charleston. Mangourit asked the governor for authorization to visit the ship to see what kind of supplies were required. To head off any possible conniving between the consul and the new arrivals, Moultrie responded that only supplies could be sent to *Maria.*[24]

The morning after Moultrie refused the consul permission to visit *Maria,* Mangourit noted a group of colonial aristocrats visiting the governor's house. This group of French were opposed to the possible debarkation of passengers from *Maria* because of the presence on board of an officer named Pierre Robequin. According to the colonial aristocrats, this officer was related by marriage to "*un chef de Nègres*" and was an "apostle of liberty for the blacks." The émigrés charged that Robequin had been sent by the "scoundrels of the civil commission of Saint-

Domingue to agitate the slaves in the United States and make them slit the throats of their masters." According to Mangourit, the émigrés were afraid to allow soldiers of the French Republic into Charleston. The émigrés feared that they would be forcibly deported by the soldiers.

The day after Mangourit had received a letter from Josnez acknowledging receipt of the supplies, Moultrie visited the consul in an angry mood. The governor handed Mangourit copies of Josnez's letters and demanded an explanation. After the consul translated the messages for the governor, Moultrie said that someone had told him that Mangourit was an operative of the *commissaires* of Saint-Domingue who was helping to stir up the local slaves. Based on this, Moultrie asked to see Josnez's original letter. Mangourit diplomatically contained his indignation at the "weakness of the old man." The consul realized that "it would be dangerous for me to indulge in an outburst when the good of our projects [referring to the Genêt projects] would require his accord with me."[25]

While protesting the violation of his correspondence, Mangourit suggested that Josnez be brought to the governor's house and, in front of witnesses, hand over the original letters. Moultrie agreed and told the consul that a group of émigrés had delivered the correspondence to the governor's office. With that, the consul took his leave of the governor, intent to investigate the colonial aristocrats. He only regretted that the courts of the United States could not send the émigrés to the "*guillotine française.*" Likewise, he wanted to "chastise the scoundrel who violated the secret of a letter" addressed to an official of France.[26]

In order to disprove the accusations leveled against the soldiers of the *Maria,* the consul resolved not to communicate with the ship without the full knowledge of the governor. Mangourit also investigated how the letters had gotten to Moultrie. He came to the conclusion that the culprit was a sailor from Cap-Français known as D. Saurine. Lieutenant Colonel Josnez told the consul that it was Saurine who had come to him pretending to be on a mission from *Commissaires* Polverel and Sonthonax. Josnez had given the letters to Saurine, only to find out later that the émigrés had sent the sailor. The colonial aristocrats hoped to bring about a rift between Moultrie and Mangourit by showing that the new refugees were agents of revolution and that the consul was a willing accomplice.[27]

While Mangourit was uncovering the émigré conspiracy to intercept his correspondence, he reported that the local allies of the colonial aristocrats were also taking steps to rally public opinion and keep the passengers of *Maria* from landing. On 8 October, a "meeting of citizens" passed resolutions "that his excellency the governor be requested to take immediate measures, that the two vessels that arrived in this harbour last week, from St. Domingo, and are now under the guns of fort [*sic*] Johnston, with their crews, passengers, free negroes and people of color, do quit the harbour and state immediately."[28] The citizens' assembly then elected a committee to observe the enforcement of the resolution. On 16 October, Moultrie gave in to the pressure from the citizens' committee. The governor issued a proclamation that began with the statement that many "people of colour" had entered the state from Saint-Domingue recently, and "that there are many characters amongst them, which are dangerous to welfare and peace of the state . . . it appears to me highly necessary that every precaution should be used to prevent any designs taking place." In conclusion, the proclamation ordered all free foreign blacks that had arrived in South Carolina less than a year before to leave the state.[29]

Many of the members of the citizens' committee were also members of the Benevolent Society, the organization to aid Domingan planters.[30] Was it merely coincidence that the same group established to render aid to the Domingans—at least as long as they were aristocrats—were now supporting measures to ban people desperately in need of assistance? This could have been seen as evidence that the colonial aristocrats exercised a good amount of influence over the activities of the Benevolent Society. Of course, the émigrés were largely white planters, so there might have been some kind of class bond between them and South Carolina planters. Both groups of planters were certainly united in their opposition to Mangourit and to slave insurrection. In the consul's eyes, the citizens' committee was nothing more than a gathering of the French colonial aristocrats. In an effort to keep the consul in the dark, the colonials were careful to have two-thirds of the committee composed of English merchants in active commerce with Britain and local Tories.[31] Mangourit's assertions about the makeup of the citizens' committee appear sound. Like the membership of the Benevolent Society, those belonging to the citizens' committee can be divided into those with British connections or anti-French convictions, those with connections to the planters of Saint-Domingue, and Federalists.[32]

Sometime before 11 October, two deputies of this "Assembly of Intimidated Citizens" visited Mangourit to ask him to ban the soldiers of the republic from Charleston. The deputies said they suspected that the soldiers had come to incite local blacks and to burn the city. The consul responded that he too had been accused of similar charges by local Tories and scoundrels from Saint-Domingue. Mangourit politely threatened the possibility of diplomatic repercussions. Although the consul's threats seemed to frighten the deputies, they maintained that the soldiers should not be allowed to come ashore.[33]

A day or so later, at the governor's house, Josnez surrendered the supposedly-damning letters to the consul and the governor. The correspondence proved to be harmless. The lieutenant colonel then gave his word that he had no other letters from Saint-Domingue for the consul. Clearly skeptical, the governor ordered a search of Josnez's belongings. After searching Josnez's quarters with some of the governor's staff, including Stephen Drayton, Mangourit returned to the governor's house for lunch.[34]

By searching Josnez's belongings, Mangourit's allies showed that they would only go so far to help the consul when their self-interest was involved. This self-interest united both the local Federalists and Republicans on the issue of a slave insurrection. Indeed, the two groups appear to have been working towards the same end. The Federalists, working through the citizens' assembly, managed to keep the soldiers on board *Maria* from landing. However, it remained for the Republicans, like Moultrie and Drayton, to actually investigate the possibility of Josnez and the new French arrivals' being involved in a slave plot. On the other hand, if the Federalists were trying to divide Mangourit and his supporters, they were certainly striking at the right spot. No governor of South Carolina could allow the possibility of a slave insurrection to go unchallenged.

The Federalists were not willing to let matters develop without further assistance. While Mangourit and Josnez were at the governor's house, a group of deputies of the citizens' committee arrived. They accused Josnez of aiding the slave conspiracy in South Carolina, which the lieutenant colonel rebutted to Mangourit's satisfaction. The consul sensed that the Federalists and the Domingan colonial aristocrats were working together. An aristocrat named Duborq, who had come in with the deputies, proposed to the governor that groups of French citizens form themselves into companies for the "safety of the city." Moultrie artfully refused Duborq's request. The consul appeared surprised at the governor's diplomatic dexterity.[35]

After searching Josnez's belongings, Moultrie was satisfied that the lieutenant colonel and his companions were not involved in any conspiracy. According to the consul, Moultrie was very polite to Josnez. Toasts were offered to the French Republic. Around four o'clock, the governor regretfully informed Josnez that the citizens' committee demanded that Josnez return to the quarantine camp on Sullivan's Island. Rather than being quarantined on the inhospitable island, the governor advised the lieutenant colonel to make good use of *Maria* and leave Charleston. Moultrie embraced Josnez, "with tears in his eyes," and the soldier departed. Shortly afterward, *Maria* sailed out of Charleston harbor.[36]

The atmosphere in Charleston during the days of 13–16 October continued to be tense. The newspapers were filled with signs of unrest among the black population and signs of fear on the part of the white population. *The State Gazette of South Carolina* reported that, on the night of 13 October, "a house near the synagogue was discovered to be on fire;—happily it was found out in the earliest stage, and was speedily extinguished.—It appears to have been done by some vile incendiary." On 15 October, an attempt was made "to set fire to a house in Hazel-street."[37]

Mangourit reported a doubling of Charleston's guard in the days prior to 15 October. From a usual complement of twenty-seven men the guard was raised to fifty-four, which Mangourit felt proved that the leaders did not really fear an uprising. From the consul's standpoint, fifty-four men had as little chance to stop a full-scale slave revolt as did twenty-seven. Mangourit later scoffed at the chances of the rumored number of fifteen thousand blacks being involved in the plot.[38]

During the night of 16 October, a quarrel took place in which no French or blacks were involved, but which does indicate the state of anxiety in the white population of Charleston. The conflict occurred on the streets of Charleston, where "a number of disorderly persons, near 40 in number . . .constituted themselves into a kind of patrole [sic] . . . attacked, insulted and threatened the main guard of this city then under the command of captain [sic] Jervey." "The matter was so serious" that the guard prepared to defend itself from the patrol. A few days later, a letter from "ONE of the PATROLE" asserted that the patrol had set up sentries to prevent any attempts at arson. The patrol's sentry asked the infantry under Captain Jervey's command to give the countersign. Jervey refused and had the sentry surrounded. Jervey then "put a pistol to one man's breast, at the same time using insolent and abusive language; but finding our patroles returning from an excursion, he thought proper to order a precipitate retreat." Although the matter was cleared up, bloodshed was narrowly avoided when a pistol was accidentally discharged.[39]

There were other signs of unrest and fear in Charleston, but the question remains: was there a slave insurrection in the offing during October 1793? There is no way to definitively answer the question. To fully investigate the rumored slave revolt, it is necessary to follow a dual hypothesis. First, if an insurrection was not being planned, then what was happening? Who had the most to gain from such rumors and what were they hoping to achieve by manipulating fears of a slave revolt? Second, if a slave revolt was being planned, what was its significance?

For a proponent of the view that white conspirators were manipulating the fear of a slave conspiracy, one need look no further than Consul Mangourit. He concluded that the colonial aristocrats were behind the rumors of a slave revolt, which they were using to try to bring about a rupture between the consul and Governor Moultrie. As early as June 1793, the émigrés were "poisoning the spirits of American's"[40] by linking French officials to an impending revolt of blacks. The émigrés set up, with their co-conspirators in Maryland and Virginia, the project of the letter of a pretended black leader. The "secret keeper" letter then found its way to the government of Virginia and, from there, to Governor Moultrie.[41]

At the same time, the aristocrats were busily trying to achieve what Mangourit saw as their real objective: to assist an English invasion of Saint-Domingue and return to the island, with "the sword of [King] George in their hands and the white cockade [of the Bourbons] on their heads."[42] The British and the Domingan aristocrats had a good reason to cooperate with each other: in September 1793, British forces invaded Saint-Domingue at Jérémie, about 100 miles west of Port-au-Prince. Aided by Domingan counterrevolutionaries, the British scored early successes. Mangourit reported a number of attempts to transport the émigrés back to assist in the conquest of Saint-Domingue.[43]

American Secretary of State Thomas Jefferson also believed that the reports of a slave revolt were false. In December 1793, Jefferson received a visit from a "French gentleman." The Frenchman repeated a rumor to Jefferson that two Frenchmen of mixed descent were going to Charleston to start a slave revolt as part "of a general plan, formed by the Brissotine party at Paris, the first branch of which has been carried into execution at St. Domingo." As to the French gentleman's source, the secretary of state "could by no means consider it as a channel meriting reliance." Jefferson questioned the Frenchman regarding the motives of the supposed insurrectionists; "he answered with conjectures which were far from sufficient to strengthen the fact." Despite his own skepticism, Jefferson forwarded this information to Governor Moultrie.[44]

The consul continued to have problems with the colonial aristocrats. Through the beginning of December, a heated exchange took place between the consulate and the Domingans over the question of whether the consulate had been distributing aid to the refugees. The émigrés, through their allies in the Benevolent Society, argued that the consulate had not aided "the distressed inhabitants of St. Domingo." One such letter used the *Maria* incident as proof that Mangourit only provided aid "to the plunderers, not to the plundered—to the authors of the calamities, not to the sufferers—to the assassins, not to the wretched remains of the massacre." Mangourit answered with his own accusations and by printing his orders from his superior, Minister Plenipotentiary Edmond Charles Genêt, not to help "either useless men, to whom France owes no assistance—or traitors, to whom it would be a crime to afford any." There were, "amongst the refugees who are spread over this continent," Genêt continued, "some counter-revolutionists, sheltered under the cloak of misfortune, [who] insinuate themselves into people's favor, and . . . accuse us of plots for extending to this country, the flames and massacre which desolate an ill-fated colony."[45]

No matter how much money the Domingan planters had, it is doubtful that they could have accomplished such a conspiracy without help in the United States. As shown by the coordination between the refugees and such groups as the citizens' committee and the Benevolent Society, the émigrés worked closely with many highly placed Federalists in South Carolina. If South Carolina's Federalists were working with the émigrés, one might expect the Federalists to show some signs of a lack of concern about the rumors of a slave revolt.

At the lower levels of South Carolina's government, however, there were signs of alarm over the possibility of a slave insurrection. In late 1793, Charleston city council passed an ordinance "for the better ordering and governing of Negroes and other slaves." Governor Moultrie advised the legislature to pass "a revision of the Negro laws." A "Bill to amend the several Acts of Assembly for the regulation of Negroes and other Slaves, Free Negroes, Mulattoes and Mestizoes" was considered by the South Carolina House of Representatives. The bill was then forwarded to the state Senate with a request for the rapid passage of the proposed legislation. However, on 7 May 1794, the Senate "thought it expedient to postpone the consideration" of the bill indefinitely. The Senate, its membership overwhelmingly of the wealthy planter class and predominately Federalist, represented the same class that had the most to lose in the event of a slave revolt.[46] This lack of concern on the part of the Senate is a possible indication that at least some senators were involved in a plot to manipulate fears of a slave revolt for political gain.

Unlike most insurrection plots, the rumored slave revolt of 1793 had interstate connections, as shown by the "secret keeper" letter. It is this difference that may well be the strongest indication of a white conspiracy: how could slaves organize a slave revolt across state lines? Although such questions cannot be answered completely, attempting to answer them leads to some interesting speculations. First, slaves were known to have communication networks, or grapevines. These grapevines worked both within and outside of individual plantations. Second, news of the revolution in Saint-Domingue "was transmitted to the North American slave population through an intricate interregional communication network operated by black seamen from American merchant ships trading in the West Indies."[47] In such networks, written notes would not only be dangerous, but unnecessary. The grapevine could carry whatever information was needed across state lines by land or by sea.

If the grapevine could carry plans for a slave revolt, what about the "secret keeper" letter from Virginia? It certainly was a coincidence that the letter found its way from the streets of Yorktown to the magistrate of York County, William Nelson. It is difficult to determine the political affiliation of Nelson, Norfolk militia commander Thomas Newton, and Lieutenant Governor James Wood. The Nelson family included prominent merchants and members of the Virginia aristocracy, so perhaps they could be considered Federalists. The Newtons were probably Republicans, while opinion on Wood ranges from Republican to a "political neutral" to Federalist. Perhaps they were all involved in a Federalist plot or perhaps they were made dupes by Virginia Federalists.[48] Nevertheless, even if they were all ardent Republicans, they had no choice but to take reports of a slave revolt seriously, as did Governor Moultrie and Thomas Jefferson. At any rate, it is as difficult to prove that there was an interstate conspiracy to manipulate fears of a slave insurrection as it is to prove that there actually was a conspiracy to start a rebellion.

The Domingan émigrés and the Federalists may have been gifted opportunists, taking advantage of a real insurrection plot to strike at their political enemies. In other words, the two possibilities regarding the slave revolt may not be mutually exclusive. However, there were signs that a slave grapevine was working to organize an insurrection. Some of this evidence comes from the "secret keeper" letter itself. The courier of the letter was supposed to be a black itinerant preacher named Garvin. Apparently, there were no black ministers named Garvin in Virginia. However, there was a free black preacher named Gowan Pamphlet in Virginia, who possibly made trips to Charleston in 1792. If Gowan Pamphlet was the mysterious courier of the "secret keeper" letter, he was in a good position to act as a messenger of black revolution. In addition to the letters already considered, two documents show interesting similarities. First, in Richmond, Virginia, John Randolph overheard a group of blacks talking during the night of 20 July 1793. "The one spoke to the other telling him that the blacks were to kill the white people soon in this place," recalled Randolph, "the one who seemed to be the chief speaker, said, you see how the blacks has killed the whites in the French Island and took it a little while ago." According to Randolph, the date for the revolt was 15 October. From a conversation overheard on the streets of Richmond to another overheard on the wharves of Charleston, the essence of the message was the same. On the evening of 26 September, a sailor overheard some blacks talking on Blake's Wharf. "They had not many Soldiers we need not be afraid of them," was clearly heard. Before the sailor could hear anything else, the blacks saw him and "withdrew into the shade or dark of the house."[49]

Since the revolt was supposed to transcend state boundaries, what signs were there in states other than South Carolina? To the north, a number of fires were set in Albany, New York, in November 1793. Three slaves were later executed for arson. Authorities in Virginia's Powhatan County discovered a group of runaway slaves. When questioned, the slaves admitted that they were to meet three hundred other slaves and begin an insurrection. A slave in Warwick County, Virginia, was executed for insurrection. In Georgia, a group of slaves murdered a doctor in July 1793. In November, an unused building burned in Savannah. In response, the commander of the city battalions placed his men on alert, which seemed warranted "especially when unpleasant communications have been received from sister states." "The effect on the mind, roused from a torpid state occasioned by sudden alarm in the night," continued the commander of the city troops, "must strongly evince the necessity of the inhabitants being always prepared with their arms and ammunition." On 17 November, a fire consumed seventy buildings in Albany, Georgia. At the end of January 1794, a plantation overseer was killed near Savannah by five runaway slaves. Taken separately, these occurrences mean very little. There was no evidence that blacks were behind any of the fires in Georgia. Also, sporadic outbreaks of violence were fairly common. Yet, taken together, something of a crescendo of resistance and fear emerges.[50]

Meanwhile, blacks and whites in Charleston remained uneasy. A black man named Cuffee was convicted of "an assault on a French lady." A free mulatto named David Grey evaded capture on the charge of assault and battery. A white inhabitant of Charleston also escaped capture after he, "in a state of inebriety, fired a musket at a negroe," and killed him. During the month of October alone, there were at least three reports of possible arson in Charleston.[51]

Arson was not the only tool of the insurrectionist. An African form of spirituality called *Vodun,* or voodoo, which most whites considered witchcraft, was an intricate part of the rebellion in Saint-Domingue. Therefore, it is interesting to note two possible occurrences of witchcraft during the months leading up to the rumored insurrection. In July 1793, a group of slaves was flogged for digging in a basement in Charleston. When asked why they were excavating, the slaves reported that one of them had tapped into the spirit world and received a vision that there was gold in the cellar. Equally mysterious was a report in early November 1793 that a slave "near the boundary line of this state and North-Carolina, was tried . . . for *witch-craft*" and hanged. It is uncertain what the accused witch was trying to accomplish, but the report was reprinted as far away as Augusta, Georgia.[52]

Charleston also experienced a rise in the number of new runaways during the months prior to October 1793. The number as reported in *The City Gazette* peaked in June, with a total of twenty. The total for the months September through November 1793 amounts to thirty-four. The same period for 1792 had only twenty. This increase in the number of runaways is circumstantial, but not conclusive, evidence that something was going on beneath the surface of South Carolina's slave society. Equally suggestive is the number of runaways who were French slaves and slaves who had some kind of maritime experience. French slaves carried first-hand knowledge of the revolt in Saint-Domingue, while sailors were one of the primary means of communication in the slave grapevine. Between September 1792 and March 1794, *The City Gazette* reported a total of 198 new runaway slave advertisements. Of these, the number of runaways who can be identified as either French or those with maritime experience was somewhere between thirty-eight and fifty. Thus nearly a quarter of the slaves who ran away during this period were potential carriers of rebellion. Also, marronage, the act of running away, played a significant role in the Haitian Revolution. Although marronage was seldom successful in North America, the French fugitive slaves were unaware of that fact and were clearly willing to attempt marronage in the United States. Voodoo and marronage are often linked to the Haitian Revolution.[53]

It is clear that Consul Mangourit was not the arms supplier mentioned in the "secret keeper" letter. Were there any other Frenchmen in Charleston who might have served as a source of weapons? It is possible that the 1793 incident may not have been the first time that Charleston was an arsenal for black resistance. Vincent Ogé, who in 1790 led an unsuccessful mulatto revolt in Saint-Domingue, visited Charleston immediately before the outbreak of violence. While in Charleston, it is "very likely" that Ogé purchased arms.[54] Of the Frenchmen in Charleston, the most likely suspect for an arms supplier is French merchant Abraham Sasportas. Sasportas supplied many of the French privateers which frequented Charleston harbor. As a French commercial agent, Sasportas no doubt handled a good amount of weapons and ammunition. Interestingly, Sasportas's nephew, Isaac Yeshurun Sasportas, was also in Charleston during the early 1790s serving as a French commercial agent. In 1799, Isaac Sasportas was arrested in Jamaica. British officials charged the younger Sasportas with having come to the island with the intent of gaining black support for an invasion from Saint-Domingue. Here Sasportas's support for black revolution ended; he was hanged in December 1799.[55]

It is possible that lessons learned during the rumored slave revolt of 1793 were carried forward in time. In 1797, Charleston authorities discovered "a conspiracy of French Negroes to fire the City and to act here as they formerly done at St. Domingo." One of the arsonists, Figaro the Younger, was the slave of a "Mr. Delaire," who was probably none other than Jacques Delaire, colonial aristocrat and Mangourit's archenemy. Obviously, Delaire's slave had learned from the Haitian experience. Since Figaro's master had intimate knowledge of the 1793 incident, one can speculate that Figaro drew on that experience as well.[56] Captain Joseph Vesey, who was a leading member of both the Benevolent Society that provided aid to the émigrés and the citizens' committee that was formed to protect Charleston from the slave revolt, had a good deal of experience in the slave trade with Saint-Domingue. As one of the dispensers of aid, many Domingan refugees made calls on Captain Vesey. When the Domingan planters visited, their slaves had a chance to speak with one of Vesey's slaves, Denmark Vesey.

Captain Vesey had purchased Denmark in 1781 on one of the captain's slaving voyages. In 1800, Denmark Vesey won $1,500 in a lottery and purchased his freedom. In 1822, Denmark Vesey led an abortive slave revolt. Charleston authorities discovered the plans and arrested those involved. During the trials, whites discovered that Vesey made deliberate appeals to both Christianity and magic as twin elements of resistance and liberation. In attempting to inspire his supporters, Vesey invoked the Hebrew liberation from Egypt. One of Vesey's lieutenants, named Gullah Jack, was a "conjurer" who, it was said, could not be killed in battle. Vesey's followers testified that their leader was inspired by the example of blacks in Saint-Domingue and that Vesey had formulated a black version of republicanism. "We are free," one of his followers reported that Vesey said, "but the white people here won't let us be so; and the only way is, to raise up and fight the whites . . . to get our liberties." Thus Vesey's objectives included one of the goals of the American Revolution and the first word in the French revolutionary slogan of "Liberty, Equality, and Fraternity." The insurrection would be successful, Vesey argued, "if we were only unanimous and courageous, as the St. Domingo people were."[57] It is possible that Figaro the Younger and Denmark Vesey learned not only from the example of Saint-Domingue, but also learned something about how to organize a revolt from what happened in 1793. If nothing else, later insurrectionists could see in the experience of 1793 the fear whites in South Carolina had of slave revolts. Later leaders could also see that the fear could be manipulated to obtain a greater degree of political and social equality within the slave South.

The rumors of a slave revolt in 1793 were either manufactured by whites or were the reflection of a genuine conspiracy. The ability to coordinate and manipulate the rumors would reveal a high level of organization in both the Domingan émigrés and the Federalist party. Both groups had motives to foster rumors of a slave revolt: the Domingans to strike at the French government whose policies were partly responsible for the exodus of planters; and the Federalists to assail their political enemies and drive a wedge between the Republicans and their French allies. However, only together could the two groups properly exploit the political gains to be made from spreading rumors of a slave revolt. Equally interesting as a sign of organization is the possibility that slaves actually did plan an interstate slave revolt. As with the cooperation between the Federalists and the émigrés, the insurgents probably had the aid of whites to do what they themselves could not do, such as procure arms. If members of the Sasportas family were involved in supplying arms to the insurgents, "then the Secret Keepers may have been connected in elusive ways to the most radical wings of the international movement inspired by the French Revolution."[58] Encouraged by events in Saint-Domingue and communicating through grapevines, the supposed insurrectionists of 1793 attempted to coordinate a surprisingly widespread effort across state lines. The 1793 example thus provides an important data point in the trajectory of slave resistance in the United States and helps to strengthen the connections between American slave resistance and the Haitian example. At the same time, the slave revolt gives testimony to the existence of a current of black republicanism in the United States. However, the black version of republicanism that took root in the United States was not influenced exclusively by the Haitian Revolution. American black republicanism was best expressed by an insurrectionist in Gabriel Prosser's rebellion of 1800. At his trial, Prosser's fellow revolutionary declared: "I have nothing more to offer than what General Washington would have to offer had he been taken by the British officers and put on trial by them: I have ventured my life in endeavoring to obtain the liberty of my countrymen and am a willing sacrifice to their cause."[59]

NOTES:

1. Secret Keeper letter enclosed in William Nelson to James Wood, 8 Aug. 1793, enclosed in South Carolina, Records of the General Assembly, Governor's Messages, 1792–1795, letter number 577, 30 Nov. 1793, South Carolina Department of Archives and History, microfilm.

2. Thomas Newton to James Wood, undated, enclosed in South Carolina, Records of the General Assembly, Governor's Messages, 1792–1795, letter number 577, 30 Nov. 1793, South Carolina Department of Archives and History, microfilm.

3. Copy of a letter signed "A Black," 10 Oct. 1793, enclosed in South Carolina, Records of the General Assembly, Governor's Messages, 1792–1795, letter number 577, 30 Nov. 1793 (South Carolina Department of Archives and History, microfilm).

4. William Moultrie to the General Assembly, 30 Nov. 1793, Ibid. See also Moultrie to General Assembly, 3 Dec. 1793, in *The State Records of South Carolina: Journals of the House of Representatives, 1792–1794,* ed. Michael E. Stevens (Columbia: University of South Carolina Press, 1988), 299.

5. "An Inhabitant of Hispaniola," (Jacques Delaire), in *The City Gazette and Daily Advertiser* (Charleston) (hereafter, *City Gazette*) 27 June 1793.

6. For biographical information, see R. R. Palmer, "A Revolutionary Republican: M. A. B. Mangourit," *William and Mary Quarterly* 3 (1952): 483–96; Robert Alderson, "Charleston's French Revolutionary Consul: Michel-Ange-Bernard de Mangourit, 1792–1794," (M.A. Thesis, University of South Carolina, 1993), 9–15.

7. On the revolution in Saint-Domingue, see Carolyn E. Fick, *The Making of Haiti: The Saint Domingue Revolution from Below* (Knoxville: University of Tennessee Press, 1990); Robert Louis Stein, *Léger Félicité Sonthonax: The Lost Sentinel of the Republic* (Cranbury, N.J.: Associated Universities Presses, 1985); Thomas O. Ott, *The Haitian Revolution, 1789–1804* (Knoxville: University of Tennessee Press, 1973). On the émigrés in America, see Frances Childs, *French Refugee Life in the United States, 1790–1800: An American Chapter of the French Revolution* (Baltimore: The Johns Hopkins University Press, 1940), 66.

8. The first references the consul made to the émigrés are in: Mangourit to Minister of Marine Monge, 10 Sept. 1792, France, Archives Nationales, Series BI, 372, Correspondance Consulaire, Charleston, tome 1, 1784–1792 (microfilm in Library of Congress, Manuscript Division [hereinafter cited as AN BI 372]), fols. 398–99 verso; Mangourit to Monge, 29 Nov. 1792, AN BI 372, fols. 408–405; and Mangourit to Genêt, 12 Feb. 1793, France, Archives des Affaires Étrangères, Correspondance Consulaire et Commerciale, États-Unis, Charleston, tome 2, 1793–1799 (Neuilly-sur-Marne, Fr.: Société d'Ingéniérie et de Microfilmage, 1992, microfilm [hereafter, AAE, CCC]), f. 009v.

9. Following the trends in France, the French society changed its name twice during Mangourit's tenure: from the French Patriotic Society to the Society of Friends of the Constitution sometime in 1792; and to the Society of Friends of Liberty and Equality in early 1793. See Mangourit to Minister of Marine Monge, 17 Dec. 1792, AN, BI 372, fols. 431–33; Michael L. Kennedy, "A French Jacobin Club," *South Carolina Historical Magazine* 91, no. 1 (Jan. 1990): 7; Michael L. Kennedy, "The Best and Worst of Times: The Jacobin Club Network from October 1791–June 2, 1793," *Journal of Modern History* 56 (1984): 637.

10. Mangourit to LeBrun, 18 June 1793, AAE, CCC, f. 042v

11. Delaire was a former municipal officer in Saint-Domingue and an administrator of the national subsidy. He had embezzled funds in his charge and hurriedly left the colony, probably with the agents of the commissioners in hot pursuit. Upon his arrival in Charleston, he became one of the leaders of the French Popular Society. He was one of the consul's most strident opponents. He died in Charleston in 1814. Mangourit to Genêt, 11 Oct. 1793, AAE, CCC, f. 093; Mangourit to Foreign Minister Deforgues, 19 Oct. 1793, AAE, CCC, f. 108v; Statement of Jacques Delaire, 3 Ventose, an III, # 370, France, Archives Coloniales, Saint Domingue, Actes, Déclarations et Dépôts Divers, Consulate du Charleston, vol. 1, 1750–An IV (Salt Lake City: Genealogical Society of Salt Lake City, 22 May 1974, microfilm); and Kennedy, "A French Jacobin Club," 10.

12. Mangourit to Genêt, 18 Sept. 1793, AAE, CCC, f. 065v

13. Mangourit to Genêt, 5 Oct. 1793 printed in Frederick J. Turner, ed., "The Mangourit Correspondence in Respect to Genet's Projected Attack upon the Floridas, 1793–1794," *Annual Report of the American Historical Association for the Year 1897* (1898): 600 (hereinafter cited as MC).

14. Mangourit to Genêt, 11 Oct. 1793, AAE, CCC, f. 095. See also Stephen Drayton to Mangourit, 12 or 9 June 1793, Papers of the Republican Society of South Carolina, (Boston Public Library: General Microfilm Co., 1971, microfilm).

15. Mangourit to Sonthonax, 29 Apr. 1793, AAE, CCC, f. 013; Mangourit to Genêt, 30 Apr. 1793, AAE, CCC, f. 017. See also George C. Rogers Jr., *Charleston in the Age of the*

Pinckneys (Tulsa: University of Oklahoma Press, 1969; University of South Carolina Press, 1987), 51–53

16. Mangourit to Genêt, 18 Sept. 1793, AAE, CCC, fols. 064–064v .

17. Of the sixteen or so members of the society, thirteen were probably hostile to the French Revolution. Members with British connections: Penman, James Gregorie, Adam Tunno, Theodore Gaillard; and with connections to Saint-Domingue: Joseph Vesey. Members who were Federalists: John Huger, H. W. DeSaussure, Dr. David Ramsay, Edward Darrell, Edward Rutledge, Nathaniel Russell, Daniel DeSaussure, John Julius Pringle. Those who are considered Federalists represent a wide spectrum of opinion: some were extremely Francophobic, while some were moderate Federalists. For list of members, see *The City Gazette and Daily Advertiser* (Charleston) 17 July 1793. The first meeting of the Benevolent Society was called early in July; see *The City Gazette,* 9 July 1793.

18. Among other reports on the political situation in South Carolina are: Mangourit to Genêt, 6 May 1793, AAE, CCC, fols. 021–24v; AAE, CCC, fols. 151–151v; Mangourit to Genêt, 3 Nov. 1793, AAE, CCC, fols. 161–62v; Mangourit to minister of foreign affairs, 21 Feb. 1794 AAE, CCC, f. 206.

19. Mangourit to minister of foreign affairs, 10 Dec., 1793, AAE, CCC, fols. 171v-72, partially printed and translated in Richard K. Murdoch, "Correspondence of French Consuls in Charleston, South Carolina, 1793–1797," *South Carolina Historical Magazine* 1 (1973): 73–74. See also the work of George C. Rogers Jr., including *Evolution of a Federalist: William Loughton Smith of Charleston (1758–1812)* (Columbia: University of South Carolina Press, 1962), 253–55.

20. See Proclamation of the Republican Society of South Carolina, August 1793, Papers of the Republican Society of South Carolina. Most of its members were Americans. Around ten people belonged to both the Republican Society and the French club. However, most Americans withdrew from the French club. See Kennedy, "A French Jacobin Club," 13 and 16; Eugene P. Link, "Democratic-Republican Societies of the Carolinas," *North Carolina Historical Review* 18 (1941): 27–28.

21. For the regulations, see *The City Gazette,* 30 Jan. 1793, 26 Mar. 1793, 10 July 1793. For reports of murder and arson, see *The State Gazette,* 17 Apr. 1793, 1 May 1793, 10 June 1793 and *The City Gazette,* 17 Apr. 1793. For reports from the French islands, see *The City Gazette,* 6 July and 20 July 1793.

22. For Delaire's remarks, see *The City Gazette,* 14 and 21 Aug. 1793. For "A Native American," see *The City Gazette,* 17 Sept. 1793.

23. *The City Gazette,* 7 Sept. 1793.

24. The arrival of *Maria* was reported in *The City Gazette,* 3 Oct. 1793. Moultrie's proclamation is in *The Columbian Herald,* 20 Aug. 1793. Mangourit's report on the arrival of *Maria* is in Mangourit to Genêt, 9 Oct. 1793, AAE, CCC, fols. 071–73.

25. Mangourit to Genêt, 9 Oct. 1793, AAE, CCC, f. 072v-73.

26. Mangourit to Pascal, 9 Oct. 1793, AAE, CCC, f. 078. Mangourit to Genêt, 9 Oct. 1793, AAE, CCC, f. 073–73v

27. Mangourit to French Foreign Minister Deforgues, 19 Oct. 1793, AAE, CCC, f. 108. See also Mangourit to Genêt, 11 Oct. 1793, AAE, CCC, f. 087.

28. *City Gazette and Daily Advertiser,* 9 Oct. 1793. Resolutions praising and emulating the Charleston resolutions soon came in from such towns as Georgetown and Beaufort, South Carolina, as well as Savannah, Georgia. See *City Gazette,* 18 Oct., 21 Oct., 22 Oct., 9 Nov. 1793.

29. Moultrie's proclamation of 16 Oct. 1793 was printed in the *City Gazette and Daily Advertiser,* 17 Oct. 1793, and the *Colombian Herald,* 17 Oct. 1793.

30. Edward Rutledge, Joseph Vesey, Edward Darrell, Nathaniel Russell, and Edward

Blake. John Huger, intendant (mayor) of Charleston, was both the chairman of the Benevolent Society and the citizen's committee. Mangourit and Huger were not on the best of terms. The consul accused Huger of helping the émigrés return to Saint-Domingue to work with the British invasion of the island. Mangourit ("*Notte Confidentielle*") to Moultrie, 23 Oct. 1793, AAE, CCC, f. 154–154v. See Terry, 48–50, and 63, who adds that high Federalist Jacob Read was in both organizations.

31. Mangourit to Genêt, 20 Oct. 1793, AAE, CCC, fols. 142v-143. See also Mangourit to Genêt, 9 Oct. 1793, AAE, CCC, f. 073v

32. Of the twenty-one or so members of the committee, at least eighteen were probably hostile to the French Revolution. Member with British connections: Edward Blake. Member with connections to Saint-Domingue: Joseph Vesey. Members who were Federalists: John Huger, Jacob Read, H. W. DeSaussure (who also had British connections), Charles Cotesworth Pinckney, Edward Darrell (who also had British ties), Edward Rutledge, Nathaniel Russell (who also had British connections), John Splatt Cripps, William Crafts, John Bee Holmes, Peter Fayssoux, John Blake, Arnoldus Vanderhorst, John Sanford Dart.

33. Mangourit to Genêt, 11 Oct. 1793, AAE, CCC, fols. 088–89.

34. Mangourit to Genêt, 9 Oct. 1793, AAE, CCC, f. 073; Mangourit to Genêt, 11 Oct. 1793, AAE, CCC, fols. 087–88. Marret to Mangourit, 6 Sept. 1793, AAE, CCC, fols. 118–8v

35. Mangourit to Genêt, 11 Oct. 1793, AAE, CCC, fols. 089–090v.

36. Ibid.

37. *City Gazette,* 19 Oct. 1793.

38. Mangourit to Genêt, 20 Oct. 1793, AAE, CCC, f. 144. For the number of blacks allegedly involved, see Mangourit to foreign minister, 10 Dec. 1793 (AAE, CCC f. 171), partially printed and translated in Richard K. Murdoch, "Correspondence of French Consuls in Charleston, South Carolina, 1793–1797," *South Carolina Historical Magazine* 1 (1973): 16.

39. *City Gazette,* 18 and 19 Oct. 1793.

40. Mangourit to Foreign Minister LeBrun, 18 June 1793, AAE, CCC, fols. 045v-046.

41. Mangourit to Genêt, 11 Oct. 1793, AAE, CCC, fols. 085–85v

42. Mangourit to Pascal, 9 Oct. 1793, AAE, CCC, fols. 078–78v. See also Mangourit to Genêt, 11 Oct. 1793, AAE, CCC, fols. 085 and 091.

43. Mangourit to Genêt, 18 Sept. 1793, AAE, CCC, fols. 064v-65v; Mangourit to Moultrie, 23 Oct. 1793, fols. 154–54v; and Mangourit to Genêt, 27 Oct. 1793, AAE, CCC, 146v-148. See also David Patrick Geggus, *Slavery, War and Revolution: The British Occupation of Saint Domingue 1793–1798* (Oxford: Clarendon Press, 1982), 61–71, and 105–7.

44. Jefferson to the governor of South Carolina, 23 Dec. 1793, *The Papers of Thomas Jefferson,* ed. John Catanzariti, vol. 27 (Princeton, N.J.: Princeton University Press, 1997), 614.

45. For Genêt's and Mangourit's arguments, see such newspapers as: *The Columbian Herald,* 16 Nov., and 17 Dec. 1793; *The State Gazette,* 21 Nov. 1793. For letters attacking the French officials, see: *The City Gazette,* 23 Nov. 1793; *The Columbian Herald,* 5 Dec. 1793.

46. For the city council's orders and the mechanics' resolutions, see *The City Gazette and Daily Advertiser,* 7 Nov. 1793. The hairdressers' resolutions are in *The City Gazette and Daily Advertiser,* 20 Nov. 1793. Moultrie to the General Assembly, 30 Nov. 1793, Governor's Messages, 1792–1795, letter number 577, South Carolina Department of Archives and History, microfilm. Mr. Bull's Report, 7 Dec. 1793, Journals of the Senate, in *The State Records of South Carolina,* 335. For the House's request of 3 May 1794, see Stevens, 534. For the Senate's response, see Stevens, 542. For the membership of the South Carolina Senate, see N. Louise Bailey, ed., *Biographical Directory of the South Carolina Senate: 1776–1985* (Columbia: University of South Carolina Press, 1986).

47. Sylvia R. Frey, *Water from the Rock: Black Resistance in a Revolutionary Age* (Princeton, N.J.: Princeton University Press, 1991), 228. For more on the network in the Caribbean,

see Julius S. Scott, "The Common Wind: Currents of Afro-American Communication in the Era of the Haitian Revolution" (Ph.D. Dissertation, Duke University, 1986). For other information on the grapevine, see Norrece T. Jones Jr., *Born a Child of Freedom, Yet a Slave: Mechanisms of Control and Strategies of Resistance in Antebellum South Carolina* (London: Weslyan University Press, 1989), 124–25.

48. For the opinions on Wood, see Robert Sobel and John Raimo, eds., *Biographical Dictionary of the Governors of the United States* (Westport, Conn.: Meckler Books, 1978), which lists him as a Republican; Richard R. Beeman, *The Old Dominion and the New Nation, 1788–1801* (Lexington: University Press of Kentucky, 1972), 202, 136, which lists James Wood as a "political neutral"; and Colleen McGuiness, *American Leaders, 1789– 1994: A Biographical Summary* (Washington, D.C.: Congressional Quarterly, Inc., 1994), 446, which lists him as a Federalist. For Newton, see Beeman; and *Virginia Magazine of History and Biography* 32 (1922): 87. For the Nelson family, see the work of Emory Gibbons Evans, including "The Nelsons: A Biographical Study of a Virginia Family in the Eighteenth Century" (Ph.D. dissertation, University of Virginia, 1957).

49. For more of Gowan Pamphlet, see: James Sidbury, "Saint Domingue in Virginia: Ideology, Local Meanings, and Resistance to Slavery, 1790–1800," *Journal of Southern History* 63 (Aug. 1997): 540–43. For the Virginia incident, see John Randolph's Deposition, 21 July 1793, in *Calendar of Virginia State Papers and Other Manuscripts,* ed. Sherwin McRae, vol. 4 (New York: Kraus Reprint Corp., 1968 [1886]), 43–44 (page references are to reprint edition). For the Charleston conversation, see: Moultrie to the General Assembly, 30 Nov. 1793, Governor's Messages, 1792–1795, letter number 577, South Carolina Department of Archives and History, microfilm

50. Herbert Aptheker, *American Negro Slave Revolts* (New York: International Publishers, 1964), 215–18; Sylvia R. Frey, *Water from the Rock,* 230–31 and James Sidbury, *Ploughshares into Swords: Race, Rebellion, and Identity in Gabriel's Virginia, 1730–1810* (Cambridge: Cambridge University Press, 1997), 41–46. See also Richard Cary to the Governor, 25 Nov. 1793, in *Calendar of Virginia State Papers and Other Manuscripts,* vol. 4, 651. For the incidents in Georgia, see *The Georgia Gazette* (Savannah): 21 Nov. 1793; 28 Nov. 1793; 19 Dec. 1793; 30 Jan. 1794. See also *The Augusta Chronicle and Gazette of the State:* 28 Dec. 1793; 8 Feb. 1794.

51. For Cuffee, see *The State Gazette,* 8 Oct. 1793. For David Grey, see *The City Gazette,* 10 Oct. For possible arson, see: *City Gazette* 2 Oct.; 19 Oct.; 1 Nov.

52. For reports of witchcraft, see *City Gazette,* 3 July 1793 and 1 Nov. 1793; *State Gazette,* 2 Nov. 1793; and *The Augusta Chronicle,* 16 Nov. 1793. For the importance of voodoo in Saint-Domingue, see Alfred N. Hunt, *Haiti's Influence on Antebellum America: Slumbering Volcano in the Caribbean* (Baton Rouge: Louisiana State University Press, 1988), 79–82; Geggus, *Slavery, War and Revolution,* 29 and 40; Sidbury, *Ploughshares into Swords,* 44–45. The importance of voodoo in the Haitian Revolution is a major theme in Fick's *The Making of Haiti.*

53. For a recent interpretation that stresses the interconnected roles of voodoo and marronage in the Haitian Revolution, see Fick, *The Making of Haiti,* 57, 60–61, 242–45. On the other hand, the evidence is equally strong that voodoo and marronage played only a minor role in the Saint-Domingue insurrection. For an interpretation along these lines, see the work of David Geggus, especially "Marronage, Voodoo, and the Saint Domingue Slave Revolt of 1791," *Proceedings of the Annual Meeting of the French Colonial Historical Society* 15 (1992): 22–35. For the importance of black sailors, both slave and free, in the grapevine, see: W. Jeffrey Bolster, *Black Jacks: African American Seamen in the Age of Sail* (Cambridge: Harvard University Press, 1997), 144–49.

54. Scott, "The Common Wind," 171. See also, Ott, *The Haitian Revolution, 1789–1804;* Fick, *The Making of Haiti,* 82.

55. Mangourit to Genêt, 11 Jan. 1794, Archives des Affaires Étrangères, Correspondance politique, États-Unis, Supplément (Paris: French Reproductions, various dates, photostats in Library of Congress, Manuscript Division), vol. 30, f. 253; Scott, "The Common Wind," 298; James William Hagy, *This Happy Land: The Jews of Colonial and Antebellum Charleston* (Tuscaloosa and London: University of Alabama Press, 1993), 180, 189. James Sidbury also believes that one or more members of the Sasportas family were arms suppliers for the conspiracy in South Carolina; see his "Saint Domingue in Virginia," 543.

56. *South Carolina Daily Advertiser,* 22 Nov. 1797; quoted in Daniel E. Meanders, "South Carolina Fugitives as Viewed Through Local Colonial Newspapers with Emphasis on Runaway Notices, 1732–1801," *Journal of Negro History* 60 (1975): 316. See also *Massachusetts Spy, or Worcester Gazette,* 20 Dec. 1797, photocopy in the South Caroliniana Library.

57. The Corporation of Charleston, *An Account of the Late Intended Insurrection among a Portion of the Blacks of This City* (Charleston: A. E. Miller, 1822), printed in *Slave Insurrections: Selected Documents* (Westport, Conn.: Negro Universities Press, 1970), 17, 34–39. See also: John Lofton, *Insurrection in South Carolina: The Turbulent World of Denmark Vesey* (Yellow Springs, Ohio: Antioch Press, 1964), 67–74 and 144–79; Aptheker, 267–76; Robert S. Starobin, ed., *Denmark Vesey: The Slave Conspiracy of 1822* (Englewood Cliffs, N.J.: Prentice-Hall, 1970), 130–51. For the development of a black version of republicanism, see: Robert M. Calhoon, *Dominion and Liberty: Ideology in the Anglo-American World, 1660–1801* (Arlington Heights, Ill.: Harlan Davidson, 1994), 86–88. For an account of Vesey's rebellion that stresses "black seamen as links in the chain of rebellion," see Bolster, *Black Jacks,* 192–94.

58. Sidbury, "Saint Domingue in Virginia," 542.

59. Quoted in Douglas Egerton, *Gabriel's Rebellion: The Virginia Slave Conspiracies of 1800 and 1802* (Chapel Hill: University of North Carolina Press, 1993), 102.

Chapter 9

The Promise of Revolution

Saint-Domingue and the Struggle for Autonomy
in Guadeloupe, 1797–1802

LAURENT DUBOIS

IN DECEMBER 1797 A REVOLT erupted in Lamentin, Guadeloupe, against the French Republican regime of Victor Hugues. The insurgents, most of whom were ex-slaves working as *cultivateurs* on plantations of the area, rallied around a cry for more political and economic power. According to Hugues's report on the incident, the leaders of the revolt rode through the countryside saying to the *cultivateurs:*

> Aren't you tired of being poor? If you are free why are you working on the land of the whites? Why doesn't all the fruit of your labor belong to you? You are three hundred against one. In Saint-Domingue everyone does what they please; all those in command are blacks; the whites have been chased away and the few that are left serve the blacks like you serve the whites. . . . Where does the money of the colony come from? From the sugar and the coffee that the blacks produce, since the whites have never worked the land. In one hour everything will be finished. The army is ours, we have to kill all the whites and the blacks and the *hommes de couleur* [free colored men] who occupy positions and who have received advantages from them, then you will have all the money of the colony, all the sugar, the coffee, the cotton and the merchandise to dress yourselves in.[1]

The insurrection, Hugues wrote, was led by four "formerly free men of color" named Eugène Rugne, Noël, Damiens and Sansan. According to the testimonies gathered from *cultivateurs* implicated in the revolt, these leaders—and others such as the ex-slave Bazile, who had been a "volunteer" in the army, and Drozin, the manager of a state-owned sugar plantation—started mobilizing insurgents on 28 December 1797. On that day, the mason Eugène Rugne visited the *cultivateur* Benjamin and told him: "We have to slit the throats of all the whites and make ourselves masters of the country." Rugne, who was known as the "representative of all the black citizens," spoke to the *cultivateur* Augustin on another plantation, and told him that the entire colony was rising up: "All the blacks are marching to kill the whites and you are here?" He added that the insurgents would soon march on Pointe-à-Pitre, the major city of the island, to "settle things there."[2]

Mobilized by Rugne's ride, the insurgents gathered the next morning at a state-owned coffee plantation called Lestier Ravine Chaude, where they formed into three companies and set out to attack the plantations. They killed three white plantation owners and managers, and sacked a number of houses. One of those killed was the Citoyen Hubert, the owner of the coffee plantation where Eugène Rugne lived. An insurgent named Gros Jacques also killed the local National Guard captain.[3] The insurgents then gathered together for an assault on the town of Lamentin, where many whites from the surrounding countryside had taken refuge. They were confronted by a small troop of soldiers led by Citoyen Modeste (described by Hugues as an old *homme de couleur* "whose boldness was so fatal to the British during the last war"), who managed, with help from the townspeople, to hold them off.[4] Despite the urging of one leader—who had asked the retreating *cultivateurs,* "since when are blacks afraid of whites?"—the insurgents, many of whom were armed only with sticks, failed in two attempts to take the town. Soon reinforcements sent by Hugues, including a mounted company of dragoons, arrived and routed the troop of insurgents gathered outside the town. The *cultivateur* Augustin, who ran and hid in a cane field, was cut seven times by the sabres of the dragoons. The insurgents who were not killed or captured fled, and soon the revolt was over.[5]

The conflict at Lamentin was played out not between slaves and masters, but between various groups of citizens whose roles were the product of the Republican regime of emancipation instituted in Guadeloupe by Victor Hugues. In 1794, Hugues had brought to the island the decree of emancipation passed that year by the National Convention in Paris, and with the help of slaves turned citizen-soldiers, had won the colony back from the British. In the next years, he continued the policy of integrating ex-slaves into the army, and Guadeloupe became the center for French Republican campaigns against the British colonies of the Eastern Caribbean. The army—and the Republican corsairs that roved the waters attacking enemy and neutral ships—provided unprecedented opportunities for social and economic advancement for many ex-slaves from Guadeloupe. The Lamentin insurrection tested the loyalty of many such slaves turned soldiers, but they showed themselves loyal and disciplined in repressing it. Hugues noted of the soldiers who fought in Lamentin that "nine-tenths of this company, the elite of the army of the Antilles, are blacks and former slaves, unequaled in their boldness and in their wise and exemplary behavior." Although some were approached to join the insurrection, they refused and instead reported the planned revolt to their superiors; "the indignation of these brave soldiers was extreme, and they were the first to convince their co-citizens that they were being trapped and misled." Artillery officer Pierre Gédéon, for instance, arrested five leaders of the conspiracy who tried to recruit him. In fact, Hugues suggested, the whites left alone would likely have fled rather than confront the insurgents. "They scorn the blacks," he wrote, "and nevertheless in all the insurrections of the Africans they are the first to run and hide. He who holds the key to the human heart seems to tell us that, in this country as in all others, tyrants, though used to commanding their slaves, always tremble in front of them."[6]

Yet those who rose up were also ex-slaves, whose experience of freedom had disenchanted them with the regime installed by Hugues. For, since 1794, while the Republican armies had become racially integrated, those ex-slaves who were not part of the army were forced to keep working on the plantations where they had been slaves, either for their former masters or under government managers appointed to oversee the functioning of "national" plantations. These had been confiscated from émigrés or royalists who had been killed fighting with the British on the island in 1794. The managers appointed by the Republican administration to manage these plantations, some of them *hommes de couleur* or ex-slaves, comprised a new and potentially powerful class of managers that had a stake in preserving the administration that had created opportunities for them. Yet some of them also complained bitterly of their lack of pay, and demanded better treatment by Hugues's regime. Many illegally supplemented their income by selling a part of plantation production for their own profit instead of handing it all over to the state, creating a circulation of smuggled goods which Hugues's regime repeatedly tried to suppress.[7] So while freedom opened up important possibilities, especially for those who joined the army, in many ways the aspirations of the ex-slaves—even those who gained positions on the plantations—were frustrated by a regime that promised much but ultimately delivered little in the way of political or economic rights. A number of the leaders of the Lamentin insurrection were men who occupied positions of some power on state-run plantations. The *cultivateurs* who had joined the insurgents also seem to have come in large numbers from state plantations where, despite repeated promises by Hugues, they were working without the pay promised to them at the time of emancipation.

The Lamentin insurrection brought to the surface some of the central contradictions of the regime of Republican emancipation in Guadeloupe, which had produced both a sense of loyalty among soldiers and of continuing dissatisfaction among *cultivateurs*. Hugues had repeatedly expressed in his correspondence the sentiment that the mission he had been given—to free the slaves while maintaining plantation production and prosecuting a war against the British—was impossible to fulfill. While he furthered the project of liberation and racial equality as he mobilized ex-slaves in the Republican war against the British, Hugues also deployed a Republican language of loyalty and self-sacrifice to justify the forced labor of ex-slaves on the plantations. He drew on the ideas of gradual abolitionists in arguing that, because of the brutalization they had experienced under slavery, the slaves could not immediately be given all the rights of citizenship. In 1797 Hugues argued that coercion was necessary in a colony where "the land is nothing, and arms are everything," and that it was only through the limitations he placed on the rights of the ex-slaves that he had avoided the violence that had plagued Saint-Domingue. Too much liberty, he warned, would make the island "a theatre of carnage and blood, like the coast of Africa which is inhabited by the most barbarous of peoples."[8]

Hugues's insistence that political rights should not be given to the ex-slaves, and that only a gradual process could transform the societies of the Antilles, contributed during the late 1790s to the increasing push for a limitation, and even a reversal, of the policy of slave emancipation. The abolition of slavery in 1794, made possible by alliances between Republicans and slave insurgents in the Antilles, had destroyed the pre-Revolutionary colonial policy of juridical and political separation between metropole and colony. In its place a system was established in which metropole and colony were, at least in principle, governed by the same laws and tied together in what one proponent of the policy, Etienne Laveaux, called in 1798 "A System of Absolute Unity." After 1799, however, with Bonaparte's rise to power, the principle of unity between metropole and colony was reversed and new laws declared that, once again, the colonies would be subjected to different laws from those of the metropole, dictated from Paris. Planters who had taken refuge from the Caribbean, as well as some who had formerly advocated emancipation, encouraged a return to pro-slavery policies. In 1801, the promise of a peace between France and Britain (finally declared in 1802 with the Treaty of Amiens) eliminated the military advantages associated with slave emancipation in the Antilles, and soon afterwards Bonaparte sent expeditions to the Caribbean to return the colonies to their "pre-1789" situation.[9]

News of the changing opinions about colonial policy in the metropole caused concern in the Caribbean. In January 1798 Hugues described how certain individuals in Guadeloupe were circulating the news of pro-slavery speeches given in France, and that such news spread "worry among the blacks that the Government had resolved that they would lose their liberty." Some pro-slavery pamphlets appeared in Guadeloupe, attacking emancipation and claiming that as a result of it "we would leave our heads on the scaffold." The effect of such news from France was compounded by the attitudes of the white planters themselves, who, according to Hugues, "still see the ownership of their former slaves as prey that has escaped them; they will seize with eagerness and greed any opportunity they have to get them between their hands." The loosening Republican legislation on émigrés meant that already in 1797–98 certain planters were returning from exile to Guadeloupe, making claims on their property and on the labor of their ex-slaves turned *cultivateurs*. The return of the departed, wrote Hugues, made it difficult "to contain the passions, the justifiable hatred, and the severity of the miserable black Africans against their former tyrants" which had exploded in the Lamentin insurrection. Indeed, if the ex-slaves, who were generally obedient, had committed "atrocious crimes" during the revolt, Hugues claimed it was to a large extent because of the inflammatory talk of their former masters, "particularly that of the wives of émigrés, of whom there are many in this colony."[10]

After 1798, as more émigrés returned and metropolitan regimes increasingly came under the sway of the arguments in favor of reversing emancipation in the Caribbean, the social groups that had fought one another in Lamentin in 1797 began to find that they had a common interest. The officer Pierre Gédéon, after helping to defuse the Lamentin insurrection in 1797, found himself urging insurrection against the metropolitan authorities in 1801. Gédéon was one among many—most notably the *homme de couleur* officer Louis Delgrès—who would respond to the actions of metropolitan administrators by defending what they saw as the true Republican policies of racial equality. For it increasingly became clear to many in Guadeloupe that fighting for Republican principles might mean fighting *against* French metropolitan authorities.

Emancipation had been administered by Republican regimes in the previous years as part of a larger, national struggle against the British. Service to the nation, both as laborers and as soldiers, became the symbol of responsible citizenship, and despite their restrictions these roles provided a context for economic and social mobility outside the lines set forth by the administrations. The Republic had been the guarantor of emancipation, even as the defense of the Republic was used to justify freedom's limits. What, then, were the Republicans of the Antilles to do as metropolitan authorities retreated from the Republican principles that had been applied in the Antilles? To whom did the people of Guadeloupe owe allegiance? If they were loyal to the Republic that had overseen the transformations on the island in the previous years, where should their loyalty lie when metropolitan authorities began to dismantle that Republic? As the people of the Antilles heard through news that arrived intermittently from across the Atlantic and from elsewhere in the Caribbean about the new directions of colonial policy, they had to decide how to react to national authorities sent to the island. They made difficult choices between national loyalty and Republican principles, and drew on their experience of freedom and its complex material and social possibilities in deciding how to act towards a Republic that was retreating from its previous policies of emancipation and racial equality.

As ex-slaves and *gens de couleur* in Guadeloupe received menacing news from metropolitan France, many looked in particular to Saint-Domingue as an example for reacting to the changing tides of metropolitan policy. Even before the Lamentin revolt, Hugues's regime had confronted insurgents who referred to their sister island as an example of what could be in Guadeloupe. In early 1797, Hugues had reported that a few *hommes de couleur* in Guadeloupe had publicly attacked his regime and lauded the increasing power of blacks and *citoyens de couleur* under the regime of Toussaint Louverture. "'Only in Saint-Domingue,' they say, 'do liberty and equality reign, men do what they wish, the agents are *de couleur*, or publicly live with *femmes de couleur*, and all the generals and the chiefs are *de couleur*, they dominate and the whites can do nothing about it.'" The receipt of letters from Saint-Domingue, Hugues claimed, had incited these claims, and a few had demanded positions in the government. One told Hugues that until there were *hommes de couleur* among the generals and the highest ranks of the administration, power would not be truly shared.[11]

The example of Louverture's regime was again invoked a few weeks before the Lamentin revolt, when a crowd descended on the main town of the Guadeloupean dependency of Marie-Galante. The "war cries" of the crowd, which was quickly dispersed by the local militia, "were that they should cut the throats of all the whites and do what was done in Saint-Domingue, where all the leaders were blacks or *de couleur*." And the insurgents of Lamentin contrasted the power structure of Saint-Domingue, which they saw as racially integrated and even black dominated, with that of Guadeloupe, where one white commissioner ruled. In fact Hugues claimed that the Lamentin revolt had been inspired by the news of Louverture's expulsion of Sonthonax from Saint-Domingue. Tellingly, he noted that news of this event traveled more quickly along informal routes than by the official ones. "We were not yet informed of this important event when a general murmur circulated among the *cultivateurs;* it was started by the Americans (who play an important role against the Republic in the Antilles)."[12]

During the years 1798 to 1802, then, the increasingly autonomous regime of Louverture provided a counter example to the increasingly repressive metropolitan authorities that arrived in Guadeloupe knowing little of the island and unilaterally established new policies. News from Saint-Domingue played a crucial role both in inciting insurrection against metropolitan authorities and in forging the vision of the possibilities of political autonomy developed in Guadeloupe. At the same time, some insurgents in Guadeloupe took pains to distinguish themselves from Louverture as they made overtures to metropolitan authorities. In a complex situation of contradictory rumors, intentional misinformation on the part of administrators arriving from France, and profound dissension among ex-slaves themselves about how best to preserve their emancipation, the conflicts in Guadeloupe and Saint-Domingue emerged symbiotically. Between 1798 and 1802, a new and hotly contested idea of what the Republic should be was articulated—and ultimately crushed—in Guadeloupe, even as events on that island contributed to the evolution of the conflict that finally created Haiti out of Saint-Domingue in 1804. The study of how the struggle for autonomy developed in Guadeloupe in relation to the events in Saint-Domingue can teach us both about the influences each conflict had on the other and about the broader conflict that ended the French Republic's experiment with emancipation and led to the creation of a new Republic in the Antilles.

In November 1798, Victor Hugues was replaced by the agent Desfourneaux, who brought to Guadeloupe his previous experience as a Republican official in Saint-Domingue. His mission was to replace Hugues and apply a law passed in January 1798 making Guadeloupe a department of France, and more broadly to bring about the integration of the island into the political life of the Republic. Despite the stated intention of his mission, however, the context of anti-emancipation writings clearly made some in Guadeloupe distrust this new official from overseas. After his arrival on the island, Desfourneaux and his entourage heard rumors that "agitators of all kinds and disorganizers provoked insurrection in the countryside and in the towns, telling everyone that the counter-revolution had taken place in France, that the royalists were dividing up the jobs, and that I had been sent to re-establish slavery and to remove the patriot administrators from all civil and military posts." The "incendiary" rumors about the re-establishment of slavery incited small-scale revolt throughout the island, and the troops became "increasingly rebellious." Desfourneaux arrested some sailors for insurrection, and his delegates "arrested black citizens daily for attacks committed as much against themselves as against whites." Since he believed that Hugues was the source of the turbulence, he also arrested him and forced him onto a ship which soon left for France.[13]

After Hugues's departure, the accusations that Desfourneaux had come to re-establish slavery increased, fed by the arrival of news from Guadeloupe's sister colony: "The unfortunate events of Saint-Domingue, the forced embarkation of

Général Hédouville, were announced by the passengers of a boat which arrived and landed before I was warned," Desfourneaux wrote. The news had encouraged the "conspirators, who blamed Général Hédouville and the people of his expedition, and compared them to us, predicting that the same disasters would happen in Guadeloupe."[14] In one of the depositions later gathered by Desfourneaux about the insurrection against him, it was reported that when conversation turned to the new arrivals in the colony, one merchant "cried with indignation that Saint-Domingue had been completely destroyed only because of the actions of similar men, and that in truth they were all *chouans.*"[15] Once he was established in Guadeloupe, Desfourneaux arrested three men named Morin, Trinchard, and Menet, charging that they had "formed a plot, to use force and the most atrocious means to oppose the establishment in the colony of the new order conforming to the Constitution of the Year 3."[16] The basis for this charge was the proof provided by nine depositions by citizens of Basse-Terre and Port de la Liberté describing speeches they had heard given to crowds at the time of the arrival of Desfourneaux. These depositions are a window into the general worry among the "new citizens" about what the change of regimes meant for the policy of slave emancipation, and give a hint of some of the plans for the future which were circulating among the ex-slaves.

On 30 November, a few days after Desfourneaux's arrival, a merchant from Port de la Liberté, Duvergé, was walking on the main square of the town when he was "attracted by curiosity to a group of black and colored citizens who seemed to press around two individuals whom he could not identify in the darkness, but who he was told were 'Gaugnet and Pignon.'" "He was struck by the audacity with which they sought to mislead these ignorant men by painting the leaders who had recently arrived in the colony as *chouans* and counter-revolutionaries, agents of a faction that was the enemy of the patriots; in their frenzy, these crazed men called on all true Republicans to join with those in whom the Citizen Hugues had always invested his confidence as the only supporters of the general emancipation he had brought to the negroes." The speakers called on the crowd to fight against the departure of their liberator and to expel the one who came to replace him in order to make the Republic triumph in Guadeloupe and all of France.[17]

The next night, outside of Port de la Liberté, in Abymes, another witness saw the same men giving a speech to a "crowd of negroes and *gens de couleur,*" claiming that Hugues, "who had brought liberty . . . was the only one who could conserve it." All the good patriots were preparing to "chase away these *chouans* who talked only in terms of 'monsieur' and 'madame'" and if they followed Trinchard and Morin, the Republic would be preserved "here as well as in France."[18] Trinchard himself was seen elsewhere speaking to a "considerable crowd," advising them to join him in repulsing these new arrivals, who had as their sole mission to "rob the blacks of their liberty and return them to the state of slavery."[19] The black fisherman Ignace overheard Trinchard talking to some friends on a state-owned plantation, saying with "a great deal of fire" that the new arrivals were "*chouans*" who had come "to put us back into slavery." An officer speaking with Trinchard responded that if they were *chouans,* "we will release the army against them," and Trinchard added that if they had come to "return us to slavery, well to hell with them." Noticing Ignace, they gave him a glass of rum, and he heard no more.[20]

Who was Trinchard? Ignace quoted him as saying that the new arrivals mean to put "us" back into slavery. Does this mean Trinchard was an ex-slave? Nowhere in the trials or the deposition was he given a racial ascription. His political vision was one in which the struggle in Guadeloupe was that last, desperate stage of the larger struggle over the future of the Republic on both sides of the Atlantic. In the anonymous letter Desfourneaux claimed that Trinchard—or one of his collaborators—had written, the colonies were represented as the last refuge of the Republic. "We can no longer doubt that Republicanism, worried and offended everywhere in France, is speaking the last words of its expiring voice, which has been suffocated by despotism." The émigrés and the priests were taking over the government—"all is counter-revolution, only the name is lacking." "A few Republican forms are observed, and vain ghosts of liberty still wander without eyes amongst a people abused, waiting for the chains they carry to be permanently attached. Liberty has fled this country, and has taken with it the Republican virtues which inflamed hearts in 1793. . . . Love of the nation has been replaced by love of gold, this metal is the god to which the positions of the government are sacrificed . . . Already the total loss of Saint-Domingue is the result of the work of the men in whom this corrupt government placed its confidence," and Guadeloupe would be next thanks to the actions of "these *chouans,* these *vendéens,* these men vomited on our shores" whose actions would destroy the prosperity of the island and lose "this rich possession" for France. "AUX ARMES CITOYENS," the letter called: "Loyal to the sacred oath we took at the foot of the tree of liberty, will we allow another conqueror of the colony to govern?"[21]

In the effervescence surrounding Hugues's removal, some put forward the idea that an even more radical uprising might be necessary to preserve liberty. A Guadeloupean *homme de couleur* named Pierre Miller, who was in exile after having been deported by Hugues in 1797, was heard saying that "the reign of the whites was over, that he was surprised Guadeloupe was still in their hands and that it had not suffered the fate of Saint-Domingue." Miller boarded a ship for Guadeloupe with two other "mulattoes who are also bad subjects," after the arrival of Desfourneaux, but he was quickly noticed by the new authorities and deported from the island.[22] Some plantation laborers—perhaps encouraged by the return of émigré plantation owners that quickly increased after Hugues's departure—rallied around a similar idea. On 25 December 1798, a few weeks after the other depositions about the actions against Desfourneaux were made, Pierre Metro, a merchant in Basse-Terre, declared that around two o'clock one afternoon he had seen a crowd gathered around "a black Citizen who was giving an incendiary speech, saying that all whites were rogues and that they had come to impose laws and that it was time to fall upon them."[23] One white plantation owner, Le Vanier, who had been part of the group that the fisherman Ignace had seen talking to Trinchard, was accused of having been aware of plans for revolution among the slaves. According to the deposition, "the blacks came to see Citizen Nicolas Le Vanier during the night, to report everything that was happening on the plantations to him, and that the said blacks took his advice and that if they cut the necks of the whites his would be preserved, because he had been able to inspire their confidence."[24] The third-hand information delivered here was certainly refracted through the fears and, perhaps, personal conflicts between those mentioned. Yet the sense that whites might be positioning themselves in relation to a future insurrection among the *cultivateurs* itself spoke volumes about the sense of danger and possibility on the island.

After Desfourneaux and the "Council of War" he had established expelled Trinchard, Menet and Morin from the island, they carried out a series of other trials against suspected enemies of the new regime. In the first of these several soldiers garrisoned in Basse-Terre were accused of having planned to march to Port de la Liberté to capture and expel Desfourneaux from the island. The accused included both ex-slaves, such as Azor, who had been born in Africa, and metropolitan whites, two of whom were executed.[25] In another trial, the central figure was Pierre Victor, a tailor who accused his former master, of having "attacked liberty and the rights of man" by having written him a letter in which he offered to "send him his liberty" for a price. Pierre Victor, however, was himself accused of having falsified the letter in order to prove that his master "doubted that liberty was a sacred right" and "in order to inflame spirits and push them towards a sedition against the authorities of the Colony." Victor was found guilty of having attempted to stir up insurrection in the colony, and was unanimously condemned to death, though his punishment was commuted to permanent exile; others who had helped him were deported from the island for ten to twenty years.[26] That such punishment could flow from the action of forgery was a mark of how tenuous was the sense of faith in the metropolitan authorities, and how dangerous even the intimation of a return to slavery could be. If the account given by the Council of the actions of Pierre Victor and his co-conspirators is true, it shows a knowledge on their part that the evocation of a return to the ties of slavery—even through a private letter presented as an offer of a personal transaction—could present a political danger in the colony.

Shortly after this trial, Desfourneaux wrote to the minister in Paris that "the public administrators of the colonies all walk on volcanoes, whose explosions constantly menace the national authority and their security." Conspiracies abounded on the island, he suggested. Some planned to imitate the expulsion of the Hédouville mission from Saint-Domingue; others wished to hand the island over to the British. Insurrection was a constant possibility.[27] Desfourneaux's regime was significant in that the *cultivateurs* were finally paid a portion of what they produced—as they never had been under Hugues—and that furthermore the first election since 1792 took place on the island. Yet his stay lasted little more than a year. Not long after having organized the successful election in 1799, Desfourneaux responded to rumors that the Directory regime in France was in danger by announcing at a dinner that if the Terror were to return he would attempt to preserve the colony from this kind of regime. A number of leaders who had served under Hugues denounced Desfourneaux as a traitor, and soon a mass movement took shape in the colony. In Basse-Terre, Desfourneaux was confronted by "a considerable crowd of men, women and children of all colors preceded by the municipal officers shouting and demanding the embarkation of 'the traitor Desfourneaux.'" The insurgents sent him, along with reports defending their actions, to the metropole, proclaiming their loyalty to the Constitution of the Year 3 (1795)—which had, however, already been abrogated by Bonaparte's Consulate at the time.[28] Among the leaders of the insurgents were army officers who had perhaps been angered by Desfourneaux's dismantling of the Republican corsairs, whose attacks on enemy and neutral ships in the region had provided many in the colony, notably ex-slaves, the opportunity to simultaneously grow rich and prove their patriotism.[29]

A provisional government set up on the island after the expulsion was soon replaced by three new administrators who had left France just as Bonaparte established the Consulate. Among them was Etienne Laveaux, the long-time ally of Toussaint Louverture, who was soon expelled by the other commissioners, Jeannet and Baco, on the pretext that he was a "negrophile." The action had been necessary, they explained, to prevent insurrection on the part of the "mulattoes" who, "always worried, always active, spy and watch over us." Confident in their numbers, they sought to influence and master the government, and waited for an opportunity to take control. "Our colleague Laveaux raised their hopes, his direct, friendly and active liaisons with them, and his indiscreet speeches, his apologies for the murders committed under the orders of Toussaint, forced us to the distressing decision to exile him." During their rule, the agents claimed to have uncovered two plots, involving a number of black soldiers, to overthrow their regime and take control of the island.[30] In order to counteract these movements, Jeannet and Baco promoted the *homme de couleur* Captain Frontin, who had participated in the expulsion of Desfourneaux, to the position of *chef de bataillon*. When they asked for confirmation of this promotion, they wrote: "The Citizen Frontin is *métis* (mixedrace) and the encouragement he will receive from the approval of his promotion can only produce the best of effects on the citizens of color, and bring them to follow the excellent conduct of this officer."[31] The commissioners clearly believed it vital to divide the army, which was increasingly becoming the center of agitation against metropolitan authorities. This was a policy that would be continued by their successor on the island, Lacrosse, although it would ultimately backfire against him. Nevertheless, divisions in the army of Guadeloupe would continue to play an important role, and ultimately make possible the repression of the move towards independence on the island.

On his arrival in Guadeloupe, Lacrosse was welcomed by a populace for whom he was part of the history of Republican transformation on the island, where he had broken royalist control and established the Republic in 1793. Lacrosse, however, discouraged the connection between his role as a liberator in 1793 and his new role in 1800. Among the guests at a dinner given in his honor on his arrival was a woman who, in 1793, had placed the red bonnet of liberty on Lacrosse's head during a ceremony at the local Jacobin club. Seeing her, Lacrosse said, "Go, citizen: Know that the Lacrosse of the year 7 is not the Lacrosse of 1793!"[32] It was Lacrosse's short tenure in Guadeloupe that led the island to the largest insurrection against metropolitan authority it ever saw.

Two of the main protagonists of this revolt were *hommes de couleur* from Martinique, Magloire Pélage and Louis Delgrès, who despite remarkably similar careers ultimately ended up as leaders on opposite sides of this conflict. Both Pélage and Delgrès joined the Republican side in the conflicts on their islands early in the

1790s. Louis Delgrès participated in the first racially integrated election in French history, held in exile in Dominica in 1792, while Pélage distinguished himself in battle against royalist forces and was promoted by Rochambeau in Martinique. Delgrès and Pélage were both taken prisoner by the British in 1794 and then arrived on Guadeloupe in 1795 as part of the *Bataillon des Antilles* formed with exiles from the Caribbean in metropolitan France. Under Victor Hugues's orders, they fought in the campaigns against the British, Pélage in St. Lucia and Delgrès first in St. Lucia and then in St. Vincent (see map, page 136). Both were eventually captured a second time by the British, and returned with Baco, Jeannet and Laveaux to Guadeloupe in 1800.[33] The story of Delgrès and Pélage, then, was inter-twined with the story of the Republican army of the Antilles to which they had belonged since the early 1790s. In 1801 they rose to leadership as a broad segment of the army of Guadeloupe, joined by *cultivateurs* of the island, reacted with vio-lence when Lacrosse began dismantling the principles of racial equality upon which this army had been constructed in the previous years. During the insurrec-tions against Hugues and Desfourneaux, the example of Saint-Domingue had inspired insurgents, and again during 1800–1802, the examples of Toussaint's autonomous power contributed to the actions of the men and women of Guade-loupe. Yet Lacrosse's expulsion from Guadeloupe in fact predated the departure of the Leclerc expedition for Saint-Domingue, and was a crucial chapter in the con-flicts that would lead to Haitian independence and to the reestablishment of slav-ery in Guadeloupe.

Why did the people of Guadeloupe turn against Lacrosse? Lacrosse arrived in May 1801, and immediately began repressing "conspiracies" he claimed were underway on the island, especially among the soldiers. On 6 June he arrested fif-teen merchants and administrators. The next day his troops arrested a number of officers and soldiers from the army, including Captain Frontin. Two of Frontin's acquaintances, Pierre Gédéon and Noël Corbet, soon became leaders of the insur-rection against Lacrosse.[34] Frontin was among the group of deportees who, once in France, wrote a report accusing Lacrosse of having placed émigrés, some of whom had served with the British army, in positions of authority in Guadeloupe. The deportees also wrote that Lacrosse had angered the *cultivateurs* by naming admin-istrators whose role was to oversee the payment of the plantation workers, but who in doing so took both took a commission out of the salaries and made the choice (previously in the hands of the *cultivateurs* themselves) of whether they would be paid in money or in the commodities they had produced. In addition, Lacrosse named a commissioner to force "vagabonds" to return to their plantations. Accord-ing to the report of the deported soldiers, "this measure had the most bloody of effects." "A black citizen named Arselle, a dependent of the Leblond plantation before the war who, since the conquest of the island, was part of the company of the artillery workers, was stopped by the commissioner Régis Leblanc in order to be brought back to the plantation. He responded that he was free and French and had a profession that he had always had the right to pursue. At that moment the plantation manager Duverger grabbed him by the collar, and Arselle pulled a dag-ger from his pocket and stabbed himself six times, saying that he knew how to die. In fact, he died the next day."[35]

As ex-slaves in the towns were told to return to their plantations, other *culti-vateurs* directly experienced the return of former masters who had left the colony before emancipation.[36] In reaction, *cultivateurs* in various parts of the island began resisting. Lacrosse's regulations on the recovery of property by émigrés, posted in Basse-Terre, were ripped down and some were smeared with excrement. In Petit-Bourg, animals were poisoned, and local officials blamed *cultivateurs.* Lacrosse placed the officer Magloire Pélage in charge of a troop that identified and executed the accused *cultivateurs.* Lacrosse then published a law declaring the penalty of death for all "poisoners."[37] Lacrosse also sent an unsuccessful mission against a group of maroons who still lived, despite emancipation, in the mountains of Basse-Terre, in what one general called "a kind of little independent Republic."[38] And he granted French soldiers more pay than the colonial soldiers, in order to reward them for their "good behavior"—which suggests he may have been attempting to assure their loyalty in fighting the colonial troops.[39] Such actions resonated ominously with the rumors about events in France that had been pushing some to resist metropolitan administrators since 1798. A citizen of Guadeloupe wrote in a letter to a friend that Lacrosse's politics towards the army which was seven-eighths "blacks and *hommes de couleur*" were sure to incite revolt: "Is it not to be feared that they will repeat in Guadeloupe all the scenes of devastation and carnage for which Saint-Domingue has for so long been the theater?"[40]

Lacrosse incited open revolt in the army when, after the French Général Bethencourt died, he put himself in charge of the army instead of promoting the *homme de couleur* Pélage. Lacrosse then imprisoned twenty-five soldiers who had protested this decision, and dissolved the battalion of which they were a part, sending the soldiers who were not arrested to hard labor.[41] One of the imprisoned soldiers, Joseph (Josie) Lagarde, angered at the actions of a guard, apparently said "they had been truly stupid to have controlled the country, and to have ceded it to rogues like that one." Then he waved his fist, bared his teeth and said, "We won't stay here forever." Lacrosse's war tribunal quickly determined that Lagarde was guilty of "having been involved in criminal conspiracies" and ordered him executed. Lagarde, like Frontin, had many connections among the other officers in the colonial army, and his execution shocked and angered many. Lacrosse followed up the execution of Josie with a call for all *gens de couleur* of Basse-Terre to gather at offices he occupied; there, he declared that they were all "enemies of the government," and threatened to deport them.[42]

Soon after Lagarde's execution, Lacrosse tried to arrest a group of popular officers, including Pélage, Pierre Gédéon, and Joseph Ignace. Ignace and Gédéon managed to elude Lacrosse's officers, and some soldiers in Pointe-à-Pitre rose up to defend them. Pélage escaped as well, and tried to control the situation as officers and soldiers rallied in insurrection. A crowd broke into the house of the police commissioner and found a list of citizens that were to be arrested, many of them *gens de couleur,* along with a letter from Lacrosse declaring that some of those already deported had been sent to Madagascar. The insurgent soldiers were joined by *cultivateurs* who, since it was a day of rest, were in town.[43] News of the uprising against Lacrosse spread quickly outside of Pointe-à-Pitre, and in addition to *cultivateurs,* many *hommes de couleur* from other towns came into the city. One elderly property owner from nearby Petit-Bourg who almost never left his house, was seen in the streets of Pointe-à-Pitre. When he was asked what he was doing there, he said, "my caste is being attacked, and all good people must unite to defend it!"[44]

Pélage quickly acted to control the situation and channel the insurrection, calming the troops and dispersing the *cultivateurs*. He then called a meeting of all the "merchants, property-owners and other notable inhabitants of Pointe-à-Pitre," who quickly took the leadership of the insurrection out of the hands of those who had started it. Pélage and his newly formed *Conseil* attempted to placate Lacrosse, who was marching on Pointe-à-Pitre with a troop to put down the insurrection. Meanwhile, however, soldiers from Basse-Terre arrived in Pointe-à-Pitre and announced that Lacrosse had arrested a number of *hommes de couleur* and placed them in chains in the holds of ships in the harbor. Some of the soldiers in Lacrosse's troop deserted to Pointe-à-Pitre; they did not want to fight, they said, "against their own color." A few days later, Pélage was brought to the fort by some officers, and there he found the troops armed and lined up in the courtyard, where they greeted him with joy and proclaimed him "General in chief of the army of Guadeloupe." According to the *Mémoire* later written in his defense, Pélage hesitantly accepted in order to prevent the passing of leadership to the more radical soldier Joseph Ignace, who, along with many of the soldiers, wished to go and attack Lacrosse immediately.[45]

Lacrosse eventually agreed to enter Pointe-à-Pitre alone, but he refused to declare an amnesty for those who had participated in the insurrection, and once in the town he spoke harshly to Pélage and others and threatened severe punishment against them. Despite Pélage's resistance, a group of black officers led by Ignace arrested Lacrosse, and Pélage negotiated his deportation from the island.[46] So the agent sent by the Consul to Guadeloupe ended up forcibly expelled at the hands not so much of Pélage himself as of a rebellious army that entered into insurrection to defend their officers and racial equality within the armed forces. Lacrosse, who established himself in exile in Dominica and went to work isolating Guadeloupe, wrote after his expulsion that "the insurgent black troops no longer follow any leader, and they refuse to put down their weapons."[47] Pélage and the *Conseil Provisoire,* staffed by two *hommes de couleur* merchants and one white lawyer, Frasans, took over the administration of Guadeloupe. They wrote to France proclaiming their continuing loyalty to the metropole and highlighting their attempts to maintain order on the plantations and protect whites on the island.[48] Pélage and his allies were perhaps influenced in their actions by the presence of the exiled *homme de couleur* François Rigaud, whose brother André had been defeated by Louverture and Dessalines in a brutal war in Saint-Domingue the year before. The example of Rigaud could well have served as a cautionary tale about the danger the *hommes de couleur* of Guadeloupe would face if they allowed the ex-slave majority to rule, and therefore encouraged Pélage in his political course during 1801.[49] Many soldiers in Guadeloupe, however, including certain *hommes de couleur,* were skeptical of Pélage's faith that the "mother country," once informed of the truth of what had happened in Guadeloupe, would forgive those Lacrosse called "rebels" and understand that they were loyal to France.

In November 1801, Lacrosse sent an envoy to Guadeloupe with copies of a newspaper which carried news about the signing of the preliminaries of the Treaty of Amiens and noted that Britain and France had joined together to "establish order and security in their respective colonies." This new alliance between the two former enemies was directly visible to the people of Guadeloupe, since it was for the most part British ships that were patrolling the waters to enforce Lacrosse's blockade against the island. For the Republican soldiers of Guadeloupe who had spent the previous years fighting the British, this reversal must have seemed particularly menacing.[50] Some soldiers in Guadeloupe said that if the treaty had been signed, "it would be necessary to reject it as the most fatal of presents, because, for the *noir* and the *homme de couleur,* this treaty is slavery." The soldiers declared further that "after having worn their uniforms for eight years they would not leave them behind to pick up the hoe under the whip of a slave-driver." Some threatened to attack the property owners.[51]

The newspaper sent from Dominica also described how a massive expedition had been sent from Brest in order to "reduce Saint Domingue and re-establish the order that existed there before." Personal letters had also arrived describing the size of forces that had already left for Saint-Domingue under the command of Leclerc, and the preparations for the mission that was to sail for Guadeloupe. Seeking allies, the *Conseil Provisoire* of Guadeloupe sent envoys to Leclerc, and took care to distinguish themselves from those who resisted the French in Saint-Domingue.[52] Yet for others in Guadeloupe, the example to emulate was that of the insurgents who were resisting French authorities in Saint-Domingue. The *Conseil Provisoire* declared that dangerous rumors were rampant in the colony, the most dangerous of which claimed that "Saint Domingue was resisting with success against the laws and orders of the metropole, and that Guadeloupe should follow this example." Those who spread these rumors were "a small number of men who in secret proclaim themselves partisans of Toussaint Louverture, and are tempted to imitate his guilty behavior." Many *cultivateurs* were deserting their plantations.[53]

These developments raised difficult questions of loyalty for members of the army. Among the officers, Ignace and Massoteau emerged as the most extreme advocates of an autonomy based on expulsion of whites from positions of authority and the arming of *cultivateurs* in preparation for the defense of Guadeloupe. A more moderate position was represented by Louis Delgrès who was not against the return of metropolitan authority in Guadeloupe, but wanted this return to be settled in a treaty that would stipulate certain conditions—including the maintenance of racial equality in the armed forces. He was wary of the actions of Lacrosse and other metropolitan authorities, and wanted to prepare for a defense of the island in order to be able to negotiate with metropolitan authorities from a position of strength. Pélage had named Delgrès commander of the important Fort St.-Charles in Basse-Terre. Delgrès, however, used this position against the *Conseil,* notably by opposing efforts by the local administration to arrest *cultivateurs* who had traveled to the towns and return them to their plantations.[54] Through the issue of the arrests, a group of leaders coalesced that later led the insurgency against Richepanse. They shared with many *cultivateurs* the concern that the *Conseil,* in being conciliatory towards the metropolitan authorities, was opening the way towards a reversal of the policies of racial equality.

Pélage clearly understood that there was a danger of an alliance between angry *cultivateurs* and soldiers. When in December 1801 six hundred armed *cultivateurs* outside Pointe-à-Pitre rose up on a series of plantations and entered into the town, instead of using the majority black troops to suppress the revolt, Pélage sent officers to make sure none of the soldiers entered the town. In fact, the insurgents were likely inspired to take action by officers from the army, and they expected that members of the army would join them when they entered the city. A few troops apparently did, briefly, take sides with the *cultivateurs,* but they were dispersed when Pélage led a troop of dragoons—who were mostly white and *de couleur*— against them. Fearful of stirring up more trouble, Pélage did not execute the three *cultivateurs* who led the insurrection, and instead had them deported from the colony.[55] Many *cultivateurs* seem to have been skeptical of Pélage's regime, and of the surrender he advocated, for when the time came, rather than follow the orders of the *Conseil,* they presented themselves in huge numbers to Delgrès and demanded weapons to fight the French.

A month later, when a white manager was killed on a plantation near Basse-Terre, Pélage oversaw the manhunt which tracked down the two domestic servants accused of having committed the crime. He also oversaw their execution, selecting a group of white and "colored" soldiers whose loyalty he trusted. On the day of the execution, "a multitude of *nègres cultivateurs* from the neighboring plantations" gathered to watch, as did soldiers from the garrison of Basse-Terre. The last man to be executed began speaking to the crowd, and "harangued the *nègres* in their idiom, and managed to make them pity his fate"; the soldiers of the firing squad, apparently fearing retribution, hesitated until Pélage intervened.[56] Throughout the next months, problems continued on plantations throughout the island. In Sainte-Rose, the local commissioner confronted *cultivateurs* who refused to work, and complained that "spiteful men have spread out through the countryside, tricking the *cultivateurs* by slandering the brave French of Europe whose arrival is announced, by making them think they are coming to attack their liberty."[57]

Pélage's position was weakened when a mission sent by the *Conseil* failed to make any headway with Lacrosse. In Pointe-à-Pitre, some members of the army were planning to take away the power from Pélage and the *Conseil Provisoire,* "and to form another government from which all the *blancs* would be excluded, and finally declare the colony independent." When a few officers in Basse-Terre responded joyfully to the (false) news of Lacrosse's imminent arrival, and suggested manning the Fort St.-Charles to greet him, Delgrès and Massoteau arrested and deported twelve suspected partisans of Lacrosse. *Cultivateurs,* "hearing of this movement, left their plantations and expanded the forces of the discontent," while in Pointe-à-Pitre soldiers and *cultivateurs* also began gathering. Pélage, fearing that arresting Massoteau and Delgrès would stir up more trouble, negotiated with them and eventually convinced them to leave the fort.[58] By the time of the arrival of the Richepanse expedition, then, an uneasy compromise had been reached between the various groups on the island. Pélage's policy of loyalty to the metropole still dominated among the political leaders on the island, who were determined to greet the French expedition with open arms. Despite a few attempts by Delgrès and other officers, no solid plan for immediate resistance to the French troops had been put into place. Many soldiers and *cultivateurs,* however, were prepared for an armed struggle. The arrival of Richepanse soon shattered the ambiguities of the situation.

A few weeks after the arrival of Richepanse's expedition in Guadeloupe, as fighting raged in the area surrounding Basse-Terre, the officer Palerme led a group of insurgents against a camp of French troops. Palerme's troop managed to close in on the camp because, when the advance sentinel of the camp called out "Qui vive?" they shouted "French Republicans!"[59] Palerme's group, many of whom had spent the previous years fighting the British, were not lying when they named themselves this way. Yet the arrival of Richepanse created a conflict over the meaning of that Republican project, and incited a battle within the ranks of the colonial army between loyalty to the French nation and loyalty to a Republican project that was no longer the project of that nation which had proclaimed it. The political splits in the army, and in the population, developed in the midst of confusion and in the context of rumor. The contradictions of the society created through eight years of freedom, which had first been expressed in a different way in the Lamentin revolt, exploded in a brutal conflict between Guadeloupean soldiers and *cultivateurs* and troops under the command of Richepanse.

The story of Richepanse's arrival in Guadeloupe contrasts sharply with the story of Leclerc's arrival in Saint-Domingue. There, Christophe refused to allow Leclerc to land without receiving orders from Toussaint Louverture, and initiated the first volley in the war that led to Haiti's independence when he set Le Cap on fire rather than hand it over to Leclerc intact.[60] In Guadeloupe, Pélage's administration greeted Richepanse with pomp and circumstance. The French troops, once in Pointe-à-Pitre, quickly began arresting black soldiers, and extensive resistance among the soldiers only developed after many troops had already been imprisoned. The insurgents of Guadeloupe therefore began fighting the French with a distinct disadvantage. Many soldiers and officers, notably Joseph Ignace, did manage to escape the French troops and made their way towards Basse-Terre, where they placed themselves under the command of Delgrès.[61] The soldiers were joined by *cultivateurs* who entered the town and demanded weapons. Consequently, despite their initial successes, the French troops encountered heavy resistance when they arrived in Basse-Terre. The Général Ménard later estimated that there had been approximately twelve thousand people fighting the French troops, of whom three thousand were soldiers who carried rifles.[62] The rest were *cultivateurs,* women and men, who fought fiercely with pikes and machetes. Throughout the region, small bands of men and women also attacked plantations, killing twenty-one whites in the region of Basse-Terre during the fighting. The difference in styles of warfare represented an important split within the ranks of the insurgents. While Delgrès occupied the Fort St.-Charles and used the tactics of traditional warfare, other groups of insurgents sought to incite large-scale insurrection and destruction of plantations as a means of driving the French troops from the island, and took up positions throughout the hills in the region of Basse-Terre.[63]

In a moment of imperial cooperation, the governor of Dominica provided ammunition for the French artillery, so the colonial troops of Guadeloupe were bombarded with British cannon balls fired out of French guns.[64] Pélage made the suggestion to Richepanse that in order to assure a victory he should release the black troops that had been imprisoned in Pointe-à-Pitre and use them to fight the insurgents. Richepanse agreed to this, and in the following days the colonial troops were released and "incorporated into the French battalions," which greatly strengthened Richepanse's position. With the support of the black troops, a number of plantations that had been held by the insurgents were taken over by the French troops, who slowly but surely surrounded the Fort St.-Charles.[65] After days of French bombardment, Delgrès decided to evacuate the fort. A group led by Ignace tried, but failed, to take Pointe-à-Pitre.[66] Delgrès, meanwhile, retreated up to the heights of Matouba, and took up a position on the Habitation d'Anglemont. Général Ménard later wrote that as the French approached Delgrès's position, "the unanimous cry of 'Live free or die!' that they constantly repeated, the care they took to remove the color white from their flag to represent their independence, all this announced that their position was desperate, and that their resistance would be terrible." On the flanks of the Soufrière volcano, the insurgents of Guadeloupe created the same flag that Dessalines, two years later, transformed into the flag of Haiti—the Republican tricolor with the white ripped out of it. Delgrès had mined the plantation at d'Anglemont, and as they French troops neared, he ordered the plantation blown up, ending the conflict with a mass suicide rather than surrender.[67]

Surrounded on all sides, the Republicans retreated to the mountains, to the old holdouts of the maroons. The clock was turned back as the regime of emancipation was dismantled and slavery was rebuilt. Mass executions and mass deportations awaited not only those who had resisted Richepanse, but eventually many who had stayed neutral in the conflict or even those, like Pélage and his officers, who had fought with the French. It is estimated that, in the course of the reestablishment of slavery, over ten thousand men and women were killed or deported.[68] But the stories of what happened in Guadeloupe crossed the waters to Saint-Domingue, unveiling the fate the French were planning for those soldiers who resisted them, and so helped initiate the last stage of the war for Haiti's independence. Officers such as Christophe and Dessalines, who had surrendered to Leclerc after the capture of Toussaint, switched sides once again. Leclerc wrote that he found himself in an untenable situation—"if my position has turned from good to critical, it is not only because of the yellow fever, but, as well, the premature re-establishment of slavery in Guadeloupe and the newspapers and letters from France that speak of nothing but slavery." In a letter written in August 1802, Leclerc again mentioned the disastrous effects of the news of the reestablishment of slavery in Guadeloupe, which he declared would cost his army and the colony "many men."[69]

After 1802, the fates of Guadeloupe and Saint-Domingue, united for eight years as part of a radical Republican project that reformulated the relationship between metropole and colony and transformed warfare and politics in the Caribbean, would be startlingly different. As Saint-Domingue emerged reborn as an independent Haiti, slavery was reconstructed in Guadeloupe, which would have to wait until 1848 for its abolition. It was only a century later, as part of the broad colonial reform of 1946, that the promise of the Revolution's policies of political integration was fulfilled as Guadeloupe became a department and its population was granted full rights as French citizens. It is no coincidence that soon afterwards the memory of those who fought against the reestablishment of slavery in 1802 began to be publicly rehabilitated in Guadeloupe. A small plaque was placed on the site of the Matouba plantation in 1948 honoring the memory of Delgrès "and his companions." In 1962, the Fort Richepanse—which had been so named at Lacrosse's request after the general's death from yellow fever in 1802— was given back its original name of Fort St.-Charles. Finally, in 1992, the writer Daniel Maximin, who had written a novel which touched on the re-establishment of slavery in Guadeloupe, and who at the time worked in Basse-Terre as Guadeloupe's regional director of cultural affairs, joined others in pushing for a new renaming. The commune of Basse-Terre had the right to rename its monuments, and so a decision was quickly made and put into effect in July 1989.[70]

Today, there are two new plaques inside the fort. One presents a chronology of the fort, which includes the actions of Delgrès. The other, also mounted in bronze, presents the last letter written by Delgrès (known from the work of Auguste Lacour), a passionate plea for racial equality and an end to slavery, addressed in strongly Republican language to "The Entire Universe." During the 1998 commemorations of the abolition of slavery in 1848, a plaque commemorating Delgrès was placed, next to one for Toussaint Louverture, in the crypt of Victor Schoelcher, as both of them were thanked by government officials for having fought the French state in defense of the principles of the Republic. For some activists in Guadeloupe today, Delgrès still stands as an inspiration for the fight for independence they see as vital for the dignity of the island. For others, his history is a reminder of the important part Antilleans played in the broader struggle for the end of slavery within the French Republic. As Guadeloupeans experience their contradictory place in the broader French Republic at the end of the twentieth century, the history of the end of the eighteenth century remains a touchstone for debates about the future in ways that highlight the continuing impact of the history of the years of conflict that created Haiti and transformed the Greater Caribbean.

NOTES

My thanks go to all the participants in the conference on the Impact of the Haitian Revolution in the Atlantic World, particularly Robin Blackburn, Rosemary Brana-Schute, David Brion Davis, Seymour Drescher, Marixa Lasso, Randy Sparks, and of course David Geggus, whose ideas and reactions helped me prepare the final version of this essay.

1. Hugues and Lebas to Minister, 24 Nivôse An 6 (13 Jan. 1798), Archives Nationales Section d'Outre-mer, Aix-en-Provence (hereafter ANSOM), C7A 50, fols. 4–11.

2. Testimony of Benjamin and Augustin taken 31 Dec. 1801, ANSOM, C7A 50, fols. 223–24, 227–28.

3. Testimony of Benjamin, Augustin, Moco and the fragment from another testimony, ANSOM, C7A 50, fols. 223–30. The Lestier Ravine Chaude plantation was the small-

est of three plantations owned by Lestier before emancipation. There was no manager residing on the coffee plantation, which was run by a *cultivateur*. See the "Etat nominatif . . . Lamentin," 1 Vendémiaire An 5 (21 Sept. 1796), ANSOM, G1 500, #12.

4. See above, n. 1.

5. Hugues and Lebas to Minister, 24 Nivôse An 6 (13 Jan. 1798), ANSOM, C7A 50, fols. 8–11. On the attack see also the testimony of Moco, Augustin, and the fragment in ANSOM, C7A 50, fols. 225–30.

6. See above, n. 1.

7. A good picture of the conflict between plantation managers and the central administration is provided in "Le Citoyen Jastram, Député de la Guadeloupe au Conseil des Cinq Cents, à ses concitoyens," in Archives Nationales, Paris (hereafter AN), AD VII 21C, #57.

8. "Les Commissaires Délégués au Ministre de la Marine et des Colonies," 4 Brumaire An 6 (25 Oct. 1797), ANSOM C7A 49, 228–29. I provide a detailed account of Hugues' regime, and of the social impact it had in Guadeloupe in "'The Price of Liberty': Victor Hugues and the Administration of Freedom in Guadeloupe, 1794–1798," *William and Mary Quarterly* 3rd series, 56:2 (Apr. 1999): 363–92. For an account of the political conflicts in Guadeloupe in the years leading up to 1794, see Anne Pérotin-Dumon, *Etre patriote sous les tropiques* (Basseterre, Guadeloupe: Société d'histoire de la Guadeloupe, 1984). For a general study of the whole period see Henri Bangou, *La Révolution et l'esclavage à la Guadeloupe, 1789–1802 : Epopée noire et génocide* (Paris : Messidor, 1989).

9. For Laveaux's formulation, see the *Discours prononcé par Laveaux, sur l'anniversaire du 16 Pluviôse An 2* (Paris: Corps Législatif, 1798), [Bibliothèque Nationale]. For a more detailed version of the events I describe in this article, and the broader shift in colonial policy during the period 1798–1802, see part 3 of my dissertation, "A Colony of Citizens: Revolution and Slave Emancipation in the French Caribbean, 1789–1802" (Ph.D. diss., University of Michigan, 1998). On colonial policy during the Directory regime in France (1795–1799), see Bernard Gainot, "La constitutionalisation de la liberté générale sous le Directoire," in *Les Abolitions de l'esclavage de L.F. Sonthonax à V. Schoelcher, 1793, 1794, 1848,* ed. Marcel Dorigny (Paris: Presses Universitaires de Vincennes, 1995), 213–29

10. See above, n. 1.

11. Hugues and Lebas to the Minister, 17 Ventôse An 5 (6 Mar. 1797), AN, AF III 209, Dossier 954, #8.

12. See above, n. 1. Hugues wrote in his letter that Toussaint Louverture was little more than the instrument of Julien Raimond, who had masterminded the plot to deport Sonthonax in order to place the *gens de couleur* in power. Sonthonax, who had the "audacity to be the first to proclaim liberty" in Saint-Domingue, had been proven wrong by the events; his policy of favoring the *gens de couleur* had turned against him.

13. Desfourneaux to Minister, 23 Frimaire An 7 (13 Dec. 1798), AN, AF III 209, Dossier 954, #10; below, n. 14.

14. Desfourneaux to Minister, 25 Frimaire An 7 (15 Dec. 1798), AN, AF III 209, Dossier 954, #22.

15. The term *chouan* was used in metropolitan France, particularly during 1793 and 1794, to describe royalist insurgents from the Vendée. See the Deposition of Fizeller, 14 Frimaire An 7 (4 Dec. 1798), AN, AF III 209, Dossier 954, #57.

16. "Extrait des régistres des arrêtés de l'agent particulier," 18 Nivôse An 7 (7 Jan. 1799), AF III 209, Dossier 954 #53.

17. Deposition of Duvergé, 12 Frimaire An 7 (2 Dec. 1798), AN, AF III 209, Dossier 954, #54. The same speech was witnessed by another man who noted that the speakers "seemed to have a great influence on all those who surrounded them," as they argued that "the point of their mission was to take freedom away from the negroes and to put them back

in the state they were in before the arrival of Citizen Hugues." See the deposition of Duchamps, 13 Frimaire An 7 (3 Dec. 1798), AN, AF III 209, Dossier 954, #55.

18. Deposition of Duchesne, 13 Frimaire An 7 (3 Dec. 1798), AN, AF III 209, Dossier 954, #56.

19. Deposition of Lambert Mauther, Frimaire An 7 (Dec. 1798), AN, AF III 209, Dossier 954, #58.

20. Deposition of Ignace, AN, AF III 209, Dossier 954, #61.

21. Copy of letter sent to the publisher Cabre, of Basse-Terre, and intercepted, in AN, AF III 209, Dossier 954, #62.

22. See the various letters about the case in ANSOM, C7A 51, fols. 77–80.

23. Deposition of Pierre Metro, 5 Nivôse An 7 (25 Dec. 1798), AN, AF III 209, Dossier 954, #59.

24. Deposition of Citoyen Beaugendre, 15 Nivôse An 7 (4 Jan. 1799), AN, AF III 209, Dossier 954, #60.

25. "Jugement rendu au Conseil de Guerre," Basse-Terre, 4 Germinal An 7, (24 Mar. 1799) ANSOM, C7A 51, fols. 46–48. For Azor, who was described in his wedding as "from the coast," which at that time meant from Africa, see ANSOM, EC Basse-Terre 9, #60, 5 Floréal An 5 (24 Apr. 1797). The accused soldiers were part of the battalion that had originally been formed by Hugues to bring together metropolitan and colonial soldiers; for a history of this battalion see Roland Anduse, "L'histoire singulière du 1er Bataillon de l'armée de la Guadeloupe: loyalisme révolutionnaire et révoltes militaires" in Martin and Yacou, eds., *Mourir pour les Antilles: Indépendance négre ou esclavage, 1802–1804* (Paris: Editions Caribéennes, 1991), 57–64.

26. "Jugement rendu par le Conseil de guerre," Basse-Terre, 15 Germinal An 7 (4 Apr. 1799), ANSOM, C7A 51, fols. 49–54. Many others were also implicated in the "conspiracy."

27. Desfourneaux to Ministre, 21 Germinal An 7 (10 Apr. 1799), ANSOM, C7A 51, fols. 42–43.

28. See the "Mémoire du Général Paris sur les événements qui ont eu lieu à la Guadeloupe dans le mois de Vendémiaire An 8," (Oct. 1799), 18 Fructidor An 9 (5 Sept. 1801), in ANSOM, C7A 51, fols. 115–19 and the attached documents in 120–27.

29. See the Report of Général Pélardy, 18 Vendémiaire An 10 (10 Oct. 1801), ANSOM, C7A 55, fols. 207–9.

30. For the naming of the new delegates, see the "Rapport au Directoire from the Ministre de la Marine et des Colonies," 17 Thermidor An 7 (4 Aug. 1799), ANSOM, C7A 51, fols. 174–79. On the expulsion of Laveaux, see Agents to Minister, 28 Ventôse An 8 (19 Mar. 1800), ANSOM, C7A 52, fols. 86–87; for Baco's comments see his letter to the Consul, 4 Thermidor An 8 (23 July 1800), ANSOM, C7A 52, fols. 115–18. For the plots, see "Jugement rendu par le Conseil de Guerre Permanent," 11 Floréal An 8 (1 May 1800), ANSOM, C7A 53, f. 299; Agents to Minister, 7 Messidor An 8 (26 June 1800), ANSOM, C7A 52, f. 94.

31. Agents to Minister, 3 Vendémiaire An 9 (25 Sept. 1800), ANSOM, C7A 52, f. 142.

32. See Hypolite de Frasans, *Mémoire pour le chef de Brigade Magloire Pélage et pour les habitants de la Guadeloupe,* 2 vols. (Paris: Desenne, An XI [1803]), 1:60.

33. For Pélage, see Frasans, *Mémoire,* 1:51–52, 53–55; see also Pélage's letter to Bonaparte, and the attached documents, in ANSOM, C7A 56, fols. 258–56. For more details on the career of Pélage, see Jacques Adélaïde-Merlande, *Delgrès: la Guadeloupe en 1802* (Paris: Karthala, 1986), 89–93. On Delgrès's participation in the 1792 election, see "Procès verbal de l'élection de l'assemblée électorale des députés pour la Martinique et la Guadeloupe," 28 Oct. 1792, AN, C181, f. 86. For biographical sketches of Delgrès, see Adélaïde-Merlande, *Delgrès,* 9–10; see also Germain Saint-Ruf, *L'Epopée Delgrès: La Guadeloupe sous la Révolution Française, 1789–1802* (Paris: Harmattan, 1977).

34. See below, n. 35; Frasans, *Mémoire*, 1:59–60. On Frontin's connections to the other officers, see the wedding in couleur," see ANSOM, EC Basse-Terre 6 (5Mi140) #34, 1 Messidor An 4 (19 June 1796).

35. "Abrégé historique des événements arrivés à la Guadeloupe pendant le mois de Prairial An 9," in ANSOM, C7A 55, 279–82.

36. In Trois-Rivières, the widow of Coquille Dugommier returned and took back the property left behind by her husband nearly a decade before. Dugommier, clearly, was thinking towards the future when she noted in particular that though four *cultivateurs* had been absent from the plantation for a long time, she knew where they were and intended to "preserve all her rights" over them. See Archives Départementales de la Guadeloupe, Dupuch 2E2/26, 14 Fructidor An 9 (1 Sept. 1801).

37. Frasans, *Mémoire*, 1:71–74. Auguste Lacour, *Histoire de la Guadeloupe* (Basse-Terre: Imprimerie du Gouvernement, 1858) 1:119–20. Lacour's text, a foundational work on the history of Guadeloupe, is indispensable for this period. Although many of the documents he used (which he unfortunately does not give references for) can still be found in the archives, others seem to have been destroyed. Lacour was also able to interview participants in the events of the 1790s.

38. Général Gobert to Minister, 21 Vendémiaire An 11 (13 Oct. 1802), in ANSOM, C7A 57, fols. 63–69.

39. See the *arrêté* in ANSOM, C7A 55, f. 43.

40. Lacour, *Histoire de la Guadeloupe*, 3:121, 126.

41. Lacrosse to Minister, 14 Fructidor An 9 (1 Sept.1801) in ANSOM, C7A 55, fols. 95–98.

42. Frasans, *Mémoire*, 1:79–87; for Lagarde's connections with other officers, notably Corbet, as well as with important leaders such as Canut Robinson, see the weddings in ANSOM, EC Basse-Terre 6, #39, 1 Floréal An 3 (20 May 1795) and in EC Basse-Terre 9, #6, 18 Brumaire An 5 (9 Nov. 1796).

43. Frasans, *Mémoire*, 1:94–99. According to Lacrosse, the list of the accused was a fake; see the "Liste des hommes tant blancs que de couleur qui ont le plus figurés dans l'insurrection de la Guadeloupe," ANSOM, C7A 55, fols. 269–78.

44. Auguste Lacour, *Histoire de la Guadeloupe* 3:141. For a description of the insurrection, see 3:129–33.

45. Frasans, *Mémoire*, 1:94–110.

46. Frasans, *Mémoire*, 1:110–23.

47. Lacrosse to Minister, 26 Frimaire An 10 (17 Dec. 1801) in ANSOM, C7A 55, fols. 102–5.

48. For the composition of the *Conseil* see the "Série de questions" in ANSOM, C7A 55, 253–56 and the "Etat nominatif de 43 individus . . . prévenus d'être auteurs ou complices de la révolte . . . contre le Capitaine Général Lacrosse," in ANSOM, C7A 55, fols. 285–86. On 28 October 1801, the *Conseil* sent a "Précis des événements" which was the first draft in a series of accounts that would eventually lead to Frasans' detailed 1805 *Mémoire*. See "Précis des événements . . . adressé aux Consuls, au Ministre de la Marine et des Colonies, et à nos Concitoyens de la Métropole," 6 Brumaire An 10 (28 Oct. 1801) in ANSOM, C7A 55, fols. 123–38.

49. For François Rigaud's presence in Guadeloupe, see Lacour, *Histoire*, 3:153–54. According to Lacour, Rigaud had been exiled from Saint-Domingue after his brother's defeat, and was among the *hommes de couleur* imprisoned by Lacrosse and released by a crowd after his expulsion. Lacour claims that François Rigaud used his experience to argue in favor of independence, but André Rigaud's alliance with the metropolitan commissioner Hédouville and his continued loyalty to metropolitan regimes makes this scenario somewhat

unlikely. I thank David Geggus for pointing out the possibility of the influence of Rigaud, and more generally the news about the fate of *hommes de couleur* in Saint-Domingue, on Pélage. On the war between Louverture and Rigaud, see Carolyn Fick, *The Making of Haiti: The Saint-Domingue Revolution from Below* (Knoxville: University of Tennessee Press, 1990).

50. Lacour, *Histoire,* 169–70.

51. Lacour, *Histoire,* 182. At the time, Lacrosse described how he and his colleagues (including Daniel Lescallier) had sent an envoy with news of the preliminaries of the peace to Guadeloupe in the hope that this would bring them back to order. Instead, however, soldiers in Guadeloupe "refused to believe" the British officer sent with the news, and mistreated him. See the "Manifeste" of 14 Frimaire An X (5 Dec. 1802) in ANSOM, C7A 55, f. 101.

52. Frasans, *Mémoire,* 1:252–53; above, n.50. Leclerc responded to the correspondence from Guadeloupe by sending two hundred soldiers, who arrived after the Richepanse expedition; see *Mémoire,* 2:332–33.

53. The "circulaire" was issued on 15 Germinal An 10 (5 Apr. 1802), and is located in ANSOM, C7A 55, fols. 119–20. According to the *Mémoire* of Frasans, "it was greatly to be feared that these deserters, these runaways, would follow the example of this too-famous rebel"—Toussaint Louverture. See Frasans, *Mémoire,* 1:256–57. See also Lacour, *Histoire,* 3:153–54.

54. Lacour, *Histoire,* 3:166–67.

55. Lacour, *Histoire,* 3:188–89.

56. Frasans, *Mémoire,* 1:207–9.

57. Riffaud to the *Conseil Provisoire,* Sainte-Rose, 22 Ventôse An 10 (13 Mar. 1802), in Frasans, *Mémoire,* 2:277–78; see also 1:254.

58. Frasans, *Mémoire,* 1:227–33.

59. Ménard's report, 18, in ANSOM, C7A 57, fols. 21–37.

60. Fick, *The Making of Haiti,* 210–12.

61. For the troops' arrival, see Général Ménard's report, ANSOM, C7A 57, fols. 21–27, and Gobert's "Particularités non-publiques sur la guerre de la Guadeloupe," sent to the minister on 22 Nov. 1802, in ANSOM, C7A 57, fols. 70–74. See also Frasans, *Mémoire,* 1:265–72 and Lacour, *Histoire,* 3:241–43, and Adélaïde-Merlande, *Delgrès.* Richepanse's report is reprinted in Frasans, *Mémoire,* 2:341–44. In Basse-Terre, a young white creole from Martinique, Monnereau, wrote a proclamation for the rebels that was signed by Delgrès and distributed in the town. The letter, addressed "to the entire Universe" expressed a certainty that the imprisonments taking place in Pointe-à-Pitre signaled the first step in a reenslavement of Guadeloupeans. See Lacour, *Histoire,* 3:253–55. The source of this proclamation, which has become one of the most famous documents in Guadeloupean history, is not identified by Lacour, and as far as I know there is no archival document that corresponds to the text.

62. Lacour, *Histoire,* 3:273–77; Ménard, 8, in ANSOM, C7A 57, fols. 21–37.

63. Lacour, *Histoire,* 3:301–6. See also Bernard Moitt, "Slave Resistance in Guadeloupe and Martinique, 1791–1848," *Journal of Caribbean History* 25 (1991): 136–59.

64. Ménard, 19–20, in ANSOM, C7A 57, fols. 21–37.

65. Frasans, *Mémoire,* 1:284–87.

66. Ménard, 21–24, in ANSOM, C7A 57, fols. 21–37. For a detailed account of Ignace's march, see Roland Anduse, *Joseph Ignace: Le premier rebelle* (Paris: Editions Jasor, 1989), 261–74.

67. Ménard, 28–30, in ANSOM, C7A, fols. 21–37. See also Adélaïde-Merlande, *Delgrès,* 149.

68. Jacques Adélaïde-Merlande, "Lendemains de Baimbridge et Matouba: 'Coureurs de bois et brigands," in Michel Martin and Alain Yacou, eds. *Mourir pour les Antilles:*

Indépendance nègre ou esclavage, 1802–1804 (Paris: Editions Caribbéennes, 1991), 203–10. See also Josette Fallope, *Esclaves et citoyens: les noirs de la Guadeloupe au XIX siècle* (Basse-Terre: Société d'Histoire de la Guadeloupe, 1992), 49–52. Pélage and the members of his *Conseil Provisoire* were put on trial but eventually acquitted; Pélage continued to fight in the French army in Europe until his death in 1813. See Lacour, *Histoire,* 3:350.

69. *Lettres du Général Leclerc,* ed. Paul Roubier, (Paris: Ernest Leroux, 1937), 201–6 and 253–59; see also generally Fick, *The Making of Haiti,* 215–22 and C. L. R. James, *The Black Jacobins* (New York: Vintage, 1963), 344–45, which provide the English translations I have used.

70. For more on the memory of Delgrès, see my "Haunting Delgrès," *Radical History Review* 78 (2000): 166–77.

Chapter 10

"A Black French General Arrived to Conquer the Island"

Images of the Haitian Revolution in Cuba's 1812
Aponte Rebellion

MATT D. CHILDS

ON 24 MARCH 1812 CUBAN MILITARY officer Vicente de la Huerta and three assistants left the fortress of La Cabaña in Havana, crossed the harbor, and headed for the predominantly free colored neighborhood called Guadalupe located just outside the city walls. Huerta and his aides had been ordered by Cuban judicial official Juan Ignacio Rendón to search houses "with the greatest thoroughness" for possible clues to a series of slave revolts that had erupted across the island in Bayamo, Holguín, Puerto Príncipe, and Havana during the last two months.[1] A week earlier, Rendón had received a special commission from the captain general of Cuba to "rapidly and promptly" find the leaders of the insurrections and end the terrifying panic voiced by the white population throughout the island.[2]

The first revolt had occurred two months earlier, near the east-central city of Puerto Príncipe. Military forces there quickly suppressed the rebellion, but not before five whites had been killed. Colonial officials responded to the bold challenge to their authority by staging a public execution. A crowd of spectators greeted with "enthusiasm" the execution of twelve slaves, and the shipment of sixty-three prisoners to St. Augustine, Florida.[3] Shortly after the suppression of the revolt, authorities reported several "black bandits" had escaped to the mountains where they planned to spread their "terrible movement" to the eastern cities of Bayamo and Holguín.[4] Rumors of a rebel slave invasion caused colonial officials to move women from the countryside to the cities, arm two hundred extra militia men, and vigorously question slaves on several plantations.[5] With the aid of a slave informer, the authorities prevented the uprising from occurring.[6] Despite the captain general's assurance in February that the "rebellions had been suppressed," a month later, slaves rose again.[7] This time, however, the revolts erupted not in the interior

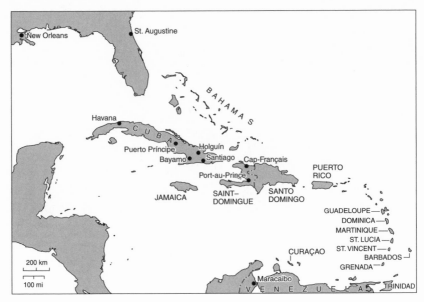

MAP 10.1: The West Indies

of the island, but "on the outskirts of the capital." As with the rebellion in Puerto Príncipe, Spanish officials quickly suppressed the rebellion and immediately questioned all those involved to calm "the public outcry."[8]

Information obtained from the interrogations of several individuals implicated in the plantation uprisings led Huerta and his assistants to the house of the free *moreno* (black) José Antonio Aponte, who had been arrested on 19 March 1812.[9] When officials arrived at Aponte's house, they discovered the door locked. Huerta forced Aponte's son Cayetano to unlock the door for authorities to search the house. Once inside, Huerta and his assistants ransacked the house for items that could serve as evidence of Aponte's role in the rebellions. Huerta discovered that Aponte's house doubled as a workshop where he earned his living as a sculptor. Many of Cuba's free and slave artisans resided in Aponte's neighborhood, where they dominated several of the skilled trades required of a bustling Atlantic port city in the early nineteenth century. Huerta also found evidence of Aponte's military background as captain of the *moreno* militia of Havana, including handwritten copies of three royal decrees spelling out the rights and benefits that members of the *moreno* militia received. Other evidence the authorities collected included items they associated with the African fraternal society of the Lucumí *cabildo,* over which, some say, Aponte presided as head official.[10]

In particular, authorities were looking for what several of the arrested conspirators had described as a *libro de pinturas* (book of paintings). Vicente de la Huerta found a "book of various plans and drawings, hidden with clothes in a dresser."[11] The book of drawings contained maps of streets and military garrisons in Cuba; depictions of black soldiers defeating whites; sketches of Aponte's father, grandfather, and King Carlos III; a drawing of George Washington; portraits of black kings from Abyssinia; and episodes in Aponte's own life. Most terrifying to Cuban authorities were reports that portraits of the Haitian revolutionary leaders Henri Christophe, Toussaint Louverture, Jean-François, and Jean-Jacques Dessalines could be found in Aponte's house. As Cuban officials investigated the rebellion, they learned that Aponte routinely showed the book to members of the free colored militia, at the *cabildo* meetings regularly held in his house, as well as to others such as the free *moreno* shoemaker Melchor Acosta.[12] Authorities concluded that the book of drawings represented a blueprint for revolution, and that Aponte used the book to illustrate and explain his plans for the rebellion. Huerta took Aponte's *libro de pinturas* and the other items recovered from his house back to La Cabaña where they provided the basis for the repeated interrogations of numerous individuals allegedly involved in what would become known as the Aponte Rebellion of 1812.[13]

Aponte was not unique among individuals who took careful notice of the historical events on the neighboring island of Hispaniola. The only successful slave revolt in human history, that enabled Cuba to capture the leading role in the world sugar market from Saint-Domingue and redirected a major tributary of the Atlantic slave trade from Hispaniola to Cuba, provided contrasting images of fear and fascination for different sectors of Cuban society. The Haitian Revolution brought to fruition dreams of wealth and extravagance for Cuban planters, but also their nightmares of an apocalyptic demise at the hands of the same slaves who filled their bank accounts. For slaves, the success of the Haitian Revolution resulted in expanding the living nightmare of human bondage throughout the island, while it encouraged many slaves to put into action their risky dreams of ending slavery through rebellion. The Haitian Revolution became a contentious point of reference around which masters and slaves defined their relationships with each other, and by extension, how they defined themselves. This essay uses the lens of the Aponte Rebellion and its documentary record to examine how images of Haiti became inseparable from ideas of slave resistance in Cuba.

While masters, slaves, and free people of color in Cuba recognized the powerful symbol of the Haitian revolution in igniting insurrection, scholars have yet to reach a consensus. Historians contributing to this collection and elsewhere share David Brion Davis's conviction that the Haitian revolution "marked a turning point in the history of New World slavery," yet disagree on for what and for whom. Eugene Genovese has shaped the scholarly debate by arguing the Haitian Revolution brought about a decisive change in the history of slave revolts from maroon runaways who rebelled against enslavement to revolutionary movements aimed at societal reorganization through the destruction of slavery as a system. Michael Craton and Michael Mullin recognize the qualitative change in slave resistance during the Age of Revolution from runaways to revolution, but argue the shift is a result of the dual process of closing the frontier and the demographic shift in the slave population from African to Creole. David Geggus has presented a systematic and detailed assessment of the Haitian revolution on rebellions, concluding abolitionism, not the ideology of the French and Haitian revolutions, most frequently stimulated rebellion. Moreover, Geggus argues the most receptive audience to the ideology of natural rights was not slaves, but free people of color. Julius Scott has examined slave revolts in the 1790s, concluding that the Haitian Revolution represented "A Common Wind" that connected rebels across national, linguistic, ethnic, and geographic boundaries in their shared resistance to slavery.[14] Robert Paquette has strongly suggested that divisions between African and Creole forms of resistance or drawing minute distinctions between abolitionist and French Revolutionary ideology "simply will not do" because "African-born slave and American-born slaves, privileged slaves and field hands, blacks and mulattoes, slaves and free people of color, slave men and slave women could at a specific historical moment under a common experience of oppression come together to attack a common target."[15] The Aponte Rebellion offers a critical case to analyze the debated role of the Haitian revolution in catalyzing slave revolts and assess if the great insurrection represented a turning point in Cuban slavery. The divergent reactions to the Haitian Revolution illustrate the uneasy social tensions that accompanied the rapid expansion of slavery in Cuba.

In the two decades following the Haitian Revolution, Cuban society underwent radical social, cultural, and economic changes. Although Cuba began to develop as a "classic" sugar plantation colony during the brief English occupation of 1762, both contemporaries and historians have tended to date the transformation of Cuban society by slavery to the 1790s.[16] Spanish officials clearly understood how the "slave insurrection on the French part of the island of Santo Domingo offered the means to develop the agriculture and crops of the island of Cuba."[17] Francisco Arango y Parreño, a spokesman for the planter class and the individual most responsible for gaining royal concessions to expand slavery and sugar production, argued that it was "necessary to look" at the "slave revolt in the French dominion of the island of Santo Domingo . . . with political eyes. . . to give our agriculture in the islands, advantage and superiority over the French."[18] For Cuban planters, the key to exploiting the "advantage" offered by the Haitian Revolution was slave labor.

For aspiring sugar planters, economic success depended on slavery, yet slaves also embodied their possible ruin, as had occurred in neighboring Haiti.[19] But Cuban elites could think of no other way to organize their economy, and repeatedly petitioned the Spanish crown to protect slaveowner interests by opening the slave trade to all competing nations.[20] The Havana *consulado,* an economic and judicial institution that represented slaveholder interests in commerce, reported to the captain general of Cuba that "slaves are their most important instrument for agriculture."[21] From 1790 to 1821, over 240,000 Africans arrived in Havana destined for a life of slavery.[22] Francisco Arango y Parreño remarked that "we can say with all frankness that the free introduction [of slaves] has allowed us to prosper."[23] Sugar and coffee plantations expanded across the island throughout the nineteenth century, fueled by the Atlantic slave trade that transported enslaved Africans to Cuba until 1867. By the 1840s, Cuba had become the world's primary producer of sugar, and the slave population exceeded the white for the first time in the island's history.

In addition to the dramatic increase in slaves imported to Havana after the Haitian Revolution, other migrants landed on Cuban shores. In the 1790s and 1800s thousands of French *émigrés* fleeing the slave insurrection that had engulfed the colony arrived in Cuba, settling mainly in the eastern part of the island.[24] Cuban slaveholders and colonial authorities expressed their "compassion" for the *émigrés,* promising to "cry perpetually" about the revolution on the nearby island.[25] The empathy of Cuban elites allowed French colonialists such as Juan Bautista Jagay to bring their slaves to Cuba and purchase land for a sugar plantation.[26] By 1808 the French *émigré* population in Santiago numbered 7,449 refugees, while nearly a thousand lived in Havana, with many others spread throughout the island.[27] Cuban officials also extended refuge to mulatto *émigrés* such as Francisco Ramón Labatitant and Pedro Viginet whom they believed could cause "no harm in any case," but rather contribute "useful work . . . performed with reputation and honor as a carpenter and a mason."[28] Cuba continued to accept many of the exiles from the Haitian Revolution until 1808, when Napoleon invaded Spain. Shortly thereafter, anti-French sentiment spread throughout the island, resulting in the expulsion of thousands of French men, women, and children, and their resettlement in places such as Jamaica, Charleston, New York, Philadelphia, and most notably New Orleans, which received over nine thousand French migrants from Cuba.[29] To Cuba's white population, the arrival in the 1790s and 1800s of thousands of French *émigrés* offered an ominous reminder of the potential dangers of relying on slave labor.[30]

If the daily presence of French refugees and their slaves provoked uneasy feelings among Cuban planters, requests by military leaders of the Haitian Revolution for arms and ammunition caused grave concern. French military officials battling the slave insurrection in Saint-Domingue often sought refuge and supplies in Cuba's nearby harbors.[31] More alarming to Cuban authorities, however, was a letter by Miguel de Arambarri, a subaltern to Toussaint Louverture, to Captain General Someruelos requesting "twenty thousand rifles . . . in order to arm volunteers" to battle the British. In exchange, Louverture offered to help Spain reconquer Jamaica. The "special agent" wrote that "General Toussaint and I have at our command troops accustomed to defeating all of the obstacles . . . of war." Arambarri urged Someruelos to act immediately, insisting that "it is not necessary to wait for orders from the King of Spain when there was such a beautiful occasion to strike the enemy of humankind."[32] As a loyal servant of the Spanish crown, Someruelos quickly responded that he could "not and will not authorize any expedition without the blessing of the King."[33] Haitian leaders also sought aid from Cuba to pursue the internal wars of the revolution that pitted Rigaud against Louverture. Rigaud requested arms and money from Someruelos to fight his archrival.[34] Military requests by Louverture and Rigaud starkly illustrated how radically the Caribbean and Atlantic worlds had changed during the era of the Haitian Revolution. A former slave and a mulatto goldsmith had become political power brokers among the major European powers.

The deep and permanent impressions caused by the Haitian Revolution in Cuban society forced colonial officials to confront the question they sought most to avoid: Could Cuba become another Haiti? Arango y Parreño confessed that "the unfortunate effects of the slave revolt in the colony of Guarico [Saint-Domingue] have persuaded us to examine the event" to "discover the origin and causes of the catastrophe."[35] Captain General Someruelos reported that "the circumstances of said island [Hispaniola] are very delicate and critical, and it is necessary for the governments of the neighboring islands to take the necessary precautions" to prevent repeated rebellions.[36] Cuban elites felt compelled to explain the causes of the Haitian Revolution in order to assure themselves that they could avert the fate of the neighboring French colony. Slaveowners and colonial authorities eased their anxiety about the expansion of slavery by developing a two-fold argument explaining that what happened in Haiti would not happen in Cuba. First, they insisted, Cuba could be effectively isolated from the ideological contagion of revolt. And second, Cuban slaves would not rebel against their masters because civil law, religion, master benevolence, and demographics would not engender the same conditions for revolt.

The most obvious way to prevent slaves emulating the example of the Haitian Revolution involved preventing the transmission of any news about the successful revolt. On 15 January 1796, Cuban Captain General Luis de las Casas issued a proclamation that "prohibited the entrance of slaves to ports of the island that were not *bozales* [slaves born in Africa] brought from the coast of Africa." Furthermore, any "slaves from the French colonies imported after the month of August of 1790" had to be "withdrawn from the island in the span of three months."[37] After slave revolts erupted in the British Caribbean, the captain general extended the expulsion of French slaves brought to Cuba after August 1790 to human cargo from the English islands imported after 1794.[38] "Extra vigilance" against the "clandestine introduction" of French slaves by smugglers had already resulted in the "apprehension of several individuals and jail sentences." In 1800, Las Casas' successor Someruelos optimistically suggested that "by these measures" they could evade "the contagion."[39]

Cuban officials clearly understood that it was not slaves alone who spread news of the Haitian Revolution. Not only did the refugees who settled in Cuba bring stories of the slave insurrection, but so did black and mulatto veterans of the war who attempted to settle on the island. In 1796, Jean-François, the leader of the 1791 revolt on Saint-Domingue's northern plain, began a life of exile. Although denied permission to settle permanently in Cuba, four years later Someruelos believed that "some of the division from Santo Domingo of the caudillo Juan Francisco still lived" on the island. Any of Jean-François' troops remaining in Cuba would be "expelled from the island" for the "ease with which they could cause distrust, hide themselves, and much more in this country."[40] Ten years later, Someruelos again rejected the request of Jean-François' troops to settle in Cuba with their families after living in Cádiz, Spain, because "they should not be trusted for the notions they bring from their country of origin."[41] Although prevented from settling permanently in Cuba, Jean-François and his troops left a long-lasting impression on the slaves and free people of color that later played an important role in the Aponte Rebellion.

Even as they tried to stave off rebellion by preventing the spread of information about the Haitian Revolution, planters tried to calm their own fears by arguing that slaves would not rise in revolt because Cuba was an entirely different colony from Saint-Domingue. Spokesman for the planter class Francisco Arango y Parreño attempted to assure fellow Cubans that the cause of the uprising in Haiti was the consequence of the awful "slave treatment" at the hands of the "French who regarded slaves as beasts, while the Spanish see them as men." According to Arango y Parreño, Cubans need not fear their slaves who were "the happiest in the world" as a result of "civil laws perfectly balancing the two extremes of the abuse of owners and the subordination of slaves."[42] The *consulado* of Havana echoed Arango y Parreño 's laudatory remarks: "We are fortunate to have a slave code, written with more humanity than those of foreigners, providing slaves with the aid of religion, and opening the doors to manumission."[43] Such self-congratulatory remarks notwithstanding, the rigors of sugar cane production and the accompanying twenty-hour work days during the harvest season rendered the effects of such laws and institutions designed to curb master authority negligible, and the treatment of slaves in Cuba and Saint-Domingue strikingly similar.[44]

Cuban officials found confidence in correctly pointing out that some of the causes of the Haitian insurgency stemmed from the turbulent uprising in France. The *consulado* concluded that "whoever knows the origin of the republican revolution in France, knows that the discord born in the metropolis over political opinions resulted in a war between the rich and the poor, and this same principle is what stripped the slaveowners of Guarico of their dominion over slaves by a declaration of liberty for four hundred thousand slaves."[45] Arango y Parreño argued that French "masters had taught their servants" about the French Revolution, "and by their own hands they had built their own ruin. Authors of anarchy should not complain."[46] By blaming the slave insurrection on the politics of the French Revolution, Cuban slaveowners avoided considering that the slaves' own desire for freedom accounted for the Haitian Revolution. Since the slave revolt merely reflected revolutionary politics and "anarchy" in far away Europe, Cuban planters denied that their slaves held similar aspirations for liberation and would risk rebellion to attain it.

Influential Cubans also concluded that the ability of slaves to stage a successful revolt rested on their demographic superiority to whites. The bishop of Havana advocated the use of slave labor for the development of Cuban agriculture. "They will work but only with the fear of the stick always raised above their backs, and if this disappears for one moment, work will be interrupted." The bishop warned that if the "island of Cuba were to reach with the aid of these arms the degree of wealth of the French part of Santo Domingo," where "sugar plantations counted more than a thousand slaves," there would be a "terrible and equal eruption."[47] In order to prevent a demographic situation similar to Haiti, Cuban planters became "census watchers," warning against the massive importation of slaves. In 1794, the publication of the Creole planter class, *Memorias de la Sociedad Económica,* recognized the danger unrestricted slave imports posed to the white planter class:

Before the calamitous ruin of the Colony of Saint-Domingue, and before the horrible destruction and unheard-of crimes committed there by the Negroes were known, the first thing that came to mind when the development of our island [Cuba] was discussed was the free and unlimited introduction of Negroes. . . Experience has shown that, although for the general development of the Island the introduction of slaves should be favored, it is necessary to proceed carefully with the *census figures in hand,* in order that the number of Negroes may not only be prevented from exceeding that of whites, but that it may not be permitted to equal that number. [emphasis added][48]

The rapidly expanding sugar economy could not be checked by arguments for the limitation of slave imports to calm master anxiety over possible revolts. As historian David Brion Davis has succinctly stated: "Fear seldom overcomes greed."[49] In the two decades after the Haitian Revolution, the slave population in Cuba nearly tripled, growing from 84,590 in 1792 to 217,400 in 1810.[50]

Despite the development of a detailed explanation to calm masters' fear over the possibility of slave insurrection, the Aponte Rebellion confirmed nightmares of a baneful Haitian-style slave revolt. Cuban authorities that suppressed the insurrection pointed to Haiti as a major influence in the rebellion. In addition to the free people of color who "seduced" the slaves to revolt, colonial officials believed the leadership "counted on the assistance of blacks from Santo Domingo."[51] Captain General Someruelos told the successor to his office that "he believed without a doubt . . . there had been here several hardened black warriors that had served in Santo Domingo with military rank."[52] Planters reported to the Havana town council that "external enemies" had been brought to Cuba by an "emissary" from the "neighboring and close island of Santo Domingo."[53] Havana's representatives to the Spanish Cortes at Cádiz stated that "it was believed, and rumors circulated, that the black Henri Christophe, ruler of the neighboring island of Haiti, would play a part in the planned [revolt, contributing] boats and arms."[54] The response by Cuban elites to the Aponte Rebellion echoed their explanations of the success of the Haitian Revolution. Because of their refusal to consider criticism of the slave system they commanded, planters proved unable to examine the rebels' motivations for revolt. Just as they explained the Haitian Revolution as the extension of French revolutionary politics to the Caribbean, they insisted that the Aponte Rebellion resulted from the external influence of the Haitian Revolution. Arango y Parreño's "happiest slaves in the world" could only be persuaded to revolt by "emissaries" outside of the Cuban slave system.

When the town council of Puerto Príncipe referred to the "mirror that is represented by our neighboring and ruined colony of Saint-Domingue," and a slaveowner stated that "the most prosperous colony of the Americas gave us the sad example of an insurrection . . . with sufficient resources to incite rebellion in all the islands of the Antilles," they pointedly revealed how slave resistance in Cuba came to be viewed through the looking glass of the Haitian Revolution.[55] As David Geggus has pointed out, "one of the difficulties of such an inquiry" into the influence of the French and Haitian Revolutions on slave revolts, "is the tendency of some white observers after 1791 to view any black resistance as an extension of the Haitian Revolution."[56] The problem Michel-Rolph Trouillot identifies in the documentary record of the Haitian Revolution as "an event that entered history with the peculiar characteristic of being unthinkable even as it happened," had been completely reversed with the slaves' triumph.[57] The previously "unthinkable" notion of a successful slave revolt now terrified most white minds recording acts of slave resistance. Despite the methodological barriers to attempting to analyze the thoughts and actions of historical actors who rarely left their own documents, the protagonists of the Aponte Rebellion clearly looked to the Haitian Revolution to animate their ideas, plans, aspirations, and voices. Free people of color and slaves called up images of the black republic to give meaning and guidance to their own forms of resistance. The voluminous testimony from the Aponte Rebellion, recording the normally voiceless and illiterate speaking boldly in their own defense to explain their own actions, provides an unusual glimpse into the multiple meanings of the Haitian Revolution for slaves and free people of color.

The most fascinating document to emerge from the Aponte Rebellion, attracting the close attention of both authorities and rebels (and long sought by historians), was Aponte's book of drawings. The book of drawings has yet to be found by scholars, but what does exist is the testimony in which for three days Aponte explained the significance of the book to authorities.[58] Colonial officials demanded that Aponte reveal where he obtained the images of the black revolutionaries that filled the pages of his book. Aponte explained that the portraits of Louverture, Dessalines, and Jean-François "were copied by myself from many other engravings acquired when the Campaign of Ballajá came to Havana."[59] He told judicial officials that he "had copied the portrait of Enrique the First [Henri Christophe] from another owned by a black who worked on the docks." Unwilling to identify the owner of the portrait, Aponte stated he did not know his name. Melchor Chirinos, one of many suspected conspirators arrested, told authorities that Aponte had drawn the portrait from a copy owned by *moreno* militia captain Fernando Núñez. Aponte later confirmed Núñez as the source for his image of Henri Christophe.[60] When asked what happened to the portraits, Aponte explained that "he had burnt them after hearing . . . they were banned illustrations."[61] Apparently, Aponte and Núñez were not the only people who owned portraits of Haitian revolutionary figures. After the rebellion had been suppressed and the principal leaders captured, another portrait surfaced when soldier Domingo Calderón "found in the street a portrait of the king Enrique."[62]

Many of the captured rebels stated that Aponte had shown them drawings of Haitian leaders in what probably amounted to lessons in the history of the Haitian Revolution. Melchor Chirinos told officials that "many asked" to see "the black King José Antonio Aponte had painted."[63] Salvador Ternero, a free black, reported that Aponte "showed [him] a book that had three painted figures . . . one a black King and two generals of the same color."[64] Free blacks Javier Pacheco and José del Carmen Peñalver stated that "Aponte showed them the portrait of the black king of Haiti named Henrique Cristóval, informing us of his coronation and recognition by the King of England and the King of Spain."[65] According to the testimony of accused rebel Clemente Chacón, Aponte's portrait of "Cristóval Henriques" contained the inscription: "Execute what is ordered."[66] Authorities concluded that "following the examples and events of those of the same class in the neighboring colony of Guarico, Aponte kept a portrait of Enrique Cristóbal, the first king of Haiti, to show the slaves."[67] Judicial official José María Nery questioned Aponte about the portraits: "Is it true that you showed Clemente Chacón three small portraits—one of Cristóbal Enriques, another of general Salinas [Dessalines], and another of a general whose name I do not remember?" Aponte responded, "It is true that I showed Chacón a portrait of Cristóbal, of Laubertú [Louverture], of Salinas [Dessalines], and of Juan Francisco."[68] The Haitian Revolution provided powerful images of a black king and military generals that provided inspiration for Aponte and others to resist their subordinate position demanded by a society based upon racial hierarchy.[69]

Slaves and free people of color questioned about their involvement in the rebellion constantly referred to rumors and stories that the insurgents would receive aid from Haitian military figures. According to Juan, a black slave who toiled on a plantation outside Havana, "word ran through Havana" that "black generals and captains from Guarico had come . . . to seek the freedom for all the slaves on this island."[70] Antonio de Quintana's slave Damato told authorities he had heard that "all of the slaves were free because two black officials from Guarico had come to give them their freedom."[71] An unnamed free black woman reportedly told her employer that "in a short period of time this land will be governed by blacks, and will have a [black] King."[72] Slave María de la Luz Sánchez allegedly repeated the same prediction to her mistress when she stated that "in a short period of time this land will be governed by the blacks."[73] After suppressing the revolts, authorities reported that "among the captured blacks there was one known as an emissary of the king."[74] Free black Salvador Ternero told authorities he had heard of the "arrival of a black French General who came to conquer the island."[75] Ternero believed that Aponte had been one of the sources of the reports of insurrectionary aid from Haiti. According to Ternero, Aponte "had been informed of the arrival of two black generals with five thousand men located in the mountains . . . to conquer the island and give freedom to the blacks."[76]

Singled out among the presumed revolutionary agents from Haiti was Jean-François, known in Spanish-speaking Cuba as Juan Francisco. Several of the arrested rebels testified to seeing and talking with Juan Francisco at the time of the rebellion. Free black Estanislao Aguilar told authorities that he had attended a "meeting in a tavern" near the "road that leads to the sugar plantations, accompanied by Juan Francisco, or Juan Fransura."[77] Juan Lisundia, a free black arrested for his involvement in a revolt on a sugar plantation outside Havana, had heard that "the black Juan Francisco . . . had arrived at the village of Guanabacoa."[78] Javier Pacheco reported that he "had dinner with other blacks and Juan Francisco, who brought two bottles of wine to toast their good success."[79] Judicial officials believed that Clemente "Chacón and Aponte carried on a friendship" with a "black Frenchman of small stature named Juan Francisco."[80] When officials questioned Chacón and Aponte about their connection with Juan Francisco, they denied any association with the "black Frenchman," and instead blamed each other. Chacón stated he had heard of "a black Frenchman of small stature named Juan Francisco or Juan Fransura" in Aponte's house. According to Chacón, Aponte had told him that Juan Francisco "was an Admiral that served under the command of the black King Cristóval of Santo Domingo, and came with his dispatches to seduce the free blacks and slaves of this island."[81] Aponte denied Chacón's assertion that Juan Francisco was his confidant. Instead, he countered that "one morning Chacón and Juan Lisundia appeared at his [Aponte's] house," where Chacón told him that

"Juan Francisco had gone to the countryside . . . to carry out . . . the orders of his King."[82]

Untangling the stories of who had seen, talked with, and talked about "Juan Francisco" and other revolutionaries from Haiti remains difficult. The life-and-death threat of imminent punishment greatly influenced how participants recounted the events of the past. Authorities later concluded from the testimony of other rebels who knew him as Juan Francisco, that Juan Barbier, a free black reputed to be from Saint-Domingue, had assumed the identity of the famous agent. Further exploration is required to place the numerous references to the Haitian Revolution by slaves and free people of color within a Cuban context to understand how they resonated with the rebels' own experience.[83]

"Juan Francisco" became intimately associated with the Aponte Rebellion for reasons stemming from his historical presence in Cuba. Jean-François had been an early leader of the Haitian Revolution who had allied with Spanish forces against the French. His inability to develop a strategy of slave emancipation or identify with the French National Convention's declaration of abolition, as had Toussaint, resulted in his declining influence. In July 1795 Spain and the Directory of the French Republic signed a peace treaty ceding eastern Hispaniola to France, leaving Jean-François and his troops without a country. "In the year 1796," Captain General Someruelos later recalled, "Juan Francisco, *caudillo* of the blacks from Santo Domingo, with other military chiefs of his," namely Georges Biassou and Gil Narciso, attempted to settle in Cuba.[84] Havana's town council barred Jean-François from living in Cuba because "several blacks had prepared functions to celebrate the arrival of Juan Francisco to show their affection toward him and his officials, although they never met them."[85] According to Cuban historian José Luciano Franco, Aponte's *cabildo* planned to participate in the festivities welcoming Jean-François.[86] The exiled troops from Saint-Domingue stayed only a brief time in Havana, prohibited by officials from disembarking while docked on the other side of the harbor to minimize their interaction with free people of color and slaves. After a short stay in Havana, Jean-François left for Cádiz, Spain, Biassou for St. Augustine, Florida, Gil Narciso for Guatemala, and other troops scattered throughout the Spanish Caribbean.[87]

Jean-François's association with Cuba did not end with his brief Havana stay in 1796. Over the next fifteen years, there would be several reports of Jean-François's soldiers visiting Havana or attempting to settle on the island.[88] Such stories may have served to transform Jean-François, the reluctant slave emancipator of Saint-Domingue defeated by Toussaint's rise to power, into "Juan Francisco," an admiral that served under the command of the black "King Cristóval." "Juan Francisco" may have even represented the black king. Salvador Ternero claimed that Aponte "assured" him "that he knew the black King, and had seen him in Havana many years ago."[89] Aponte may have been referring to the "many years ago" when Jean-François had briefly stayed in Havana. Reports of aid from "Juan Francisco" for the Aponte rebellion took on a life of their own. A year before the revolts erupted, Jean-François had died in Cádiz, Spain. Available sources do not reflect whether those involved in the rebellion knew of Jean-François's death. In any case, the currency of Cuban rumors about "Juan Francisco" and the aid he would provide the rebellion revealed how the powerful image of the Haitian Revolution served as a point of reference for rebels seeking to transform their own society.[90]

Just as revolts erupted across the island during the first months of 1812, authorities in Havana arrested soldiers who had once served under Jean-François. At the end of December 1811, "twenty blacks from the island of Santo Domingo with six heads of family" arrived in Havana. Captain General Someruelos housed the blacks from Saint-Domingue at the military fort Casa Blanca, provided a "ration in silver specie" to buy goods and supplies, and allowed them to stay in Havana while they prepared to return to Hispaniola.[91] Sometime before 24 March 1812, colonial officials detained Gil Narciso and three of his aides, Juan Luis Santillán, José Gaston, and Isidro Plutton, for suspected involvement in the rebellion. Santillán explained that it was not the first time that he and the others had been to Havana: "We came in a boat from Bayajá [Fort-Dauphin] when Juan Francisco had also come, and after staying awhile, we went with Gil Narciso to the Kingdom of Guatemala."[92] Narciso told authorities that while in Guatemala, he had been informed of a royal order from Cádiz "for all of the migrants of said island [Hispaniola] to return to their origin." Jean-François's former soldiers explained that they had only stopped in Havana en route to Santo Domingo. Cuban authorities did not ask questions specifically related to their possible involvement in the rebellion, but only whether they had contact with blacks from Havana. Narciso admitted he had visited the free colored and slave neighborhoods located outside the city walls of Havana. "Greeted by various people of color, mulattoes as well as blacks," Narciso had been "asked from where he had come and where he was headed."[93] José Gaston told authorities that several blacks and mulattoes "on various occasions, asked if it was true that among him and his companions there was a Brigadier." Gaston noted that he was "asked" that the brigadier "be shown in uniform."[94] The interest expressed in seeing the "brigadier" may refer to Gil Narciso's military rank while fighting under Jean-François in the service of the Spanish crown.[95] Likewise, the "people of color in the neighborhoods outside the city walls," showed an interest in the military uniform of Isidro Plutton.[96] Just one day after questioning Narciso, Santillán, Gaston, and Plutton for the first time, Captain General Someruelos ordered that "the blacks who are imprisoned at Casa Blanca should leave today for Santo Domingo."[97]

The brief questioning, prompt release, and unspecified dates of detention in Havana, make it difficult to establish the relationship of Jean-François' former soldiers to the Aponte Rebellion. Someruelos may have decided to release the prisoners in the belief that Gil Narciso and those under his command intended to aid the rebellion; thus, by sending them to Santo Domingo, he followed the familiar policy of isolating Cuba from the contagion of radical insurgents. On the other hand, the captain general may have believed that while unconnected to the rebellion, the soldiers' presence in Havana and the interest shown by people of color in their uniforms fanned the flames of an already insurrectionary situation. It is also possible that Narciso and the others had intended to join the rebellion, but learning of its quick suppression, opted to continue on to Santo Domingo. Gil Narciso may have been a man in search of revolution. The same year Narciso arrived in Santo

Domingo, he participated in a slave revolt.[98] At the very least, the presence of Gil Narciso and his troops served to legitimate rumors of "Juan Francisco's" participation in the revolt, if not provide the inspiration for such reports. Indeed, the arrival of Narciso's troops in 1812 confirmed Someruelos' prediction made twelve years earlier: The troops of "Juan Francisco" could "easily . . . hide themselves and much more in this country."[99]

While it is unclear if Jean-François's former soldiers planned to participate in the rebellion, several free people of color and slaves sought them out to ask them why they had come to Havana. Isidro Plutton noted—as had Gil Narciso and José Fantacia Gaston—that several people had come to visit him and his companions.[100] Among those who wanted to see and talk with the troops of Gil Narciso was Salvador Ternero, who "proposed to go to see them and ask if they were Brigadiers as it had been said."[101] Ternero crossed Havana's harbor and went to the small military fort of Casa Blanca where the former soldiers of Jean-François had been quartered during their stay in Havana. Ternero reported that there he spoke with three of the soldiers, but did "not see the French general that Aponte told him" about. Ternero had seen Aponte's "book that had three painted figures . . . a black King and two generals of the same color." Ternero "asked the soldiers if the portraits" drawn by Aponte represented anyone at "Casa Blanca, but they assured him that they did not."[102] Ternero also "asked these officials if they had come to participate in plotting the conspiracy; to this they answered no."[103] The free black Juan Barbier also went to Casa Blanca to see the soldiers.[104] According to Clemente Chacón, Barbier told several at a meeting at Aponte's house that "the blacks at Casa Blanca are his people and they have come to conquer this land for the people of color as they had done numerous times."[105] Aponte denied seeking out the Saint-Domingue military veterans at Casa Blanca, but he did admit that on "two occasions Chacón brought the secretary of the brigadier to his house between six or seven in the morning."[106] Apparently, Aponte and others seized upon the opportunity provided by the presence of former soldiers of Jean-François to project an image of a powerful movement supported by the only independent black country in the Western Hemisphere born from the liberating destruction of a slave revolution.

Orders sent out across the island for the arrest of Hilario Herrera, a "resident of the village of Azua" on the Spanish border dividing "the island of Santo Domingo," added another dimension to the international aspect of the rebellion. During the last days of February 1812, Puerto Príncipe's lieutenant governor, Francisco Sedano, concluded that "Hilario Herrera, alias the Englishman," had been "the primary organizer of the bloody uprising" in the eastern part of the island. Previously wanted for "stealing a cow," according to Sedano, Herrera had escaped capture, spread the rebellion to the cities of Bayamo and Holguín, and was attempting to return to Santo Domingo to evade arrest.[107] Colonial officials ordered a manhunt for Herrera in Santiago, Bayamo, Holguín, and even in Santo Domingo.[108] Historian Franco wrote that Herrera "served as the agent of the conspiracy planned by Aponte in the eastern zone of the island," providing the link with the leadership in Havana. Herrera may have attempted to coordinate "on the day of the rebellion the arrival in an undetermined place on the northern coast a boat from Haiti carrying three hundred rifles for the rebels."[109] The search for the elusive rebel in several cities only turned up the barren report that the "black Hilario Herrera boarded as a passenger on the Spanish sloop *Dos Amigos*" bound for Santo Domingo on 1 February.[110] Herrera left behind a trail of unanswerable questions for colonial officials and historians on his role in the Aponte rebellion. He did not leave in Cuba his revolutionary activities. In the same year Herrera escaped from Cuba, he participated in a slave revolt in Santo Domingo.[111]

In addition to stories of Haitian assistance and the presence of Saint-Domingue veterans in Cuba, the rebels creatively invoked the imagery of the Haitian Revolution as a recruitment strategy in planning the insurrection. After the rebellion had been repressed, a slave named Joaquín owned by José Domingo Pérez told the mayor of San Antonio Abad that at the time of the revolt, he had seen a "black with a uniform from Guarico."[112] Unless Joaquín was from Haiti, somebody must have influenced his ideas of what a "uniform from Guarico" looked like. Clemente Chacón reported to authorities that he had been introduced to Juan Francisco, who was "dressed in a blue military jacket demonstrating he was a great subject, indicated by his line of yellow buttons on his jacket, some with the image of an anchor and an eagle."[113] Estanislao Aguilar testified that when he traveled to the plantation to recruit slaves for the rebellion, "Juan Francisco . . . entered a slave hut and returned dressed in a blue military jacket and military pants, taking off the clothes he had worn."[114] Several other rebels questioned about the revolts provided similar descriptions of soldiers in uniform.[115] Military uniforms could have been obtained relatively easily from members of the free colored militia. When authorities searched Aponte's house, they found his "blue military jacket" in a closet.[116] The success of the Haitian Revolution added new meaning to the familiar sight of blacks in military uniforms throughout the Caribbean. In recruiting others to their cause, the leaders of the Aponte Rebellion refashioned their own military experience in Cuba to wed it with the imagery of the Haitian Revolution.

Just as Cuban military uniforms could be employed by rebels to alter the wardrobe issued by the Spanish colonial government into the appearance of a liberating Haitian leader, so could discussions of emancipation in Spain be transformed to appear as emanating from Haiti. Rumors of abolition circulated widely in Cuba during 1811–12. As a result of the French occupation of the Iberian peninsula, the weakened regency had conceded parliamentary representation to the colonies. On 26 March 1811, a Mexican representative to the Cortes at Cádiz proposed that "slavery as a violation of natural law, already outlawed by the laws of civilized countries . . . should be abolished forever."[117] The shocking suggestion quickly crossed the Atlantic, prompting Captain General Someruelos to write the Cortes, urging them "to treat the issue with all the reserve, detailed attention, and thought that its grave nature requires in order to not lose this important island." News of the debate over slavery circulated in Havana through the *Diario de sesiones de Cortes,* causing "a significant sensation among the inhabitants of the capital, and a very sad series of grumblings . . . throughout the island, requiring all of the government's vigilance."[118] William Shaler, the United States commercial agent in Havana, wrote to Washington that the prospect of abolition moved planters to suggest to him that "the Island of Cuba ought to become part of the United States."[119] The question of the abolition of slavery attracted the attention of a wide and varied audience from masters concerned about their property, Spanish officials seeking to maintain the colonial status of Cuba, and pre-Monroe Doctrine Americans eager to expand their power in the hemisphere. Perhaps nobody showed as much interest as the slaves who had the most to gain.

Captain General Someruelos claimed that the "contagion . . . of false and attractive news and promises that the extraordinary sessions of the Cortes had decreed the slaves free, and the government of this island had concealed from them this extremely important point," resulted in "the slaves becoming involved in the criminal project."[120] Slaves such as Maria Candelaria explained their participation in the revolt "because in spite of having granted the slaves their freedom, it had been denied to them" by their masters.[121] Several slaves, however, reported that it was not the Spanish Cortes that had declared them free, but the King of Guarico. At the time of the rebellion, several of those arrested were found in possession of proclamations from Saint-Domingue that had reportedly been shown to others.[122] "Havana was very agitated," slave José Antonio had heard, "because some black generals from Guarico had come with an order from the black King to tell the governor of Havana to give the slaves freedom."[123] Another bondsman reported that "one or two black captains from Guarico had ordered the Governor to free the slaves in the name of the King of Guarico."[124] Slave Joaquín Belaguer had "talked in his excessive inebriation" about the elaborate "coronation of Cristóval" that resulted in slaves regarding Henri Christophe as the liberating king.[125] As the only nation to abolish slavery in the Americas, Haiti seemed, to many Cuban slaves, a logical origin for an emancipation decree.

In addition to proclamations from Saint-Domingue, several letters in French were found by authorities that required the translating expertise of the "Public Interpreter for his Majesty in Foreign Languages," Don Gabriel Pantelon de Escarti.[126] Leaders of the rebellion referred to the French letters as they planned the revolts, claiming they declared "the freedom of the slaves."[127] The translation of the supposedly "seditious" French material revealed no insurrectionary slogans or declarations for abolition, but rather, the timid description of a sick French slave named Tomás and an advertisement in English for a stationery store in Philadelphia.[128] Aponte claimed that the "Brigadier's secretary " carried to the plantations "insignias and papers underneath his jacket."[129] The panic expressed by Cuban officials and the interest of people of color in the "French" papers reveals how perceptions of slavery had quickly and radically changed in Cuba. In the aftermath of the Haitian Revolution, pieces of paper in French brought fear to masters, and to people of color, catalysts for rebellion.

While colonial officials brutally and quickly crushed the revolts that erupted across Cuba during the first months of 1812, the public execution of Aponte and other leaders did not destroy the dreaded thought that other rebellions would occur in the future. The town council of Puerto Príncipe asked "who is capable of believing that after the contamination" of the slaves with rebellion "they will return to their duties because we have killed ten or twelve of the principal leaders?" Council members recognized that the "contamination" from the Aponte Rebellion could last for a long period of time because "more than five years" of insurrection "passed in the other colony [Saint-Domingue] until it finally ended in catastrophe."[130] In 1814, colonial officials would continue to link the Aponte Rebellion to the Haitian Revolution, as an "uprising in this island with a plan equal to that in Guarico."[131] Images of the Haitian Revolution became inseparable from the Aponte Rebellion for masters, slaves, and free people of color. For Cuban elites and colonial officials, the Aponte Rebellion served to confirm their deepest apprehensions of a Haitian-style slave revolt, whereas for slaves and free people of color, the Haitian Revolution inspired pride and gave shape to their own movement. The divergent reactions to the Haitian Revolution expressed by people of European and African ancestry in the form of fear and fascination, abomination and admiration, and disgust and delight would not end with the Aponte Rebellion. During the extensive La Escalera slave conspiracy of 1844, the struggle for independence in the second half of the nineteenth century, the massacre of the Partido Independiente de Color in 1912, and at other moments of revolutionary change, the image of Haiti would reappear, metaphorically revealing how racial divisions continued to structure Cuban society.[132]

NOTES

The author gratefully acknowledges financial support from the Conference on Latin American History, the Southwest Council of Latin American Studies, the Institute of Latin American Studies at the University of Texas at Austin, the Ford Foundation, the Johns Hopkins University, the Fulbright-Hays Program, and the Social Science Research Council to conduct research in Cuba and Spain.

1. Archivo Nacional de Cuba, Havana, fondo Asuntos Políticos (hereafter ANC-AP), 12, no. 17, fol. 4v.

2. Apodaca to Cano, 14 Dec. 1812, Archivo General de Indias, Seville, fondo Santo Domingo (hereafter AGI-SD), 1284, no. 71, fol. 1v.

3. Sedano to Someruelos, 1 Feb., 4 Feb., and 22 Mar. 1812, Archivo General de Indias, Seville, fondo Papeles de Cuba (hereafter AGI-PC), 1640; Archivo Histórico Provincial de Camagüey (hereafter AHPC), Actas Capitulares, no. 27, fols. 35–121.

4. Arminan to ?, 17 Feb. 1812, Archivo Histórico Provincial de Holguín (hereafter AHPH), Tenencia de Gobierno, 69, exp. 2048.

5. Archivo del Museo Provincial de Holguín, fondo Colonial, 1700–1867 (hereafter AMPH-Colonial), no. 191; AHPH-Actas Capitulares, no. 64, exp. 1936, fols. 9v-14; AHPH-Tenencia de Gobierno, no. 69, exp. 2042, fol. 5.

6. ANC-AP, 12, no. 9; Corral to Someruelos, 16 Feb. 1812, AGI-PC, 1649, no. 66; Corral to Suares de Urbina, Bayamo, 27 Feb. 1812, and Arminan to Suares de Urbina, Holguín, 16 Mar. 1812, AGI-PC, 1548.

7. Someruelos to Pezuela, 14 Feb. 1812, Archivo General de Indias, Seville, fondo Ultramar (hereafter AGI-UM), 84, no. 343.

8. ANC-AP, 13, no. 15, fol. 70.

9. Hitar to [Rendón?], 20 Mar. 1812, ANC-AP, 12, no. 14, fol. 33.

10. ANC-AP, 12, no. 17, fols. 3–5, 7–12, 33v-35v. A more systematic search of the house itemizing everything from clothing to sculpting tools to furniture was conducted on 15 Apr. 1812, ANC-AP, 12, no. 26. fols. 7–14. For the role of the *cabildos* in the Aponte rebellion see,

Philip A. Howard, *Changing History: Afro-Cuban Cabildos and Societies of Color in the Nineteenth Century* (Baton Rouge: Louisiana State University Press, 1998), 74–80.

11. ANC-AP, 12, no. 17, fol. 3v.

12. ANC-AP, 12, no. 14, fol. 92; no. 17, passim; and no. 18, fols. 25, 28. Cuban historian José Luciano Franco has reprinted some of Aponte's explanation of the book of drawings in *La conspiración de Aponte* (Havana: Publicaciones del Archivo Nacional, 1963), 66–72, 74–97; and Idem, *Las conspiraciones de 1810 y 1812* (Havana: Editorial de Ciencias Sociales), 109–63. I would like to thank archivist Jorge Macle for finding ANC-AP, 12, no. 17 that had been declared missing.

13. I have employed the title "Aponte Rebellion" instead of "Aponte Conspiracy"—as it known in the historiography—because the term "conspiracy" in studies of slave revolts generally connotes a foiled rebellion.

14. David Brion Davis, above, ch. 1; Eugene D. Genovese, *From Rebellion to Revolution: Afro-American Slave Revolts in the Making of the Modern World* (Baton Rouge: Louisiana State University Press, 1979); Michael Craton, *Testing the Chains: Resistance to Slavery in the British West Indies* (Ithaca, N.Y.: Cornell University Press, 1982); Michael Mullin, *Africa in America: Slave Acculturation and Resistance in the American South and the Caribbean, 1763–1831* (Urbana: University of Illinois Press, 1992); David Patrick Geggus, "The French and Haitian Revolutions and Resistance to Slavery in the Americas: An Overview," *Revue Française d'Histoire d'Outre-Mer* 76 (1989): 107–24; Idem, "Slavery, War, and Revolution in the Greater Caribbean, 1789–1815," in *A Turbulent Time: The French Revolution and the Greater Caribbean,* eds. David Barry Gaspar and David Patrick Geggus (Bloomington: Indiana University Press, 1997), 1–50; Julius Sherrard Scott, "The Common Wind: Currents of Afro-American Communication in the Era of the Haitian Revolution" (Ph. D. diss., Duke University, 1986).

15. Robert L. Paquette, "Social History Update: Slave Resistance and Social History," *Journal of Social History* 24 (1991): 683.

16. Manuel Moreno Fraginals, *El ingenio: Complejo económico social cubano de azúcar,* 3 vols. (Havana: Editorial de Ciencias Sociales, 1978), 1:67–68; Pablo Tornero Tinajero, *Crecimiento económico y transformaciones sociales: Esclavos, hacendados, y comerciantes en la Cuba colonial (1760–1840)* (Madrid: Ministerio de Trabajo y Seguridad Social, 1996), 169–71; Hugh Thomas, *Cuba: The Pursuit of Freedom* (New York: Harper & Row, 1971), 77; Matt D. Childs, "'Sewing Civilization': Cuban Female Education in the Context of Africanization, 1800–1860," *The Americas* 54 (1997): 86–88; Franklin W. Knight, *Slave Society in Cuba During the Nineteenth Century* (Madison: University of Wisconsin Press, 1970), 11–13; David R. Murray, *Odious Commerce: Britain, Spain and the Abolition of the Cuban Slave Trade* (Cambridge: Cambridge University Press, 1980), 19; Laird W. Bergad, Fe Iglesias Garcia and María del Carmen Barcia, *The Cuban Slave Market, 1790–1880* (Cambridge: Cambridge University Press, 1995), 28. Allan J. Kuethe, *Cuba, 1753–1815: Crown, Military and Society* (Knoxville: University of Tennessee Press, 1986) and Sherry Johnson, "'Honor is Life': Military Reform and the Transformation of Cuban Society: 1753–1796" (Ph. D. diss. University of Florida, 1995) argue that the military embodied the defining institution of Cuban society throughout the eighteenth century.

17. "Favores dispensados a la agricultura y comercio de la Habana desde 1792," 23 Feb. 1796, AGI-SD, 1157.

18. Francisco Arango y Parreño, "Representación hecha a su S. M. con motivo de la sublevación de esclavos en los dominios francés de la Ysla de Santo Domingo," 22 Nov. 1791, Biblioteca Nacional José Martí, Colección Francisco Arango y Parreño (hereafter BNJM-Arango y Parreño), fol. 60.

19. Robert L. Paquette provides an excellent discussion of this dilemma in the chapter

"Cuban Whites and the Problem of Slavery," in *Sugar is Made with Blood: The Conspiracy of La Escalera and the Conflict between Empires over Slavery in Cuba* (Middletown, Conn.: Wesleyan University Press, 1988), 81–103.

20. The 1789 *Real Cédula* declaring free trade in slaves can be found in Archivo General de Indias, Seville, fondo Indiferente General (hereafter AGI-IG), 2823.

21. Consulado de la Habana to Someruelos, 29 Oct. 1802, Biblioteca Nacional José Martí, Havana, Colección Vidal Morales y Morales (hereafter BNJM-Morales), tomo 79, no. 61, fol. 217v.

22. Calculated from the monthly receipts for slaves imported to Cuba from 1790 to 1820 in AGI-SD, 2207.

23. Francisco Arango y Parreño, "Representación manifestando las ventajas de una absoluta libertad en la introducción de negros, y solicitando se amplíe a ocho años la prórroga concedida por dos años," 10 May 1791, BNJM-Arango y Parreño, fol. 38.

24. Archivo Histórico Provincial de Santiago de Cuba (hereafter AHPSC), Juzgado de Primera Instancia, 376, no. 2, fol. 2; AHPSC-Protocolos, 241, fols. 49v, 108; 242, fol. 86; 357, fol. 331v; 358, fol. 92v; AHPH-Protocolos, Escribano Rodríguez, año 1810, fol. 66v; Escribano Fuentes, año 1809, fol. 40; año 1810, fol. 20v; AHPC-Protocolos, Escribano Mora, año 1810, fol. 171v; Murrilo to Someruelos, Baracoa, 2 July 1804, and Murrilo to Someruelos, 22 Aug. 1806, AGI-PC, 1785; Suares de Urbina to Apodaca, Santiago, 15 June 1812, AGI-PC, 1702; "Noticia de los franceses existentes en el Barrio de Guadalupe," 1809, AGI-SD, 1284, no. 330; Someruelos to Ignacio de la Pezuela, 8 Jan. 1812, AGI-SD, 1284.

25. Arango y Parreño, "Representación hecha a su S. M con motivo de la sublevación de esclavos . . . ," BNJM-Arango y Parreño, fol. 60; AHPC-Actas Capitulares, no. 27, fol. 55v.

26. Murrilo to Someruelos, Baracoa, 2 July 1804, AGI-PC, 1648.

27. Juan de Dios Zayas, "Resumen general de los moradores franceses que comprehende la ciudad de Cuba," Santiago de Cuba, 27 July 1808, ANC-AP, 142 no. 86; Someruelos to ?, 5 Mar. 1800, Archivo Histórico Nacional, Madrid, fondo Estado (hereafter AHN-Estado), 6366, caja 1, exp. 4. Nearly thirty years ago Bohumil Badura corrected, with archival sources, the incorrect estimate of thirty thousand French refugees in Santiago by Ramiro Guerra that continues to be cited. "Los Franceses en Santiago de Cuba a mediados del año de 1808," *Ibero-Americana Pragensia* (Prague) 5 (1971): 157–60.

28. Someruelos to Ignacio de la Pezuela, 8 Jan. 1812, AGI-SD, 1284, no. 330.

29. AHPH-Tenencia de Gobierno, 68, no. 2007; AMPH-Colonial, no. 103; AHPC-Actas Capitulares, no. 25, fols. 190–190v, 265v; no. 26, fol. 155; below, Paul Lachance, chap. 14, pp. 350–55.

30. For French *émigrés* to Cuba, see William R. Lux, "French Colonization in Cuba, 1791–1809," *The Americas* 29 (1972): 57–61; Alain Yacou, "Esclaves et libres français à Cuba au lendemain de la révolution Saint-Domingue," *Jahrbuch für Geschichte von Staat, Wirtschaft und Gesellschaft Lateinamerikas* 28 (1991): 163–98; Idem, "La présence française dans la partie occidentale de l'île de Cuba au lendemain de la Révolution de Saint-Domingue," *Revue Française d'Histoire d'Outre-Mer* 74 (1987): 149–88; Gabriel Debien, "Les colons de Saint-Domingue réfugiés à Cuba (1793–1815)," *Revista de Indias* 13 (1953): 559–606, and 14 (1954): 11–36.

31. AHPSC-Juzgado de Primera Instancia, 375, no. 4; AMPH-Colonial, no. 649.

32. Arambarri to Someruelos, 19 Feb. 1800, AHN-Estado, 6366, caja 1, exp. 3, no. 3.

33. Someruelos to Arambarri, 28 Feb. 1800, AHN-Estado, 6366, caja 1, exp. 3, no. 3.

34. Someruelos to ?, 12 Aug. 1800, AHN-Estado, 6366, caja 1, exp. 16, no. 2.

35. Arango y Parreño, "Representación hecha a su S. M. con motivo de la sublevación de esclavos ," BNJM-Arango y Parreño, fols. 55–56. Guarico was used in Spanish to refer to the city of Cap-Français, but also generically to Saint-Domingue and Haiti.

36. Someruelos, "Observaciones relativas al estado actual de la Isla de Santo Domingo," 16 May 1811, AGI-PC, 1749, fol. 1.

37. Someruelos to ?, 27 Jan. 1800, AHN-Estado, 6366, caja 1, exp. 2.

38. AHPC-Actas Capitulares, no. 27, fol. 22.

39. Someruelos to ?, 27 Jan. 1800, AHN-Estado, 6366, caja 1, exp. 2.

40. Ibid.

41. Someruelos to Bardari y Azara, 10 Feb. 1811, AGI-SD, 2210.

42. Arango y Parreño, "Representación hecha a su S. M. con motivo de la sublevación de esclavos ," BNJM-Arango y Parreño, fols. 57–58.

43. Consulado de la Habana to Someruelos, 29 Oct. 1802, BNJM-Morales, tomo 79, no. 61, fol. 221.

44. Gwendolyn Midlo Hall, *Social Control in Slave Plantations Societies: A Comparison of St. Domingue and Cuba* (Baltimore: Johns Hopkins University Press, 1971), 81–112.

45. Consulado de la Habana to Someruelos, 29 Oct. 1802, BNJM-Morales, tomo 79, no. 61, fol. 220v.

46. Arango y Parreño, "Representación hecha a su S. M. con motivo de la sublevación de esclavos ," BNJM-Arango y Parreño, fol. 56.

47. Obispo de Cuba,"El obispo de Cuba informa Sobre el fomento de esta parte occidental de la Isla," 30 Nov. 1794, AGI-SD, 2236.

48. *Memorias de la Sociedad Económica* (1794): 54–55, in Duvon C. Corbitt, "Immigration in Cuba," *Hispanic American Historical Review* 22 (1942): 284–85.

49. See David Brion Davis, above, ch. 1.

50. Ramón de la Sagra, *Historia económico, político y estadística de la isla de Cuba* (Havana: Imprenta de las Viudas de Azora y Soler, 1831), 3–10; Alexander von Humboldt, *Ensayo sobre la isla de Cuba* (Paris: Jules Renouard, 1827), 108–113.

51. ? to Sres. Presdte. y Oydor de la Rl. Audiencia, 25 Apr. 1812, ANC-AP, 12, no. 27, fol. 3.

52. Apodaca to Ministro de Guerra, 29 Oct. 1812, AGI-PC, 1849, no. 184.

53. "Informe presentado al cabildo . . . relativo a la moción de la Cortes para abolir al tráfico de negros," 23 Mar. 1812, BNJM-Morales, tomo 78, no. 8, fol. 90.

54. Andres de Jauregui and Juan Bernardo O'Gavan, "Memorial de los diputados de la Habana sobre una insurrección de esclavos en el ingenio de Peñas Altas," Cádiz, 23 May 1812, BNJM-Morales, tomo 79, no. 72, fol. 292.

55. AHPC-Actas Capitulares, no. 27, fol. 55; ? to Someruelos, 8 Apr. 1812, Archivo Histórico de la Oficina del Historiador de la Ciudad, Havana (hereafter AHOHCH), Actas Capitulares, no. 84, fols. 223–223v.

56. Geggus, "French and Haitian Revolutions," 112.

57. Michel-Rolph Trouillot, *Silencing the Past: Power and the Production of History* (Boston: Beacon Press, 1995), 73.

58. Most of Aponte's testimony discussing the book of drawings with authorities is found in ANC-AP, 12, no. 17, titled "Expediente sobre declara José Antonio Aponte el sentido de las pinturas que se hallan en el libro que se le aprehendido en su casa." Cuban historian José Luciano Franco has reprinted some of the documents in *La conspiración de Aponte,* 66–72, 74–97, and *Las conspiraciones de 1810 y 1812,* 109–63.

59. ANC-AP, 12, no. 17, fol. 78v. The "campaign of Ballajá" refers to the exodus of the Spanish-allied black Saint-Domingue troops from the city of Fort-Dauphin in 1795.

60. ANC-AP, 12, no. 18, fols. 27–28.

61. Ibid., no. 17, fol. 80.

62. Ibid., no. 18, fol. 41.

63. Ibid., fol. 25.

64. Ibid., no. 14, fol. 92.

65. Ibid., no. 1, fol. 316. Christophe's coronation took place in June 1811.

66. Ibid., no. 17, fol. 16.

67. Ibid., no. 15, fol. 18v.

68. Ibid., no. 17, fols. 78–78v.

69. People of African ancestry throughout the Americas had great admiration for revolutionary leaders from Haiti. Only a year after Haitian independence, free people of color as far away as Rio de Janeiro wore necklaces bearing the image of Dessalines. See above, introduction, p. iv.

70. ANC-AP, 12, no. 26, fols. 37v-38.

71. Ibid., fol. 33.

72. ? to Somereulos, 22 Mar. 1812, ANC-AP, 12, no. 14, fol. 48.

73. ANC-AP, 12, no. 20, fol. 9.

74. ? to Somerulos, 8 Apr. 1812, AHOHCH, Actas Capitulares, no. 84, fol. 227.

75. ANC-AP, 12, no. 14, fol. 91.

76. Ibid., no. 18, fol. 31.

77. Ibid., fol. 6.

78. Ibid., no. 16, fol. 12.

79. Ibid., no. 1, fol. 49.

80. Ibid., no. 14, fol. 85.

81. Ibid., fol. 70. The "Admiral" was the title Jean-François called himself while fighting with the Spanish against the French during the early years of the Haitian Revolution. Knowledge of his title may reveal the detailed information received by blacks in Cuba on events in Saint-Domingue. C. L. R. James, *The Black Jacobins: Toussaint L'Ouverture and the San Domingo Revolution,* 2d ed. (New York: Vintage, 1963), 94.

82. ANC-AP, 12, no. 18, fol. 29v-30.

83. ANC-AP, 12, no. 14, fol. 73; no. 16, fols. 4–5, 13–14; no. 18, fols. 8–9, 34v; ANC-AP, 13, no. 1, fols, 83v-84; no. 15, fol. 18v. Invoking the Haitian Revolution through assuming the name of revolutionary figures also occurred in the Curaçao rebellion of 1795. Among the leaders executed by Dutch authorities, one called himself Toussaint, and another was known by the nickname Rigaud. See Scott, "The Common Wind," 264.

84. Someruelos to Ministro de Estado, 1 Sept. 1800, AHN-Estado, 6366, caja 1, exp. 20, no. 1, fols. 2v-3; Luis de las Casas to ?, 13 Jan. 1796, AGI-Estado, 5–A, no. 28.

85. AHOHCH-Actas Capitulares, 4 Dec. 1795, fols. 204v-205; García to Príncipe de la Paz, 3 Mar. 1796, no. 48, *Cesión de Santo Domingo a Francia: Correspondencia de Godoy, Garcia, Roume, Hedouville, Louverture, Rigaud, y otros, 1795–1802,* ed. Emilio Rodríguez Demorizi (Trujillo: Impresora Dominicana, 1958), 75.

86. Franco, *La conspiración de Aponte,* 9.

87. Jane G. Landers, "Rebellion and Royalism in Spanish Florida: The French Revolution on Spain's Northern Colonial Frontier," in *A Turbulent Time,* ed. Gaspar and Geggus, 163–70; Jacques Houdaille, "Negros Franceses en América Central a fines del siglo xviii," *Antropología e historia de Guatemala* 6 (1954): 65–67; Francisco Fernández Repetto and Genny Negroe Sierra, *Una población perdida en la memoria: Los negros de Yucatán* (Mérida: Universidad Autónoma de Yucatán, 1995), 55.

88. Someruelos to ?, 27 Jan. 1800, AHN-Estado, 6366, caja 1, exp. 2; Someruelos to ?, 31 July 1804, AGI-PC, 1778–B; Someruelos to Bardari y Azara, 10 Feb. 1811, AGI-SD, 2210.

89. ANC-AP, 12, no. 14, fol. 93.

90. Franco, *La conspiración de Aponte,* 10; David Patrick Geggus, "Slave Resistance in the Spanish Caribbean in the Mid-1790s," in *A Turbulent Time,* eds. Gaspar and Geggus, 153, n. 52; Renée Méndez Capote, *4 conspiraciones* (Havana: Gente Nueva, 1972), 14.

91. ANC-AP, 214, no. 28, fols. 2–3v.

92. ANC-AP, 12, no. 16, fol. 6. These men probably were part of the group that arrived in December.

93. Ibid., fol. 4.

94. Ibid., fol. 8v.

95. Luis de las Casas to ?, 13 Jan. 1796, AGI-Estado, 5–A, no. 28.

96. ANC-AP, 12, no. 16, fol. 10.

97. Ibid., fol. 22.

98. Franco, *La conspiración de Aponte,* 33; Geggus, "Slavery, War, and Revolution," 15; Méndez Capote, *4 conspiraciones,* 38.

99. Someruelos to ?, 27 Jan. 1800, AHN-Estado, 6366, caja 1, exp. 2, fol. 3v.

100. ANC-AP, 12, no. 16, fol. 10.

101. Ibid., no. 14, fol. 91.

102. Ibid., fol. 92.

103. ANC-AP, 12, no. 16, fol. 21.

104. Ibid., no. 14, fol. 88.

105. Ibid., no. 16, fol. 18.

106. Ibid., no. 17, fol. 74v.

107. Sedano to Suares de Urbina, 23 Feb. 1812, ANC-AP, 214, no. 46, fols. 1–2.

108. Suares de Urbina to ?, 29 Feb. 1812, ANC-AP, 214, no. 54; Suares de Urbina to Gobernador Político Interno de Santo Domingo, 29 Feb. 1812, ANC-AP, 214, no. 55; Buenaventura to Suares de Urbina, 1 Mar. 1812, ANC-AP, 214, no. 56; and Suares de Urbina to Teniente Gobernador de Holguín, 29 Feb. 1812, AHPH-Tenencia de Gobierno, no. 71.

109. Franco, *La conspiración de Aponte,* 31–33. I could find no sources in Havana or provincial archives to document Franco's statements.

110. Suares de Urbina? to Teniente Gobernador del Puerto Príncipe, 3 Mar. 1812, ANC-AP, 214, no. 61; Suares de Urbina? to Governador de Santo Domingo, 3 Mar. 1812, ANC-AP, 214, no. 60.

111. Franco, *La conspiración de Aponte,* 31; Geggus, "Slavery, War, and Revolution," 42, n. 115; Méndez Capote, *4 conspiraciones,* 38.

112. ANC-AP, 12, no. 26, fol. 30.

113. ANC-AP, 12, no. 14, fol. 73. Yellow buttons may have caught the attention of Chacón because "buttons of gold" were often included in wills of free people of color, see AHPSC-Protocolos, 63, fol. 26v; 64, fol. 156; 243, fol. 118; Archivo Histórico Provincial de Granma, Bayamo, Protocolos, 11, libro 3, fol. 52

114. ANC-AP, 12, no. 18, fol. 9, 34v.

115. ANC-AP, 12, no. 13, fols. 21v-23v, 31, 36–37; no. 17, fol. 72.

116. ANC-AP, 12, no. 26, fols. 7–14.

117. "Proposiciones del Sr. don José Miguel Guridi Alcocer," Cádiz, 26 Mar. 1811, *Documentos de que hasta ahora se compone el expediente que principiaron las Cortes Extraordinarias sobre el tráfico y esclavitud de los negros* (Madrid: Imprenta de Repulles, 1814), 87. For an account of the issue of slavery in the Cortes debates, see James F. King, "The Colored Castes and American Representation in the Cortes of Cádiz," *Hispanic American Historical Review,* 33 (1953): 33–64; Murray, *Odious Commerce,* 29–34; Franco, *Las conspiraciones de 1810 y 1812,* 15–16; Tornero, *Crecimiento económico y transformaciones sociales,* 80–89; and Alain Yacou "La conspiración de Aponte (1812)," *Historia y Sociedad* (Rio Pedras) 1 (1988): 48–49.

118. "Representación que el Capitán General de la isla de Cuba, Marques de Someruelos, elevó a las Cortes," 27 Mayo 1811, *Documentos . . . sobre el tráfico y esclavitud de los negros,* 102–3.

119. Shaler to Smith, 14 June 1811, National Archives of the United States, General

Records of the Department of State, Despatches from United States Consuls in Havana, 1783–1906, roll 2, vol. 2.

120. "Bando del Capitán General de la Isla D. Salvador José de Muro y Salazar, fecha Habana 7 de Abril de 1812, acerca de las medidas acordadas con motivo de la alternación del orden. . . " ANC-AP, 12, no. 24. Emancipation rumors served as a common catalyst for numerous rebellions and conspiracies in the Americas during the eighteenth and nineteenth centuries. David Geggus has counted "more than twenty" for the years 1789–1832. See "Slavery, War, and Revolution," 7–9.

121. ANC-AP, 12, no. 9, fol. 7v; ANC-AP, 13, no. 15, fols. 42–43; AHPC-Actas Capitulares, no. 27, fol. 35.

122. ANC-AP, 12, no. 14, fols. 9, 19–24, 34, 70.

123. ANC-AP, 12, no. 26, fol. 34.

124. Ibid., fol. 36.

125. ANC-AP, 12, no. 27, fols. 13v-14v. In Puerto Rico similar reports of Christophe as a liberating monarch circulated throughout the island in 1812. See Guillermo A. Baralt, *Esclavos rebeldes: Conspiraciones y sublevaciones de esclavos en Puerto Rico (1795–1873)* (Río Piedras: Ediciones Huracán, 1982), 27.

126. ANC-AP, 12, no. 18, fol. 15.

127. Ibid., fols. 7, 34.

128. ANC-AP, 12, no. 14, fols. 50, 64; no. 18, fols. 12v-15.

129. ANC-AP, 12. no. 17, fol. 72.

130. AHPC-Actas Capitulares, no. 27, fols. 55–55v.

131. Consulado de la Havana to Larizbal, 16 Aug. 1814, BNJM-Morales, tomo 78, no. 45, fol. 576.

132. Manuel Barcia Paz, *La resistencia esclava en las plantaciones cubanas (1790–1870)* (Pinar del Río, Cuba: Ediciones Vitral, 1998), 9; Paquette, *Sugar is made with Blood,* 115, 180, 211, 242; Ada Ferrer, "Social Aspects of Cuban Nationalism: Race, Slavery, and the Guerra Chiquita, 1879–1880," *Cuban Studies* 21 (1991): 43; Aline Helg, *Our Rightful Share: The Afro-Cuban Struggle for Equality, 1886–1912* (Chapel Hill: University of North Carolina Press, 1995), 17, 78–80, 121, 229, 240; Marc C. McLeod, "Undesirable Aliens: Race, Ethnicity, and Nationalism in the Comparison of Haitian and British West Indian Immigrant Workers in Cuba, 1912–1939," *Journal of Social History* 31 (1998): 601, 611.

Chapter 11

A Fragmented Majority

Free "Of All Colors," Indians, and Slaves in Caribbean
Colombia During the Haitian Revolution

ALINE HELG

[They] were the descendants of army and navy deserters, of numerous Spanish stowaways, of blacks, runaway slave men and women
. . . and many Indian men and women who, mixed with mestizo,
black, and mulatto women, propagated an infinity of racial mixes
(*castas*) difficult to verify.

— Antonio de la Torre y Miranda, 1776

IN 1799, THE SPANISH RULERS of New Granada (modern Colombia) and
Venezuela became seriously alarmed. In a six-week period, they discovered two
conspiracies, one in Cartagena, the other in Maracaibo, which in their eyes threatened to transform the Caribbean coast of South America into another Haiti. In
both cases they found that the leaders were men of color from Saint-Domingue
who were able to recruit to their schemes Creole people of African descent, free and
slave. Moreover, some Spanish authorities thought that the two attempts were part
of a larger revolutionary plan connected with conspiracies in Santiago de Cuba,
Santa Marta, and Riohacha, and supported by the Guajiro Indians and the French
consul in Curaçao.[1] Yet both conspiracies were nipped in the bud, and the
Caribbean region was spared the "total ruin" of Saint-Domingue.[2]

In reality, Spain's fear of an alliance between the region's free people of African
descent, unconquered Indians, and slaves never materialized. Neither in 1799 nor
in the next five decades while slavery remained legal in Colombia—including during the turmoil of the wars for independence—did the subaltern groups attempt to
unite forces to impose their rule in the Caribbean coast. After analyzing these two
incidents, I will attempt to explain this lack of united challenge to the region's elite.
First, I will briefly expound why racial, color, status, and ethnic differences
between the urban dwellers of Cartagena made the first conspiracy hopeless.[3] Sec-

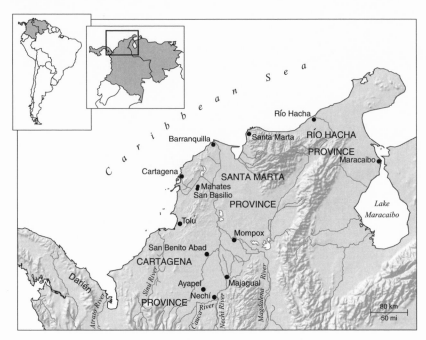

MAP 11.1: New Granada's Caribbean Coast

ond, I will examine in detail why the extreme fragmentation of the territory and social fabric of the vast Caribbean region precluded mass rebellion.

In Cartagena during the Holy Week of 1799, a group of black French slaves recently acquired by naval officers and wealthy *cartageneros* allied with some African-born and Creole black slaves and allegedly planned a major slave rebellion. On 2 April, the accusation went, they were to kill the province's Spanish governor, seize several fortresses, then massacre the whites and plunder the city. They had rallied a black sergeant of the artillery to their cause and they had hidden arms and ammunition in the vicinity. One day before its launching, however, the conspiracy was denounced to the governor, Anastasio Zejudo, by a *pardo* (mulatto) corporal, Manuel Yturen. The slave conspirators had attempted to mobilize him with his pardo militia unit, convinced that the latter "would easily take part because of the advantages that freedom brings."[4]

Colonial authorities immediately arrested six French slaves and some local slaves. The French belonging to officers claimed that they were originally free and had been captured and illegally reduced to slavery. However, the public prosecutor believed that they were slaves who had participated in the rebellions of the French colonies and had been sold to Spanish officers, in violation of a 1791 royal decree that allowed the free importation of slaves directly from Africa, but not from other American territories. If such was the case, he argued, the slavetrader should also be prosecuted for indirectly "sowing the seed of sedition and mutiny to which [these slaves] were accustomed."[5]

Despite prompt security measures, two slave conspirators were able to escape capture and burned a hacienda in the vicinity of Cartagena. Nevertheless, one week after the discovery of the alleged plot, the governor of the province proudly noted that the arrest of the French blacks and others suspects "has not caused the slightest sign of unreasonableness or discontent among the remaining Blacks . . . entertained [*sic*] in their respective occupations."[6] His confidence was shared by the viceroy of New Granada, Pedro Mendinueta.[7] Still, Zejudo asked for additional troops from Spain to reinforce the military presence along the Caribbean coast, mostly comprised until then of militiamen of African descent and "dull" soldiers from the Andean interior who could easily "become corrupted by the detestable maxims of liberty and disobedience."[8]

Most annoying to the governor was the fact that the black artillery sergeant and the slave sailors implicated in the alleged conspiracy requested the military *fuero,* a privilege that allowed them to be prosecuted by military, rather than ordinary, courts.[9] Zejudo predicted a lengthy trial in which some defendants would be sentenced by military judges, others by ordinary ones, when swift and exemplary justice in one single trial was necessary. His opinion was countered by the viceroy, who favored letting justice follow its normal course.[10] Both men agreed, however, on the necessity to publicly reward Yturen, the pardo corporal who had denounced the plot, with a promotion to sergeant and to ask Madrid to award him a Merit Medal. Zejudo thought that with such a "dignified example" the love and gratitude for the king of all pardo militiamen would be "strengthened and stimulated," which were keys to "the conservation of these dominions."[11] Mendinueta added that such a generous gesture would have an incommensurable effect on "this very numerous class of people of color in that province who so far have not belied their loyalty, and whose corruption would be of irreparable consequences."[12] Spain agreed and granted Yturen the award.[13]

On 19 May 1799, on the very day New Granada's viceroy praised the loyalty of the province of Cartagena's pardos, another conspiracy was discovered in Maracaibo, on the Caribbean coast of Venezuela. The white veteran corporal Tomás Ochoa reported to the governor of the province of Maracaibo that two mulatto French captains, the brothers Jean and Augustin Gaspard Boze, their black and mulatto crew, and the pardo second lieutenant of the city's pardo militia, the tailor Francisco Javier Pirela, intended to "introduce in [the city of Maracaibo] the same system of freedom and equality that has reduced to total ruin . . . the French ports of the island of Saint-Domingue."[14]

Ten days earlier, the two French corsairs and their British prize had entered the Bay of Maracaibo, not without raising the suspicion of the governor, because the captains were mulatto, and "those of this class had caused so many revolutions in the French Possessions of the Island of Saint-Domingue." Since then, Augustin Gaspard Boze allegedly gained the trust of Pirela, whom he contracted as a tailor. Pirela gave him confidential information on the customs of the town and the residence of its principal authorities. Boze confided to Pirela his plan to "form a revolution like in his land." The pardo second lieutenant was to provide him with two hundred men who would seize arms and occupy the city's main buildings. They would also set fire to one neighborhood and, taking advantage of the confusion it would produce, kill the city's leaders. Once the revolt triumphed, Pirela would become the new governor of Maracaibo.

According to the governor, Ochoa's denunciation, which was rewarded with an immediate promotion to sergeant, spared the city "a bloody revolution." With many troops away, the governor claimed to have subdued the French rebels by mobilizing most of Maracaibo's men against the fully armed French corsairs. The crew surrendered with arms and ammunitions, although a few managed to run away. Sixty-eight men were arrested, causing serious problems of custody due to the lack of secure jails and the prisoners' supposed complicity with free men of color.[15]

The events in Maracaibo had a rapid impact on Cartagena. Linking the two alleged conspiracies, the Council of War in Madrid denied the military *fuero* to the black artillery sergeant and the slave sailors implicated in Cartagena's plot and demanded their prompt condemnation and execution. Arguing that these slaves "were from the French colonies, where in the past disturbances they learned false ideas of freedom," the council ordered strict obedience to the Royal Decree of 1791 prohibiting the importation of foreign slaves not born in Africa to prevent the ideological "contamination" of Spanish American ports. Such slaves already in the Spanish colonies should be isolated from others of similar origin and submitted to the special vigilance of their masters, who should report suspicious slaves and relinquish them if necessary.[16]

The fate of Cartagena's defendants, as well as that of Pirela in Maracaibo, remains unknown. However, we know that in the latter case, the conspiracy was confirmed in a trial that concluded with long prison terms, but not the death penalty, for the mulatto French captains and part of their crew. Indicative of the continuing fear of a general uprising on the Caribbean coast is the alarm expressed by New Granada's viceroy to Spain when he learned that some of the Maracaibo prisoners would be transferred to Cartagena and Panama: "In one and the other provinces and their capitals there are plenty of black slaves, in the majority foreign, and people of color who favor and support them. The slaves don't need much incentive to conceive ideas of freedom in view of the pernicious example of those from the French colonies, and prudence suggests that all that could help to stir up and promote [those ideas] be avoided as much as possible," he wrote.[17]

In 1803, Viceroy Mendinueta's fear of a revolution along Haitian lines in Caribbean Colombia rose again with the alleged landing in the Guajira Peninsula of two hundred blacks and mulattoes from Guadeloupe, presumably deportees. Three of them were turned in to the governor of the province of Riohacha by a friendly indigenous community routinely rewarded for catching runaway slaves. The governor faced a difficult dilemma: if he accepted more French captives from the Indians, he told the viceroy, the former could spread ideas of freedom in the region; if he refused them, "these barbarous [Indians]" could kill them and resume hostilities against Spain.[18] Mendinueta recommended that he encourage the pacified Indians to bring as many captives as possible to Riohacha to obtain intelligence about their landing and about conditions in the French Caribbean. They should then be rapidly returned to a French colony, despite New Granada's need for additional laborers. A more interventionist policy, such as the sending of troops to capture the French blacks still hiding in Guajiro territory, could break the fragile truce recently reached between Spain and the Guajiro, he argued. Indeed, he dreaded that the mere communication between "a class of people infested with the ideas of freedom, equality and so on, who have been so pernicious and have caused so much devastation and horror in the unfortunate French islands" and the numerous, hardened, and well-armed Guajiro "always ready to hurt and always enemies of the Spanish name" could produce "a terrible and cruel domestic war."[19]

Indeed, the demography of Caribbean New Granada seemed to justify the viceroy's fear. Everywhere, whites (a category that included the *blancos de la tierra,* or so-called whites) were a small minority—about one in ten—whereas free people of color constituted the absolute majority in the three provinces of Cartagena, Santa Marta, and Riohacha. Almost two inhabitants in ten were "civilized" Indians, and only the slaves were slightly less numerous than the whites.[20]

Yet, as already stated, the viceroy's fear of an alliance uniting the nonwhite population never materialized. I will first examine briefly why the slave conspiracy failed in Cartagena in 1799, despite the fact that in the provincial capital, about three *cartageneros* out of four were of full or partial African descent, and about one cartagenero in six was a slave.[21] Indeed, it was not entirely coincidental that all the conspirators were blacks who, unable to rally the support other slaves and free persons of color, were denounced by a free pardo. In reality, in the walled city, color, ethnicity, status, and class worked together to preclude the formation of a broad racial consciousness among the population of African descent.

Color and status mattered, as exhibited by the 1777 census, which showed cartageneros' preference for endogamous marriages. Whites tended to marry with whites, quadroons with quadroons, pardos with pardos, *zambos* (of mixed Indian-African descent) with zambos, blacks with blacks, free with free, and slaves with slaves.[22] Moreover, racial categories often came with certain economic attributes, indicating a clear hierarchy of professions corresponding with the color hierarchy. Some hard manual occupations, such as mason and carpenter, were overwhelmingly in the hands of black men and included some men of mixed ancestry but no whites. Occupations requiring more qualifications, such as barber and tailor, were held predominantly by pardos and mulattoes, and a few whites but no blacks, while those such as storekeeper and baker were the prerogative of whites and of a few men of mixed ancestry but, again, comprised no blacks.[23]

Slaveownership was not the privilege of any racial group, but the whiter the head of household, the more likely he or she was to own slaves. Also, white slaveowners tended to have a higher number of slaves than persons of mixed African ancestry, whereas there were only a handful of black slaveowners and these had no more than one or two slaves. Yet the mere fact that in the popular barrio of Santo Toribio, for example, one household of color out of seven included slaves provided an effective obstacle to the formation of a racial consciousness uniting the free and the slave of African descent.[24]

Ethnicity also mattered. Despite the waning of the slave trade, the African-born still had *cabildos de nación* corresponding to their region of origin where they met separately from the Creoles. In addition, among its leaders and followers the

1799 conspiracy counted several French and African-born slaves who could not speak Spanish and communicate well with most of the city's slave population.[25] Moreover, Cartagena's slaves were scattered throughout the city, making concerted action difficult. Many lived separately from their masters, sometimes in couples; although they were obliged to make payments to their owners, they enjoyed a certain degree of independence that they probably would hesitate to risk.[26]

Also crucial in the failure of the conspiracy was its denunciation by a pardo militia officer.[27] Formed in the 1770s, the militia corresponded to the color hierarchy at work in employment: highest in prestige was the militia of whites, then followed the mostly mixed militia of pardos, and at the bottom was the darker militia of the artillery.[28] Nevertheless, only able and self-supportive men could be enlisted. Although race restricted certain promotions, all militiamen, regardless of color, benefited from the military *fuero* and other corporate privileges. Thus, belonging to the militia gave free men of color a sense of equality grounded in the shared defense of the community. It also put them in a position of power regarding the lowest strata of society: the free destitute, the Indians, and the slaves, as exemplified during the military campaign against the Indians in Darién in the mid-1780s and in the failure of the Cartagena's 1799 slave conspiracy.[29] Indeed, in the colonial city, color, class, ethnicity, and status were meaningful categories that effectively militated against a rebellion uniting free and slave blacks and mulattoes.

I will turn now to a more extensive analysis of the reasons for the absence of mass rebellions outside of Cartagena, in the vast Caribbean region: mainly the extreme fragmentation of its territory and social fabric. Significantly, from the 1760s to the 1800s, the Spanish viceroys expressed the same diagnostic: the coastal region was underpopulated and lacked a system of communication, reliable civil servants, and church personnel, which prevented its becoming a profitable and "civilized" colony. In other words, the region remained superficially conquered.

The Caribbean coast had no secure border. The approximately one thousand miles of seashore extending from the Gulf of Urabá to the Guajira Peninsula were easily accessible to foreign corsairs, contrabandists, pirates, and invaders. In the 1690s, the attempt by Scots to establish a colony in Darién and the successful seizure of Cartagena by a French fleet under the command of Admiral Pointis had fully exposed the vulnerability of the coast to attacks from the sea. Since then, Spain sought to increase control by adding new fortifications and by forming in 1775 a *matrícula de mar* (navy register) to expand the coast guard.[30] Despite these efforts, Dutch, British, and French contrabandists and corsairs still called in, even near Cartagena.[31] Understandably, during the Haitian Revolution, news that rebellious French slaves and free men of color were deported to Caribbean shores or escaped by sea alarmed New Granada's authorities.[32] With the threat of a slave revolt from the sea, the coastal region seemed all the more uncontrollable.

The borderlands were also unsafe. In the east, the Guajira Peninsula was the unconquered territory of some thirty thousand Guajiro Indians, who periodically attacked settlements in the Riohacha Province. In the west, the territory was almost entirely controlled by unsubdued Indians: the Emberá in the south of the Sinú and San Jorge valleys, the Cuna in the region of the Atrato River and in Darién.[33] The mountains of the Sierra Nevada between Riohacha and Santa Marta belonged to three indigenous groups: the Arhuaco, the Kogi, and the Arsario. The Andean Cordillera between Riohacha and Ocaña comprised several areas in which the Motilón still held firm. The hilly region east of the Magdalena River was the stronghold of about ten thousand Chimila Indians.

Indigenous defiance of Spain meant that these regions favored Spain's enemies and were sites of active contraband. Both the Cuna and the Guajiro, in particular, had intense commercial relations with the British from Jamaica and the Dutch from Curaçao who traded clothes, arms, and ammunition against cacao and tortoise shell in Darién, lumber, dyewood, cattle, and mules in the Guajira.[34] It also meant that they gave refuge to "other Indians already converted and to licentious people."[35]

Weakened by unconquered Indians on the periphery, the vast frontier territory of the Caribbean coast was far from being an integrated unit. Although well connected to the Caribbean Sea through the ports of Cartagena and Santa Marta, the coast was not a major player in the global Caribbean economy, mostly because Spain restricted New Granada's trade. As a result, the region had no real system of communication and transport supporting tropical plantations as in other parts of the Caribbean. Unlike central Colombia, which is divided by three high-peak cordilleras, the coastal region is mostly a fertile tropical lowland, with the exception of the Sierra Nevada and the arid Guajira Peninsula. It has a complex network of rivers running from the center of the viceroyalty to the Atlantic Ocean, the most important of them being the Magdalena, which meets the Cauca River near Mompox and flows into the Caribbean Sea near Barranquilla. However, neither the Magdalena, nor the San Jorge or the Sinú, the other two major rivers in the region, were easily navigable. Beside the rivers, there were some narrow and dangerous trails linking colonial towns and villages, but the rainy season rendered them virtually impassable. Neither Cartagena nor Santa Marta, the two largest cities on the coast, had direct access to the Magdalena River. As a result, the journey between Cartagena and Santa Fe de Bogotá took several weeks, first by trail to the Magdalena River, then by small boats up the river to Honda, and then by trail again to the viceroyalty's capital—that is, longer than the voyage between Cartagena and Spain.[36]

Illustrative of the difficulty of communication within the province of Cartagena are the ordeals suffered by the bishop of Cartagena, José Díaz de Lamadrid, when he visited his diocese during the dry season in 1779 and 1780. He faced all kinds of dangers on rough trails, tumultuous rivers, and the unpredictable sea; he had to endure the region's suffocating heat and voracious insects; on several occasions he lacked food and drinking water. Although he survived, both his chaplain and his secretary died of disease and exhaustion during the journey.[37]

Not surprisingly, with such an embryonic system of communication, large portions of the Caribbean region not controlled by Indians escaped the supervision of the colonial institutions. State and church authority hardly extended beyond the cities of Cartagena, Mompox, Santa Marta, and the major towns established along the rivers. Until the 1770s, an estimated sixty thousand people lived on the margin of the colony, in small illegal settlements called *rochelas,* established in the forests, hills, and swamps along the rivers. Most *arrochelados* were runaway slaves, poor free people of color, breakaway Indians, Spanish stowaways, fugitives and deserters, consenting or abducted slave or indigenous women, and their children. According to one of their conquerors, the Spanish lieutenant colonel Antonio de la Torre y Miranda, "they propagated an infinity of racial mixes (*castas*) difficult to verify."[38]

However, most rochelas were not egalitarian communities living beyond the reach of priests and *hacendados*. According to another conqueror, the Franciscan friar and veteran army officer Joseph Palacios de la Vega, some were characterized by internal violence and abuse, especially against women and children.[39] In addition, the arrochelados in the area near Nechí, for example, were under the despotic rule of a rich landowner and his associate, the parish priest, who performed the holy sacraments only after substantial payments in goods and specie. Arrochelados also often lived close to the routes of New Granada's contraband, which gave them a source of revenue, but made them dependent on the big contraband bosses in Mompox and Cartagena.[40]

Although several colonial reports claimed that arrochelados lived a life of idleness, pleasure, and intoxication,[41] the French traveler Gaspar Mollien portrayed them as busy settlers and farmers in a hostile environment.[42] No doubt, they resisted the Catholic Church norms on marriage and joyful celebration, but otherwise they did not oppose Catholicism but rather accommodated it to their conditions of relative isolation.[43]

In addition to rochelas, several *palenques* (communities of runaway slaves) continued in existence since their formation in the early seventeenth century around Cartagena and in the lower Cauca River.[44] Although by the 1690s many had been destroyed by military expeditions, some became officially recognized as peaceful hamlets of free blacks. For example, the 1780 census returns of the village of Santa Catalina, between Cartagena and Barranquilla, included two haciendas and one palenque comprising three households and thirteen inhabitants.[45] More famous is the case of Palenque de San Basilio, near Cartagena, which was granted the status of an autonomous black community in the 1710s, after all attempts at conquest had failed.[46] In exchange for a general pardon and freedom, the *palenqueros* agreed not to shelter new runaway slaves.[47] In 1772, Cartagena's bishop, Diego de Peredo, noted that they "keep to themselves without mixing with other peoples," talking "a particular language" they taught to their children. The only outside authority in the community was the priest, who ministered to a total of 396 parishioners as well as 90 slaves from adjacent haciendas.[48] The fact that slaves could be kept on haciendas in the direct vicinity of San Basilio shows that the palenqueros fully complied with the agreement reached earlier in the century and made no attempt at uniting with slaves.

In the 1770s, several other palenques survived, but without enjoying the status of autonomous black communities. The mangrove swamps of Matuna and the thickly covered Mountain of María near Cartagena still sheltered small groups of runaway slaves who lived a life contrary to the Catholic canon and harassed nearby haciendas.[49] South of Mompox, the palenques formed by slaves from the gold mines of northern Antioquia in the seventeenth century continued to exist, protected by their difficult access and by Spain's relative neglect after the decline of the region's gold production.[50] Most notable among them were the palenques of Guamal and Palizada, which, according to Palacios de la Vega, lived by fishing and robbing passengers on the Magdalena and Cauca Rivers, and in an appalling state of sin.[51]

In sum, if the hundreds of blacks living in palenques are added to the tens of thousands of insubordinate Indians in the periphery and to the estimated 60,000 arrochelados of all racial mixtures, those who escaped the control of the government, the Church, and the law probably amounted in the 1770s to some 100,000 persons. This figure, in contrast to the total of 162,272 inhabitants officially counted in the region by the 1777 census, indicates that out of every ten inhabitants on the Caribbean coast almost four lived on the colony's fringes.

To confront this problem, from the 1740s to the 1780s, the viceroys promoted several expeditions of conquest and forced resettlement against unsubdued Indians on the periphery and against arrochelados and palenqueros within the Caribbean region. The means of pacifying the borderland Indians ranged from military conquest followed by colonization to the reduction of Indian communities under caciques on the Spanish payroll.[52] Both policies proved a failure,[53] except with the Chimila and Motilón Indians, who were forced by repetitive military campaigns and intense missionary activity to cease hostilities.[54] The solution chosen by the governor of Riohacha in 1776 to deal with the Guajiro seemed the most successful: he allegedly diverted the royal budget destined to a military campaign to "give the Indians corn, brandy, linen clothes, meat, and other things so that they do not rebel."[55] Two decades later, the Guajiro still held to their territory and traded openly with the British and the Dutch, but they did not attack settlements anymore, "owing to the governors' obsequiousness."[56] In contrast, despite costly military expeditions, the entire region between the south of the Sinú River and Portobelo in Panama (including the Atrato River, principal access road to the Chocó's gold mines) remained under undisputed Cuna control, and in 1803 viceroy Mendinueta estimated their "reduction . . . an almost desperate matter."[57]

Four campaigns were launched against rochelas and palenques. The first one, entrusted to José Fernando de Mier y Guerra, focused on the east bank of the Magdalena River, in order to secure the main route between the coast and the interior of New Granada. It lasted from 1744 to 1765, during which time twenty-two settlements were founded with an estimated total of eight thousand inhabitants.[58] Simultaneously, a second campaign, led by the commissioned judge Francisco Pérez de Vargas, attempted to bring some colonial order to the region of Tierradentro, around Barranquilla, by separating Indians from the free population illegally residing in their pueblos. Indians were forcibly resettled in new pueblos and non-Indians in legal villages and towns.[59]

The third and most extensive campaign was headed by Antonio de la Torre y Miranda, from 1774 to 1778, and focused on the valleys of Sinú and San Jorge as well as on the plains of Tolú. In total, de la Torre founded or relocated forty-three settlements with a total of 43,133 inhabitants, most of them arrochelados of all colors and Indians, as well as blacks from the illegal palenques near Cartagena.[60] The fourth and last campaign was undertaken by Joseph Palacios de la Vega in the southeast of Cartagena Province in 1787–88. Under the direct orders of archbishop-viceroy Caballero y Góngora, he was to destroy rochelas and palenques and to resettle their dwellers in Christian villages. Brandishing the sword more often than the cross, he is credited with the forced settlement of about two thousand people but was recalled before completing his mission.[61]

These campaigns facilitated the formation and consolidation of large land-holdings belonging to few owners, generally the descendants of recent Spanish immigrants residing in Cartagena and Mompox. Simultaneously, thousands of small cultivators, arrochelados, palenqueros, and Indians lost the lands they tilled and were forced to become dependent on haciendas or to try elsewhere.[62] Most affected by this process were the areas of Mahates, Tierradentro, the plains of Tolú, San Benito de Abad, and Ayapel. Not surprisingly, with less land available to inde-pendent cultivation, tensions among the rural population, notably between free people of color and Indians, increased.[63] Hacendados expanded their landholdings by buying the land that had become property of the king after the suppression and relocation of several Indian pueblos and after the 1767 expulsion of the Jesuits. Another form of land acquisition was the *composición,* or declaration of ownership and purchase of the property titles of untitled lands cultivated by small peasants and arrochelados.[64] According to historian Hermes Tovar, the process of land con-centration was such that in Cartagena Province, 77 percent of all the land adjudged between 1699 and 1800 benefited fourteen individuals; in the Santa Marta Province 78 percent of the land was awarded to seventeen proprietors. Among them, three families managed to accumulate 170,000 hectares between the 1730s and the 1770s. Not only were the magnates laws unto themselves, their holdings were parts of larger enterprises involved in legal trade and contraband.[65]

The new holdings principally consisted of cattle ranches in the Tolú plains and along the Magdalena, Sinú, San Jorge, and César rivers; sugar cane haciendas around Cartagena and Mompox; and cacao haciendas south of Mompox.[66] They used a labor force composed mostly of slaves, which often represented an impor-tant portion of a hacienda's total value.[67] They also employed sharecroppers (*arren-datarios*), peons (*matriculados* and *concertados*), and Indians, whose labor became increasingly accessible after the campaigns of resettlement.[68]

The slave haciendas were ruled with almost no outside interference. Many slaveowners and overseers did not respect their obligation to adequately feed, dress, protect, and teach the rudiments of the Christian doctrine to their slaves.[69] More-over, masters often gave no days of rest to slaves and prohibited them to attend mass on Sundays and feast days, requiring that instead they work in order to "earn to have clothes."[70]

In the 1780s, bishop Díaz de Lamadrid took a series of drastic measures to bring the Catholic doctrine to rural slaves. He recalled to all parishioners—masters, overseers, free individuals, as well as male and female slaves and servants—their duty to go to mass. He ordered several slaveowners to build decent churches for their dependents and to entrust their slaves to priests for basic catechization. In order to prevent masters from forcing their slaves to work on days of compulsory church attendance, Díaz de Lamadrid instructed priests to explain to the slaves and the free that "their owners were compelled to give them the necessary sustenance and clothing as well as to teach them the Christian doctrine."[71] Finally, in 1782, he imposed the penalty of excommunication on masters who, after three admonitions, continued to force slaves to work on religious days. In response, Cartagena's ecclesiastical cabildo, a stronghold of slaveowners, petitioned to have the 1782 decree nullified. The Council of the Indies validated it but replaced the penalty of excommunication with one that gave ample room for manipulation due to hacendados' patronage networks: the reporting of disobedient slaveowners to the royal authorities (*jueces reales*) in charge of enforcing compliance.[72]

More generally, the colonial institutions were ill equipped to challenge the power of the local magnates, despite the fact that the campaigns of resettlement increased state and church control of the Caribbean region. The state lacked basic police forces to make people respect the law. The few authorities that did exist outside the main cities and those serving in small towns and villages often fell under the influence of local bosses related to the big hacendados, who not only mistreated communities but also defrauded the royal treasury. Physical abuse and corruption were especially widespread in the villages, where it was not uncommon to see captains collude with priests to exploit the indigenous population.[73]

The Church was in no better condition to exercise control than the state. At the root of the problem were the endemic shortage of priests and the immense poverty of the majority of the population, who lacked the means to support a minister and a church. As a result, few priests were willing to serve outside the main cities, and among those who went, many were incompetent, abusive, or immoral.[74]

In addition, in many places the Church received no support from the civil authorities supposed to make people respect the law, as already noted regarding hacendados' duties toward their slaves. Parishioners disobeyed the priests, ignored the threats of excommunication, and knew that the royal authorities would not intervene.[75] Symptomatic of the lack of state support for the church in the 1770s and 1780s is the viceroys' overruling of diocesan edicts that banned *bundes* (popular dances held in the coastal region on the eve of the most popular religious celebrations). Whereas the bishops claimed that the bundes were sources of sexual promiscuity and intoxication, the viceroys saw them as moments of public enjoyment.[76]

Given the weak presence of colonial authorities at the local level, most of the Caribbean region resembled a vast patchwork of fiefdoms with undefined borders on a background of unconquered lands. The fiefdoms were ruled by powerful hacendados who were able to place men from their patronage network into most royal and ecclesiastical positions. The magnates also controlled the population residing in small towns and villages in their area through various patron-client relations, including labor and land contracts, recruitment in the militia, and access to natural resources. Finally, their power extended to the rochelas and palenques on the fringe of their fiefdoms.[77]

As a result, villages and pueblos showed little concern for the colonial order, except in their geometrical organization around central squares. The campaigns of reconquest produced intense demographic transfer and mixing that blurred racial and ethnic boundaries. Along the Magdalena River, Indians from distinct communities were forcibly resettled together in single pueblos. Some subjugated Indians from Darién and the Chocó were deported to pueblos in the newly colonized regions of the Sinú and San Jorge rivers. Arrochelados and palenqueros were brought together to form new villages.[78] Hacendados, officials, and other men in positions of power contributed to the racial mixing by taking advantage of women. Moreover, to the horror of Bishop Peredo, in such occasions as the bundes, "Indians, mestizos, mulattoes, blacks and zambos, and other people of the lower class: all congregate together without order or separation of the sexes, the men mixed with the women."[79]

Also representative of the blurring of racial boundaries was Spain's difficulty in establishing disciplined militias along color lines in the 1770s. Whereas the fortified city of Cartagena and the district of Barranquilla counted separate companies of whites, pardos and *morenos* (blacks), in the rest of the region the classification was limited to units of whites and of *todos los colores* (all colors). By the 1780s, there were so few light-skinned men in the white militia that Spain opted for having only militia of all colors in most of the coast, including Santa Marta.[80]

Yet this very lack of colonial order benefited to some extent the rural population. Several viceroys noted the general resistance of the population to outside interference. In the words of one of them, people were still free to obey or resist the law, because "there was no force, arms, or means to ensure that superiors be respected and obeyed."[81]

As the daily wages of peons had remained stagnant since the 1750s, in contrast with the rapid rise of the prices of goods and of the hacendados' profits, many chose to beg rather than to work.[82] Disobedience was particularly noticeable in the religious realm, in part because the local elite profited from the weakness of the church. Bishops Peredo and Díaz de Lamadrid, who extensively visited the province of Cartagena in the 1770s and 1780s, lamented "the universal relaxation and corruption of the faithful's mores," who failed to baptize their children at birth, ignored the Catholic doctrine, and lived in concubinage.[83] Although they attributed this situation to the region's general poverty and the acute shortage of priests, in some cases people simply refused to pay for a priest, and parents resisted sending their children to be catechized, "giving as an excuse that they are not Indians who have to be taught the doctrine."[84]

Moreover, the eighteenth-century campaigns against Indian territories, rochelas and palenques were only partly successful. On the frontier, the Guajiro and the Cuna remained invincible and continued to provide refuge to fugitives. Palacios de la Vega's aborted campaign left many rochelas and palenques south of Mompox intact. Several illegal settlements situated outside or on the fringe of the areas being colonized still existed. In addition, many of those forcibly resettled along the Magdalena, Sinú, and San Jorge rivers fled individually or in small groups to join or form rochelas further in the hinterland.[85]

Indeed, individual flight, not joint rebellion, was the principal means of resistance by subordinate groups in the coastal region. As accurately noted by the archbishop-viceroy Caballero y Góngora in 1789, in the absence of measures to limit land concentration, "Most of the free population are truly a vagrant and unsettled population who, forced by the landowners' tyranny, move around with the ease granted by the light weight of their furniture, the small value of their hut, and their lack of love for the font where they were baptized . . . This comes from [their] old and deeply rooted freedom of avoiding one another in order to be able to live as they please without fearing to be noticed in their infamous and vile behavior."[86]

Although there are no figures to quantify the magnitude of flight among slaves, the fact that rochelas and palenques still existed in the early nineteenth century shows that it was an important phenomenon. The lack of security forces in most of the region also increased slaves' chances of successfully running away. In addition, the availability of unconquered backlands made the prospect of becoming a free peasant, and, south of Mompox, of finding gold, all the more possible.[87] Arguably, individual escape could also have been tacitly accepted by owners as a security valve in the slave system. By letting the most rebellious slaves run away, masters indirectly protected their holdings by removing potential leaders of rebellions.

Indeed, only a few local slave rebellions have been recorded on the Caribbean coast, notwithstanding that most haciendas were relatively isolated and often counted more slaves than free persons on their lands. In one case, on a cattle-raising hacienda in the province of Santa Marta in 1768, the slaves rebelled after killing their overseer, but then successfully used the threat of destruction and flight to the "wild Indians" to force their master into negotiations over labor conditions.[88] In another, unsuccessful, occurrence on a hacienda in the jurisdiction of Mompox in 1799, slaves rebelled against the takeover of the property by their owner's heirs after his death and in arms refused "to serve any white." They resisted until 1802, when some slaves betrayed the others, who were taken to Mompox to be sold.[89] Here, as in the first case, slaves stayed in their workplace, but rejected any new authority over them, acting as if the hacienda had become theirs at the death of their master.

Similarly, few rebellions were reported among the free population of color. They took place generally in response to forced resettlement, and were not autonomous lower-class movements, but promoted or led by local magnates. For example, the Franciscan Palacios de la Vega claimed that near Nechí he faced alone three hundred armed men and two hundred "armed concubines," all Indian, zambo, mulatto, and black arrocheldos. The rebels were headed by the "mulato-indio" Antonio López, acting under the orders of a magnate and a priest who ruled the area unchallenged. "Thanks to God's help," the officer-friar managed to escape death.[90] In the plains of Tolú, the destruction of rochelas deprived some powerful hacendados of access to their inhabitants' services and products. One landlord did not hesitate to mobilize and arm dozens of lower-class men of color to attempt to chase former arrocheldos out of their new settlement and bring them back into his fief.[91]

Apart from these isolated incidents, at the time of the Haitian Revolution the Caribbean coast was peaceful, despite the continuing domination of its periphery by unconquered Indians and arrocheldos. According to viceroy Mendinueta in 1803, crimes and murders were rare, and in general the population was docile and laborious.[92] As for those still in rochelas, they were content "with freely vegetating." In fact, the viceroy noted with foresight that unrest was coming from the more civilized cities rather than from the wild mountains and swamps.[93]

Whereas in the city of Cartagena, divisions based on color, status, class, and ethnicity, in addition to basic logistics, explain the failure of the 1799 slave conspiracy, in the rest of the coast, the nonwhite majority's inability to rebel against the white elite was due principally to overall fragmentation. Lacking a system of communication, the coastal territory was surrounded by unconquered Indians and consisted of a patchwork of rival cities, small towns, pueblos, fiefdoms dominated by landlords, and backlands sheltering rochelas and palenques. Such division was not conducive to mass revolt. Rochelas and palenques owed their survival to their relative isolation and noninfringement of the magnates' fiefdoms. Therefore they generally kept to themselves and avoided conflicts and alliances with outsiders, except to protect their territory.[94] Simultaneously, the social fabric of the region had been profoundly affected by the Spanish campaigns of resettlement of the rural population and by ensuing land concentration. As pueblo Indians, arrochelados, palenqueros, and isolated peasants were forcibly relocated, they had to create new identities and ties of kinship in an environment where limited land was available. Longtime residents in established towns and villages had to accommodate themselves to decreasing purchasing power and reduced access to land and resources. The formation of viable lower-class alliances in this changing context was all the more difficult in that they did not face a well-defined force of domination. The hacendados were the most visible and nearest incarnation of power, yet daily dependence on them and ties of patronage and kinship tended to prevent open challenge. The colonial state and the Catholic Church were weak and often at odds with each other, thus not easily perceived as joint institutions against which to mobilize.

Neither was the demography of the Caribbean coast conducive to lower-class rebellion. Unlike in the French or British Caribbean, where slaves were in the majority, in Caribbean New Granada they comprised only about 10 percent of the official population, despite their leading role in the colonial economy. As a result, they had no chances of successfully revolting, except in alliance with other social groups. Of these, the Cuna and Guajiro Indians were the best organized and armed and the most vehemently opposed to Spanish colonialism. However, their struggle was a territorial one situated on the periphery that could not connect with the slaves' struggle. The Indians residing in legal pueblos outnumbered the slaves by two to one. Divided by ethnicity and scattered in communities throughout the region, they were rapidly losing the struggle against mestizaje and encroachment on their lands by landlords and free people of color. As for the free population of color, although increasing dependence of the large haciendas brought them closer to the slaves, the forces of localism and patronage, and, in the case of those recently resettled, the lack of deep roots in and commitment to their new communities hindered collective action. Indeed, individual protest, principally in the form of flight, seemed the best option in a fragmented region characterized by unconquered borders and backlands.

Ten years after the great fear of a revolution along Haitian lines in Caribbean New Granada, the region began its struggle for independence as fragmented as it was in 1799. Whereas Mompox and Cartagena declared their independence in 1810 and 1811, respectively, they waged a war against each other, and Santa Marta remained the stronghold of the Spanish monarchy. Subregions and fiefdoms aligned themselves to one or the other side according to circumstance. As a result, the coastal region suffered as much from its own civil war as from Spanish reconquest in 1815. In the early 1810s, the free people of color of Cartagena and Mompox proclaimed their equality on the basis of the ideals of the French Revolution of 1789, but they continued to act under white leadership and they did not demand the abolition of slavery. Nowhere in the Caribbean coast did the free and slave subaltern groups of full and partial African descent unite to attempt to establish a black republic on the model of the Haitian Revolution.[95]

NOTES

1. Pedro Mendinueta to Francisco de Saavedra, 19 July 1799, Archivo General de Indias, Seville (hereafter AGI), Estado, 52, no. 81, fols. 1–2; General Gouvion Saint Cyr to Pedro Cevallos, 29 Prairial (May) de l'an 10 de la République française, AGI, Estado, 71, no. 5, fols. 9–11.

2. Marquis of Santa Cruz to Manuel de Guevara Vasconcelos, 21 May 1799, AGI, Estado, 71, no. 3, fols. 23–25, 29–31.

3. For an in-depth analysis of Cartagena's society, see Aline Helg, "The Limits of Equality: Free People of Color and Slaves during the First Independence of Cartagena, Colombia (1810–15)," *Slavery and Abolition* 20 (1999): 1–30.

4. Anastasio Zejudo to viceroy, 9 Apr. 1799, AGI, Estado, 53, no. 77, fol. 10.

5. Josef Munive y Mozo to Zejudo, 24 Apr. 1799, AGI, Archivo General de Simancas (hereafter AGS), Secretaría Guerra, 7247, exp. 26, fols. 122–23.

6. Zejudo to viceroy, 9 Apr. 1799, AGI, Estado, 53, no. 77, fols. 9–11; also Mendinueta to Saavedra, 19 May 1799, AGI, Estado, 52, no. 76, fols. 5–7.

7. Mendinueta to Saavedra, 19 May 1799, AGI, Estado, 52, no. 76, fols. 5–7.

8. Zejudo to Saavedra, 30 Apr. 1799, AGI, Estado, 53, no. 77, fols. 1–4.

9. Lyle N. McAlister, *The "Fuero Militar" in New Spain, 1764–1800* (Gainesville: The University Presses of Florida, 1957), 1–15; Allan J. Kuethe, *Military Reform and Society in New Granada, 1773–1808* (Gainesville: The University Presses of Florida, 1978), 27–28.

10. Zejudo to Mendinueta, 9 Apr. 1799, AGI, Estado, 53, no. 77, fol. 12; Joaquín Francisco Fidalgo to Zejudo, 20 Apr. 1799, AGI, AGS/ Secretaría Guerra, 7247, exp. 26, fols. 109–10; Mendinueta to Zejudo, 29 Apr. 1799, AGI, Estado, 52, no. 76, fols. 25–27; Mendinueta to Juan Manuel Alvarez, 19 May 1799, AGI, Estado, 52, no. 76, fols. 29–35.

11. Zejudo to Mendinueta, 10 Apr. 1799, AGS, Secretaría Guerra, 7247, exp. 26, fols. 149–50.

12. Mendinueta to Alvarez, 19 May 1799, AGI, Estado, 52, no. 76, fols. 147–48. The viceroy alludes to the anti-Bourbon Comunero Revolt in 1781, which had been an Andean, not a coastal affair, and during which black and mulatto militiamen from the province of Cartagena had shown loyalty to Spain. See John Leddy Phelan, *The People and the King. The Comunero Revolution in Colombia, 1781* (Madison: University of Wisconsin Press, 1978), 144–45.

13. Resolución del Consejo de Guerra, 2, 4, and 8 Oct. 1799, AGS, Secretaría Guerra, no. 7247, exp. 26, fols. 18–20, 22–23, 157.

14. Marquis of Santa Cruz to Manuel de Guevara Vasconcelos, 21 May 1799, AGI, Estado, 71, no. 3, fols. 23–25, 29–31.

15. Marquis of Santa Cruz to Guevara, 21 May 1799, AGI, Estado, 71, no. 3, fols. 24–27, 32–33; Guevara to marquis of Santa Cruz, 3 and 4 June 1799, AGI, Estado, 71, no. 3, fols 35–40.

16. Consejo pleno extraordinario de guerra, 9 Oct. 1799, AGS, Secretaría Guerra, 7247, exp. 26, fols. 34–45.

17. Mendinueta to Josef Antonio Caballero, 19 Nov. 1800, AGI, Estado, 52, no. 102, fols. 1–3.

18. Ignacio Sánchez de Texada to Pedro Mendinueta, 28 Feb. 1803, AGI, Estado, 52, no. 137, fols. 15–16.

19. Mendinueta to Pedro Ceballos, 19 Apr. 1803, AGI, Estado, 52, no. 137, fols. 1–10. See also Mendinueta to Sánchez de Texada, 9 Apr. 1803, AGI, Estado, 52, no. 137, fols. 16–18.

20. According to the 1777 Spanish census, the total population of the province of Cartagena amounted to 118,382: 64 percent free people of color, 16 percent Indians, 12 percent whites, and 8 percent slaves; the province of Santa Marta had a total of 39,940 inhabitants, 57 percent free of color, 21 percent Indians, 11 percent whites, and 10 percent slaves; as for the province of Riohacha, its total population amounted to only 3,950: 64 percent free of color, 16 percent Indians, 9 percent whites, and 11 percent slaves. See Anthony McFarlane, *Colombia before Independence. Economy, Society, and Politics under Bourbon Rule* (Cambridge: Cambridge University Press, 1993), 353. These figures do not include the thousands of Indians and free people of color living on the periphery (see below).

21. Hermes Tovar Pinzón, *"Convocatoria al poder del número." Censos y estadísticas de la Nueva Granada* (Bogotá: Archivo General de la Nación, 1994), 484–503. The figures were 3,612 whites (including 223 ecclesiastics), 7,612 free of all colors, 2,107 slaves, and 65 Indians.

22. Padrón del barrio de Sto. Thoribio, año de 1777, in Archivo Histórico Nacional de Colombia, Bogotá, Sección Colonia (hereafter AHNC, CO), Fondo Miscelánea (hereafter MI), tomo 41, fol. 1078v; Padrón que comprehende el barrio de Nra. Sa. de la Merced, y su vecindario, formado en el año de 1777, AHNC, CO, Fondo Censos Varios Departamentos (hereafter CV), tomo 8, fol. 164; Razón del barrio de San Sebastián, Año de 1777, in AHNC, CO, MI, tomo 44, fol. 957. Santo Toribio was the most densely populated and racially mixed barrio in Cartagena, with a majority of free persons of color and about one-third of the city's slaves. It is also the barrio with the most complete census, which explains why much of my evidence is based on its Padrón.

23. Padrón del barrio de Sto. Thoribio. This comment takes into account the proportion of each racial category in the barrio's population.

24. Padrón del barrio de Sto. Thoribio.

25. Ibid.; Munive to Zejudo, 24 Apr. 1799, AGS, Secretaría Guerra, 7247, exp. 26, fols. 122–23. For the same trends in the 1810s, see Joaquín Posada Gutiérrez, *Memorias histórico-políticas,* 4 vols. (Bogotá: Imprenta Nacional, 1929), 2:195–209.

26. Padrón del barrio de Sto. Thoribio; Padrón . . . [d]el barrio de Nra. Sa. de la Merced; Razón del barrio de San Sebastián.

27. For a discussion of the militia see Kuethe, *Military Reform.*

28. Relación que comprende los artesanos que viven en el Barrio de Sn. Sebastián de esta ciudad con expresión de sus nombres, casas, edades y los que son milicianos, AHNC, CO, MI, Rollo 31, fols. 1014–15v; Relación que manifiesta los artesanos que existen en el Barrio de Sto. Thoribio el presente año de 1780, AHNC, CO, MI, Rollo 31, fols. 148–54v.

29. Kuethe, *Military Reform,* 28–30, 141–43.

30. McFarlane, *Colombia before Independence,* 24–26; Kuethe, *Military Reform,* 23.

31. Representación de los comerciantes de Cartagena al Secretario de Estado Don Diego Gardoqui, 30 Apr. 1795, AGI, Santa Fe, 1019.

32. Mendinueta to Ceballos, 19 Apr. 1803, AGI, Estado, 52, no. 137, fol. 5.

33. Consejo Regional de Planificación de la Costa Atlántica, *Mapa cultural del Caribe colombiano* (Santa Marta: Consejo Regional de Planificación de la Costa Atlántica, 1993), 130–34, 153–55.

34. Francisco Antonio Moreno y Escandón, "Estado del Virreinato de Santafé" (1772), in Germán Colmenares, ed., *Relaciones e informes de los gobernantes de la Nueva Granada,* 3 vols. (Bogotá: Banco Popular, 1989), 1:153–87; Francisco Xavier Monty, "Reconocimiento y exploración de la costa de Carolina y golfo del Darién" (1761), in Antonio B. Cuervo, *Colección de documentos inéditos sobre la geografía y la historia de Colombia,* 4 vols. (Bogotá: Imprenta de Vapor de Zalamea Hermanos, 1891), 1:483–84.

35. Moreno, "Estado del Virreinato," 1:182–87.

36. Joaquín Francisco Fidalgo, "Expedición Fidalgo" (1790s), in Cuervo, *Colección de documentos inéditos,* 55 n, 76 n; Consejo Regional de Planificación de la Costa Atlántica, *Mapa cultural,* 51, 85; Theodore E. Nichols, *Tres puertos de Colombia: Estudio sobre el desarrollo de Cartagena, Santa Marta y Barranquilla* (Bogotá: Banco Popular, 1973), 39–41; McFarlane, *Colombia before Independence,* 39–40.

37. José Fernández Díaz de Lamadrid], "Informe del Obispo de Cartagena sobre el estado de la religión y la iglesia en los pueblos de la Costa, 1781," in Gustavo Bell Lemus, *Cartagena de Indias: de la colonia a la república* (Bogotá: Fundación Simón y Lola Guberek, 1991), 153.

38. Antonio de la Torre y Miranda, "Noticia individual de las poblaciones nuevamente fundadas en la Provincia de Cartagena" (1774–1778), in José P. Urueta, ed., *Documentos para la historia de Cartagena,* 6 vols. (Cartagena: Tipografía de Antonio Araújo L., 1887–1891), 4:43. See also Gaspar Mollien, *Voyage dans la république de Colombia, en 1823,* 2 vols. (Paris: Arthus Bertrand, 1824), 1:45.

39. Joseph Palacios de la Vega, *Diario de viaje del P. Joseph Palacios de la Vega entre los indios y negros de la provincia de Cartagena en el nuevo reino de Granada, 1787–1788,* ed. Gerardo Reichel Dolmatoff, (Bogotá: Editorial ABC, 1955), 72–73, 94, 105, 104; Diego de Peredo, "Noticia historial de la provincia de Cartagena de Indias, año 1772," *Anuario Colombiano de Historia Social y de la Cultura* 6–7 (1971–1972): 147.

40. Palacios, *Diario de viaje,* 49–52, 104. See also ibid., 47–48, 71, 75–76, 93, 95, 100; De la Torre, "Noticia individual," 4:47, 55–56; Francisco Gil y Lemos, "Relación de D. Francisco Gil y Lemos" (1789), in Colmenares, ed., *Relaciones e informes,* 2:17–18.

41. Antonio Caballero y Góngora, "Relación del estado del Nuevo Reino de Granada," (1789), in Colmenares, ed., *Relaciones e informes,* 1:410; De la Torre, "Noticia individual," 4:44, 60.

42. Mollien, *Voyage,* 1:49. See also ibid., 1:45–50.

43. De la Torre, "Noticia individual," 4:49, 60; Palacios, *Diario de viaje,* 96.

44. On palenques, see María del Carmen Borrego Pla, *Palenques de negros en Cartagena de Indias a fines del siglo diecisiete* (Sevilla: Escuela de Estudios Hispanoamericanos, 1973); Anthony McFarlane, *"Cimarrones* and *palenques:* Runaways and Resistance in Colonial Colombia," *Slavery and Abolition* 6 (1985): 131–51; Orlando Fals Borda, *Capitalismo, hacienda y poblamiento en la costa atlántica* (Bogotá: Punta de Lanza, 1976).

45. Padrón del sitio de Santa Catalina, año 1780, in AHNC, CO, CV, rollo 21, fols. 143–51v.

46. De la Torre, "Noticia individual," 4:47–51.

47. Aquiles Escalante, "Notas sobre el Palenque de San Basilio, una comunidad negra de Colombia," *Divulgaciones Etnológicas* 3 (1954): 228–29; McFarlane, *"Cimarrones* and *palenques,"* 134–35.

48. Peredo, "Noticia historial," 140.

49. De la Torre, "Noticia individual," 4:47–51.

50. Ann Twinam, *Merchants and Farmers in Colonial Colombia* (Austin: University of Texas Press, 1982), 16.

51. Palacios, *Diario de viaje,* 105; also ibid., 96.

52. Pedro Messía de la Zerda, "Relación del estado del Virreinato de Santafé . . . Año 1772," in Colmenares, ed. *Relaciones e informes,* 1:137–38, 144–47; Moreno, "Estado del Virreinato," 1:188–89; Francisco Silvestre, "Apuntes reservados particulares y generales del estado actual del Virreinato de Santafé de Bogotá" (1789), in Colmenares, ed. *Relaciones e informes,* 2:80–82, 102.

53. Fidalgo, "Expedición," 184–85 n.

54. Silvestre, "Apuntes reservados," 2:103. Also Gil, "Relación," 2:19–22; Orlando Fals Borda, *Historia doble de la Costa,* 4 vols. (Bogotá: Carlos Valencia Editores, 1979–1986), 1:103AB-114AB.

55. Anonymous letter quoted in Juan Marchena Fernández, *La institución militar en Cartagena de Indias en el siglo XVIII* (Seville: Escuela de Estudios Hispanoamericanos, 1982), 172.

56. Fidalgo, "Expedición," 1:48–49, 38–41 n.

57. Pedro Mendinueta, "Relación del estado del Nuevo Reino de Granada. Año 1803," in Colmenares, ed. *Relaciones e informes,* 3:167. See also Luis Arguedas, "Diario de una expedición reservada" (1786–1787), in Cuervo, *Colección de documentos inéditos,* 1:385–89; Caballero, "Relación," 1:459–67; Silvestre, "Apuntes reservados," 2:104–5; Josef de Ezpeleta, "Relación del gobierno . . . en este Nuevo Reino de Granada" (1796), in Colmenares, ed., *Relaciones e informes,* 2:154–58; Fidalgo, "Expedición," 188 n; Kuethe, *Military Reform,* 130–44.

58. Fals, *Historia doble,* 1:103AB-114AB.

59. José Agustín Blanco Barros, *Atlántico y Barranquilla en la época colonial* (Barranquilla: Ediciones Gobernación del Atlántico, 1994), 77–106.

60. De la Torre, "Noticia individual," 4:43. See also Pilar Moreno de Angel, *Antonio de la Torre y Miranda, viajero y poblador* (Bogotá: Planeta Colombiana Editorial S.A., 1993), 4:34–35, 39.

61. Palacios, *Diario de viaje,* 105–6; Moreno de Angel, *Antonio de la Torre,* 33–34.

62. Germán Colmenares, "El tránsito a sociedades campesinas de dos sociedades esclavistas en la Nueva Granada, Cartagena y Popayán, 1780–1850," *Huellas* 29 (1990): 19; McFarlane, *Colombia before Independence,* 45. Colmenares shows that during the same period, Cauca witnessed a process of land parcelization that benefited the rural poor.

63. Hermes Tovar Pinzón, *Hacienda colonial y formación social* (Barcelona: Ediciones Sendai, 1988), 119.

64. Ibid., 31–33, 36, 42.

65. Ibid., 39.

66. Peredo, "Noticia historial," 137–38, 140–43, 146–50, 153–54; José Fernández Díaz de Lamadrid, "Visita pastoral de la ciudad y diocesis de Cartagena de Indias, 1778–1781," in Gabriel Martínez Reyes, ed., *Cartas de los obispos de Cartagena de Indias durante el período hispánico, 1534–1820* (Medellín: Editorial Zuluaga, 1986), 660–62, 673–74, 693–97. See also Tovar, *Hacienda colonial,* 28, 94.

67. Tovar, *Hacienda colonial,* 102.

68. Adolfo Meisel Roca, "Esclavitud, mestizaje y haciendas en la provincia de Cartagena, 1533–1851," in Gustavo Bell Lemus, ed., *El Caribe colombiano. Selección de textos históricos* (Barranquilla: Editorial Uninorte, 1988), 123–24; Colmenares, "El tránsito," 19.

69. Díaz de Lamadrid, "Visita pastoral," 696; [Díaz de Lamadrid], "Informe del Obispo," 156.

70. Díaz de Lamadrid, "Visita pastoral," 693; also ibid., 673–74, 695–97; [Díaz de Lamadrid], "Informe del Obispo," 156.

71. Díaz de Lamadrid, "Visita pastoral," 696.

72. Martínez, ed., *Cartas de los obispos de Cartagena,* 569–62.

73. Moreno, "Estado del Virreinato," 156–57; Palacios, *Diario de viaje,* 49–52, 71.

74. Díaz de Lamadrid, "Visita pastoral," 656, 660; Peredo, "Noticia historial," 149–50; [Díaz de Lamadrid], "Informe del Obispo," 155. See also Guy Bensusan, "Cartagena's Fandango Politics," *Studies in Latin American Popular Culture* 5 (1984): 128.

75. [Díaz de Lamadrid], "Informe del Obispo," 155–56; Díaz de Lamadrid, "Visita pastoral."

76. Bensusan, "Cartagena's Fandango Politics," 127–32.

77. Moreno de Angel, *Antonio de la Torre,* 48–62.

78. Peredo, "Noticia historial"; Díaz de Lamadrid, "Visita pastoral."

79. [Díaz de Lamadrid], "Informe del Obispo," 156–57.

80. Kuethe, *Military Reform,* 161–62, 196–97.

81. Messía, "Relación," 1:147. See also Caballero, "Relación," 1:410–11.

82. Mendinueta, "Relación," 3:53. See also Ezpeleta, "Relación," 2:207.

83. [Díaz de Lamadrid], "Informe del Obispo," 154. See also Peredo, "Noticia historial," 125–54; Díaz de Lamadrid, "Visita pastoral," 639–98.

84. Díaz de Lamadrid, "Visita pastoral," 684.

85. Moreno, "Estado del Virreinato," 1:182–87; Blanco, *Atlántico y Barranquilla,* 77–106; Peredo, "Noticia historial," 153; Fals, *Historia doble,* 4:119A.

86. Caballero, "Relación," 1:410.

87. On New Granada in general, see McFarlane, *"Cimarrones* and *palenques,"* 138–43.

88. Ibid., 138–39.

89. Jaime Jaramillo Uribe, *Ensayos sobre historia social colombiana,* 2 vols. (Bogotá: Tercer Mundo Editores, 1989), 1:67; Hermes Tovar Pinzón, *De una chispa se forma una hoguera: Esclavitud, insubordinación y liberación* (Tunja: Universidad Pedagógica y Tecnológica de Colombia, 1992), 24–31.

90. Palacios, *Diario de viaje,* 49–61.

91. Moreno de Angel, *Antonio de la Torre,* 55.

92. Mendinueta, "Relación," 3:53. See also Ezpeleta, "Relación," 2:207.

93. Mendinueta, "Relación," 3:55–56. As foreseen by the viceroy, the movement of independence began in such cities as Cartagena, Mompox, and Santa Fe, not in the rural areas.

94. On a fascinating case in the province of Cauca, see Francisco U. Zuluaga R., *Guerrilla y sociedad en el Patía: Una relación entre clientelismo político y la insurgencia social* (Cali: Universidad del Valle, Facultad de Humanidades, 1993).

95. On New Granada as a whole, see Anthony McFarlane, "Building Political Order: The 'First Republic' in New Granada, 1810–1815," in Eduardo Posada-Carbó, ed., *In Search of New Order: Essays on the Politics and Society of Nineteenth-Century Latin America* (London: Institute of Latin American Studies, 1998), 8–33.

Chapter 12

Haiti as an Image of Popular Republicanism in Caribbean Colombia
Cartagena Province (1811–1828)

MARIXA LASSO

...Vs se han de joder porque correrá la sangre como en Santo Domingo:
A broadside that appeared overnight on Mompox's walls, 1823

IN THE WAKE OF THE Spanish American Wars of Independence, the *pardo*[1] mayor of a small town in the province of Cartagena was accused of threatening the local white elite with a new and bloodier war, just as had happened in Haiti. In 1823, in the city of Mompox, an anonymous broadside threatened the whites with being chopped with the machete until their blood ran as it had in Saint-Domingue. And in 1828, in the city of Cartagena, two *pardo* veterans of the War of Independence protested that they, who had built the fatherland, would not be able to enjoy their liberty without first finishing off the whites. What is the connection between these bloody threats of repeating Haitian violence and the Wars of Independence in Caribbean Colombia? What can they tell us about the political culture and aspirations of the region's lower classes in the aftermath of the Independence Wars?

This essay on *pardo* political use of Haitian images aims to address these questions using some hitherto unexploited documentation.[2] My analysis of the first Republic of Cartagena suggests that the local *pardo* population had several opportunities to be familiar with the events of the Haitian Revolution. In addition, three particular episodes—the 1822 trial of Arcia, a *pardo* mayor and carpenter, the 1823 disturbances in the city of Mompox, and the military turmoil in Cartagena in 1828—illustrate the strength of the Haitian Revolution as an image of popular republicanism. Indeed, when the Wars of Independence were over, the Haitian model offered a possible political alternative that both the elite and the lower classes could either fear or desire.

Although the republican rhetoric of Spanish American founding fathers has been the subject of considerable and often excellent scholarship, little is known about the republican imagery of the lower classes and their contacts with the Age of Revolution, a surprising oversight given the close links between revolutionary Haiti and the Spanish Caribbean. Works on the Spanish American Independence Wars allude to Haiti, either to explain the royalist inclination of the slaveholding elite as the result of their fear of slave rebellion along Haitian lines,[3] or to point out Pétion's military aid in return for Bolívar's promise to abolish slavery.[4] The possible influence of the Haitian Revolution on the popular political culture of the Independence period is never considered. Yet, Bolívar did not travel alone. Numerous sailors and soldiers traveled back and forth between Haiti and New Granada. What new experiences and expectations did these men bring with them? The answer to this question addresses crucial debates over the nature of popular politics during the Independence era. Although recent works have challenged the traditional assumption that the lower classes neither participated in, nor influenced, the formation of the political ideology of the Independence period, the nature of popular politics and historical change during these crucial years remains unclear. Indeed, the very revolutionary character of these wars is contested. Was it a revolution from above? The dominant historiographical tendency so argues. According to Eric Van Young, one of the most thoughtful analysts of popular culture for this period, the traditional, backward-looking aspirations of the lower classes were quite detached from the liberal-enlightened ideology of the elite.[5] Yet, some recent works on popular politics suggest otherwise. Peter Guardino's work on the liberal inclinations of the peasants of Guerrero, Silvia Arrom's article on the 1828 Parián riot in Mexico City, and Virginia Guedea's analysis of the changing political ideology of Indian governors in Mexico City from 1808 to 1816 challenge the assumption of a strong ideological divide between the elite and the lower classes.[6]

The controversy over ideological differences between the elite and lower classes is closely connected to the question of whether the lower classes were familiar with the eighteenth-century revolutions. The literature on slavery has highlighted the importance of lower class, geographically mobile, men and women in disseminating news concerning the Haitian Revolution and abolitionist politics among the Caribbean slave population.[7] Unfortunately, there has been little dialogue between this rich literature and the historiography of the Independence Wars. Even new revisionist studies of popular liberalism, such as Guardino's, remain confined within national boundaries.

In the Colombian case, a disregard for lower-class connections to international events has limited historians' questions, and thus affected their conclusions about the nature of popular politics. Thanks to the works of Francisco Zuluaga and Alfonso Múnera, we know some of the reasons behind lower-class decisions to follow the royalists or to fight for independence,[8] and the active role played by *pardos* in the independence movement and their agency in achieving their aspirations for legal racial equality.[9] Moreover, Margarita Garrido has shown the shifts in the political language of the lower classes during the transition from colonial to republican rule, showing how peasant communities quickly learned to use the new republican rhetoric. However, the fundamental issue of whether changes in popular politics involved presenting old aspirations in a new language or genuine changes in aspirations remains controversial. We do not know what kind of political future the populace of Colombia imagined, or the type of government they expected to replace the Spanish one. Garrido argues that the substance of lower-class demands and grievances remained the same: "There was absent in New Granada a model of radical democracy like those of Morelos and Artigas."[10] My analysis of the appeal of Haitian republicanism to the lower classes of Cartagena challenges this assertion since, at least for a brief period, a sector of the *pardo* population appears to have imagined a radically different future.

Finally, since Cartagena supported a large free *pardo* lower class and a relatively small number of slaves, I have chosen to focus on the free population. The analysis of *pardos* who not only enjoyed freedom but also legal equality seeks to provide a different perspective to the discussions about the influence of the Haitian Revolution, which have traditionally centered on the slave population.[11]

A REPUBLIC OF PARDOS AND SAILORS, CARTAGENA 1811–1815

When the Wars of Independence finally came to an end, the populace of Cartagena had encountered a broad range of radical republican experiences that would be crucial in determining their aspirations and programs for the new nation. As the inhabitants of a Caribbean port city, lower class Cartageneros had multiple opportunities to learn about the events of the Atlantic revolutions. Sailors, soldiers and slaves probably brought news to the lower-class neighborhood of Cartagena.[12] For example, in May 1803, the Spanish authorities apprehensively discussed what to do about two French government commissioners from Saint-Domingue and Martinique, who had proudly displayed the tricolor flag in the house they occupied in the lower-class neighborhood of Getsemaní.[13] How the people of Getsemaní interpreted that flag, or what versions of the French and Haitian revolutions they received, we do not know. Thanks to the work of Múnera, we do know that the *pardos* from Getsemaní followed with interest the debates in the Cádiz Cortes and, after learning that the Spanish parliament had denied citizenship rights to people of African descent, became determined supporters of the Independence cause.[14] Indeed, it was the armed people of Getsemaní who in November 1811 forced the hesitant Creole elite to declare total independence from Spain.[15] Although it remains unclear what their aspirations for the new political system were, it would have been extremely difficult, according to the royalist witness Fernández de Santos, to convert Cartagena's populace back to the royalist cause. Cartageneros had become "enchanted with promises of happiness and frenetic egalitarianism, and [were] contented with their poverty as long as their disorders [were] not corrected."[16] That egalitarianism was associated not only with republicanism, but also with Jacobinism.[17]

It was Year One of the Republic of Cartagena. Beginning with the introduction of a new calendar, the new republic emulated the rhetoric of the French Revolution.[18] During the following four years the pressure of lower-class "frenetic egalitarianism" turned Cartagena into one of the first republics of the hemisphere that guaranteed equal political rights to free *pardos* and whites. The 1812 constitution eliminated legal color distinctions, guaranteed suffrage rights to all free men but vagrants and servants, and, although it did not abolish slavery, it outlawed the slave trade. In addition, *pardos* of modest origin became members of the constitutional assembly, the war council, and the parliament.[19]

The political contacts of Cartagena's populace with the outside world subsequently increased during the short-lived republic. When in desperate need of funds, the government transformed Cartagena into a haven for Caribbean corsairs in 1812, French and Haitian sailors became a common sight in the city. In addition, Cartageneros and Haitians sometimes joined together as pirates, and Haitians served as sailors in the new republic's navy.[20] The government effort to print bilingual (French-Spanish) city ordinances, and Spanish efforts to win the French population to their side during the 1815 siege are yet other indications of the importance of the French and Haitian presence in Cartagena. Indeed, we know with certainty that during the defense of Cartagena a fifty-man garrison was formed exclusively with Haitians.[21] When in 1812 the defeated Venezuelan revolutionary army found refuge in Cartagena, its soldiers added an additional component to the cosmopolitanism of these years. From them Cartageneros probably heard stories about Boves's campaign, the emancipation of the slaves who fought for the royalists, and their bloody treatment of the Venezuelan elite. It was in Cartagena, with a dominant Haitian following, that in 1813 Briceño prepared his Venezuelan *guerra a muerte*.[22] Again in 1814 these men returned defeated and with additional stories to tell.

Cartageneros' contacts with Haiti outlived the Republic. When the Spanish army won the siege, a significant number of residents left the port in privateering vessels, finding final refuge in Pétion's Haiti.[23] Some of them would return to play a crucial role in the local politics of the post-independence period.

A SEDITIOUS PARDO MAYOR, MAJAGUAL 1822.

To Valentin Arcia, the Wars of Independence were not just a bloody event that left colonial social structures untouched. He was a successful thirty-one-year-old *pardo* carpenter, who sometimes traveled as a small merchant from his hometown Majagual to Popayán in the far south. He had recently been elected the *alcalde* (mayor) of Majagual, a small town in the province of Cartagena (see map, page 158). As such, he enjoyed political power over the rich white *vecinos* (townsmen), and expected to be treated as their social equal. Arcia was also concerned with national policy, and was fond of writing about political issues.[24]

Yet, things did not flow as placidly as he may have wished. Whereas as a representative of the state he enforced military recruitment and faced lower-class desertion, as a *pardo* mayor and carpenter, he confronted the hostility of the local elite. Indeed, from 1822 to 1824, the white elite of Majagual and the nearby town of Algarrobo simultaneously accused him of promoting a race war and of exceeding his power as *alcalde* in his attempt to enforce enlistment. His predicament illustrates the political culture surrounding this literate *pardo* artisan, and reveals the different meanings that such terms as republicanism and independence acquired for the competing class and race interests of the region.

In May 1822, Valentin Arcia, no doubt proud of his latest written work, went to the house of the other mayor, where some members of the town elite had gathered. After exchanging greetings, he read his work. It was a dialogue between a *pardo* mayor and a *labrador* (peasant). According to Arcia, the dialogue was based on a real conversation between himself and a local peasant. Therefore, it offers a rare opportunity to understand the concerns of small landowners and peasants at the end of the Independence Wars. Both the *alcalde* and the *labrador* were concerned with the decline of commerce in their town. The *labrador* protested against government requisition and military conscription. The *alcalde* complained of the difficulties he confronted as a humble craftsman made mayor; his poverty prompted people to accuse him of charging the fees attached to his position with unusual exactitude. Finally, they both lamented the degree of inequality people of color still were subjected to. Local members of the elite considered all of this extremely radical for a representative of the state. Some days later, one of them wrote to the provincial government of Cartagena accusing Arcia of sedition. In consequence, Arcia was arrested and a trial that would last three years began.

According to the man that denounced Arcia, his discussion of racial inequality included a comment, "the war [of independence] will never end because a new and bloodier war against the whites will start, just as it had in Guarico."[25] However, the witnesses' depositions, including that of Arcia himself, indicate that Arcia's words were a bit less threatening. He had only said, "if people of his rank are as ill-treated in the rest of Colombia as they are in Majagual, God forbid, a new war against the whites may start."[26]

What aroused Arcia to the point of uttering such menacing words? When in the aforementioned meeting he complained of the ill-treatment people of his "class" received in Majagual, whites responded with the argument, what else could they possibly want than to have a *pardo* mayor? However, Arcia was unsatisfied. He also expected to be treated as a social equal by the white elite. He took offense when the white ladies highlighted his humble origins by denying him the polite treatment appropriate to a gentleman,[27] and strongly resented challenges to his political authority by the male members of the white elite.[28]

Despite his disenchantment, Arcia was a convinced supporter of the new republican system. Not even his most vehement accusers doubted his republicanism. The prosecutor, local elite, and Arcia himself agreed on one thing: under the new system people like Arcia had gained tangible benefits impossible under Spanish rule. But the elite feared the supposed radicalism of Arcia's republicanism. Both Arcia's support for the new government and his radicalism can be seen in this proclamation exhorting the people of Majagual to be good patriots and enlist in the army:

> "*Despertad Majagualeños; no estén aletargados*
> *mirad que quien tiene enemigos no duerme . . .*
> *En todo Colombia el despotismo no tiene lugar;*

> *los Americanos a las Bayonetas lo han de desterrar*
> *El yugo tirano no se vea en Majagual*
> *pues de lo contrario habéis de esperar*
> *la muerte propicia a nuestro umbral."*[29]

"Awaken Majagualeños; don't be lethargic.
Be aware, he who has enemies, should not sleep . . .
There is no place for despotism in all of Colombia;
Americanos with their bayonets must root it out.
The tyrant's yoke shall not be seen in Majagual
Otherwise, you can expect
Deserved death on our doorstep."

Although his obvious intention was to recruit soldiers for the republican army, the violent tone of the proclamation seemed too dangerous to be used by a *pardo* mayor. A rumor spread among whites that Arcia was trying to organize the colored classes against the whites. Yet, Arcia's goal was to reach the Majagualeños who did not share his republican convictions, those for whom the Republic meant little. The war, with its economic and human suffering, was their real concern. Their solution, to run to the wilderness and prudently wait for a Spanish or American final victory, was what Arcia lamented in his proclamation: "You fill yourselves with confidence; you say I have always run to the hills to avoid serving Colombia . . . Some people will say: Men, let's take things easy, step by step. Maybe the present government will not last, and then we will have a hard time with the Spanish. I believe, sirs, that all these people are wrong."[30]

Eventually, Arcia was set free. The central government in Bogotá believed that he did not intend sedition, and three years spent in jail waiting to be tried served as more than enough punishment for whatever strong words he may have uttered. Arcia's trial reveals that if for a section of the population the establishment of a republican government was inconsequential, for others it meant a real change. The elite faced the possibility of being governed by a *pardo* craftsman "with no more means of subsistence than his tools."[31] For the lower classes it entailed the possibility of being governed by one of their own. At stake was how much further these changes would go. Would the "Arcias" of New Granada have to be satisfied with a bit of political power without its correspondent economic power and social recognition, or would conflicts escalate to the point of race war? At the time, both options were believed possible. If the new republican state failed to fulfill Arcia's aspirations, the image of Haiti, a republic commanded by blacks, was available, and made his threat of a "new war against the whites" plausible.

THE THREAT OF THE MACHETE:
THE MOMPOX DISTURBANCES OF 1823

That the concerns of white Majagualeños were more than just paranoia becomes evident with the 1823 popular disturbances in Mompox. At the time of Independence, Mompox was the most important city of the lower Magdalena. It was the center of all commerce between the coast and the highlands, and the gathering place of ten thousand *bogas,* free colored river boatmen, who enjoyed a large degree of mobility. Their travels allowed them to keep in touch with news from the coast and the highlands, and, unlike other lower-class mobile men such as sailors and soldiers, the nineteenth-century *bogas* were not subject to a disciplinary regime. They were known for their "unruliness" and opposition to regimented labor; their desertion was a common problem travelers had to contend with.[32] Thus, it is not surprising that the Mompox disturbances began just as the army attempted to recruit Mompox men for the Maracaibo campaign.

Conflicts began when Commandant Robledo replaced the *pardo* general commandant of Mompox, Colonel Remigio Márquez, an elected member of the senate.[33] This replacement signaled a radical turn in the way the local Republican government approached the lower classes. According to military reports, Márquez's government had bestowed on the populace far too many liberties; Mompox had become a place of "insolence and licentiousness."[34] The inhabitants, the reports complained, had grown accustomed to a "weak governmental indulgence," and were under the assumption that "they could serve the government according to their own free will."[35]

The presumption of Mompox's lower classes that they could serve the government according to their own inclinations did not fit with the military needs of the new state. To the dismay of the military officials, only government employees and merchants responded to enlistment calls; perfectly able-bodied men walked the streets without fear of the authorities. The impunity enjoyed by the masses under Márquez had made them "bold and criminal."[36] However, enforcing enlistment was not simple. Mild methods such as giving special privileges to enlisted Momposinos, promising that they would not be taken away from their region and that their service would not last more than one month, met with little success. Coercion also failed. When a military patrol attempted to impose itself on the lower-class Barrio de Abajo neighborhood, it was ejected with stones and machete blows. It was impossible for the government to get into a neighborhood where "neither political judge, nor military commandant, nor anybody else is obeyed." Moreover, as the military officers feared, a stronger military presence and repression would only result in people fleeing to the wilderness.[37] As if this lower class "anarchy" was not threatening enough, Márquez's government began to enforce anti-contraband laws, thus confronting the traditional practices and interests of the local merchant elite.[38] "All respectable men had suffered some vexation from Márquez," lamented his opponents.[39]

In April 1823, Robledo, a commandant more sympathetic to the interests of the local elite, replaced Márquez. Yet, military control did not improve. To the surprise of the military officers, Mompox's populace continued to be ungovernable despite the absence of its leader. When in May Márquez returned to Mompox on his way to the senate in Bogotá, the opposition to military enlistment escalated to the level of racial conflicts. Márquez was accused of disrupting previously harmonious relations and fomenting "class conflicts" (*divisiones de clase*). Every night the "lowest class" (*última clase*) visited him and played drums on the doorsteps of his house. At night, masked men strolled in the streets, and every morning threatening anonymous broadsides appeared on the walls. Fortunately, one of these broadsides has survived, providing a splendid and rare example of how Mompox's popular classes expressed political grievances and aspirations.

"Señor juez político
  No me dirá usted porque no han seguido los pasquines? Pues yo se lo diré.
  Es porque han sabido los blanquitos de mierda . . . que la gente quiere al Sr. Marques y temen que ande el machete carájo.
  Usted no quiere que el Sr. Marques sea juez político porque se le quita la chupadera de aguardiente. El Sr. Robledo no quiere cortar el mando *porque se le quita el robo con la tropa. . . . al fin Vs se han de joder porque correrá sangre como en Santo Domingo."*[40]

"Señor juez político
  Won't you tell me why the broadsides have not continued? Well, I'll tell you.
  It is because the damn whites learned . . . that the people want Mr. Márquez, and they fear the chop of the machete.
  You don't want Mr. Márquez to be the political judge because it deprives you of rum. Mr. Robledo doesn't want to leave his command *because his robbing the troops would cease. . . . In the end, you will all be f...d because blood will run like in Saint-Domingue."*

How should we interpret the broadside and the complaints about Momposino unruliness? What do they tell us about popular aspirations at this crucial time? The broadside claimed that the "people loved" Márquez. Why? They may have identified with a *pardo* governor who participated in their dances (*tamboras).* They may also have approved of his style of administration. The broadside applauded his confronting the elite's corruption, because it halted the robbing of the troops. In addition, the lower classes no doubt approved his lenience. As previously mentioned, government officials complained that the masses had grown accustomed to "a weak governmental indulgence" and were "under the assumption they could serve the government according to their own free will." It may not be too far-fetched to conclude that the Momposinos interpreted the new republican liberty as the right to live under a government that did not control but *was controlled* by the populace.

Moreover, the broadside tightly interwove racial and political claims. What was the relationship between political claims and threats of bloody Haitian violence? Was it just a convenient political tool for producing fear and obtaining results, or did Haiti embody Momposinos' republican aspirations? Perhaps, we can assume from the broadside that Haiti had become an alternative model of popular republicanism, that Momposinos' imagined Haiti as a place where blacks not only ruled themselves, but also enjoyed an honest government that did not oppress the lower classes. In other words, Haiti had developed into a utopian image for the lower classes.

When Márquez finally left, the tumult did not cease. To the bewilderment of the elite, masked men continued to wander at night, and threatening broadsides continued to appear in the morning. Indeed, the central government eventually found Márquez innocent of promoting racial war.[41] Whatever happened in Mompox was not the result of his political machinations, but of the beliefs of the local inhabitants.

"THIS IS A GOOD NIGHT TO FINISH OFF THE WHITES": A *PARDO* CONSTITUTIONAL REVOLT AGAINST BOLÍVAR, CARTAGENA 1828.

Although the unrest in Mompox did not result in a massacre of whites, the threat of racial war did not disappear from the provincial political scene. In March 1828, the lower classes of Cartagena revolted against Bolívar's attempts to reform the 1821 constitution. An examination of this revolt illuminates an interesting array of political agendas that combined threats against the whites with cries favoring liberty against military dictatorship, and rejection of Bolívar's constitutional project.

The Benemérito de la Patria, Admiral José Padilla, a *pardo* sailor who became a general during the Independence Wars, was the organizer and best known figure of this revolt. His career merits discussion because it provides a good example of the contact with the Atlantic revolutions that numerous colored men of the coast engaged in maritime activities may have had. In 1792, when he was fourteen years old, he became a cabin boy in the Spanish Royal Navy. Eventually, he managed to become boatswain, a high position for a *pardo* Creole. In 1805, he participated in the battle of Trafalgar, and was taken prisoner by the English. Padilla remained in England until the peace of 1808, when he returned to Cartagena.[42] By this time his travels had no doubt made him familiar with stories about the French Revolution, the Haitian Revolution, and English abolitionism. In 1815, after the fall of Cartagena, he took refuge in the Haitian port of Les Cayes, from which, thanks to the support of President Pétion, he returned with Bolívar to continue the fight for independence.[43] In 1823, he became a national hero for his role in the republican victory at Maracaibo. His ascendance over Cartagena's populace was probably the result of his humble racial and social origins, his military feats, and his worldly experience.

On 5 March 1828, a group of people from the lower-class neighborhood of Getsemaní informed Padilla that they had come to distrust the military, because its hostility toward the Great Convention was a threat to liberty.[44] The concerns of the people of Getsemaní were part of the national struggle between Bolívar and Santander over the need to reform the Constitution of 1821.[45] A section of the Gran Colombian elite, of which Bolívar was the principal representative, believed that contemporary political problems resulted from the excessive liberalism of the 1821 Constitution, and that a stronger state was needed. Part of their program was to adopt the Bolivian constitution, which, among other measures, called for a life presidency. Consequently, Bolívar organized a national convention to devise a new constitution. The national elections for the convention, however, favored Santander's faction. In reaction to this unfavorable outcome, the Bolivarian faction began a campaign to thwart the convention. In Cartagena, as in other parts of the country, Bolívar's military followers proceeded to write *representaciones a la convención,* that were threats to the elected representatives to the convention. Padilla decided to defend the convention and voiced his personal support for all the officers who refused to sign the threatening *representación.* He counted on the support of the people of Getsemaní who opposed the military men that were a threat to liberty. The governor of Cartagena's explanation for these protests by Getsemaní's residents was the underpayment of the troops and the hunger of the lower classes. He also predicted turmoil.[46] Indeed, the following day the populace gathered under the leadership of Padilla and the civilian Dr. Ignacio Muñoz, deposed General Commandant Montilla, and proclaimed Padilla *Intendente* and general commandant of the department.

Why did the populace express their material discontent in antagonistic terms toward the Bolivarian faction, and what hopes did they have in electing Padilla? Some answers to these questions appear in the testimonies of fifteen *pardo* and white witnesses, interrogated in summary proceedings.[47] Their versions of Padilla's speech provide a window into what he thought were the issues that could arouse lower class political interest. In addition, their disparate stories reveal multiple readings of the revolt, and how rumors and conversations shaped and reshaped political goals.

The first issue that emerges is the strong appeal that the defense of the liberal constitution had for Cartagena's populace. In his speech to the people, Padilla affirmed that, "after the people had sacrificed itself for the cause of liberty, Montilla [the city's general commandant] aimed to destroy the laws and Constitution, and to dissolve the Convention." According to one witness, Padilla had said, "General Montilla should die because his purpose is to subjugate the people of Colombia to tyranny." In another deposition, Padilla was reported as saying, "the *Carta Boliviana* [the conservative Bolivian constitution] provides no advantages to the second class, who fought on the battlefields to suppress tyranny." According to a third testimony, he had asked the people if they "would recognize him as their commander, and if they wanted to be slave or free, obtaining the response of some that, yes, they indeed recognized him, and they wanted to be free."[48]

Secondly, racial antagonism was interwoven with the Bolívar-Santander constitutional conflict. Two days after the populace declared Padilla general commandant of Cartagena, rumors about massacring the whites spread. One witness overheard somebody in a group of five to six persons, "whose clothes reveal their belonging to the people" saying that "this would be a good night to finish off the whites."[49] On the same day, another witness overheard two corporals saying, "it's getting necessary to finish off the whites."[50] A Venezuelan *pardo* officer, Captain Ibarra, who had lived in Haiti and was considered by some white officers a danger to the city, stated, "he feared that people would turn to the last resort of declaring war on the whites."[51]

These testimonies reveal the popular classes' support for liberal institutions, that they held to be the product of their effort and sacrifice on the battlefield. The lower classes of Cartagena thought that conservative institutions and a stronger state did not address the needs of the *segunda clase* (second class, which can be understood as either the lower classes or people of color). Yet, for a sector of the populace, it was not enough to defend liberal institutions. Liberty could not be enjoyed as long as the whites were in power. Their goal was a republic without whites. Two *pardo* soldiers were heard commenting that, "They themselves had created the fatherland, they were its founders but, without destroying the whites, they would never enjoy their freedom."[52] Their goal was both *pardo* and republican, a "Haiti" in Colombia.

On 8 March, Padilla reached an agreement with the legal government of Cartagena and left for Mompox to seek Bolívar's pardon. However, he did not succeed. In the eyes of Bolívar, always fearful of *pardocracia*, Padilla's color, political stature, and ascendancy over the *pardos* of the Caribbean coast were too dangerous. Accused of sedition, he was executed in Bogotá in October 1828, thus becoming a martyr and hero for the people of the *Costa*.

CONCLUSION

In the interstitial period between the Wars of Independence and the consolidation of the Republic, Haitian images permeated some of the sociopolitical conflicts of Caribbean Colombia. The uses of these images reveals of some of the fears and aspirations that emerged during the Independence Wars. The three cases here examined arose from the conflicts over locally powerful *pardos* who had achieved positions of political and military power during the independence struggles. In all three cases, local elites attempted to discredit well-known *pardos* with the accusation of promoting race war, or, more specifically, a second Haiti in Colombia. Yet, elite accusations were not mere machinations. Haitian images had become part of the republican ideology of some sectors of Cartagena's *pardos*. This should not be surprising considering the close ties between the populace of Cartagena and Haiti. After fighting a bloody war that radically altered people's conception of the state, and with the Haitian example a recent memory, the possibility of escalating the struggle to the point of abolishing not only Spanish but also white rule seemed feasible to some sectors of the lower classes. The sentiments expressed in the words of the Alcalde Arcia, "if people of [my] rank [continue to be] mistreated . . . a new war against the whites may start," certainly were in the mind of many.[53]

However, to reduce the aspirations of Cartagena's inhabitants to racial antagonism is to simplify their political views, and to isolate them from the political currents of their time. If Haiti was a political image, it is worth asking what type of political image it was. In other words, what did Haiti symbolize in terms of the ideal relationship between the people and the state? The cases examined above suggest a strong linkage between racial demands and a radical interpretation of republicanism with a forceful dislike for a strong state. The lower classes of Mompox revolted on the assumption that they had the right to be governed by a man with whom they could identify, and to serve the state according to their own free will. They did not want to be controlled, but to be in control of the state. The Majagualeño peasant dreamed of a government without military requisitions and conscriptions. Finally, the people of Cartagena favored the 1821 liberal constitution against Bolívar's conservative programs because, in the words of Padilla, the *Carta*

Boliviana provided no advantages to the "second class," which had fought on the battlefield to suppress tyranny.

It is also necessary to ask whether lower class invocations of Haiti reflected a clear understanding of Haitian reality or if Haiti had become a vague utopian image. The populace of Cartagena may have admired Pétion's Republic—the part of Haiti they had the strongest ties with, rather than the northern state where forced labor was maintained until 1820. Haitian ex-slaves had strenuously opposed Toussaint Louverture's attempt to reinstate a plantation economy. Pressured by them, Pétion initiated a radical program of agrarian reform that transformed southern Haiti into a republic of small independent peasants.[54] However, for most of its independence, at least part of Haiti had known authoritarian rulers, styled emperor or king, and, in the mid-1820s, the Haitian Republic founded by Pétion sought to abandon its land reform and revive the plantation economy. In any event, none of the three cases here studied mentions Pétion or any concrete aspect of Haitian reality. Haiti was invoked as a bloody threat to express local aspirations and discontent; Haiti may have symbolized a purification process that had to take place for the lower classes to achieve their political aspirations. According to the Mompox broadside, elite corruption would cease and the people would be governed by a man of their liking only after blood ran as in Saint-Domingue. In a similar vein, two soldiers in Cartagena stated that they would never achieve their liberty without first destroying the whites. Apparently, Haiti had become a utopian image, a place where *pardos* not only governed themselves, but also enjoyed an unobtrusive republican government that did not oppress the lower classes.

Can we assume from all of this that Haiti played for the Spanish Caribbean a role similar to that of Inca utopias in the post-conquest Andes and, therefore, merits similar attention? I believe it is not a far-fetched possibility. Indeed, according to the Spanish general Morillo, rumors grew during the Independence Wars that General Piar, a Venezuelan *pardo,* planned to create a black republic in the Orinoco with the aid of Pétion.[55] Be that as it may, what remains is the appeal of Haitian images among some sectors of the *pardo* population of Caribbean Colombia. To further explore this appeal will enhance our understanding of lower-class reasons for fighting on the Republican side during the Wars of Independence and of the political claims *pardos* sought to impose on the new republican government.

NOTES

1. This paper uses the term *pardo* to refer to all free people of African descent. I have chosen *pardo* over black or mulatto because none of the documents consulted used the word *moreno* (black). Although it is a subject that requires further study, the documentation seems to reveal that, during the Independence period, colonial distinctions between *morenos* (blacks) and *pardos* (mulattoes) gave way to the generalized use of the word *pardo* for free people of African descent. This trend is also observable in the large reduction of the percentage of *morenos* and the rising percentage of *pardos* in the late eighteenth-century census.

2. The search for the Haitian Revolution's influence on Cartagena's popular politics led me to new sources and previously unknown events, such as the trial of Arcia and the disturbances of Mompox. Due to the fame of its leader, José Prudencio Padilla, the revolt of

Cartagena is better known. Yet, previous analyses have focused on Padilla and his personal conflicts with Bolívar, ignoring the sources that allow us to understand popular aspirations and participation in this event.

3. Jorge Domínguez, *Insurrection or Loyalty: the Breakdown of the Spanish American Empire* (Cambridge: Harvard University Press, 1980).

4. Paul Verna, *Petión y Bolívar: cuarenta años de relaciones haitiano-venezolanas y su aporte a la emancipación de Hispanoamérica* (Caracas: Imprenta Nacional, 1969), 157–61.

5. Eric Van Young, "Quetzalcóatl, King Ferdinand, and Ignacio Allende Go to the Seashore; or Messianism and Mystical Kingship in Mexico, 1800–1821," in Jaime Rodríguez ed., *The Independence of Mexico and the Creation of the Nation* (Los Angeles: Latin American Center Publications-UCLA, 1989), 111.

6. Sylvia M. Arrom, "Popular Politics in Mexico City," in Silvia M. Arrom, Servando Ortoll eds., *Riots in the Cities: Popular Politics and the Urban Poor in Latin America, 1765–1910* (Wilmington: Scholarly Resources, 1996), 71–96; Virginia Guedea, "De la infidelidad a la infidencia," in Jaime E. Rodríguez ed., *Patterns of Contention in Mexican History* (Wilmington: Scholarly Resources, 1992), 95–123; P. Guardino, *Peasants, Politics, and the Formation of Mexico's National State: Guerrero, 1800–1857* (Stanford, Calif.: Stanford University Press, 1996).

7. Julius S. Scott, "The Common Wind: Currents of Afro-American Communication in the Era of the Haitian Revolution" (Ph.D. diss., Duke University, 1986); D. B. Gaspar and D. P. Geggus eds., *A Turbulent Time: The French Revolution and the Greater Caribbean* (Bloomington: Indiana University Press, 1997).

8. Francisco Zuluaga, "Clientelismo y Guerrilla en el Valle del Patía, 1536–1811," in Germán Colmenares, ed., *La Independencia: ensayos de historia social* (Bogotá: Instituto Colombiana de Cultura, 1986), 111–36.

9. Alfonso Múnera, "Failing to Construct the Colombian Nation: Race and Class in the Andean-Caribbean Conflict, 1717–1816" (Ph.D. diss., University of Connecticut, 1995).

10. Margarita Garrido, *Reclamos y Representaciones: Variaciones sobre la Política en el Nuevo Reino de Granada, 1770–1815* (Bogotá: Banco de la República, 1993), 296.

11. For the debates on the influence of the Haitian Revolution see Eugene Genovese, *From Rebellion to Revolution: Afro-American Slave Revolts in the Making of the Modern World* (Baton Rouge: Louisiana State University Press, 1979); Scott, "Common Wind"; David Patrick Geggus, "Slavery, War, and Revolution in the Greater Caribbean, 1789–1815," and "Slave Resistance in the Spanish Caribbean in the Mid-1790s," in Gaspar and Geggus, eds., *A Turbulent Time*.

12. I am building upon Julius Scott's analysis of the role played by sailors and other lower class mobile men and women in the dissemination of news about the Haitian Revolution among the slaves of the Caribbean port cities.

13. Archivo General de la Nación, Colombia (hereafter AGN) Sección Colonia, Fondo Milicias y Marina, 113, fols. 76–87.

14. Múnera, "Failing to Construct," 237.

15. Ibid., 238–40.

16. "Porque su plebe paladeada con el vicio, con quiméricas promesas de felicidad, y con una frenética igualdad, se hayan bien con la miseria, con tal que no se les corrijan sus desórdenes," in "Noticias sobre el estado de la Plaza de Cartagena," 15 Oct. 1812, AGN, Archivo Anexo, Fondo Historia, fols. 445–53.

17. "Respecto a que el Obispo es Fernandino, que salga Jacobino." Ibid.

18. See, for example, Edicto del Presidente Manuel Rodriguez Torices, AGN, Archivo Restrepo, 5, fol. 51.

19. For the active participation of *pardos* in the Republic of Cartagena, see Múnera, "Failing to Construct," chapter 6.

20. Paul Verna, *Petión y Bolívar,* 337, 316.

21. "Allí mandaba yo cincuenta haitianos corsaristas que se pusieron a mis ordenes," a Cartagenero wrote in his account of the siege. See Manuel Corrales, comp., *Documentos para la historia de la Provincia de Cartagena de Indias, hoy Estado Soberano de Bolívar, en la Unión Colombiana* (Bogotá: Imprenta Medardo Rivas, 1883), 183.

22. Paul Verna, *Petión y Bolívar,* 312.

23. Ibid. 334.

24. The discussion on Arcia is based on "Causa criminal contra Valentin Arcia, alcalde ordinario de segunda nominación de Majagual por hablar mal contra los blancos y contra el gobierno" AGN, República, Asuntos Criminales (hereafter R-AC) 61, fols. 1143–1209, and 96, fols. 244–322.

25. "Jamás se concluiría la guerra porque había de despertarse luego una más sangrienta contra los blancos como sucedió en Guarico." AGN, R-AC, 61, fols. 1143–1209. Guarico was the Spanish name for Cap-Français, where the Haitian Revolution had begun.

26. "Si en todos los lugares de Colombia se trataba a los de su calidad con el mismo desprecio, no quisiere Dios que se suscitase otra guerra de aquellos contra los blancos." AGN, R-AC, 61, fols. 1143–1209.

27. Arcia mentions with bitterness an instance when a white lady did not offer him a chair in a social meeting she hosted.

28. The documents describe a lengthy quarrel between Arcia and the white witnesses over an incident in which the male members of the white elite ignored Arcia's demand for the entire town to gather after mass.

29. AGN, R-AC, 61, fols. 1143–1209.

30. Ibid.

31. AGN, R-AC, 96, fols. 244–322.

32. "Mompox es el lugar de reunión de los bogas, que llegan a ser cerca de 10,000, y no existe una buena ley que los regule y están mal administrados. Son ellos mismos los que determinan términos del viaje y, además, cobran por adelantado despareciendo frecuentemente con el dinero." Charles Stuart Cochrane, *Viajes por Colombia 1823 y 1824: diario de mi residencia en Colombia* (Bogotá: Banco de la República, 1994), 53. Throughout his travel on the Magdalena river, Cochrane continues to complain about the boatmen's "bad" work habits and "unruliness": Ibid., 59–70.

33. My discussion of the turmoil in Mompox is drawn from several reports that the military officers stationed there sent to their superiors in Cartagena and Bogotá. AGN, R-AC, 66, fols. 804–11. AGN-R, Secretaría de Guerra y Marina, 30, fols. 342–50, 368–69, 564, 616–21.

34. AGN-R, Secretaría de Guerra y Marina, 30, fols. 324–50.

35. AGN-R, Secretaría de Guerra y Marina, 30, fols. 616–21.

36. Ibid.

37. Ibid.

38. For the conflicts between Márquez and the local merchants see David Bushnell, *The Santander Regime in Gran Colombia* (Westport, Conn.: Greenwood Press, 1970), 65, 85.

39. AGN-R, Secretaría de Guerra y Marina, 30, fols. 324–50.

40. AGN, R-AC, 66, fols. 804–11. Emphasis added. This is from a copy that a local official sent to his superiors in Cartagena. The tone of this broadside was typical, the official complained.

41. AGN-R, Congreso, 9, Apr. 1824, fols. 455–56.

42. For the details of Padilla's life, see Enrique Otero D'Costa, *Vida del Almirante José Padilla (1778–1828)* (Colombia: Imprenta y Litografía de las Fuerzas Militares, 1973).

43. Verna, *Petión y Bolívar,* 167–254.

44. Official account of Intendant Ucros, cited by Enrique Otero D'Acosta, *Vida del Almirante,* 92.

45. For a good brief description of the liberal-conservative conflicts, see Bushnell *The Santander Regime.* For a brief description of Padilla's revolt, trial, and execution in the context of the Independence Wars and the abolition of slavery, see John Lynch, *The Spanish American Revolutions, 1808–1826* (New York: Norton, 1973), 256, 265–66, and Robin Blackburn, *The Overthrow of Colonial slavery* (London: Verso, 1988), 263.

46. Enrique Otero D'Acosta, *Vida del Almirante,* 92.

47. "Cartagena, Sumaria averiguación para aclarar asuntos relacionados con la seguridad pública y con la subordinación y disciplina en las clases del ejército," AGN-R, AC, 44, fols. 86–118.

48. Ibid.

49. "Que esta era una buena noche para acabar con los blancos." Ibid.

50. "Acabar con los blancos se iba haciendo necesario." See above, n. 47.

51. "Temía que el pueblo recurriera al último recurso . . . de declararle guerra a los blancos." See above, n. 47.

52. "Ya sería siendo necesario concluir con el color blanco, pués la patria ellos la habían hecho, y que siendo ellos sus fundadores sin destruir a estos jamás gozarán su libertad." See above, n. 47.

53. AGN, R-AC, 61, fols. 1143–1209.

54. Robert LaCerte, "The Evolution of Land and Labor in the Haitian Revolution, 1791–1820," in Hilary Beckles, Verene Shepherd, eds., *Caribbean Freedom: Society and Economy from Emancipation to the Present* (Kingston: Ian Randle, 1993), 42–47.

55. Morillo based his report on letters intercepted by the Spanish, that he himself had not seen. See Asdrubal González, *Manuel Piar* (Caracas: Vedell Hermanos Editores, 1979), 185.

PART FOUR

REFUGEES

Chapter 13

Étrangers dans un Pays Étrange

Saint-Domingan Refugees of Color in Philadelphia

SUSAN BRANSON AND
LESLIE PATRICK

THROUGHOUT THE LAST DECADE OF the eighteenth century and the early years of the nineteenth century, ships carried thousands of white refugees, their slaves, and free people of color from Saint-Domingue to port cities in the United States. Many arrived in Norfolk, Virginia, and chose to remain there. Some did not have the financial resources to go elsewhere, and others remained because Virginia permitted slavery (though several other slave states denied entry to any owners with slaves from Saint-Domingue). Many could not bear to travel further north to a climate where winters could be severe. Yet Philadelphia, despite its abolition law and its colder weather, was the destination of thousands of Saint-Domingans. This wave of emigration, propelled by the warfare and consequent upheaval in the West Indian colony, resulted in the creation of a large francophone community in the City of Brotherly Love. Whites, *gens de couleur* and slaves all faced the prospect of new lives in this North American city.[1] This essay examines the experience of people of color, both slave and free, as strangers in a strange land. It departs from seemingly similar examinations of this population in its interpretation of the documentary evidence, drawing less sanguine conclusions about the black emigrés' lives.[2] Religion and language set the refugees apart from their host community, but it was skin color that primarily determined a refugee's experience. Whereas white Saint-Domingans reconstituted ties with fellow refugees, promoted the development of a francophone social and cultural community, or at the very least managed to find employment, people of color, both slave and free, were much more isolated and had far fewer resources than their white counterparts. Laws, prejudices, and fear of rebellion tightly constrained the social, economic and legal status of these survivors of revolution. These people figured centrally in white imaginations filled with fear of witnessing another black revolt. Despite these limitations, Saint-Domingue's refugees of color attempted to achieve their freedom and establish a community in their new homeland.

For people of African ancestry the American, French, and Haitian Revolutions all appeared to exhibit at least one characteristic in common—the idea of freedom. Curiously, little attention has been given to the black individuals who emigrated from Saint-Domingue to Philadelphia and what freedoms they "enjoyed" upon doing so. These people were swept along on the tidal wave of the three revolutions washing over the Atlantic world. Although each revolution promised liberty, the meaning of the term varied in each geographical and temporal context.[3]

On the one hand, it takes little effort to discern why whites and *gens de couleur,* both of whom could own slaves, were anxious to leave Saint-Domingue. What remains a mystery is why their slaves accompanied them, since it was only the revolution in Saint-Domingue which promised liberty to enslaved people. The motives of slaves who journeyed to Philadelphia cannot be easily discerned. Although many probably had no choice in the matter when owners snatched them away, others may have willingly left at their owners' sides. The records of those who arrived with the white refugees reveal that most were from urban areas. They may not have had the ideological investment that rural slaves had in overturning the slaveowning regime. Frances Sergeant Childs speculates that many slaves who accompanied fleeing whites "were loyal enough to prefer exile with their owners than freedom at home."[4] This interpretation, of course, follows from the contemporary belief that there were no good reasons for the revolution in Saint-Domingue. The fact is, the great majority of bondspeople arrived before slavery was abolished in Saint-Domingue.

Pennsylvania should not have been the destination of choice for whites fleeing Saint-Domingue who intended to keep their slaves. Yet they suddenly appeared in significant numbers in 1793, thirteen years after the act for the gradual abolition of slavery had passed into law. The 1780 law embodied a number of points that would have a direct effect on whites bringing slaves from Saint-Domingue. The law required such owners to register their slaves within six months if they intended to remain as residents in the commonwealth and to free those aged over 21. The law further stipulated that no child born after its passage would be a slave for life. Rather, children born to enslaved parents would be bound servants for 28 years and thereafter freed, or if the slave in question was under 21 years of age, he or she would be bound for no more than seven years before achieving freedom. Only "foreign Ministers and Consuls" were permitted to retain "domestic slaves attending upon" them. White refugees from Saint-Domingue did not meet this latter requirement.[5]

Despite the uprisings that had begun in 1791 and the 1794 decree that abolished slavery in the French colonies, slaveholders who migrated to Philadelphia from Saint-Domingue persisted in holding on to their human property. Once in Philadelphia, some protested that neither the 1780 nor the 1788 acts for the abolition of slavery should apply to them. As early as 1793, shortly after the first sizable group arrived, the émigrés "petitioned the legislature to amend the gradual emancipation acts to allow them to bring slaves into the state."[6] Individuals also protested the legislation. One such instance of protest occurred when Jean-Baptiste Seapointe challenged the law by claiming that the slaves Marie Louise and her daughter Mélanie belonged to him, while he resided in l'Arcahaye. Marie Louise had been born in Port-au-Prince and sold to Seapointe, who in turn gave the slave to his sister, Madam Olive, who lived in Port-au-Prince. Seapointe asserted that on 6 May 1798, "when the British left Port-au-Prince the said Marie Louise went on board of a vessel with Madam Olive." They arrived in Philadelphia, where "she lived with her in this city near one year," when Madam Olive "went to France leaving defendant here." Subsequent to Madam Olive's departure Marie Louise gave birth to her daughter Mélanie. The defendants, however, drew upon the 1780 and 1788 Pennsylvania legislation to claim that slaves who "shall be brought into this state by persons inhabiting or residing therein, or intending to inhabit or reside herein shall be immediately considered, deemed and taken to be free to all intents and purposes." William Shoemaker, Alderman for the city, agreed with the defendants' claims and judged them "free . . . from confinement."[7] Marie Louise and her daughter Mélanie were fortunate, unlike other bondswomen brought to the City of Brotherly Love.

Although the refugees entered a bustling community where there had been a longstanding black presence, it was not a presence without problems for the *gens de couleur* and former slaves. Newspapers and other institutions reveal ambivalence at best toward the black refugees. Contemporary observers, though critical of "the conduct of the greatest number of the colonists," were awash in sympathy for whites that had fled the island, and they simultaneously referred to the "more than savage barbarity" of the black insurgents in Saint-Domingue. No one seemed to show sympathy for the plight of the slaves who accompanied their owners, and the free people of color who were quite as likely to have been "reduced to misery and want" as the whites.[8] Until the more recent past, historians have followed the lead of contemporary observers, expressing pity for whites from Saint-Domingue and outrage at blacks who had revolted, while ignoring the darker hued refugees arriving in American cities. Philadelphians witnessed slaves, *gens de couleur,* and whites as they stumbled off ships that often had visited numerous ports before arriving in Philadelphia. Weeks of privations at sea would have left them ragged, tired, and desperate. They were "strangers in an alien land begging news of each other."[9] The Philadelphia into which the immigrants streamed provided fortune for a few and misery for many.

Émigrés of color arrived in Philadelphia at a time when the city's population of African Americans was rapidly increasing. Although the number of slaves in Philadelphia had declined since passage of Pennsylvania's 1780 gradual abolition act to only 387 in 1790, the number of black people taking up residence in the city increased dramatically due to the state's proximity to slaveholding states and its abolition law.[10] Depending on whose figures one uses, the black populace increased by either 210 or 176 percent between the censuses of 1790 and 1800.[11] Émigrés from Saint-Domingue contributed to this burgeoning community, adding roughly five hundred individuals to a black population that numbered around twenty-one hundred in 1790.[12]

When the City Directory of 1795 was compiled, it listed "the names of 105 African American heads of households, including 22 women."[13] Most African

Americans in Philadelphia, as recent scholars have shown, intended to carve out a meaningful and legitimate existence. But, as Darlene Clark Hine and Kathleen Thompson observe, "In some ways, freedom did not change the lives of African Americans nearly so much as they had hoped." Most free black men continued working in ports, as laborers, or artisans, while black women "continued to work in white homes." Unless they were indentured and then sold or they achieved freedom unconditionally, the immigrants from Saint-Domingue, like many African Americans, remained as servants to whites and most likely lived in white households until the end of their indenture. The household of white émigré Louis Morin Duval exemplified this arrangement between 1795 and 1798. Duval, his wife Antoinette Félicité La Roux, their three children, and "two black servants" arrived in Philadelphia on 18 June 1795. Required by Pennsylvania's gradual abolition law to free any slave who had resided in the state for six months, he waited until the last possible moment, 2 December 1795, to first free, and then indenture, the two slaves, Hippocrate and Hortence. Hippocrate, a male aged twenty, remained indentured for seven more years until he reached the age of twenty-eight and Hortence, a female aged thirty, also waited for seven years before achieving freedom.[14]

Most slaves from Saint-Domingue whose owners manumitted them eventually joined the ranks of other free people of color in Philadelphia and, most likely, they suffered from the same discrimination and poverty faced by African Americans who had been born in the city.[15] Though they did not necessarily speak English, and should have been recognized as foreign, they were not identified as such. Nor did white Philadelphians make the subtle distinctions of skin color found in the West Indies. First and foremost they were considered black, and thus relegated to the inferior status reserved for all such people.

As such, these refugees were denied the relief supplied by both the French and Americans. The federal government, as well as private donors, gave aid to whites that were forced to leave their possessions and their property behind. Local groups also stepped in to contribute to the relief effort. In 1794 Philadelphians raised $14,000; $3,000 was used to send 150 refugees back to Saint-Domingue.[16] Another $4,000 paid the passage of 200 Saint-Domingans returning to France. White refugees also received aid from the private organization, Société Française de Bienfaisance de Philadelphie, and from individual Philadelphians. Nine hundred dollars of the money raised by Philadelphia was given to widows whose husbands had died in Saint-Domingue.

Nor did members of the elite African American community, such as pastor Richard Allen, publicly acknowledge the arrival of the destitute gens de couleur from Saint-Domingue or offer any assistance. Allen's silence may have had to do with the unfortunate timing of their presence. At the very moment when the refugees arrived, Richard Allen and Absalom Jones "who had spent a year trying to raise $3,500 [for their church], must have watched in dismay as $12,000—enough to build three black churches—was raised in a few days," for white refugees.[17] Allen never mentioned the refugees' arrival nor the fact that his labors to raise money had been halted as a result.[18] Although there is no evidence that the founders of the African Methodist Episcopal Church held ill will toward the newcomers, neither is there evidence that Jones and Allen (or the other black elite of

Philadelphia) necessarily embraced them as fellow blacks suffering under the yoke of racial oppression.

Thrown back on their own diminished resources, émigrés of color, especially women, had few options open to them. Contemporary accounts also suggest that some of these French women of color continued their roles as paid companions, not only to Saint-Domingan refugees, but to Americans and Frenchmen as well. Philadelphians were shocked by a sight which was common in Saint-Domingue, but unheard of in Philadelphia: "Mestizo ladies, with complexions of the palest marble, jet black hair, and eyes of the gazelle, and of the most exquisite symmetry . . . escorted along the pavement by white French gentlemen, both dressed in West Indie fashion, and of the richest material." Many white Saint-Domingans were accompanied through the city streets by their former slaves: "coal black negresses, in flowing white dresses, and turbans of 'mouchoir de Madras.'"[19] Not just the Saint-Domingan planters, but mainland French, such as the exiled Talleyrand, were to be seen strolling the streets "in Contemporary open daylight, with a colored woman on his arm."[20] Moreau de Saint-Méry recorded his observations about these female émigrés, claiming that they lived "in the most obnoxious luxury," which "can only be provided by the French and by former French colonials." To Saint-Méry, "the contrast of their condition with the mass of their compatriots is revolting."[21] Despite Moreau de Saint-Méry's assertions about their lives of obnoxious luxury, life proved difficult materially and emotionally for most females of African ancestry who involuntarily immigrated to Philadelphia. Making the transition to a foreign culture proved especially arduous because American cultural practices denied many the status and opportunities available to them on the island.[22]

Poverty also endangered the prospects for some black immigrants' successful transition to Philadelphia. The almshouse might appear to be a logical place to find those people who could not secure employment, or depend on the attentions of men, once they achieved freedom. Yet during the years between 1791 and 1800, black women from Saint-Domingue seem almost to have successfully avoided the almshouse. The almshouse was probably not a viable alternative to living without the security of shelter and food. As recent historians have shown, "the regulations of the house *were* demeaning to the poor; in many ways, it resembled a prison."[23] Wishing to remain invisible in Philadelphia was not the only reason black émigrés did not appear frequently in the almshouse; one needed a "recommendation" to be admitted.[24] Despite these restrictions and obstacles, some of the black people from Saint-Domingue did turn to the almshouse for care. The reasons for their admission clearly reveal difficulties they must have encountered in adjusting to Philadelphia's climate and their ambiguous status as servants. Although more men than women received admission to the almshouse, there were a few women whose specific circumstances resulted from their involuntary residence in Philadelphia.

Elizabeth had only been in Philadelphia for four months when Messrs. Ware and Baker recommended that she be admitted to the almshouse on 9 November 1796. That she was diagnosed by the steward as apparently consumptive would not be unexpected since Elizabeth was probably not physically prepared for the dramatic change in climate that she encountered and endured once in the mid-Atlantic region. And her probable destitution would have also contributed greatly to her fragile health, especially if she had no permanent residence. Although the steward recorded that Elizabeth needed medical aid the moment that she arrived, Elizabeth languished and died three weeks later.[25]

Another tragedy occurred in 1798 when Pelisha, "a French Negress," arrived at the almshouse in search of a temporary dwelling. Pelisha, or the men who superintended her admission, informed the steward that she was pregnant by an unnamed black man, and that she was a servant whose master had turned her out of doors because of her parturience. Pelisha's pregnancy, no doubt, would cost her master and bring little benefit to him. Pelisha's master, it turns out, was Monsieur L'Comb of Ninth Street, quite possibly the same Lacomb who in 1803 would charge Pierre Paul forty-eight silver dollars to purchase his wife's indenture. In this instance, however, it was L'Comb who would be charged; Mr. Preston, an overseer, intended to make Pelisha's master pay for her support.[26]

Clearly, Americans were in conflict over the new black immigrants whose circumstances and ambiguous status defied the requirement widespread throughout the United States that slavery be upheld. The most tangible example of this conflict occurred in 1799–1800, when Absalom Jones and Richard Allen submitted a petition to Congress in session at Philadelphia. Jones and Allen asked the Congress to immediately abolish slavery, overturn the fugitive slave law, and plan for the future emancipation of all black people.[27] Nothing in that brief document suggests direct influence by the revolutionary events in Saint-Domingue. Yet the reaction of congressmen, northern as well as southern, is most instructive, for their virtually unanimous response revealed their commitment to rights in property over the rights of persons. Moreover, it was members of Congress who inferred the influence of the French and Haitian revolutions, for "The Eastern States were now suffering from the streams which issued from this great and dangerous fountain." According to John Rutledge Jr. of South Carolina, the "new-fangled French philosophy of liberty and equality" had impressed upon slaves in Saint-Domingue ideas they could not have arrived at on their own. In his fury at the petitioners, Rutledge exclaimed, "They now tell the House these people are in slavery—I thank God they are! if they were not, dreadful would be the consequences." John Brown, Rhode Island's representative, was equally averse to threats against the rights of property. Although he did not own slaves, Brown had profited a few years earlier from equipping "a slaver in violation of both Rhode Island and the federal law." Now Brown proclaimed "he was as much for supporting the rights and property of those who did . . . [and] considered [slaves] as much personal property as a farm or a ship, which was incontestably so." Even the petition's sponsor, Robert Waln, from Pennsylvania, capitulated in the end allowing the petition to die.[28]

As their protests over the petition reveals, members of Congress imagined the threat of revolutionary influence imported from Saint-Domingue. Those members of Congress who objected to the petition's submission resembled slaveowners who had fled Saint-Domingue; both groups were concerned with the protection of property in the slave. Moreover, they were not about to return to the question of slavery that had been settled by the Constitution: "Gentlemen were sent to that House to protect the rights of the people and the rights of property. That property which the people of the Southern States possess consisted of slaves, and therefore

Congress had no authority, but to protect it, and not take measures to deprive the citizens of it."[29]

But one instance of black protest, linked explicitly to Saint-Domingue, did occur in 1804 when

white Philadelphians believed they saw concrete evidence that the virus of rebellion was spreading when several hundred young blacks commemorated the twenty-eighth anniversary of American independence in their own way. Assembling in Southwark on the evening of July 4, they formed themselves into military formations, elected officers, and then, armed with bludgeons and swords, marched through the streets. Whites who crossed their paths were subjected to rough treatment, and at least once they entered the house of a hostile white and pummeled him and his friends. On the evening of July 5, the militant young blacks gathered again, terrorizing those whom they encountered, 'damning the whites and saying they would shew them Saint-Domingo.'"[30]

Despite whites' fears, it is not possible to know whether any of the "several hundred young blacks" had connections to their counterparts in the Caribbean. The American black elite was slower to take up the revolution's goal in a systematic manner. In this particular instance, however, some members of Philadelphia's black populace, though most likely not the elite, did embrace the cause of liberty taken up by the slaves of Saint-Domingue.[31]

Such attitudes among American lawmakers contributed to the prolonged state of servitude and dependence that Saint-Domingan slaves were forced to endure. A number of institutional and legal mechanisms accompanied a pernicious animosity to ensure they would not disrupt a fragile social stability. Public institutions such as the Vagrants Ward and the Jail and Penitentiary House represented the most dramatic form of this control. And the Pennsylvania Abolition Society, uncritical of the limitations to which they contributed, ensured that these men and women, legally released from slavery but not freed, remained firmly controlled by their former owners, men and women alike.

Despite the white refugees' protests and the refusal of the United States Congress to confront the question of slavery, between 1793 and 1796 the Pennsylvania Abolition Society's officers recorded 456 manumissions of French slaves.[32] These men, women and children became indentured servants or free residents of Philadelphia between 1790 and 1796. Their ages ranged from three months in the case of Victoire who came with her mother, Marion, aged fifteen.[33] The oldest slave to be manumitted and indentured was Fanchon, age fifty in 1793. Although Fanchon was well past the age when manumission should have been immediate, the remaining term of service mandated was seven more years.[34] Most of the slaves were in their teens, and they may not have been living apart from a parent before being spirited away with an owner. Female slaves outnumbered male slaves slightly. Perhaps females were preferred for life in an urban setting, since in Saint-Domingue they had been "strongly represented among the domestic slaves as house servants, washerwomen, and, occasionally seamstresses."[35] The average age of these slaves was fifteen; younger slaves may have been easier for the fleeing masters to control.

Some slaveowners, however, did not lose all of their investment, despite the law's requirement that they eventually release their bondspeople. Some left the state before expiration of the six-month period that they had to register their slaves prior to manumission. Others retrieved some of their costs by selling an ex-slave's indenture to another Philadelphian. This practice occurred on 26 November 1793 when Marinette of Cap-Français sold the remaining eighteen years of her slave Irène's indenture to "Adalaide, spinster, of Cape Français" for fifty pounds.[36] The slave named Clere had been brought to Philadelphia with the gentleman David Somayrac, her master, in 1794. Somayrac, rather than retain Clere as an indentured servant, sold her indentures to Peter Victoire Dorey for $112. Fourteen years of age at the time of this transaction, Clere had another fourteen years of service before she would know freedom.[37]

Determined not to lose their investment in its entirety, some slaveowners drove hard bargains once they arrived in Philadelphia. In 1803 Pierre Paul, a man of African ancestry, purchased the remainder of the slave woman Fanny's indenture from Peter Lacomb. Lacomb had purchased Fanny for seventy dollars in 1801, when she was twenty-two years old and he continued her indentures for six more years. At some point Pierre Paul had married Fanny, but that domestic circumstance appears to have made little difference to Lacomb; Paul paid him 48 silver dollars for his wife's indenture.[38]

Despite a law designed to free slaves by a determinate time, the status of some of these men and women often remained ambiguous. Mary Francis Argine, "a woman of color," had been brought to Pennsylvania from Port-au-Prince in 1803. Although Argine's owner, Francis Dumas, had manumitted her she remained in the family's household "for some years while he resided at Chester near Philadelphia." Between 1803 and 1817 Argine gave birth to five children, four males and one female. The first child, a male named Sebastian, died; two of the male children were bound to a Dr. Blenneau, who also lived near Philadelphia, and the third male child remained with his mother.

When Dumas' daughter, Anestaliores, married, he transferred Argine's daughter Frances to Anestaliores "to wait upon her." Shortly after their marriage the couple "went to New York and took shipping to New Orleans." Apparently Frances had traveled to New York and New Orleans with the couple; but Argine had received a letter from her daughter "dated at Norfolk Virginia . . . stating that she [had] been brought there to be sold." In 1825 Argine approached the city authorities on behalf of her only daughter, Frances. Dumas had since gone to France. Argine came before the mayor of Philadelphia, Joseph Watson, to seek assistance in bringing her daughter back to Pennsylvania. Watson directed that documents be sent to "the Mayor of Norfolk and to Doctor Lenac Main at Norfolk," presumably with the intention of ensuring that Argine's daughter Frances would not be sold into slavery. At the core of Argine's argument was the contention that she "had acquired her freedom by being brought into the State of Pennsylvania." What remains unstated, but might be inferred from Argine's persistence in seeking her daughter's return, is that her progeny should also have been free by virtue of having been born in the same state. The fate of Argine's daughter Frances remains unknown.

If some whites played fast and loose with Pennsylvania's abolition law as a way to control their human property, others took advantage of vagrancy laws, which allowed them to place recalcitrant servants in the city jail. Those who were slaves, servants, or who had sought employment as freed men and women, often found the conditions of their employ intolerable. Examples abound of women and men who were committed to the Vagrants' Ward, the east wing of the jail and penitentiary house on Walnut Street. Vagrants' apartments held idle and disorderly persons, prisoners awaiting trial, and runaway slaves and servants. Instances of black men and women who accompanied white refugees from Saint-Domingue suggest relations fraught with tension and resentment on both parties' part; no longer did masters have complete and absolute control over their servants. And, it would seem, these individuals had their own ideas about the prospect of freedom, as they were willing to challenge the conditions of their servitude.

These cases also indicate differences between white male and female refugees' experiences with their servants. The majority of male masters committed their servants for running away. In December 1791, Crispo was committed for absconding from his master, Monsieur D. Artis. Another of Artis's servants, Crispin, was twice committed for absconding. Female servants were just as likely to run away as male servants. Sophia, for example "absconded from Master Monsieur Gobert's service" in 1792.[39] This is not to say that servants never ran away from mistresses. For instance, in 1794 the spinster Ermine Dugay arranged for the woman Zaire's freedom to begin seven years hence. Zaire, already 28, would be Dugay's servant until 1801. In 1796, however, Zaire decided in favor of her freedom, and in September that year she absconded from Dugay. For her bid to be free, Zaire spent one month in the Vagrants' Ward.[40]

Although white women were a minority of the Saint-Domingans in the city, they represented a majority of owners whose ex-slaves were committed to the Vagrants' Ward for public disturbances. It is unclear just what this circumstance indicates. Possibly more ex-slaves chose the uncertainty of freedom over an extended, perhaps tumultuous, stay with their master. Or perhaps women, many of whom may now have been without any family or support network, had more difficulty controlling their ex-slaves. Whatever the reason, slaves like Justine and Leonora, owned by Madame Mobart, refused "obedience to her orders," in May 1794. Calypso was incarcerated for "being very ill-tempered and . . . behaving very insolent towards her mistress, Madame Antonie." Worse yet, Desire was charged by his mistress, Madame Beaverneau, "with having at divers times embezzled money and spent the same in lewd houses." This is not to say that women could not handle their slaves or servants and men could. There are a few cases of masters committing their servants for bad behavior. Joseph Gardette committed Claudine in December 1794 for "disobedience" and "associating herself with people of infamous character and in the night time admitted them into her said master's house without his leave and knowledge." Though American Southern slaveowners spoke of their fear of "contagion" from the Saint-Domingan revolts, refugees may have been equally wary of their slaves having easy access to, and daily interaction with, Philadelphia's free people of color.

A few *gens de couleur* did make a successful transition from Saint-Domingue to North America. Some of these individuals brought both skills and money needed to begin anew. And a few, perhaps, because of their light skin color, became part of the African American elite community, which observers noted "contained a disproportionate number of mulattoes."[41] John Appo was one such individual of mixed racial ancestry who immigrated to Philadelphia from Saint-Domingue and prospered. Appo appears to have immigrated between 1790 and 1800. That he was of mixed racial ancestry is confirmed by the confusion of census takers between 1800, when he and his family were listed as white, and 1810, when they were listed as free black people. At the time of the 1810 census, the Appo family lived in what was referred to as the Cedar Ward, which was where the largest number and proportion of black people lived in the city.[42] When Appo died in 1818, his wife and three children inherited real estate that included fixtures and furniture valued at roughly $150. Ann Appo, his widow, inherited one-third of the estate if she remained unmarried, while the children received the remaining two-thirds to divide among themselves. By 1822, the estate had generated considerable income, amounting to about $2,227. When Ann Appo died in 1825 she was buried in the St. Thomas' Episcopal graveyard, one of the two black churches in the city.[43]

Not only was the Appo family relatively well off, they also circulated among Philadelphia's black elite and were known and respected in black circles beyond Philadelphia. James Forten, Philadelphia's wealthy sailmaker, was an executor of Appo's will. Forten also belonged to St. Thomas' Episcopal Church, where Ann Appo was buried.[44] Furthermore, although the Appo daughters remained in Philadelphia, they were clearly prominent among the black elite outside of the city. When Ann Appo, the daughter, died in 1828, the African American New York paper *Freedom's Journal* carried notice that her death would be "deeply lamented by a large circle of friends and acquaintances."[45] Her sister, Ellen Appo, would join in business with Mrs. H. Johnson in Philadelphia to "commence the Milenary and Fancy Dress Making business" in 1837. The *Colored American,* another New York African American newspaper carried the announcement.[46]

Though the Appo family joined the majority of Philadelphia's blacks in worship at a Protestant church, refugees also built a community based upon their Catholic faith. Unlike their Protestant counterparts, Catholics recognized people of African ancestry as members of the church, baptizing and marrying, though not burying, them. This recognition extended to people of color from Saint-Domingue, though status and race determined the degree of attention given to recording particular details of the ceremonies. The refugees were welcomed by the three Catholic churches in the city, St. Joseph's, St. Mary's and Holy Trinity, all near to where the French were living. White, mulatto and black Saint-Domingans worshiped there, although not always together. Separate services were often conducted for the blacks. But priests did not discriminate in recording births and baptisms. They listed children of color along with whites in the same book.[47] In the Sacramental Registers at St. Joseph's 31 baptisms of French refugee children, including slaves or black indentured servants, were recorded in 1796.[48]

Although the characteristics of black sacraments did not for the most part change over time, one aspect of the ceremonies did. By 1796, it would appear that in some instances black women and men were acting as sponsors at baptisms. Previously either whites, who sometimes had French surnames, or the priest acted as the sponsor:

> ——, James; negro, born July 8, 1786, of Saul, and Fener, negroes; baptized July 8 [1796], by the [Rev. M. Ennis]; sponsor: Mary Josephine, negress.
> —— [27 May 1797], by Rev. M Ennis, Mary Catharine, born Jan. 1st, of Sophia and —— de la Violette, negroes, sponsor, Stanislaus, negro.[49]
> ——the 19th [August 1797], by Rev. R. Houdet, Peter, negro, born on the 14th, of Elizabeth ——, sponsor Peter and Magdalen.

Registration of non-white sacraments and marriages were scant on details and sometimes carelessly recorded.[50] For instance, Henry, who had no surname, had been born probably in November 1792; although notice of his baptism appeared in St. Joseph's records for 1793 and it mistakenly showed him having been born that year. He was the son of Joseph and Theresa Sophia, "free negroes," both of whom were Catholics. On 19 January 1793 Reverend F. A. Fleming conducted Henry's baptism, and Peter and Mary Antoinette Zemia, also Catholics, sponsored it. That the witnesses possessed a surname suggests that they were not of African descent.[51]

During the late eighteenth century, a very small number of people of African ancestry possessed surnames. One immigrant of African descent from Saint-Domingue, Louisa Robert, acquired a surname when arrangements were made for her manumission. When John Sovis, a geographer from Saint-Domingue, registered Louisa in 1795, she was 14 years of age. At that point Louisa acquired the surname Robert, but not her freedom, which she would not gain for another fourteen years.[52] Nor did church officials record surnames of black people or *gens de couleur* who married or had their children baptized, although they assiduously documented these individuals' racial ancestry. Mary Stanislaus LaChaise was rare among black children who possessed a surname when baptized at St. Joseph's.[53] Nicholas Laupair's marriage to Anisette August at St. Joseph's in 1813 was another rare instance of "Negroes" who possessed a family name.[54] Men of mixed racial ancestry, however, more commonly possessed family names than did "Negroes" or even "octoroon" women. Weddings in which both individuals of mixed racial ancestry possessed surnames were very rare. Philip Barbarani and Sophia Narvaille married on 20 December 1816 at St. Joseph's. Barth, the priest, noted that all parties were "octoroons of African stock."[55] More common were marriages that occurred among octoroons, such as the wedding of John Dutruil to Dieudonné, a woman who came to the union with no surname.[56] To the extent that the observations of the priests can be relied upon, the marriage records reveal that people of varying degrees of African ancestry married within their color caste: Negro, quadroon, and octoroon.

By 1811 the "Directory of Coloured Persons" revealed a number of black men and women who had acquired surnames. Although not many women appeared in the directory, a few possessed family names of French origin. M. Louisa Chapateau, for example, was a seamstress living at 159 Cedar Street. Another black woman's name, Fortune Sharloe, suspiciously resembled that of Mary Charlotte Fortuné, the same woman who witnessed marriages between black men and women from Saint-Domingue at St. Joseph's.[57]

Marriage among émigrés of color was sanctioned by the Catholic church and proved to be another way that émigrés slowly but steadily established themselves as permanent residents in this strange land. As was the case with baptisms, class and race determined the degree of attention given to the details of the ceremony, the most elaborate descriptions having been reserved for white émigrés of high standing. For instance, when "Pierre Morin of San Domingo" married Marie Ann Victoire Armaignac "of the parish of St. Peter of Larcahayé" on 16 December 1799, not only were there two witnesses, but also six further signatures attesting to the union.[58] Yet when the black couple John Francis and Mary Magdalen married on 15 September 1812, only three men witnessed their wedding.[59] No one recorded details of their birthplaces or genealogies as had been the case in the Morin-Armaignac marriage and those of other high-ranking whites.

Despite this distinction that endured until at least 1825, the black Catholics continued to marry at St. Joseph's. Moreover, their presence as witnesses at each other's weddings suggests that they continued to be a community of people who maintained an identity forged by birth in Saint-Domingue. Mary Fortunée Charlotte seems to have known many of the couples, as she attended their weddings and acted as a witness on numerous occasions between 1813 and 1824.[60] Priests may not have recorded many details about each couple, but they scrupulously documented their racial origins, refining distinctions among people of African ancestry. Reverend P. Kenny made such a distinction between "octoroons" and "Negroes," on 26 May 1813, when "Jean Pierre, at point of death and Veronica, (negroes)" were married in a ceremony witnessed by the ubiquitous Mary Fortunée Charlotte and another woman, Rosette.[61] It would appear from the extant records that Fortunée Charlotte also drew distinctions; she was only recorded as a witness for marriages between "Negroes."

Circumstances such as these suggest that some of these people who had emigrated from Saint-Domingue established a community that revolved around their common religion and their estrangement from a familiar, if oppressive, milieu. Language, religion, and culture appear to have created a distinct and unassimilated group of black people who identified with one other as black Catholics from Saint-Domingue. This also raises questions about the extent to which these emigrants were embraced by and incorporated into Philadelphia's black community.[62] The Appo family may have been an exception to the rule.

With the exception of the affluent blacks and *gens de couleur* from Saint-Domingue the scant evidence suggests that the Philadelphia black elite did not immediately or openly embrace the masses of African-descended people who arrived from the island or the revolt that sent them abroad. Perhaps these émigrés were viewed by the American black population as they were by the writer, Frances

Sergeant Childs, who described these refugees as "loyal enough to prefer exile with their owners than freedom at home."[63] Their infrequent appearance as part of the black elite's concerns suggests that these émigrés did not conform to black Americans' perception of what constituted an appropriate revolution.

As the 1804 protest illustrates, the refugees brought with them a troubling legacy of revolution. White fears of the consequences of freedom for enslaved people propelled efforts to curtail the refugees' freedom. Yet by the second decade of the nineteenth century these émigrés, many of them forcibly taken by their masters from Saint-Domingue on the eve of achieving freedom, gained a tenuous foothold as free people in American society. Despite social, economic, and legal restrictions, they found employment, a cultural community, and identity in the City of Brotherly Love. They were no longer strangers in a strange land.

NOTES

1. By the end of the decade there may have been as many as five thousand French refugees living and working in the city. This estimate comes from Anne Catherine Hebert, "The Pennsylvania French in the 1790s: The Story of Their Survival" (Ph.D. diss., University of Texas at Austin, 1981), 50, and Gary B. Nash, *Forging Freedom: The Formation of Philadelphia's Black Community, 1720–1840* (Cambridge: Harvard University Press, 1988), 141. An estimated sixteen thousand French, of whom ten thousand were from Saint-Domingue, arrived in the United States between 1783 and 1820. Hans-Jürgen Grabbe, "European Immigration to the United States in the Early National Period, 1783–1820," in *The Demographic History of the Philadelphia Region, 1600–1860,* ed. Susan E. Klepp (Philadelphia: American Philosophical Society, 1989), 197.

2. The most recent examination will be found in Gary B. Nash "Reverberations of Haiti in the American North: Black Saint Dominguans in Philadelphia" *Pennsylvania History: A Journal of Mid-Atlantic Studies, Explorations in Early American Culture* 65 (1998): 44–73. An earlier examination of these emigrés will be found in Susan Branson, "St. Domingan Refugees in the Philadelphia Community in the 1790s, in *Amerindians, Africans, Americans: Three Papers in Caribbean History* (Mona: University of the West Indies, 1993): 69–84.

3. David Brion Davis, *The Problem of Slavery in the Age of Revolution, 1770–1823* (Ithaca, N.Y.: Cornell University Press, 1975), especially 73–74, 76–77 discusses the significance of Saint-Domingue's revolution to the U.S.

4. Frances Sergeant Childs, *French Refugee Life in the United States, 1790–1800: An American Chapter of the French Revolution* (Baltimore: Johns Hopkins University Press, 1940), 56.

5. *Laws of the Commonwealth of Pennsylvania* (Philadelphia: John Rioren, 1810), I:495, III, IV, X. Because slaveowners were attempting to avoid the requirement that they register their slaves within six months, the 1788 legislation was passed to strengthen the force of the law by declaring "all and every slave and slaves who shall be brought into this state, by persons inhabiting or residing therein, or intending to [do so], shall be immediately considered, deemed and taken to be free, to all intents and purposes." *Laws of the Commonwealth of Pennsylvania,* vol. II: 443, II.

6. Paul Finkelman, *An Imperfect Union: Slavery, Federalism, and Comity* (Chapel Hill: University of North Carolina Press, 1981), 53.

7. Absalom Shoemaker, "Extract from Docket concerning enslavement of a black French Citizen," 11 Dec. 1806, Pennsylvania Abolition Manuscript Collection, 6:167.

8. *Pennsylvania Gazette,* 10 July 1793 [Item # 79087], 17 July 1793 [Item # 79109 and 79104]. Source: Accessible Archives Search and Information Server.

9. J. H. Powell, *Bring Out Your Dead* (Philadelphia: University of Pennsylvania Press, 1949), 4.

10. Edward R. Turner, *The Negro in Pennsylvania: Slavery—Servitude—Freedom, 1639–1861* (New York: Negro Universities Press, Repr. 1911), 253.

11. James Oliver Horton and Lois E. Horton, *In Hope of Liberty: Culture, Community and Protest Among Northern Free Blacks, 1700–1860* (New York: Oxford University Press, 1997), 83, using Nash, *Forging Freedom,* 137, Table 4.

12. Nash, *Forging Freedom,* 143, Table 5. Turner, *The Negro in Pennsylvania,* 253, however, declares the number of blacks in Philadelphia was 2,102 during the same year.

13. Darlene Clark Hine and Kathleen Thompson, *A Shining Thread of Hope: The History of Black Women in America* (New York: Broadway Books, 1998), 37.

14. Although the ship on which Duval arrived had originated in Jamaica, he was not unlike other Saint-Domingans who had traveled to other ports before disembarking at Philadelphia. The record of his arrival will be found in National Archives, Naturalization Petitions to the U.S. Circuit and District Courts for the Eastern District of Pennsylvania, 1795–1930, RG M-1522, Microfilm roll 369. Duval's arrangements to indenture Hippocrate and Hortence are documented in Pennsylvania Abolition Society, *Manumission Records,* Historical Society of Pennsylvania, Philadelphia [hereafter PAS-MR], Book D, 6.

15. Leon F. Litwack, *North of Slavery: The Negro in the Free States, 1790–1860* (Chicago: University of Chicago Press, 1961), 64–112; John K. Alexander, *Render Them Submissive: Responses to Poverty in Philadelphia, 1760–1800* (Amherst: University of Massachusetts Press, 1980), 78–79; Billy G. Smith, *The "Lower Sort": Philadelphia's Laboring People, 1750–1800* (Ithaca, N.Y.: Cornell University Press, 1990), 150–75; Horton and Horton, *In Hope of Liberty,* 109–110.

16. Gary B. Nash and Jean R. Soderlund, *Freedom By Degrees: Emancipation in Pennsylvania and Its Aftermath* (New York: Oxford University Press, 1991), 89, 86.

17. Nash, *Forging Freedom,* 120–21.

18. Richard Allen, *The Life Experience and Gospel Labors of the Rt. Rev. Richard Allen . . .* (New York: Abingdon Press, 1960; the date of its original writing cannot be confirmed.)

19. John F. Watson, *The Annals of Philadelphia and Pennsylvania,* 3 vols. (Philadelphia: Edwin S. Stuart, 1905), 1:181.

20. Comte de Moré, quoted in Hebert, "Pennsylvania French," 131.

21. Kenneth Roberts and Anna M. Roberts, trans. and eds., *Moreau de St. Méry's American Journey [1793–1798]* (Garden City, N.Y.: Doubleday, 1947), 311

22. David Geggus notes that though women "had much less access than their male counterparts to positions of independence, skill, and prestige," they found ways to accumulate wealth, and sometimes achieve freedom. Their scarcity put a premium on their sexual favors. Many acquired jewelry and expensive muslin textiles in exchange for their favors. This practice, judging from comments made by Philadelphians, continued during their exile in America. David P. Geggus, "Slave and Free Colored Women in Saint Domingue," in D. Barry Gaspar and Darlene C. Hine, eds., *More Than Chattel: Black Women and Slavery in the Americas* Bloomington: Indiana University Press, 1996), 260–61, 265, 268.

23. Alexander, *Render Them Submissive,* 94. Emphasis in original. Billy G. Smith also argues that the almshouse was prison-like in *The Lower Sort,* 167.

24. Guardians of the Poor, Daily Occurrences Dockets, Microfilm Reel 2, 1797 to Dec. 1802 Philadelphia City Archives, Department of Records.

25. Ibid.

26. Ibid., 21 Dec. 1798.

27. Herbert Aptheker, *A Documentary History of the Negro People in the United States: From Colonial Times Through the Civil War* (New York: Citadel Press, 1963 [1951]), 1: 44.

28. Congressional debate will be found in *Annals of Congress* 6 Cong., I Sess., 229–45. Quotes are taken from 230, 232. This petition and responses to it are also discussed in Winthrop D. Jordan, *White Over Black: American Attitudes Toward the Negro, 1550–1812* (Chapel Hill: University of North Carolina Press, 1968), 328–30, quote about Brown profiting from the slave trade will be found on 329; and Larry Tise, *Proslavery: A History of the Defense of Slavery in America, 1701–1840* (Athens: University of Georgia Press, 1987), 232.

29. *Annals of Congress* 6 Cong., I Sess., 231.

30. Nash, *Forging Freedom,* 176.

31. Julie Winch, *Philadelphia's Black Elite: Activism, Accommodation, and the Struggle for Autonomy, 1787–1848* (Philadelphia: Temple University Press, 1988), 49–69. This became more apparent after the 1820s. Between 1827 and the 1850s black newspapers carried memorials to Toussaint Louverture and Haiti. Cf *Freedom's Journal, The North Star, The Colored American, The National Era, The Provincial Freeman, The Frederick Douglass Paper.*

32. Gary B.Nash, *Forging Freedom,* 142. We have calculated 548 slaves from Saint-Domingue, based on the manumission records.

33. PAS-MR, Book B, 262.

34. PAS-MR, Book A, 197.

35. Geggus, "Slave and Free Colored Women," 260.

36. PAS-MR, Book A, 160.

37. PAS-MR, Book B, 76.

38. PAS-MR, Separate Folder.

39. Inspectors of the Jail and Penitentiary House, Vagrancy Dockets, 1790–1797, Microfilm Reel 1 (1790–1797), Record Group 38.44, Philadelphia City Archives, Department of Records.

40. PAS-MR, Book C, 126; Vagrancy Dockets, 2:366, Philadelphia City Archives.

41. Winch, *Philadelphia's Black Elite,* 33, 50. The immigrants of African ancestry from the Caribbean have been described as "not altogether of an undesirable character . . . nearly all of [them] were skilled in some kind of art or craft." Richard R. Wright, *The Negro in Pennsylvania: A Study in Economic History* (Philadelphia: AME Book Concern, 1912), 52.

42. Census, 1810. Blacks comprised 1,779 out of 6,664 people (26.7%) living in this district.

43. The authors wish to thank Julie Winch for providing information about the Appo family: Register of Wills, 1818, No. 151, Book 6, 623; Inventory of Estate; Board of Health Records, 15 Nov. 1825 for death of Ann Appo; Census Data: 1800, Philadelphia County, 135; 1810 Philadelphia, Cedar Ward, 262. The quote about churches is taken from Nash, *Forging Freedom,* 192.

44. Nash, *Forging Freedom,* 182.

45. *Freedom's Journal,* 26 Dec. 1828 [Item #1731 on Accessible Archives Search and Information Server]

46. *The Colored American,* 30 Sept. 1837 [Item #2889 on Accessible Archives Search and Information Server]

47. Joseph L. J. Kirlin, *Catholicity in Philadelphia* (Philadelphia, 1909), 129. Rev. Laurence Phelan began preaching in French to his parishioners in 1793.

48. Soderlund and Nash, *Freedom By Degrees,* 64.

49. [Francis X. Reuss], "Sacramental Registers at St. Joseph's Church, Philadelphia, Pa., of the Eighteenth Century," *Records of the American Catholic Historical Society* [hereafter

RACHS] 16 (1905): 330, 373, 380. Stanislaus also had acted as a sponsor for Eleanor and Peter when they baptized their child Henry in 1796. [Reuss], "Sacramental Registers," *RACHS* 16 (1905): 341.

50. For the more prominent white émigrés, however, great care was taken in recording the baptism of their infants: Vendryés, Louise Frances Alexander, born 5 Nov. 1792, of Louis Vendryés, Commissioner of Marine in the colony of San Domingo, and his wife Marie Antoinette Adam, baptized on [9 Aug. 1793], by Anthony Joseph Larroque, Vice-prefect of the missions of Guadeloupe, sponsors Jean Bapt[ist] François, Chevalier Volante, native of San Domingo, Joseph Ant. Mercier, Superior Councilor of Guadeloupe, Porris, Resseneour, Vendryre. See [Reuss], "Sacramental Registers," *RACHS* 15 (1904): 466. Of course, given the number of baptisms that occurred in any given year, only the more prominent families received such detailed attention. In 1793, for example, there were 284 baptisms performed; in 1794, 183; in 1795, 299; in 1796, 357; in 1797, 440; in 1798, 450; in 1799, 344; in 1800, 419—and these are only the baptisms that were performed at St. Joseph's. St. Mary's and St. Augustine's sacramental records are not as easily available. [Reuss], "Sacramental Registers" *RACHS* 16 (1905): 53–68, 202–23, 314–43, 361–90; 17 (1906): 4–32, 322–47, 457–85.

51. [Reuss], "Sacramental Registers" *RACHS* 15 (1904): 457.

52. PAS-*MR*, Book B, 246.

53. [Reuss], "Sacramental Registers," *RACHS* 16 (1905): 336. Her parents, however, were another matter. Although the priest identified her father, Peter LaChaise, Mary Stanislaus' mother was not named. The parents, however, were listed as "negroes."

54. "Marriage Registers at St. Joseph's Church, Philadelphia, Pa., 1809–1825," *RACHS* 20 (1909): 137.

55. Ibid., 151.

56. Ibid., 147.

57. Jane Aitken, *Census Directory for 1811,* "Directory of Coloured Persons."

58. [Reuss], "Marriage Registers at St. Joseph's Church, Philadelphia, Pa. From December, 1799, to December, 1808," *RACHS* 20 (1909): 25.

59. [Reuss], "Marriage Registers,1809–1825" 137.

60. Mary Fortunée Charlotte's name appears in at least eight ceremonies where black people married, though it is often spelled differently.

61. [Reuss], "Marriage Registers, 1809–1825," 138. Cf. ibid, 144, 145, 147, 151, 153, 155.

62. In *Forging Freedom,* 141, Gary B. Nash asserts "their presence also politicized Philadelphia's resident free blacks, for they came bearing firsthand reports of the most extensive black revolution in two centuries of slavery in the Western Hemisphere."

63. See above, note 3.

Chapter 14

Repercussions of the Haitian Revolution in Louisiana

PAUL LACHANCE

THE THEME OF THE IMPACT of the Haitian Revolution on the Atlantic World raises very large questions. First, how did its outcome affect the balance of power in the region? In depriving France of what had been the most valuable colony in the Americas in the eighteenth century, did it remove any effective counterweight to British hegemony for decades to come? Secondly, what were the international economic ramifications of the revolution? To what extent were the important shifts in population, distribution of crops, and commercial exchange in the Caribbean between 1750 and 1830 consequences of the elimination of the largest sugar producer in the world economy?[1] Thirdly, did the revolution hasten or delay the abolition of slavery in other colonies and countries? General answers to these questions are treated in this essay as hypotheses and tested against results of research on how the revolution affected a specific place on the edge of the Atlantic world.

In 1791, the year in which slaves in the North Province of Saint-Domingue revolted, approximately forty thousand free and enslaved persons of European and African descent inhabited Spanish Louisiana.[2] Over the next dozen years, the Haitian Revolution directly and profoundly affected this colony in three ways corresponding to the large questions articulated above. Geopolitically, the situation in Saint-Domingue influenced Napoleon's decisions first to obtain retrocession of Louisiana from Spain in 1800 and then to sell it to the United States in 1803. As regards economics, Louisiana planters converted from tobacco and indigo to sugar and cotton production in the 1790s. One stimulus to make the transition to sugar was its high price on the international market due to the decline in exports from Saint-Domingue during the revolution.[3] Thirdly, the abolition of slavery in Saint-Domingue in 1793, confirmed by the French Convention and extended to all French colonies in 1794, inspired several rebellions by Louisiana slaves in the 1790s. It also motivated the ruling elite to take the danger of slave revolts very seriously, attempt to avert them by restrictions on the slave trade, and crush them quickly and ruthlessly when they occurred. These were effects of the Haitian Revolution as it was happening. After it ended with the declaration of Haiti's independence by Jean-Jacques Dessalines on 1 January 1804, over ten thousand refugees sought asylum in New Orleans, where they continued to influence the course of Louisiana history.

Napoleon would never have sold Louisiana to the United States in 1803 if he had succeeded in reimposing French rule over Saint-Domingue. Retrocession of Louisiana to France by the second Treaty of San Ildefonso with Spain in 1800 was a first step in his grand design to reconstruct an empire centered on Caribbean islands exporting sugar, coffee and other tropical products to France and Europe. In the revived imperial system, the role assigned to Louisiana was to furnish the French West Indies with foodstuffs and lumber, thereby avoiding dependence on the United States for supplies. The second step was the Peace of Amiens, negotiated in 1801 and signed in 1802, by which Great Britain returned Martinique to France and accepted a truce that left Napoleon free to mount a military expedition to the Caribbean. The third step was the dispatch to Saint-Domingue of twenty thousand French troops under the command of his brother-in-law, General Charles Victor Emmanuel Leclerc. His mission was to occupy the colony by ruse if possible or by force if necessary, deport Toussaint Louverture and all the black generals, disarm all the blacks and force them to return to agricultural production.[4]

The debacle of the Leclerc expedition made the Louisiana Purchase possible. By the summer of 1802, the French army was ravaged by a renewed black insurgency and yellow fever. The epidemic claimed the life of Leclerc himself in November 1802. Reinforcements met the same fate as the soldiers they replaced. Military losses eventually totaled 50-55,000 of 60-65,000 men sent to Saint-Domingue.[5] Once it became clear Saint-Domingue was irrecoverable, Napoleon had neither the means nor the incentive to take control of Louisiana. Not only did its sale to the United States refill his depleted coffers, it also increased the chances of the buyer pursuing a policy of friendly neutrality, if not openly siding, with France when war with Great Britain inevitably resumed.[6] Transferring sovereignty over Louisiana to the United States served the same purpose as its cession by France to Spain after the Seven Years' War. It kept the territory out of British hands.

Too much of a slaveholder to continue the realpolitik of his Federalist predecessors with respect to Toussaint Louverture and as yet uninformed about Napoleon's plan to take possession of Louisiana as soon as Saint-Domingue was pacified, Thomas Jefferson endorsed in the summer of 1801 the prospect of a French military expedition to recover the colony. "Nothing would be easier," he assured Louis-André Pichon, the French chargé d'affaires in Washington, "than to furnish your army and fleet with everything and to reduce Toussaint to starvation."[7] Once the president realized the connection of Louisiana to Saint-Domingue, he failed to follow through with measures to prevent American merchants from continuing to supply the black insurgents and made clear his opposition to a French takeover of Louisiana. Access to the sea through the port of New Orleans for trans-Appalachian farmers and planters remained a major objective of American foreign policy. A delegation journeyed to Paris in January 1803 with instructions to acquire the island between the Mississippi River and Lake Pontchartrain on which New Orleans was located. When Talleyrand offered to sell all of Louisiana, Jefferson's ambitions adjusted accordingly.[8] He obtained this immense territory without going to war or compromising American neutrality. Yet it is doubtful that he could have done so without the defeat of Napoleon in Saint-Domingue, leading Henry Adams to remind "the American people [of] the debt they owed to the desperate courage of five hundred thousand Haytian negroes who would not be enslaved."[9]

The Haitian Revolution also contributed indirectly to Louisiana's economic growth in the antebellum period. In 1791, Saint-Domingue produced approximately 30 percent of the world's sugar.[10] Sugar exports declined from seventy thousand tons in 1789 to nine thousand tons in 1801. Although Haiti continued to export some sugar even after independence, it was no longer a supplier of any importance to the world market. Only sixteen tons were exported in 1826.[11] British and Spanish colonies quickly took the place of Saint-Domingue and satisfied most of the burgeoning international demand for sugar.[12] World production rose from 245,000 tons in 1800 to 572,000 tons in 1830, an increase of 233 percent in thirty years.[13] As in Cuba, but on a much smaller scale, sugar production took off in Louisiana during the Haitian Revolution. Successful granulation was first achieved on Étienne de Boré's plantation in 1795, and his crop made twelve thousand dollars. Within seven years, sixty to seventy plantations on both banks of the Mississippi River above and below New Orleans were producing a total of 2,250 to 3,100 tons of sugar annually.[14] By 1840, Louisiana produced 51,712 tons of sugar, 8 percent of international production.[15] It can be counted among the places on which the Haitian Revolution had a positive economic impact by opening markets formerly dominated by Saint-Domingue to other producers.

In addition to its geopolitical and economic impact, the political and cultural shock wave emanating from an uncontainable slave insurrection was felt by slaveholding societies throughout the Americas. A "common wind," Julius Scott's evocative metaphor for the channels of popular communication of a seafaring world, carried news of events in the colony of Saint-Domingue to enslaved peoples and sympathetic allies everywhere, tempting them to attempt the no-longer-impossible as well.[16] Sensitive to the danger, planters and governments in the same societies responded by extraordinary measures to deter revolts and subdue those that occurred before it was too late.

Louisiana in the 1790s furnishes dramatic examples of both the contagion of revolution and counterrevolutionary response. In October 1791 a free New Orleans mulatto, Pierre Bailly, was tried on hearsay evidence for having declared that he and his companions were awaiting word from Saint-Domingue to mount a *coup* like the one at Cap-Français.[17] In the spring of 1795 a conspiracy on one of the Poydras plantations in Pointe Coupée caused one alarmed Creole to write: "If our information is correct, the Saint-Domingue insurrection did not have a more violent beginning."[18] Other slave conspiracies were discovered at Opelousas post in February 1795, and in Pointe Coupée and on the German Coast in February, March and April 1796.[19] Acting on petitions from "countless inhabitants," the

Cabildo (town council) demanded and received from the Spanish governor, Francisco Louis Hector Carondelet, a temporary ban on all slave importations in 1795 and indefinite extension of the suspension in 1796. In 1800, notwithstanding the opposition of six of eleven members of the Cabildo, Nicolás Vidal, Carondelet's successor as governor, reopened the African slave trade; but the prohibition of Saint-Domingue slaves remained in force.[20]

Besides restrictions on the slave trade, measures were taken to maintain control over a slave population viewed as increasingly defiant. Spanish governors and Louisiana planters clashed over the most effective means to avoid insurrection. Carondelet authorized the execution of twenty-one slaves and the deportation of fifty others for participating in the 1795 Pointe Coupée conspiracy; but he also heard complaints of slaves and punished several planters for disobeying rules against brutal treatment of slaves.[21] Vidal blamed the insolence of slaves on their masters and called for respect of legitimate authority and the laws in force: Christian education of slaves, humane correction when required, and proper food and clothing so they would not have to steal and prostitute themselves to survive.[22] Planters, for their part, demanded unconditional authority to use whatever means necessary to keep their slaves in line.[23] Their insistence on restrictions on the slave trade reflects a fundamental lack of confidence in the gentler means recommended by Spanish officials.

Louisiana was **not** the preferred asylum of refugees from the Haitian Revolution while it was happening. Colonists fleeing Saint-Domingue between 1791 and 1803 sailed first to the closest open seaports. When slaves from the surrounding hills descended on Cap-Français in June 1793, ten thousand colonists sought safety on the fleet in the harbor which took them to Atlantic ports in the United States.[24] Approximately two thousand collaborators retreated to Jamaica with British occupation forces after their defeat by Toussaint Louverture in 1798.[25] Colonists also fled to the Spanish part of Hispaniola and to Cuba well before the final mass exodus in 1803.[26] Refugees at first expected to return to Saint-Domingue, as many in fact did when Toussaint Louverture restored a fragile peace and order to the colony.[27] The greater the hope of returning, the less attractive was a relatively remote refuge such as Louisiana.

The paranoiac reaction in Spanish Louisiana to the Haitian Revolution also discouraged refugees from seeking asylum there. Even white refugees found themselves the object of judicial proceedings for suspicious behavior. Paul Alliot related how he had been arrested in New Orleans in 1802 and accused of allowing a Negro to hold a new-born child over the baptismal font, drinking with men of color in public places and encouraging them to revolt, and addressing a mulatress as *"citoyenne."*[28] Measures forbidding entry of slaves who might spread news of events in Saint-Domingue were a particular obstacle to refugees who had managed to escape with several of their slaves. "Without that rigorous interdict," wrote Berquin-Duvallon in his *Vue de la colonie espagnole,* "French colonists gathered at the north of America (in a country whose language they did not understand and whose climate was hostile to them) . . . would have come here in great numbers to settle." Slaves belonging to refugees were seized and kept in prison at their owners' expense. Berquin-Duvallon warned refugees not to expect any sympathy from

Louisiana Creoles: "There is no little scamp of a creole in this savage colony, who has never been out of sight of the shores of the Mississippi, and who has never drank other water than that of this river, who does not consider himself authorized, by the example of the chief men among them, and like the ass in the fable, to insult an unfortunate stranger—I mean even a Frenchman, a colonist like himself, escaped from the upheaval and massacres of San Domingo, and a refugee in this country with some little remnants of his fortune."[29]

The number of Saint-Domingue refugees making their way to New Orleans increased after the change from Spanish to American sovereignty. Two factors made Louisianians more willing to risk the entry of refugees with slaves. Enactment by the territorial legislature of a slave code in 1806 gave planters greater personal power over their workers. Plans of Americanization pursued by the United States government, by assimilation of the French population if possible, but especially by encouragement of Anglo-American immigration, threatened the ascendancy of French-speakers.[30] A thousand or so refugees from Jamaica arrived in 1803 and 1804.[31] More than ten thousand arrived by way of Cuba in 1809.

We can be reasonably certain how many came in 1809 because the mayor of New Orleans kept track of them. Although his report has disappeared, the *Moniteur de la Louisiane* published aggregate figures based on it.[32]

The 9,059 refugees counted by the mayor were more numerous than the 8,475 persons comprising the total population of New Orleans and its suburbs in 1805. They were over half as many as the 17,001 persons enumerated in rural as well as urban areas of Orleans parish in 1806.[33] In addition to the refugees arriving from May to December 1809, as many as a thousand remained of several thousand who had arrived prior to 1809, and at least a thousand more refugees followed in the first months of 1810.

Comparison of the composition of the 1809 migration with the census of New Orleans just before their arrival suggests how these refugees, if they took up residence, modified the racial and age structure of the population and exacerbated its already imbalanced sex ratios.[34]

First and most important, the refugee influx substantially increased the proportion of free persons of color in the total population. Over a third of the refugees

TABLE 14.1: Race and Condition, Age and Sex of Saint-Domingue Refugees Arriving from Cuba in 1809

	MEN	WOMEN	CHILDREN UNDER AGE 15	TOTAL
Whites	1,373	703	655	2,731
Free persons of color	428	1,377	1,297	3,102
Slaves	962	1,330	934	3,226
Total	2,763	3,410	2,886	9,059

Source: Report of the Mayor of New Orleans on 18 January 1810, published in the *Moniteur de la Louisiane,* no. 1001(27 January 1810).

TABLE 14.2: Characteristics of Population of New Orleans in 1805 and of Saint-Domingue Refugees Arriving from Cuba in 1809

	RACIAL DISTRIBUTION		CHILD-WOMAN RATIO		ADULT SEX RATIO	
	NEW ORLEANS IN 1805	1809 MIGRATION FROM CUBA	1805	1809	1805	1809
Whites	43.2%	30.1%	1.378	0.932	131	195
Free persons of color	19.0%	34.2%	1.233	0.942	36	31
Slaves	37.8%	35.6%	0.866	0.702	67	72

Sources: Census of New Orleans, 5 August 1805 (see note 34); mayor's report on refugees arriving in 1809 (see Table 14.1).

Notes: Racial distributions sum to 100% by column. Child-woman ratios are children under age 16 per women over age 15. Adult sex ratios are the number of men over age 15 for every 100 women over age 15.

were free persons of color, compared to less than a fifth of the residents of the city of New Orleans in 1805. Secondly, the child-woman ratios of the 1809 migrants were lower than in New Orleans in 1805. In terms of the strain that a large number of refugees put on the host society, fewer children meant they were less dependent on its aid than they might have been. The mayor commented in August 1809 that over six hundred adult male refugees with a trade were already "usefully employed."[35] In January 1810 he complimented free black carpenters for their "uncommon industry. Many houses have been built in little time and at less cost than before."[36] Thirdly, the adult sex ratios of both white and non-white free refugees were more imbalanced than those of corresponding elements of the New Orleans population prior to their arrival. The direction of the imbalance, however, was the same. The 1809 migration from Cuba reinforced in this respect a previously existing characteristic of the city's population.

In several ways, the 1810 census confirms the expected impact of the refugees. Their arrival should have augmented the urban population relative to the rural population of Orleans parish; and it did. Between 1805 and 1810, residents of New Orleans and its suburbs increased from around half to over two-thirds of the parish population.[37] The growth rate of the city during these five years was 15.3 percent per annum, higher than between any two previous or subsequent censuses between 1726 and 1860. It was 25.9 percent for free persons of color, raising them from 19 to 29 percent of the urban population. Among whites, the child-woman ratio dropped from 1.378 in 1805 to 1.231 in 1810 while the adult sex ratio increased from 131 to 155 males per 100 females, again consistent with the direction of change expected from comparison of characteristics of refugees arriving in 1809 with the population of New Orleans in 1805.[38]

The absolute increase in population, 8,767 persons in New Orleans from 1805 to 1810, 7,551 in the entire parish from 1806 to 1810, was less than the number of refugees who arrived in 1809 and 1810. If the urban death rate were higher in these years than the birth rate, the population growth since 1805 could imply a net immigration of around 10,000 persons. Refugees, however, were not the only immigrants between 1805 and 1810; nor did all those who arrived from Cuba in 1809 remain in the city or parish a year later when the census was taken, either because they had themselves died in the meantime or because they had emigrated. While comparison of the mayor's report with censuses suffices to show the number of arrivals relative to the population before and after the influx, the census recapitulations do not distinguish refugees from non-refugees. Census manuscripts do not enable us to identify refugees without already knowing their names, and then only heads of households. Without identifying refugees, we do not have direct evidence of how many remained in New Orleans. Arrival is one thing; establishing residence is quite another.

By far the most valuable source for identifying refugees is the collection of sacramental records in the archives of the Diocese of New Orleans. In 1810, all Catholic baptisms, marriages and funerals were performed at the St. Louis Cathedral or at the Ursulines Chapel.[39] The records of both churches are extant and complete for this year. Separate registers were kept for whites and non-whites, the latter including both free and enslaved persons of color. Several entries provide a sense of the information on refugees to be found in this source.[40]

On 24 January 1810, Claude Thomas, himself a former *curé* in Saint-Domingue, baptized Jean-Baptiste Drouillard, the white son of Jean-Vincent Drouillard, a native and former planter from the district of Croix des Bouquets in Saint-Domingue. The infant's mother and godparents were born in Philadelphia.[41] Among persons of color baptized in 1810, one finds Manuel de Silva, a free quadroon, the natural son of a Portuguese immigrant and a free mulatress born at Môle Saint-Nicolas in Saint-Domingue. The child's godfather was white and his godmother was a free mulatress, neither of whom was identified as coming from Saint-Domingue nor as related by blood to the child.[42] The first entry in 1810 in the St. Louis Cathedral register of baptisms of persons of color was for Charles, a five-week-old Negro, the natural son of Marie-Josephe, Negro slave of Madame Duverger, a resident of Cap-Dame-Marie in Saint-Domingue. The child's godparents were also slaves, the godfather belonging to the rich Louisiana planter Bernard Marigny and the godmother to Doctor Bugard, a former inhabitant of the Artibonite in Saint-Domingue. The act was annotated "all refugees in this city," although that wasn't true for Marigny.[43]

Since slaves could not marry, marriage records exist only for whites and free persons of color. In 1810, Jean-Baptiste Rossignol Desdunes Leclair, a white refugee from Saint-Marc in Saint-Domingue who later became one of New Orleans' largest bakers, married the daughter of the Louis Moreau Lislet, a refugee from Cap-Français famous in Louisiana history as the compiler of the 1808 Digest of the Civil Code. In addition to the parties to the marriage and their fathers, the marriage act contains the signatures of five witnesses, at least four of whom other records reveal to be Saint-Domingue refugees as well.[44] The Desdunes-Lislet marriage ended tragically in 1831 when the wife was murdered by the baker's apprentice, whose mistress she had become after deserting her husband. The only marriage in 1810 of free persons of color from Saint-Domingue was between Pierre Jessé and Hortense Noleau. Both were mulattoes born in Saint-Marc, but the hus-

TABLE 14.3: Saint-Domingue Refugees Arriving in 1809 as a Proportion of Total Population of New Orleans in 1810, and Percentage of Sacramental Records Referring to Refugees in 1810

RACE	ARRIVALS FROM CUBA (1809)	POPULATION OF NEW ORLEANS (1810)	REFUGEES AS PROPORTION OF POPULATION	BAPTISMS OF REFUGEE CHILDREN		REFUGEE SPOUSES		FUNERALS FOR REFUGEES	
Whites	2,731	8,001	34.1%	68	27.6%	28	20.6%	100	38.3%
F.p.c.	3,102	5,727	54.2%	107	40.2%	2	7.7%	129	54.2%
Slaves	3,226	10,824	29.8%	48	10.0%			132	39.4%
Total	9,059	24,552	36.9%	223	21.7%	30	18.5%	361	43.3%

Sources: Mayor's list of arrivals in 1809 cited in Table 14.1; aggregate returns for Orleans parish in *Third Census of the United States, 1810: Population*, 82; and sacramental records of St. Louis Cathedral and St. Mary's Church (in reality, the Ursulines chapel) listed in note 40.

band was a legitimate child while the bride was the natural daughter of a white man and a Negro mother. The husband being seriously ill, the purpose of the marriage was to legitimize their four children before he died.[45]

Entries for Saint-Domingue refugees in sacramental records in 1810 are evidence of the number still present in New Orleans in that year. Since sacramental records do not include Protestants and unbaptized slaves, the source overstates the proportion of refugees in the total population. This bias is offset by the absence from the mayor's report on arrivals in 1809 of several thousand additional refugees who arrived prior to 1809 and in the first months of 1810. Thus comparison of the two sources provides a fairly accurate impression of the proportion of arriving refugees who stayed in New Orleans for at least a year.

Having observed in Table 14.2 lower child-woman ratios for refugees in 1809 than in the population of New Orleans in 1805, it comes as no surprise that the percentage of refugee baptisms is also less than the ratio of arrivals in 1809 to population in 1810. Both child-woman ratios and the percentage of baptisms are evidence of the low fertility of all categories of refugee women, perhaps compounded by greater than usual infant mortality. The exceptionally low percentage of baptisms of slaves belonging to refugees is consistent with lower child-woman ratios among refugee slaves than among free refugees. By contrast, in a census of Santiago de Cuba in 1808, the child-woman ratio of slaves owned by Saint-Domingue refugees was as high as for white refugees and higher than the ratio for free persons of color from Saint-Domingue. Moreover, the adult sex ratio of refugee slaves in Cuba had been balanced, in contrast to only seven adult male slaves for every ten adult female slaves brought by refugees from Cuba to New Orleans.[46] One may infer the separation of some slave families by the expulsion of refugees from Cuba in 1809.

Temporary impoverishment of some of the refugees in the 1809 migration could explain why the percentage who married in 1810 was less than the percentage of arrivals. The average value of assets in marriage contracts drawn up for white refugees in New Orleans between 1804 and 1820 was well below the norm in all contracts for whites: $3,216 for grooms born in Saint-Domingue compared to $8,034 for all grooms, $2,530 for brides born in Saint-Domingue compared to $3,849 for all brides.[47] These spouses were refugees who arrived with sufficient assets to compete immediately in the marriage market. Others arrived with too little to do so.

The welfare committee formed to aid white refugees in 1809 exaggerated in describing the "majority [as] in an absolute want of objects of prime necessity."[48] The rapid employment of refugees with skilled trades has been noted. From the average number of slaves per owner in refugee inventories from 1810, it appears that half of the white refugee families were able to profit from the sale or rental of slaves they brought with them.[49] Nevertheless, notations in the funeral records from 1810 reveal an unusually large number refugees who lacked the means to pay for their interment. Funerals were provided *gratis* for 27 percent of the white refugees who died in 1810 compared to 16 percent of other whites. Half of Saint-Domingue free persons of color could not pay for their burial, in contrast to 14 percent of other free persons of color. Three-fourths of refugees' slaves were buried for free, compared to a third of those belonging to other masters.

The proportion of funerals for refugees and slaves belonging to refugees is as high or higher than the ratio of arrivals in 1809 to the population in 1810 for these groups. Adding deaths of Protestants and unbaptized African slaves to entries in the Catholic funeral register diminishes somewhat the percentage of funerals for refugees. From a recapitulation of vital events in the *Moniteur,* we know that 1,046 persons in Orleans Parish died in 1810, 20 percent more than the 833 entries in the Catholic funeral registers.[50] Dividing entries in the funeral register for refugees by 1,046 rather than 833 reduces their proportion of all deaths from 43.3 percent to 34.5 percent.

If the multiple factors affecting baptisms, marriages and deaths preclude certainty about how many refugees were present in New Orleans in 1810, the 223 refugees who were baptized and the 361 who died in that year do permit us to narrow down the probable number who stayed in the city. The method is simple: calculation of vital rates implied by sacramental events for refugees and comparison of their vital rates to those of the remainder of the population of Orleans parish as reported in the *Moniteur.* Without a yellow fever epidemic, 1810 was a healthy year for antebellum New Orleans. The unadjusted crude birth rate for the entire population was 37.5 per thousand.[51] The general crude death rate was 42.6 per thousand.[52] Table 4 shows the rates for refugees and for the rest of the population for different estimates of the number of refugees in the parish.

Since child-woman ratios indicate a lower birth rate for refugees than for the rest of the population and since it is likely that their death rate was above average, we can infer a minimum of seven thousand and a maximum of eight thousand refugees in Orleans parish in 1810, or 58 to 67 percent of an estimated twelve thousand refugees arriving over the preceding two decades, and 70 to 80 percent of the ten thousand who arrived in 1809 and 1810. The difference between the number of baptisms and deaths of refugees in 1810 strongly suggests they were incapable of reproducing themselves by endogamous marriages and consensual unions. Attrition through natural causes compounded by out-migration from New Orleans was

TABLE 14.4: Estimated vital rates of Saint-Domingue refugees and the rest of the population of Orleans parish in 1810

	SAINT-DOMINGUE REFUGEES			REST OF THE POPULATION	
	223 BIRTHS	361 DEATHS		698 BIRTHS	685 DEATHS
	BIRTH RATE	DEATH RATE		BIRTH RATE	DEATH RATE
5000	44.6	72.2	19,552	35.7	35
6000	37.2	60.2	18,552	37.6	36.9
7000	**31.9**	**51.6**	**17,552**	**39.8**	**39**
8000	**27.9**	**45.1**	**16,552**	**42.2**	**41.4**
9000	24.8	40.1	15,552	44.9	44
10000	22.3	36.1	14,552	48	47.1

Source: See Table 3.

Notes: The birth and death rates are per 1,000 persons. The highlighted rows are the more probable estimates.

only partially offset by new arrivals of refugees after 1810. Refugee movements differ from other types of migration in being more sharply delimited in time. Although they may suddenly inflate the population of the host society, subsequent in-migration is minimal.

The minimum estimate of seven thousand Saint-Domingue refugees in 1810 remains a very large number relative to the size of New Orleans at the time. The sacramental records also furnish evidence of a high rate of persistence in the decades that followed. Refugees born in Saint-Domingue accounted for 13 percent of four thousand entries in the white funeral register from 1815 to 1828. They represented 18 percent of white French-speaking spouses from 1810 to 1819, 13 percent from 1820 to 1829, and 3 percent in the 1830s. They were an even higher proportion of free persons of color who married in New Orleans during these three decades: 25 percent from 1810 to 1819, 33 percent in the 1820s, and 15 percent in the 1830s.[53]

Entries in the sacramental records show that the process of absorption of the refugees into the French-speaking population of New Orleans had already begun in 1810. The godfather of the baptized slave, although born in Saint-Domingue, had been purchased by the Louisiana slaveholder Bernard Marigny. Among twenty-three white marriages in 1810 involving natives of Saint-Domingue, five were with a spouse born in Louisiana; and among ninety-seven baptisms of white refugee children, nine had one parent from Saint-Domingue and the other from Louisiana. Conversely, several documents point to behavior at odds with immediate assimilation into the Gallic community. The parents of the baptized child Drouillard are an example of a refugee who married into an American rather than into a Louisiana Creole family. Manuel de Silva was the offspring of a consensual union between a Portuguese immigrant and a free woman of color from Saint-Domingue. Like the marriage of two mulatto refugees from Saint-Marc in 1810, free persons of color born in Saint-Domingue married endogamously much more often than their white counterparts in subsequent years. Their behavior is evidence that refugees remained a distinct subgroup among free persons of color in New Orleans longer than they did among whites.[54]

In addition, the sacramental records reveal relationships among subgroups of the refugee population itself. First, white refugees included many French-born colonials as well as Creoles, or natives, of Saint-Domingue. The proportion of each is difficult to determine because one also finds in New Orleans many Frenchmen who immigrated directly or by routes that did not pass by French islands in the Caribbean. In 1810, twice as many Frenchmen from France as men born in Saint-Domingue married Saint-Domingue women. No Frenchwoman from France married a native of Saint-Domingue. Among white children baptized in 1810, forty-five had a father born in France and a mother born in Saint-Domingue, compared to thirty-eight with both parents born in Saint-Domingue. No child had a father born in Saint-Domingue and a mother born in France. We can conclude from this evidence that practically all white refugee women were Creoles of Saint-Domingue, while half to two-thirds of white refugee men were born in France.

Secondly, the sacramental records reveal the frequency of interracial relationships within the refugee community as well as in the population of New Orleans as a whole. Only five of fifty-seven free children of color born in 1809 or 1810 and baptized in the first four months of 1810 were legitimate. In this respect, refugee behavior was the same as that of the rest of the population. Among free children of color with refugee mothers, two out of twenty-seven were legitimate. Not only were the vast majority of children of all free persons of color born out of wedlock, most were baptized with no mention even of their natural father. He was named in the entries for only 37 percent of free children of color, and for no slave children. Manuel de Silva's father, who was present at his son's baptism, who recognized him as his natural son, and who accepted that he bore his last name, was atypical, if not altogether exceptional. Comparison of the phenotypes of baptized children and their parents (mothers and, when mentioned, fathers) reveals that 61 percent of all free children of color and 35 percent of all slave children in New Orleans had white fathers. Among refugees the proportions were 63 and 50 percent respectively.

Besides their demographic impact, which reinforced the "three-caste" racial hierarchy in New Orleans and augmented the Gallic community at the beginning of a period of economic, political, and cultural confrontation with Anglo-American immigrants, Saint-Domingue refugees perpetuated two of the three ways in which the Haitian Revolution had already affected Louisiana prior to their arrival. Although they contributed less than is often claimed to the development of sugar production in Louisiana, they did play an important part in repulsing the British attack on New Orleans at the end of the War of 1812, thereby preserving the Louisiana Purchase which the Haitian Revolution had made possible. Above all, the refugees collectively reinforced the counterrevolutionary impact of the Haitian Revolution on attitudes and behavior with respect to slavery in Louisiana.

The development of sugar production in Louisiana is often associated with Saint-Domingue refugees. In what remains the major monograph on the sugar industry in the American South, J. Carlyle Sitterson cites, among the factors contributing to its development in the first decade of the nineteenth century, "the growing tide of immigrants from the West Indies, many of whom were familiar with sugar culture and some of whom were themselves sugar makers and sugar engineers." Then, referring to the refugee influx of 1809, he asserts, "Indeed, the amazingly rapid progress made by this new culture in the years after 1795 must be attributed in no small degree to the experience, knowledge, and industry of these newcomers."[55] In the major monograph to date on the influence of the Haitian Revolution on the United States, Alfred Hunt writes, "St. Domingans contributed significantly to the agricultural development of Louisiana, especially in transplanting successful sugar production into the underdeveloped territory." He credits not only white refugees for this contribution, but also their slaves: "St. Domingans brought semi-skilled slaves into Louisiana to work the cane fields and others to tend the kettles during the crucial cooking process."[56]

Evidence to support such generalizations is in truth slim. Antoine Morin, a chemist and sugar maker originally from Saint-Domingue, was employed by Étienne de Boré in 1795; and advertisements in newspapers do show that some refugees sought employment on sugar plantations and that some of their slaves may have been hired to help in the harvest of sugar crops. Hunt's one example of a Saint-Domingue refugee who became a sugar planter in Louisiana, Paul Mathias

Anatole Peychaud, in fact spent his active life involved in municipal politics and only moved to the country when he retired. His sugar plantation in St. Tammany parish worked by twenty slaves was hardly a major operation. There is no equivalent for Louisiana of Gabriel Debien's partial list of 135 Cuban coffee farms run by Saint-Domingue planters in 1807.[57]

The technology used in the manufacture of sugar in Louisiana up to 1830 was the traditional open kettle method used everywhere in the Caribbean. The real takeoff of sugar production in Louisiana occurred in the 1830s.[58] It owed much to a "French connection" described well by John Heitman, but none of the French chemists and engineers that he mentions were Saint-Domingue refugees. The interest in sugar chemistry of the apothecary J. B. Avequin, for example, dates from a trip he made to Santo Domingo in the 1830s. Another path by which French scientific and technological knowledge was applied to the production of sugar in Louisiana was education in France of Louisiana Creoles like the quadroon Norbert Rillieux, who studied at the École polytechnique in Paris and, some time after returning to Louisiana, patented a multiple-effect evaporation system in 1843. Another Creole, Valcour Aimé, learned about new methods of manufacturing sugar on a trip to Cuba in 1845.[59]

If it is an exaggeration to attribute to Saint-Domingue refugees a key role in the development of sugar production in Louisiana, their part in defending the Louisiana Purchase at the Battle of New Orleans just as often goes unrecognized in histories of the War of 1812 written from an American nationalist perspective. Napoleon's sale of Louisiana to the United States is emblematic of the geopolitical consequences of the Haitian Revolution. Although the failure to reestablish French control over Saint-Domingue weakened France to the point that it could no longer rival British power in the Atlantic, Napoleon limited his losses by arranging for the transfer of sovereignty over Louisiana to the United States before France suffered further defeats in the Caribbean.[60]

In the long run, the elimination of France as a major power in the Atlantic world was compensated by the rise of the United States to a position where it could challenge British hegemony. In the short run, the United States let itself become involved in the last phase of the Napoleonic Wars as an enemy of Great Britain, if not a formal ally of France. The British invasion of Louisiana at the end of the War of 1812 put Napoleon's strategy in jeopardy. Since the treaty ending the war was signed before the Battle of New Orleans, although the news did not reach the combatants in time to avert the battle, and since the American victory did not affect the terms of peace, it is impossible to say what would have been the consequences of a British victory. It is conceivable, though, that Great Britain would have repudiated the Treaty of Ghent and claimed the interior of the North American continent as the spoils of victory. Saint-Domingue refugees in Louisiana helped to prevent that scenario by fighting on the side of the United States in the Battle of New Orleans.

At the time of the 1809 migration from Cuba to Louisiana, no one foresaw these developments. On the contrary, the association of Saint-Domingue refugees with Napoleonic ambitions in the Americas was a matter of concern even to Louisiana Creoles who gave them a friendlier reception than they had given to Alliot and Berquin-Duvallon.[61] The unexpected arrival of thousands of French-speaking refugees in 1809 especially upset promoters of the rapid Americanization of Louisiana. For their part, refugees tried to disassociate themselves from Napoleon by posing as nonpartisans in search of a shelter from the revolutions and wars of their time. Their reply to an invitation to join the West Florida Revolt in 1810 demonstrates their political posture. At the same time as American rebels alluded to the Bonapartist threat represented by the refugees in their plea to be annexed to the United States, they negotiated through Charles Audibert, formerly representative of the government of Guadeloupe in Santiago de Cuba, for support of the refugees in the event of military action against Spain. In response to American assurances that "any attachment to Bonaparte should be no offense to the Country," Audibert insisted that the refugees "had used Bonaparte's name to please the Spaniards who had vexed them, but as Citizens of their new Country they'd Rather Remain independent than to submit to any master." All that was necessary to get them to fight for the West Florida Convention was to promise them part of the vacant land.[62]

Whatever their attitude toward Napoleon—and by 1809 many refugees may have felt abandoned by him—they continued to see England as their nemesis. They had not forgotten the blockade of the coasts of Saint-Domingue by the British fleet and the aid given to insurgents in 1803. A refugee from Cuba recounted how English spies had offered to supply the refugees with arms so that "we and the Spanish could cut each other's throats, and who no doubt regret that we did not repay with the vilest perfidy the hospitality that the government of Cuba had so generously offered us, but which political reasons prevented it from continuing." The abstract allusion to "political reasons" was a way of exculpating Cuban authorities. According to the same refugee, the true authors of their misfortune were the English: "If we escaped the rapacity of English warships, it is only because they were busy elsewhere and realized they would have been hindered by such a large population. Bandits like certain officers in the British navy who sold in Kingston the clothes and furniture of the unfortunate women who fled from Saint-Domingue would certainly not have had any qualms about plundering us a second time, if they had found the least advantage in doing so."[63]

The lingering rancor of Saint-Domingue refugees against the English took on importance when the United States declared war against Great Britain in 1812. The British invasion of Louisiana and attempt to capture New Orleans at the end of 1814 put them in a position where they had to take sides. Their Anglophobia led them to choose the American camp. White refugees fought mainly in the Battalion of Orleans. Among 109 veterans of this unit of 600 soldiers whose birthplace has been determined by Ronald Morazan, 28 percent were natives of Saint-Domingue. Two companies in the battalion were commanded by refugees: the *Compagnie des Dragons* by Henri de Ste.-Gême and the *Compagnie des Chasseurs* by Augustus Guibert.[64] Before and after the Battle of New Orleans, several refugees requested to be exempted, as French citizens, from militia duty; but during the battle itself, according to the French consul in New Orleans, only one Frenchman did not answer Andrew Jackson's call to arms in 1814.[65]

The Second Battalion of Free Men of Color was essentially the Santo

Domingo garrison commanded by lieutenant-colonel Joseph Savary, a mulatto, which had retreated to New Orleans early in 1810.[66] The same Savary organized the battalion of men of color that saw action in the Battle of New Orleans under the command of a white baker from Saint-Domingue, Louis d'Aquin. Baratarian privateers included many of the same men who had used Baracoa and Santiago de Cuba as bases to attack British shipping up to 1809. They, too, fought alongside the Americans. Before the battle, an English officer had met their leader, Jean Lafitte, to offer him thirty thousand dollars and rank of captain in the British navy if he and his men would help the British to invade Louisiana. Lafitte refused. Given American harassment of the privateers—his brother was at that moment incarcerated in New Orleans on the charge of smuggling—his refusal of the British proposition makes better sense if one takes into account the birth of the two brothers in Saint-Domingue, like many other Baratarians. In informing Paris of the victorious battle that followed, the French ambassador to the United States remarked that "these privateers are former French filibusters driven from our islands by British conquest or by the insurrection they fomented . . . They provided General [Jackson] with 800 soldiers and especially with excellent gunners."[67]

The Battle of New Orleans was one of those exceptional moments in history when individuals participate directly in an event that decides the future. In a sense, the English invasion of 1814 is comparable to the arrival of the Leclerc expedition in Saint-Domingue, that had required colonists to take a position for or against Napoleon's plan to restore the authority of the metropole and put blacks back to work on plantations. In supporting this counterrevolution, they suffered the consequences of its failure. Six years later, as refugees in Cuba, they had to react to the order of Cuban officials to swear loyalty to Ferdinand VII, whom Napoleon had just replaced by his brother as king of Spain. In refusing to take the oath, they paid the price of expulsion. In Louisiana, their decision to fight against the British invasion contributed to the American victory. They finally chose the winning side. In preserving New Orleans as a permanent refuge, they made possible their own long-term impact on the host society. At least with respect to the institution of slavery, it was counterrevolutionary.

The slaves whom refugees took first to Cuba and then to Louisiana are evidence of a visceral attachment to slavery. They also acted as if they were still the masters of those whom they had left behind. Marriage contracts of refugees in New Orleans frequently contained references to property in Saint-Domingue, including slaves. In 1806, for example, the contract of Anne Louis de Tousard mentioned properties in Jérémie and "all his Negroes remaining in Saint-Domingue."[68] In 1810, the marriage contract of Luce-Charlotte Mérillon cited, as property from her first marriage, a lot in Port-au-Prince and a plantation with fifteen slaves in the district of Mirebalais "usage of whom events have deprived her."[69] In 1819, Marie Claveaud, born in Santiago de Cuba, declared her rights to "lands, houses, and slaves abandoned by her father and mother during the evacuation Saint-Domingue."[70]

As in other cities of the American South, slavery declined in New Orleans over the course of the antebellum period.[71] Between 1810 and 1860, slaves fell from

TABLE 14.5: Frequency of Slaves in Successions in New Orleans, 1809–1860

Year	Refugee inventories			Other inventories		
	Slaveholders	Slave assets	N	Slaveholders	Slave assets	N
	%	%		%	%	
1809–10	95.8	56.2	24	55.4	14.8	74
1820	91.7	54.3	12	29.7	7.3	64
1830	85.7	27.7	7	46.3	8.0	95
1840	75.0	31.5	8	46.6	6.1	131
1850	100.0	7.2	2	36.4	12.0	349
1860	60.0	9.9	5	29.6	9.5	301

Source: Inventories of successions in New Orleans, City Archives, New Orleans Public Library.

34.6 to 8.3 percent of the city's total population. The actual number of slaves increased steadily from 1810 to 1840, then declined over the next two decades, dropping back by 1860 to the level reached in 1830.[72] While Saint-Domingue refugees participated in this trend, they were also the element of society that offered the greatest resistance to it. The inventories of refugees at death reveal that they invested a larger part of their fortunes in slaves than any other group of property-holders in the city up to and including 1840. A higher percentage of refugee inventories listed slaves through 1860.

It was not only by continuing to own slaves that refugees reinforced the institution of slavery, but also and especially by the image many of them conveyed of the Haitian Revolution as a "long series of misfortunes and bloody episodes," of which they were the living witnesses and which they passed on to the next generation. The famous Creole pianist Louis Moreau Gottschalk, whose grandmother was a refugee, wrote in his journal of the "somber memories" and "grievous recollections" associated with the name of Saint-Domingue: "our dwellings burned, our properties devastated, our fortunes annihilated"; the massacre of all his great-uncles; "their daughters and wives, fallen into the power of their former slaves, . . . put to death after having been subjected to the most horrible outrages."[73]

To be sure, not all Saint-Domingue refugees shared this image of the Haitian Revolution. It would be unfair to cite Gottschalk as I have just done without mentioning that he expressed in the next paragraph an enlightened understanding of the deeper historical significance of the revolution. Some of the many refugees involved in interracial unions remembered the revolution as a situation that forced them to choose between family ties and racial or political solidarity. Furthermore, the refugees were hardly responsible for introducing counterrevolution into Louisiana. Fears of slaves from the French West Indies antedated the Haitian Revolution. The Creole planter elite reacted immediately to news of the slave uprising in Saint-Domingue in 1791 by prohibiting the importation of slaves from the French Antilles capable of transmitting to Louisiana slaves the contagious virus of revolution. They did not need to be advised by refugees to crush without procrastination or leniency attempts at insurrection in Louisiana. Nevertheless, the public image of refugees as victims of revolution, flesh-and-blood examples of defeat, dispossession, and violent death of family members, obviously an image that fit free refugees better than their slaves, reinforced in Louisiana the apocalyptic vision of what would happen if control over slaves were relaxed.

NOTES

The author wishes to thank Thomas Fiehrer and David Geggus for comments.

1. These shifts are described in Stanley Engerman and B. W. Higman, "The demographic structure of Caribbean slave societies in the eighteenth and nineteenth centures," and David Eltis, "The slave economies of the Caribbean: Structure, performance, evolution, and significance," in *The Slave Societies of the Caribbean,* vol. 3 of the *General History of the Caribbean,* ed. Franklin Knight (London and Basingstoke: UNESCO Publishing, 1997), 45–137.

2. The population of Louisiana in 1788 was 42,611, according to the "Résumé général du recensement fait dans la province de la Louisiane, District de la Mobile et Place de Pensacola en 1788," Archives des Affaires Etrangères, Paris, Correspondance consulaire pour la Nouvelle-Orléans, 1 (1804–1817), f. 55.

3. John Clark, *New Orleans, 1718–1812: An Economic History* (Baton Rouge: Louisiana State University Press, 1970), 218. On the movement of sugar prices during the Haitian Revolution, see also J. H. Parry and P. M. Sherlock, *A Short History of the West Indies* (London: Macmillan, 1971), 172.

4. E. Wilson Lyon, *Louisiana in French Diplomacy* (Norman: University of Oklahoma Press, 1974 [1934]), 109. Napoleon's instructions to Leclerc have been published as an appendix to Paul Roussier, ed., *Lettres du Général Leclerc, commandant en chef de l'Armée de Saint-Domingue en 1802* (Paris: Société de l'histoire des colonies françaises et Librairie Ernest Leroux, 1937), 263–74.

5. Claude and Marcel Auguste, *L'expédition Leclerc 1801–1803* (Port-au-Prince: Henri Deschamps, 1985), 316. Because their estimate of troops includes naval personnel, it is higher than the figure of 44,000 given by most historians. The expedition, of course, also took the lives of many blacks. Claude and Marcel Auguste estimate between 100,000 and 130,000 black victims.

6. Rayford Logan, *The Diplomatic Relations of the United States with Haiti, 1776–1891* (Chapel Hill: University of North Carolina Press, 1941), 143–44.

7. Thomas Jefferson in his meeting with Louis-André Pichon, 20 Jul. 1801, as reported by Pichon to Talleyrand on 22 Jul. 1801, Archives des Affaires étrangères, Paris, États-Unis, 53, fols. 177–84, cited in Carl Lokke, "Jefferson and the Leclerc Expedition," *American Historical Review* 33 (1928): 324. For context, see Michael Zuckerman, "The Power of Blackness: Federalists, Jeffersonians, and the Revolution in San Domingo," in *La Révolution française et Haïti: filiations, ruptures, nouvelles dimensions,* ed. Michel Hector, 2 vols. (Port-au-Prince: Henri Deschamps, 1995), 2:109–50; Marie-Jeanne Rossignol, *Le ferment nationaliste: Aux origines de la politique extérieure des États-Unis, 1789–1812* (Paris: Belin, 1994), 207–39; Robert Paquette, "Revolutionary Saint Domingue in the Making of Territorial Louisiana," in *A Turbulent Time: The French Revolution and the Greater Caribbean,* ed. David Barry Gaspar and David Patrick Geggus (Bloomington: Indiana University Press, 1997), 204–25.

8. Documents related to the Louisiana Purchase have been compiled and published in *State Papers and Correspondence Bearing upon the Purchase of the Territory of Louisiana* (Washington: Government Printing Office, 1903); and in Richard Skolnick, ed., *1803: Jefferson's Decision: the United States Purchases Louisiana* (New York: Chelsea House, 1969).

9. Henry Adams, *History of the United States of America during the Administrations of Thomas Jefferson* (New York: Literary Classics of the United States, 1986 [1889]), 316.

10. French colonies produced 39 percent of the world's sugar in 1791, and Saint-Domingue accounted for 78 percent of French production in 1789. See Dale Tomich, *Slavery in the Circuit of Sugar: Martinique and the World Economy 1830–1848* (Baltimore and London: John Hopkins University Press, 1990), 15; Michel Devèze, *Antilles, Guyanes, La Mer des Caraïbes de 1492 à 1789* (Paris: S.E.D.E.S., 1977), 267.

11. Franklin W. Knight, *The Caribbean: The Genesis of a Fragmented Nationalism* (New York: Oxford University Press, 1978), 241.

12. Tomich, *Slavery in the Circuit of Sugar,* 23–26 (on British colonial sugar production), 30–31 (on Cuban production).

13. Sidney Mintz, *Sweetness and Power: The Place of Sugar in Modern History* (New York: Penguin, 1986), 73.

14. Clark, *New Orleans: An Economic History,* 218–19.

15. Tomich, *Slavery in the Circuit of Sugar,* 15. As J. H. Galloway remarked in *The Sugar Cane Industry: An Historical Geography from its Origins to 1914* (Cambridge: Cambridge University Press, 1989), 190, Louisiana supplied primarily a United States market protected by high tariffs. The Louisiana Purchase, rendered possible by the Haitian Revolution, was a necessary condition for the willingness of Congress to guarantee the United States market to Louisiana planters.

16. Julius Scott, "The Common Wind: Currents of Afro-American Communication in the Era of the Haitian Revolution" (Ph.D. diss., Duke University, 1986).

17. Kimberly Hanger, *Bounded Lives, Bounded Places: Free Black Society in Colonial New Orleans, 1769–1803* (Durham, N.C.: Duke University Press, 1997), 155.

18. Charles Fleuriau to the Cabildo, 25 Apr. 1795, in City Archives, New Orleans Public Library, Records and Deliberations of the Cabildo [hereafter Cabildo Records], 4: 2–3. Other examples of the paranoia in New Orleans in the 1790s are given in Scott, "The Common Wind," 266–74; and Hanger, *Bounded Lives,* 148–52. The most thorough discussion is Thomas Fiehrer, "The Baron of Carondelet as Agent of Bourbon Reform: A Study of Spanish Colonial Administration in the Years of the French Revolution" (Ph.D. diss., Tulane University, 1977), 466–505.

19. Gwendolyn Hall, *Africans in Colonial Louisiana: The Development of Afro-Creole Culture in the Eighteenth Century* (Baton Rouge: Louisiana State University Press, 1992), 355, 372, and in general chap. 11.

20. Shifts in policy on importation of slaves during the 1790s and the great debate of 1800 over reopening the slave trade are examined in my article, "The Politics of Fear: French Louisianians and the Slave Trade, 1786–1809," *Plantation Society in the Americas,* 1 (1979): 164–76.

21. Baron de Carondelet to the Cabildo, 1 May 1795, Cabildo Records, 4: 7.

22. Nicolás Maria Vidal to the Cabildo, 21 Oct. 1800, in ibid., 4: 198. For additional evidence of Spanish policy of slave control, see James Thomas McGowan, "Creation of a Slave Society: Louisiana Plantations in the Eighteenth Century" (Ph.D. diss., University of Rochester, 1976), 276–85.

23. McGowan, "Creation of a Slave Society," 223–24, 288.

24. C. L. R. James, *The Black Jacobins* (New York: Vintage, 1989 [1963]), 126–27. Frances Childs, *French Refugee Life in the United States, 1790–1800* (Baltimore: John Hopkins University Press, 1940), 15, 395.

25. Gabriel Debien and Philip Wright, "Les colons de Saint-Domingue passés à la Jamaïque (1792–1835)," reprint of an extract from the *Bulletin de la Société d'Histoire de la*

Guadeloupe, no. 26 (1975), 70; David Geggus, *Slavery, War and Revolution: The British Occupation of Saint-Domingue, 1793–1798* (Oxford: Clarendon Press, 1982), 271–72, 314.

26. Gabriel Debien, "Les colons de Saint-Domingue réfugiés à Cuba, 1793–1815," *Revista de Indias* 13 (1953): 559–605; 14 (1954): 11–36; Alain Yacou, "L'émigration à Cuba des colons français de Saint-Domingue au cours de la révolution" (Ph.D. diss., Université de Bordeaux, 1975).

27. Between 25 Jun. 1799 and 30 Oct. 1801, the United States State Department issued more than four hundred passports to refugees to return to Saint-Domingue. The list has been published by Nellie Fowler, "Santo Domingo Passports, 1799–1801," *National Genealogical Quarterly* 41 (1968): 263–75.

28. "Alliot, Médecin, Propriétaire en Nègres et en Terres de St-Domingue, Déporté de la Louysiane; aux Habitans de la commune de Lorient et à tous les Français, [publ.] aux Prisons de Pontaniou, à Lorient, 26 Messidor an XI." My notes are from a copy of the pamphlet sent to Gabriel Debien by René LeGardeur, 30 Dec. 1965. A copy is also found in the Jefferson papers; and large excerpts are published under the title "Historical and Political Reflections on Louisiana," in *Louisiana under the Rule of Spain, France, and the United States, 1785–1807,* 2 vols. (Freeport, N.Y.: Books for Libraries Press, 1969 [1910–1911]), ed. James Robertson. See especially the editor's biographical sketch of Alliot, 1:148–49.

29. Berquin-Duvallon, *Vue de la colonie espagnole du Mississippi ou des provinces de Louisiane et Floride occidentale, en l'année 1802, par un observateur résidant sur les lieux* (Paris, 1803), as translated in ibid., 1: 190–91, 194. His case and Alliot's are discussed, with long excerpts from their writings, in Gabriel Debien and René LeGardeur, "The Saint-Domingue Refugees in Louisiana," in *The Road to Louisiana: The Saint-Domingue Refugees, 1792–1809* (Lafayette: Center for Louisiana Studies, 1992), ed. Carl Brasseaux and Glenn Conrad, 167–73.

30. Lachance, "Politics of Fear," 184–85.

31. Debien and Wright, "Colons de Saint-Domingue passés à la Jamaïque," 170–74.

32. The data were reprinted in the *Moniteur de la Louisiane* (hereafter *Moniteur*), no. 1017, 24 Mar. 1810, with a note that the arrival in Louisiana since the mayor's first report of refugees on several ships from Cuba that had stopped first in Jamaica brought their total number to more than ten thousand.

33. Report of the Mayor of New Orleans, 18 Jan. 1810, published in the *Moniteur,* 27 Jan. 1810; census of New Orleans, 5 Aug. 1805, by Matthew Flannery, reprinted in *New Orleans in 1805: A Directory and a Census* (New Orleans: Pelican Gallery, 1936); and the returns for Orleans parish in the "Recensement général du Territoire d'Orléans au 1er du janvier 1807," item 1 in Joseph Dubreuil de Villars papers, William R. Perkins library, Duke University, Durham, N.C.

34. The contrast in racial distribution is even sharper when the 1809 refugees are compared with the 1807 census of Orleans parish, according to which 37 percent of the population was white, 14 percent were free persons of color, and 49 percent were slaves. The 1807 census does not provide the information necessary for comparison of the other parameters at the parish level.

35. James Mather to William Claiborne, 9 Aug. 1809, in *Official Letter Books of W.C.C. Claiborne, 1801–1816,* ed. Dunbar Rowland, 6 vols. (Jackson, Miss., 1917), 4: 406.

36. Letter of James Mather, 18 Jan. 1810, published in the *Moniteur,* 27 Jan. 1810.

37. While the total number of persons living in the parish increased from 17,001 in 1806, according to the census dated 1 Jan. 1807, to 24,552 in 1810, residents of New Orleans and its suburbs increased from 8,475 in 1805 to 17,242 in 1810 (*Third Census of the United States, 1810: Population,* 82; see note 34 for references to the 1805 and 1807 censuses).

38. Lack of breakdowns by age and gender for free persons of color and slaves in the 1810 census does not allow us to observe changes in the structure of these elements of the population after 1805.

39. Sacramental records of the Roman Catholic Church of the Archdiocese of New Orleans, Archives of the Archdiocese of New Orleans: St. Louis Cathedral Baptisms, 1809–1811 (B22); St. Louis Cathedral Baptisms of Slaves and Free Persons of Color, 1809–1811 (B23); Libro primero de matrimonias de negros y mulatos de la parroquia de San Luis de la Nueva Orleans, 1777–1830 (SLC, M3); St. Louis Cathedral Marriages. 1806–1821 (SLC, M6); St. Louis Cathedral Funerals, 1803–1815 (SLC, F7); St. Louis Cathedral Funerals of Slaves and Free Persons of Color, 1806–1810 (SLC, F8); St. Louis Cathedral Funerals of Slaves and Free Persons of Color, 1810–1815 (SLC, F8); St. Marie Baptisms. 1805–1838 (SMNO. B1); Baptèmes des personnes de couleur libres et des esclaves, 1805–1844 (SMNO, B2); St. Marie Marriages, 1805–1837 (SMNO, M1). The abbreviations are those used in the abstracts of the *Sacramental Records of the Roman Catholic Church of the Archdiocese of New Orleans,* vol. 10, *1810–1812,* ed. Charles Nolan (New Orleans: Archdiocese of New Orleans, 1994).

40. Not only do the sacramental records name Saint-Domingue refugees who married, gave birth to children, and died in New Orleans, they also reveal the names of members of their families and other refugees who served as godparents or witnesses to baptisms and marriages. Recorded systematically, they offer the possibility of reconstructing the remnants of families and kinship networks that survived the displacement of the refugees by revolution and forced migration.

41. *Sacramental Records,* 10:150, Jean-Baptiste Drouillard, baptized 14 Jan. 1810, born 20 Dec. 1809.

42. *Sacramental Records,* 10:139, Manuel de Silva, baptized 20 Jan. 1810, born 8 Nov. 1809. In an entry for his sister on page 408 under the name Silvas, the birthplace of the father and the spelling of the name of the mother are different.

43. Charles, baptized 1 Jan. 1810 (act not abstracted in *Sacramental Records* because no family name is given for the baptized child).

44. *Sacramental Records,* 10:138, marriage of Juan Bautista Desdunes with Isavel Althea Julia Moreau Lislet, 1 Oct. 1810.

45. *Sacramental records,* 10:240, marriage of Pedro Adriano Jessé with Ortanza Noleau, 13 Mar. 1810.

46. Census of Santiago de Cuba, 27 Jul. 1808, transcribed in Bahumil Badura, "Los Franceses en Santiago de Cuba a medianos del Año 1808," *Ibero-Americana Pragensia* (Prague), 5 (1971): 157–60.

47. Paul Lachance, "Were Saint-Domingue Refugees a Distinctive Cultural Group in Antebellum New Orleans?: Evidence from Patterns and Strategies of Property Holding" (paper presented at 29th annual conference of the Association of Caribbean Historians, Martinique, 9 Apr. 1997), 11 (Table 3: "Percentage of Marriage Contracts and Average Declarations of Wealth by Gender, Race, and Origin, New Orleans, 1804–1820"), to appear in *Revista / Review Interamericana.*

48. Proceedings of Council Meetings, City Archives, New Orleans Public Library, 24 May 1809.

49. In 1810, 24 refugees died with sufficient property to warrant an inventory. All except one owned slaves. The 88 slaves named in these estates were distributed relatively equally, no refugee possessing more than seven. If the 3,226 slaves from Cuba were also divided among refugees at an average of 3.8 per owner, 849 refugees were slaveholders. Judging from inventories, less than 5 percent of these refugee slaveholders were free persons of color. Controlling for race and considering couples as a single owner, around half of the

white refugee households included slaves. This analysis is based on a sample of inventories in New Orleans for selected years between 1804 and 1860 from the manuscript collection in the City Archives, New Orleans Public Library. Out of 1,289 inventories examined, 92 were for Saint-Domingue refugees.

50. "Récapitulation de l'année 1810," in the *Moniteur,* no. 1105, 12 Jan. 1811.

51. The crude birth rate is based on 1,029 acts in the Catholic baptismal records and 1,034 baptisms reported in the *Moniteur* in 1810. Neither source included Protestants. In a table of vital events in the last nine months of 1808 in Barthelemy Lafon, *Annuaire louisanais pour 1809* (New Orleans, 1808), 182, only 2 of 38 white children and none of 76 non-white (*gen. C.*) children who died were Protestants. At the same proportion, there were an additional 14 white births for Protestants in 1810. I also subtracted 127 baptisms of adult slaves, mostly recently imported African slaves, to arrive at a birth rate to 37.3 per thousand using baptisms in the church records, 37.5 using the *Moniteur* count.

52. For the crude death rate, I divided the 1,046 deaths in the recapitulation in the *Moniteur,* which include Protestants as well as Catholics, by 24,552, the population of Orleans parish in 1810.

53. Paul Lachance, "The 1809 Immigration of Saint-Domingue Refugees to New Orleans: Reception, Integration, and Impact," in *The Road to Louisiana,* 264.

54. Paul Lachance, "Intermarriage and French Cultural Persistence in Late Spanish and Early American New Orleans," *Histoire sociale / Social History* 15 (1982): 74.

55. J. Carlyle Sitterson, *Sugar Country: The Cane Sugar Industry in the South, 1753–1950* (Lexington: University of Kentucky Press, 1953), 11. His statistics and graph on pages 27–30 belie his generalization about the "amazingly rapid progress" of sugar production from 1795 to 1810.

56. Alfred Hunt, *Haiti's Influence on Antebellum America: Slumbering Volcano in the Caribbean* (Baton Rouge: Louisiana State University Press, 1988), 62–63. Another example of the argument is José Morales, "The Hispaniola Diaspora, 1791–1850: Puerto Rico, Cuba, Louisiana, and Other Host Societies" (Ph.D. diss., University of Connecticut, 1986), 51: "It is obvious that the French refugees from Cuba were important to the development of Louisiana between 1809 and 1810, for many brought slaves and technology, and served as owners, overseers, and technicians in Louisiana's infant sugar industry. . . . There seems to be a correlation between the increase in sugar production and the influx of French refugees from St. Domingue and, later, Cuba, both premier sugar-producing colonies."

57. Debien, "Les colons de Saint-Domingue à Cuba," 13, 595–601. After listing these 135 names, Debien remarks they were only a fraction of the refugees who succeeded in starting new coffee plantations, and goes on to name a dozen others.

58. See the graph in Sitterson, *Sugar Country,* 29. Prior to 1839, sugar production in Louisiana surpassed 100,000 hogsheads (50,000 tons) only in 1828 and 1834.

59. John Heitman, *The Modernization of the Louisiana Sugar Industry, 1830–1910* (Baton Rouge: Louisiana State University Press, 1987), 9–16.

60. On French defeats in the Caribbean after the loss of Saint-Domingue, see Jean Meyer, *Histoire du sucre* (Paris: Éditions Desjonquères, 1989), 159.

61. My argument on the association of refugees with Napoleonic ambitions is based on evidence originally presented in a paper read at the Colloque international du bicentenaire de la Révolution française in Port-au-Prince (Haiti), 5–8 Dec., 1989, and published under the title, "Les réfugiés de Saint-Domingue à la Nouvelle-Orléans: leur impact à court et à long terme," in *La Révolution française et Haïti,* 2: 90–108.

62. C. M. Audibert to F. Skipwith, 4 Sept. 1810, in James A. Podgett, "The West Florida Revolution of 1810, as told in the Letters of John Rhea, Fulwar Skipwith, Reuben Kempers, and Others," *Louisiana Historical Quarterly,* 21 (1938): 87–88.

63. Letter to the editor signed "Un réfugié de St. Yague de Cuba," *Courrier de la Louisiane,* 10 Jul. 1809.

64. Ronald Morazan, comp., *Biographical Sketches of the Veterans of the Battalion of New Orleans, 1814–15* (Baton Rouge: Legacy, 1979).

65. Anne Louis de Tousard to John Clement Stocker, 6 Jan. 1815, in Norman Wilkinson, "The Assaults on New Orleans, 1814–1815," *Louisiana History* 3 (1962): 49.

66. Roland C. McConnell, *Negro Troops of Antebellum Louisiana: A History of the Battalion of Free Men of Color* (Baton Rouge: Louisiana State University Press, 1968), 67–71. See also the interesting information on Savary's activities prior to the Battle of New Orleans in chap. 2, "The Republican Cause and the Afro-Creole Militia," of Caryn Cossé Bell, *Revolution, Romanticism, and the Afro-Creole Protest Tradition in Louisiana, 1718–1868* (Baton Rouge: Louisiana State University Press, 1997), 41–64.

67. Report of Louis Sérurier on the Battle of New Orleans, 7 Feb. 1815, Archives des Affaires Étrangères, Paris, Correspondance politique: États-Unis, 72, fols. 25–26.

68. Narcisse Broutin, notary, marriage contract between Anne Louis de Tousard and Anne Marie Geddes, 26 Jun. 1806, Orleans Parish Notarial Archives.

69. Marc Lafitte, notary, marriage contract between Antoine Marie Goysson and Luce Charlotte Mérillon, 5 Dec. 1810, Orleans Parish Notarial Archives.

70. Narcisse Broutin, notary, marriage contract between Remy Leon Viennot and Marie Manuel La Caridad Claveaud, 13 Apr. 1819, Orleans Parish Notarial Archives.

71. Richard Wade, *Slavery in the Cities: The South 1820–1860* (Oxford: Oxford University Press, 1964), 3; Claudia Goldin, *Urban Slavery in the American South 1820–1860: A Quantitative History* (Chicago: University of Chicago Press, 1976), 1.

72. Federal censuses of Orleans parish enumerated 5,961 urban slaves in 1810, 7,355 in 1820, 13,945 in 1830, 23,448 in 1840, 18,068 in 1850, and 14,484 in 1860.

73. Louis Moreau Gottschalk, *Notes of a Pianist,* ed. Jeanne Behrend (New York: Alfred Knopf, 1964), 12.

Chapter 15

The Caradeux and Colonial Memory

DAVID P. GEGGUS

OF THE HUNDREDS OF FRENCH refugees who crowded into Charleston in the early 1790s, Jean-Baptiste de Caradeux (1742–1810), was perhaps the most notable. This was partly because he stood 6'4" and was completely bald, but also because he was a man with a past, whose name was well known to Saint-Domingue exiles. A rich aristocratic planter, recently commander of the National Guard of that colony's West province, he had played a prominent role in the early years of the Haitian Revolution. Charlestonians called him "General Caradeux." Whereas many French colonists arrived in the city destitute, especially those who fled the burning of Cap-Français in June 1793, Caradeux was exceptional in reaching Charleston with at least a modest remnant of his fortune. Unlike the northern part of Saint-Domingue that was laid waste in 1791, plantations in the Cul-de-Sac plain, where the Caradeux family had its property, were still largely intact in the summer of 1792, when Jean-Baptiste shrewdly decided it was time to leave.[1]

In 1792 Jean-Baptiste de Caradeux was fifty years old, a recently widowed father of three young children. Besides his children, household servants, and their children, he brought with him his widowed sister Marie-Louise, an overseer's daughter, and about twenty-five slaves.[2] Caradeux had prepared his departure by previously shipping to Charleston a large quantity of sugar, which (thanks to the revolution) sold at sky-high prices, and on arrival he sold a quantity of diamonds, doubtless his late wife's.[3] He was able to purchase a house on the city's outskirts, and in 1797 he built a plantation home on a thickly forested tract of land about ten miles north of Charleston. Cedar Hill, on the Wando River in St. Thomas parish, was more of a farm than a plantation.[4] The family established a brickworks and lumber business there, supplying the Charleston market by boat, and they proved rich enough to provide hospitality for more than a decade to a succession of relatives and other Saint-Domingue refugees.

Such refugees were attracted to South Carolina for its climate and its support of slavery, and perhaps because of its Acadian/Huguenot community. Louisiana was then still a struggling frontier settlement, whose Spanish government most French perceived as a baneful influence. Around the time Caradeux left, Saint-Domingue newspapers were carrying for-sale adverts of South Carolina plantations.[5] At least five hundred refugees arrived in Charleston in the period 1791–1793, when the city had about seventeen thousand residents.[6] By early 1794, the city had French schools, a French theater, and an entire district where French or creole was the main language. Two years later, a visitor found it "full of French," and in 1816, there were supposedly three thousand French living there.[7]

With French fashions very popular in the early republic, white Americans tended to admire the refugees for their refinement and cultivation, while disapproving their sexual license and political boisterousness. Their gambling, dueling, and cruelty to slaves also attracted comment in some quarters. Moved at the sight of so many plunged from opulence into poverty, Americans funded public subscriptions to assist their settlement.[8] While many once-wealthy individuals had to reinvent themselves as musicians or dance teachers, clerks or fencing instructors, Jean-Baptiste de Caradeux was unusual in remaining a landowner and in retaining the patriarchal lifestyle that then defined a gentleman. Although he never learned to speak English well, Cedar Hill gained a reputation for hospitality to passing travelers. The French naturalist Descourtilz praised the "delectable plantation" with its "perfectly chosen library" and the "sumptuous abundance" of its welcome, when he visited in January 1799, having been rowed from Charleston by six African oarsmen. He commented also on the intolerable heat of the living room with its two fireplaces loaded with logs, suggestive of the Creoles' difficult adaptation to winter weather.[9]

Despite his political past, Caradeux seems to have kept a low political profile. One finds no trace of him in the local French Jacobin club that was founded in January 1792 and in 1793 became dominated by fellow colonists from Saint-Domingue, and he was not among those denounced as counterrevolutionaries by the French consul.[10] We do not know how he reacted to the fall of the French monarchy or to Britain's intervention in Saint-Domingue but, like most colonists, he no doubt shared the growing hostility of local opinion toward revolutionary France. According to a family story told in the nineteenth century, Caradeux once in the mid-'90s had to defend his house against a French privateer crew that set out from the harbor to kill or capture "the old aristocrat."[11] He became an American citizen in February 1795.

During the next decade, as Saint-Domingue was fitfully transformed into Haiti, letters from the colony informed the exiles of their plantations' demise and slow rebirth as peasant villages. Sugar production and shipments to Charleston continued on Jean-Baptiste's estate into 1793, despite the growing assertiveness of the workforce, but in that year it experienced the successive shocks of slave revolt, war, and the abolition of slavery. In October 1796 the plantation was described as ruined with few workers and growing only vegetables.[12] The judgment was somewhat premature, as in the late 1790s the estate was leased to the black general Dessalines, which guaranteed it a certain degree of preservation. After avoiding sequestration during the British occupation of 1793–1798, the estate had been seized as absentee property by the French Republic.[13] Jean-Baptiste's younger brother, Laurent (1752–?1822), known as La Caye because of his impressive plantation house, was deported by the French colonial administration in 1793 and again in 1798. Though he managed to return to Saint-Domingue in late 1799, when allowed back by the governor, Toussaint Louverture, he did not get the sequestration order lifted until December 1802.[14] This was midway through the apocalyptic war of independence, and by 1804 the colony was gone for good.

The lure of slaveowning and Caribbean plantations remained strong in the family. In 1806, the elder Caradeux sent his twenty-year-old son, Jean-Baptiste Jr., nicknamed "Hercule," to Cuba, where the plantation economy was booming and where several thousand Domingan refugees had settled. In a letter expressing paternal concern for his health and sorrow at the death of his dog, he instructed the young man to report back on slave discipline, the nature of plantation life, the influence of priests, and the "manner of rendering justice."[15] By that time, Jean-Baptiste's two other children had died at Cedar Hill, both aged fifteen; they had succumbed to malaria, a disease which would later claim one, if not two, of his three grandchildren. His sister died in 1807.[16] Though Hercule's visit to Cuba came to nothing, Laurent de Caradeux also seems to have visited the island around this time. Perhaps a victim of the mass expulsion of French residents in 1809, he apparently moved on to Puerto Rico, where the plantation economy was similarly expanding, and it is there he died.[17] Having outlived most of his family, Caradeux *aîné* himself died 25 May 1810. His newspaper obituary hailed him as a man universally esteemed, a pillar of strength in the struggles of white Saint-Domingue, and his tombstone awarded him the rank of "General and Commander in Chief of the island."[18]

Most of what is known about the Caradeux in South Carolina comes from a family memoir written in the late-nineteenth century by James Achille de Caradeuc, grandson of Jean-Baptiste.[19] Reverentially recreating the familial atmosphere of Cedar Hill, the memoir recalls a large house, women of beauty and business sense, men of imposing physique and refined manners. Items of jewelry and portraiture providing links to their generation are described with affection. As is typical of the genre,[20] Achille recounts the dramatic escapes from Saint-Domingue of certain relatives, the general poverty of refugee life, and the charity and fortitude it inspired. Proud of his aristocratic lineage, he tallied the number of his great-aunts and their daughters who married counts and marquesses (the vast majority). He contrasts Jean-Baptiste, "respected by all," with his "reckless, spendthrift" younger brother, Laurent, who married beneath his social class; and he briefly evokes his father, Jean-Baptiste Jr., "a number one shot" who reveled in hunting the Carolina countryside with hounds of French descent.[21]

The family slaves form part of the portrait and a generally familiar cast of characters. After the faithful and elderly house servants, cared for in old age, one reads of the Caradeux children's African wet nurse, whom they called Mama Monkee. "She kept a little kind of store on the plantation and worked only for herself. We all loved her very dearly, she had several fine children who turned out well and good, some mulattoes and some black." Pedro, also from Africa, was remembered as "a great rogue, always stealing; my mother, when her children were young, was always afraid of him, as he had repeatedly told her that nothing was nicer than children's hands and feet, and he would smack his lips and laugh!" Kyric, in contrast, was "said by the other negroes to have been the son of a king in Africa, he was a very strong, fine looking negro, exercising powerful influence over the negroes, not only on our plantation but on the neighboring. He was never guilty of a lie, nor of stealing, nor of impertinence, as faithful a slave as ever lived, he truly was a noble negro." There were also "two great cooks, real French cooks," one of them in the French tradition, a man. He was Alcindor, the young scullion of 1792, who voluntarily joined the Caradeux after their departure.[22] He and his wife, Dolinde, became in South Carolina Alexander and Dolly, and finally Old Daddy and Old Grannie, dying in 1863.[23] The reader is evidently meant to deduce that, despite the moral failings of the enslaved (promiscuity, theft, vestigial cannibalism), slavery was not incompatible with moral attainment, skilled work, and mutual affection between owner and owned.

Born in 1816, Achille in fact knew few of the exiled generation except his mother, who had fled Saint-Domingue as a child.[24] His account of the revolution is perfunctory and garbled, and largely limited to proclaiming his grandfather's importance. Without regard for basic chronology, he attributes Jean-Baptiste's departure to the abolition of slavery and a Jacobin hunger for guillotining nobles. If his memoir is a less than reliable witness to the death throes of Saint-Domingue, his own life is clear testimony to the survival of certain Gallic traits in the now American family. Not least was his abandon of his first name, James, in favor of Achille; he also gave his own children French names and married into a Catholic family of Italian origin. His wife was educated in Madame Talvande's French school in Charleston. When he became a planter in Aiken, S.C., around 1840, he grew grapes and imported French vineyard workers to make wine; the estate was named Montmorenci for distant relatives of the Caradeucs. Like many of his colonial predecessors, he was an accomplished artist, and also botanist. Fundamental in shaping his life was the fact he spent his adolescence in Paris. There he revisited the world of the colonial émigrés, expanded his sense of family, and also studied at the prestigious École Polytechnique. His training in engineering stood him in good stead, for after his plantation was destroyed in the Civil War, he was obliged to begin a new career as a railroad engineer.

Achille de Caradeuc was described by those who knew him in old age as a taciturn patriarch, a lover of French culture, and a man "of strong prejudices" who was loyal to the Old South and to monarchical France.[25] Two of his sons died fighting for the Confederacy. Long after the Civil War he retained tangible links to Saint-Domingue in the form of the periodic indemnity payments that arrived from France in compensation for the family's losses in the Haitian Revolution. This "French money," as it was called, provided the occasion for ritual distributions of cash to each member of the family.[26]

Achille's mother did not die until 1870, and in 1877 he had a surprise encounter with the last of the slaves brought from Saint-Domingue, then a blind centenarian. "She remembered all my ancestors," he was pleased to note.[27] When Achille died in 1895, his obituary gave almost as much space to memorializing his grandfather (who had been dead eighty-five years) as to himself. Three times in a few paragraphs it described Jean-Baptiste as "lieutenant of the marshals of France" and "general-in-chief of the King's troops in San Domingo."[28]

For a white Southern culture fond of military titles and aspiring to aristocracy, Jean-Baptiste de Caradeux enjoyed iconic status from the time he got off the boat in 1792. For a defeated South, and for Caradeux's aging grandson writing in the Civil War's aftermath, his image was even more resonant, a reminder of not one, but two, lost worlds. By the decade of *Gone With the Wind,* Achille's memoir had gained perhaps still more symbolic capital, when in the depths of the Depression, his granddaughter chose to publish it. Finally, in the era of the Civil Rights Movement, we find the image of Jean-Baptiste reappearing in an article on the French refugees that was contributed to a South Carolina history journal. Its author clearly felt there was a strong parallel between the French slaveholders facing interference from European abolitionists in the 1790s and the southern states threatened by federal authority in the late 1950s, as well as the mid-nineteenth century.[29]

Other southerners and descendants have looked back to this founding father from different standpoints. Carole Ione's *Pride of Family* is an eloquent and evocative history of a black family that traces its descent, uncertainly, from the Caradeux. William Rollin, born in 1815, shortly before Achille de Caradeuc, appears to have been his out of wedlock half-brother.[30] Son of Hercule (Jean-Baptiste Jr.) and a woman of color presumably of Domingan descent, he was of course not mentioned in Achille's memoir. A French-speaking Catholic, tall and near-white in complexion, Rollin became the prosperous owner of a lumber yard that had some connection to the Caradeuc family's business. Miscegenation and the endowment of illegitimate children had been common in Saint-Domingue, and though Charleston already had a distinctive "brown" middle class by the 1790s, the influx of refugees with Caribbean *mores* doubtless gave impetus to its expansion.[31] William Rollin owned slaves, married a woman from the Caribbean, and sent his daughters to French school.

The Rollin sisters enjoyed a degree of national fame during the Reconstruction era as "aristocrats of color" in the new South.[32] They evidently had no contact with their other aristocratic relatives, as their awareness of their ancestry seems to have been rather sketchy. Frances, the eldest and best-known of the sisters, thought Achille de Caradeuc was her father's nephew. When a young woman, she wrote in her diary, along with comment on "the great Toussaint," that her father was "a descendant of one the proudest and most honored families of Santo Domingo." Her sister Charlotte, a pioneer feminist, told a *New York Times* reporter that, unlike certain rising politicians who were "negroes," her family was "French." Frances's daughter, born in 1872, passed on confused stories of William Rollin's brother being the governor of Saint-Domingue and that the wealthy original migrant from the colony had two families, one white, the other colored, both of which he recognized.[33] Though these were politically progressive women of social conscience, active in the black community, they seem to have looked back on their white slaveowning ancestors with some pride. Although separated by an insuperable social barrier, both the Rollins and Caradeucs had owned slaves, shared a francophone culture, and came close to being ruined by the Civil War.

Researching her family history in the 1980s, writer Carole Ione, great-great-granddaughter of William Rollin, had to be more ambivalent on reading of her ancestors' commitment to slavery. "Born patrician masters within a vile system . . . the French ancestors I'd finally found were not a family I could be proud of; whatever pride there was would have to be mixed with shame."³⁴ She briefly alludes to Jean-Baptiste de Caradeux ordering the decapitation of slaves, which is mentioned in many histories of the Haitian Revolution. Yet overall her account of the exiles stays close to that of Achille. She depicts a tight-knit family of distinguished lineage, loyal to France, and conservative. Jean-Baptiste appears as a colony-wide military leader in a struggle between "French nobility and rebelling slaves," and the hated enemy of republicans.

The images of Jean-Baptiste de Caradeux recalled by his descendants and those presented in Haitian Revolution historiography not surprisingly diverge. As to his aristocratic lineage, at least, there is no doubt. Although Saint-Domingue had its share of phony *comtes* and *marquis,* and "aristocrat" was used as a generalized smear-word in the Revolution, specifically applied to colonists as "aristocrats of the skin," the Caradeucs' nobility can be traced back to the fourteenth century. In the late seventeenth century, Jean-Baptiste's grandfather had left his native Brittany, a region famous for impoverished noble families, and settled in Saint-Domingue, where he became an early sugar planter. The migrant's son, Jean-Jacques (1704–1775), made a fortunate marriage in 1739, which linked him to the very wealthy and childless Jean-Martin Aubry (c.1683–1763). The marriage produced six children, Jean-Baptiste, Laurent, and four sisters, who each inherited one-eighth of great-uncle Aubry's property in the Cul-de-Sac plain. Aubry also paid for Jean-Baptiste's education in France.³⁵ As a young man, he served as aide-de-camp to three governors of Saint-Domingue, was presented at court on a visit to France in 1772–73 and became second captain of the militia dragoons of Port-au-Prince parish. In 1784, during another stay in France, he purchased for 6,000 livres tournois (about $1,125) the title of *lieutenant des maréchaux de France* for the district of Rambouillet.³⁶

It was during this visit that Caradeux, aged forty-two, married his nineteen-year-old niece, Agathe, who brought with her a dowry of 200,000 livres ($37,500).³⁷ As the Caradeux sisters had married local planter aristocrats, this marriage further consolidated the family's property holdings in the plain behind Port-au-Prince. Jean-Baptiste was personally nowhere near as wealthy as some historians have thought (mistaking his sisters for his daughters), but he was at the center of one of Saint-Domingue's great family fortunes. He owned somewhere between 190 and 250 slaves, and he and his brother each owned sugar estates worth respectively $268,000 and $275,000, which was average for the Cul-de-Sac.³⁸ The brothers also shared the Aubry ranch, worth some $40,000. In addition Jean-Baptiste developed a coffee plantation for one of his nieces and rented the neighboring Châteaublond plantation from his sister Marie-Louise, whose husband had gone insane. On behalf of his absentee sister Ursule and her husband (who were also his parents-in-law) he became "overseer" of the Latoison Rocheblanche estate, the most valuable in the colony ($715,000). Most of the family plantations formed a contiguous bloc a few miles from the colonial capital, Port-au-Prince.

The Caradeux fortune was not entirely solid. Several relatives or supposed relatives of the Aubrys laid claim to a share of their estates; a major law suit was in progress when the revolution broke out.[39] Moreover, Jean-Baptiste ran up considerable debts in France; he owed one merchant more than $40,000.[40] But the ability to extract this amount of credit of course reflected his wealth and reputation. Contemporaries called him a great administrator and one of the best sugar-makers in the colony. An innovator, he was among a select few who in the late 1780s participated in government-sponsored experiments to improve manufacturing methods. He used the plow and ample irrigation, and even bred camels to test their suitability as draft animals.[41] The onset of the French Revolution found this Creole-born scion of the provincial nobility firmly ensconced in the social elite of the Caribbean's most important colony.

Act one, scene one of the Haitian Revolution consisted of wealthy white colonists who wanted free trade and self-government secretly organizing to seek representation in the States-General that was to meet in France. Jean-Baptiste de Caradeux took a leading role in this movement early in 1789, and became president of the Committee of the West.[42] Under working class white pressure, the initially elite movement became more democratic toward the end of the year. Caradeux, in contrast to most Cul-de-Sac planters, allied himself with the unruly and virulently racist *petits blancs* of Port-au-Prince and made the city his power base. Unlike his followers, however, he often took a less harsh, if elusive, stance on the question of racial equality and sought on several occasions to avert conflict between whites and free people of color. The grievance-list of the Committee of the West paid at least lip service to free colored interests. And when extremists in the new colonial assembly proposed a "general proscription" of free coloreds, he headed off the measure by suggesting instead controls on their movement and carrying arms, but at the same time placing them under the assembly's protection.[43]

Caradeux stood for a politics of extreme colonial autonomism that put troops under the control of the colonial assembly, envisaged no political role for the National Assembly or royal governor, and left the king only a weak veto power. There are strong grounds for believing he supported the colony's right to independence, if "oppressed" by France.[44] His brother La Caye was jailed by the royal administration for his political activity in 1790 and his fellow parishioners in the Cul-de-Sac tried to have him prosecuted, though the courts proved too timid to do so.[45] An important turning point in the elder Caradeux's career came in March 1791, when the Port-au-Prince Regiment, supported by local radicals, mutinied and publicly killed its colonel, mutilating his body. The colonial governor fled the city, its royalist administration collapsed, and Caradeux was chosen head of the local National Guard, which he had already reorganized. He was publicly accused of participating in the killing, but apparently unjustly.[46] Backed by gangs of foreign sailors, led by a long-haired Italian, he had become a very controversial figure.

The following July colonists flew into an uproar when news arrived that the National Assembly had made some limited concessions to the free people of color. Some talked openly of secession or seeking a British protectorate. Caradeux presided over a "general federative assembly" that united the West province's radical political bodies to concert resistance should France send troops to enforce the new measures. Envoys were secretly sent to Jamaica to seek British support, doubtless with his complicity.[47] It was at this tense moment, following slave revolts on three local estates, a planter wrote with an air of bravura: "If anyone has qualms about cutting off heads, we will call in citizen General Caradeux; he made fifty or so fly during the time he was tenant of the Aubry estate and, so that everyone knew, stuck them on stakes like palm trees around his plantation."[48]

Shortly thereafter, the colony exploded. While thousands of slaves rebelled in the Northern plain, the free coloreds of the West province took up arms to win racial equality. In the Cul-de-Sac plain, most white planters decided to support them as the most prudent course of action. Caradeux's allies in the capital, however, tried to crush the free coloreds. They failed miserably. It seems that, with British warships in Port-au-Prince harbor, Caradeux then offered his opponents a deal of racial equality in return for supporting a bid for independence, which they refused. French troops in the capital called for his punishment, but backed down when the town council claimed the charges were false.[49] After a lengthy stand-off, he then negotiated a concordat in October that accorded all the free coloreds' demands. Peace was briefly restored. Caradeux became commandant general in the West province of a fully multiracial National Guard. Some have seen his actions at this time as statesmanlike mediation. Others have termed them disingenuous maneuvering, for, thanks to the hostility of the white urban workers and unemployed, the rapprochement soon fell apart. Months of bitter fighting ensued between the free people of color, supported by the white planter class, and the radical urban whites led by Caradeux. The richest quarter of Port-au-Prince was burnt to the ground by his followers, atrocities were widespread, and lynch law prevailed in the capital.

Unlike the figure of family memory, admired by South Carolinians, the historical Caradeux was hardly a defender of king and France, but rather a populist and something of a class traitor. Achille de Caradeuc completely reversed reality when, in his *Memoir,* he falsified a contemporary letter to present his grandfather as "loved and respected by *the higher class and rich* but . . . a subject of terror & hatred *by the republican rabble.*"[50] Republic and monarchy were scarcely issues in Saint-Domingue at this time, and Caradeux was, as an observer reported, the "only person of consequence and standing" among the Port-au-Prince radicals.[51] His enemies were, first, royal absolutism and metropolitan control, and then free people of color who demanded political rights. He never had to confront abolitionist officials (they came later); and he fought very little against insurgent slaves (for the same reason). In fact he was among the first whites in Saint-Domingue to arm a body of slaves to fight his opponents. They received bounties for bringing in the severed heads of mulattoes.[52]

Evidently, the significance of these events faded as the Haitian Revolution progressed and came to stand simply for the eclipse of white power by insurgent slaves. A millionaire aristocrat who led a multinational urban mob and battalion of armed slaves against fellow planters, who flirted with the British, and oscillated between embracing racial equality and fiercely defending white supremacy: such a figure fit awkwardly into the abridged master narrative of the Haitian Revolution that lodged in public consciousness. Filial piety, of course, also played its part in filtering family memories, and, once in the United States, Caradeux may have made his own personal voyage from radicalism to conservatism, living to regret some of his political activity.

Much remains unclear about the man's career. Contemporaries were themselves sometimes confused.[53] The Port-au-Prince magistrate who wrote the generally even-handed manuscript history known as the "Précis Historique" described him as a stubborn autonomist but motivated primarily by personal ambition. The abbot Félix Ouvière claimed he joined the Patriot party simply out of revenge, when his (unspecified) proposals to the Colonial Assembly were ignored. And his sometime collaborator, the Port-au-Prince merchant, Gamot, called him "gigantic in size, insufferably conceited, and of unusual stupidity in political matters."[54] Of Haiti's two great nineteenth-century historians, Thomas Madiou believed he took the lead in trying to force Port-au-Prince to accept the concordat policy of rapprochement and racial equality, whereas Beaubrun Ardouin argued he worked against it and, far from being swept along by the masses, he was the evil genius behind the urban mob.[55]

Certainly, once the October rapprochement broke down, Caradeux obstructed further attempts to negotiate with the people of color and pursued a military solution with destructive results.[56] Taking advantage of the civil war, slaves around the West province generally put down tools and revolts multiplied. Slavery would be a long time dying in the region, and production generally revived in summer 1792. Yet the anarchy unleashed in this period surely was one of the factors that persuaded the elder Caradeux it was time to leave. Of critical importance was the National Assembly's voting racial equality on 28 March, which all over Saint-Domingue precipitated a strengthening of conservative forces and the decline of the Patriots. Caradeux also clashed with the civil commissioners sent from France. Ordered to join an expedition sent against rebel slaves in nearby Léogane, he refused to be subordinate to the local military commandant, which even the radical colonial assemblies mandated, and he threatened to resign. This dispute was nothing to do with the abolition of slavery, as Achille de Caradeuc imagined, but was a petulant quarrel about personal precedence, which greatly assisted the slave insurrection in Léogane.[57]

As his year as National Guard commander came to an end, Caradeux prepared to turn his back on Saint-Domingue, and on his debts in France. For years he had avoided repaying the large credits advanced him by his merchant correspondents by sending his sugar to different factors.[58] Ignoring the now desperate situation of his French creditors—those who had made large loans to North province planters were facing ruin—he shipped 118 barrels of sugar to the radical Charleston merchant Abraham Sasportas. The two men had met in Saint-Domingue, and had already discussed investments in South Carolina.[59] Some time in July, Jean-Baptiste de Caradeux left behind his revolutionary past and set out for a new life in the United States.[60]

However, it was not just the details of his revolutionary career that faded from view in his new country. His prerevolutionary past also vanished from memory. But this was not the case in independent Haiti. Four years after Caradeux's death, one of King Henry Christophe's ministers, the Baron de Vastey, published in the former Cap-Français *Le système colonial dévoilé* (The colonial system unmasked).[61] Vastey's book is a litany of atrocity stories, which indicts a large proportion of Saint-Domingue's famous names. As such it is easy to dismiss as a propaganda piece. It was written in 1814 at a critical moment to galvanize international opinion against French plans to reconquer the former colony.[62] Haiti's image had been tarnished by the massacres that followed independence, and the author was charged with the state's public relations. Moreover, Vastey was only a child at the time of the Revolution and had lived all his life in the North province, far from the Cul-de-Sac. Whatever its reliability, the book inevitably leaves the reader with a nagging uncertainty, for it speaks to an unresolveable issue central to the study of slavery: the incidence of overt cruelty.

In *Le système colonial dévoilé* Caradeux *aîné* is remembered as a slaveowner who ordered punishments of two hundred lashes for small faults and sometimes buried slaves up to the neck and left them to die. Though this is perfectly plausible, the skeptical reader might begin to suspect a caricature on reading that the death of Caradeux's young wife was due to his kicking her, when she interceded between him and a female victim. Then again, one might wonder why the death was remembered, if there had been nothing unusual about it. However, the author's claim that the man depopulated his plantation to such a degree that merchants refused to supply him would seem clearly to veer into the domain of the preposterous, did it not bring to mind the letter about the "fifty or so" decapitations. As for the image of Caradeux attacking merchants with chains and kicks, when they asked for repayment of debts, it looks like a composite metaphor for the excesses of Caribbean slaveowning, rather than a historical fact; though Vastey does name a merchant with whom the angry debtor fought a duel.

Since slavery times, some have argued that the economic rationality of slaveowners precluded widespread atrocities. Others doubt the force of this argument applied to a milieu known for reckless gambling, abusing credit, and fighting duels, and that rested precariously on an extreme imbalance of power. If few can doubt that slaveowning encouraged brutality and permitted atrocities, it remains all but impossible to gauge exactly how typical of the institution these features were. The issue is central, too, to understanding the Haitian Revolution, because in the literature of slavery Saint- Domingue has a particularly bad reputation. Yet, since court records have not survived, documented atrocities are few. General assessments by contemporaries were vague and contradictory. Should we believe, then, that, in addition to his other faults, Caradeux was extravagantly sadistic?

Probably, yes, given the variety of evidence that points in that direction. *Le système colonial dévoilé* looks rather more credible when it is read in conjunction with another work published the same year in Paris. It, too, tells the story of a slave buried up to the neck by Caradeux (who then crushed his head with a rock), and of white women interceding. Although the author admired the planter, he described him as ferocious, violent, and cruel, especially so toward his sugar-boilers. Far from being the work of a young Haitian propagandist, this book was written by Charles Malenfant, a French plantation manager who had lived a short distance from the elder Caradeux's estate.[63]

The most memorable portrait of the man, however, comes from the father of Haitian history, Thomas Madiou. Madiou lived in Port-au-Prince and collected oral testimony for his *Histoire d'Haïti* (1847–1848) in the decade after 1835. He was not a propagandist like Vastey, though he was concerned to justify the violence used against the French, and the local memory he recounted referred to events already a half-century old. Madiou called Caradeux "perhaps the cruelest white who existed in Saint-Domingue. . . . On his lands he was a petty potentate with the right of life and death over his subjects. When he gave parties, he invited the most distinguished white families and made the slaves dance in their presence on the terrace of his splendid house. In the afternoon the guests showed off their skill to the ladies: a slave was placed thirty paces away with an orange on his head. He who knocked off the golden apple with a pistol shot was awarded the crown by the ladies. Happy was the slave who finished these games without a broken limb or without being killed."[64]

If this callous Caribbean version of a frivolous *fête champêtre* formed part of his upbringing, it is fortunate Hercule was raised to become "a number one shot." Madiou's description, however, does not stop there. As with Vastey's book, the account takes a turn that leaves the reader wondering what to believe, though with a better grasp perhaps of why the planter left Saint-Domingue so quickly. "Other games followed these. Caradeux had young or elderly people tied naked to long planks and whipped them till they were covered with blood. The joy of the spectators was noisy and the victims' agony elicited no compassion. The torture to which Caradeux generally condemned his slaves was to bury them up to the waist and leave them to die in the sun with their head covered with molasses...His baseness was such that Haitian peasants today still tell of his atrocities, when showing travelers the ruins of his plantation and the terrace where he stood, when he ordered a slave flayed alive."[65]

Sixty years later, when Léon Descos was French ambassador in Port-au-Prince, both the plantation ruins and the oral tradition still haunted the landscape. "Among the blacks," the ambassador wrote, Caradeux's name "remains surrounded with an aura of untold extravagance and legendary harshness."[66] Even in the 1980s, Jacques de Cauna found, along with the estate's surviving ruins, that the name of "Caradeux le cruel" is not forgotten in the Haitian countryside.[67]

Refracted through the prism of the Haitian Revolution, the picture Jean-Baptiste de Caradeux bequeathed to posterity has been split into three contrasting images. In the United States, family memory and a slaveowning environment preserved a positive portrait of a defender of class and racial privilege. In the historiography of the revolution, Caradeux is generally recalled as a racist rabble-rouser hostile to metropolitan interests, albeit unpredictable on the race question. In Haiti, among elite and masses, the dominant image is of "Caradeux le cruel," the sadistic planter. None of our sources inspires total confidence; question marks remain over all three of these images. Caradeux's career thus speaks to a larger issue of assessing the causes of the Haitian Revolution and how much of the history of slavery has been silenced and how much remembered.

NOTES

I thank Paul Lachance for offering helpful comments on this chapter.

1. "Cul-de-Sac plantations will be worth more than the mines of Peru," wrote a local colonist 1 May 1792, anticipating record prices for the harvest. See Marin plantation papers, Archives Départementales des Bouches-du-Rhône, Marseille, 1Mi 34/26.

2. James Achille de Caradeuc, *Memoirs of the de Caradeuc Family,* ed. Maude Heywood (NP: privately printed, 1931), 13, 18; Mabel Webber, "Copy of some Loose Pages found among the Manigault Papers," *South Carolina Historical and Genealogical Magazine* 40 (1939): 15–20. Some claim he took with him fifty or sixty slaves. See Charles Malenfant, *Des colonies et particulièrement de celle de Saint-Domingue* (Paris, 1814), 32, 199; Pamphile de Lacroix, *Mémoires pour servir à l'histoire de la Révolution de Saint-Domingue,* 2 vols. (Paris: Pillet, 1819), 1: 188; Beaubrun Ardouin, *Études sur l'histoire d'Haïti* ([1853] Port-au-Prince: Dalencour, 1958), 1: 80. However, according to the 1800 U.S. Census, his household included twenty-five slaves and one free person of color.

3. See below, note 59; Webber, "Loose Pages," 15–20. Selling at around fifteen *gourdes* per cwt., the sugar would have fetched about $24,000.

4. Jacob Milligan, *The Charleston Directory* (Charleston: W. Young, 1794); Webber, "Loose Pages," 15–20; De Caradeuc, *Memoirs,* 13. The U.S. Censuses show the household slaveholding increasing between 1800 and 1810 from twenty-five to seventy-three slaves and falling back to twenty-seven slaves in 1820. I suspect the middle figure reflected a temporary arrangement with French colonists arriving from Cuba in 1809.

5. *Moniteur Colonial* (Cap-Français), July and August 1792. Indigo was then in decline; cotton had yet to take off.

6. Winston Babb, "French Refugees from Saint Domingue to the Southern United States: 1790–1810" (Ph.D. diss., University of Virginia, 1954), 382. The French consul claimed in December 1793 there were six hundred men from Saint-Domingue in the city. See Richard Murdoch, "Correspondence of the French Consuls in Charleston, S.C., 1793–1797," *South Carolina Historical Magazine* (hereafter *SCHM*) 74 (1973): 16.

7. Charles Fraser, *Reminiscences of Charleston* (Charleston: Garnier, 1854), 35–45; Michael Kennedy, "A French Jacobin Club in Charleston," *SCHM* 91 (1990): 4–22; James Hagy, Bertrand Van Ruymbeke, "The French Refugee Newspapers of Charleston," *SCHM* 97 (1996): 139.

8. Frances S. Childs, *French Refugee Life in the United States, 1790–1800* (Baltimore: Johns Hopkins University Press, 1940), 195–200; Babb, "French Refugees," 380–407; Althéa de Puech Parham, ed., *My Odyssey: Experiences of a Young Refugee from Two Revolutions* (Baton Rouge: Louisiana State University Press, 1959); Alfred de Laujon, *Souvenirs et voyages,* 2 vols. (Paris: Vernet, 1835), 2: 83–132. Domingan refugees in the United States were probably more likely to be destitute that those who migrated to Jamaica and Cuba. They had less time to prepare their departure (so many fleeing the burning of Le Cap) and more time at sea to be robbed by British privateers.

9. Michel-Etienne Descourtilz, *Voyage d'un naturaliste,* 3 vols. (Paris: Dufart, 1809), 1: 281–91. He in addition described encountering on a hunting trip a fugitive slave who supposedly was trying to kill Caradeux.

10. Kennedy, "Jacobin Club in Charleston," 4–22; Childs, *French Refugee Life,* 171.

11. Notes by Achille de Caradeuc in Georgia Historical Society, Savannah, De Caradeuc Papers (hereafter GHS), item 1, vol. 2. French republican seamen earned a turbulent reputation in Charleston and other U.S. ports in these years. See Melvin Jackson, *Privateers in Charleston, 1793–1796* (Washington, D.C., Smithsonian Institution, 1969), 58, 69–73.

12. Juré aîné to Caradeux, 22 Oct. 1796, University of North Carolina, Southern Historical Collection, Caradeuc Papers (hereafter UNC), folder 3.

13. Caradeux La Caye to Caradeux aîné, 10 Fructidor an 10 (10 Aug. 1802), GHC, folder 4.

14. Bibliothèque Nationale, Paris, Manuscrits (hereafter BN), Nouv. Acq. Fr. 14879, f. 140; Nellie Fowler, "Santo Domingo Passports," *National Genealogical Quarterly;* 41 (1968): 267; lifting of sequestration order, 2 Nivôse an 11, UNC, folder 5. Laurent de Caradeux had had the good fortune to sell his own plantation early in 1791, but his house was temporarily sequestered during the British occupation. See records dated 9 May 1796, Public Record Office, London, T 226B/10C; and 8 and 15 Feb. 1796, T 81/17.

15. J.-B. Caradeux, *aîné* to J.-B. Caradeux, *fils,* 23 Oct. 1806, UNC, folder 4. All the translations from French are my own.

16. The children were Louise Agathe (1787–1802) and Achille (1789–1804); the sister, Marie Louise (1746–1807), widow of Louis-Henri Taveau, marquis de Chambrun de Châteaublond. Built like his father, Hercule (1786–1820) would later die in a hunting accident. Though Catholic, all the family were buried in the local Protestant church.

17. Laurent married Marie-Jeanne Ledoux in 1777 two weeks after coming of age. According to de Caradeuc, *Memoirs,* 15, he died blind in Cuba around 1804 and his wife went to Puerto Rico alone. Puerto Rican sources suggest he migrated there with thirty thousand pesos and that his wife was already there in 1800: personal communication, Diana M. García. His will, written in Puerto Rico, 8 July 1822, is mentioned in item 48, GHS, folder 7.

18. "Marriage and Death Notices," *South Carolina Historical and Genealogical Magazine* 35 (1934): 32–33; de Caradeuc, *Memoirs,* 32. Caradeuc genealogies of uneven reliability can be found in item 55, GHS; several notices in *Généalogie et Histoire de la Caraïbe* 33 (1991): 446; 36 (1992): 539–41; 98 (1997): 2108; and below, note 35.

19. See above, note 2; the original manuscript is in GHS, folder 5; a printed copy, in UNC, folder 5. Only the Saint-Domingue generations of the family spelled their name with an X instead of a C. Written in 1894, the memoir was published by his granddaughter in 1931 in a limited edition of thirty copies.

20. See sources cited above, note 8; Paul Lachance, "La Révolution haïtienne dans la mémoire des réfugiés de la Nouvelle-Orléans," in *Mémoire privé, mémoire collective dans l'Amérique pré-industrielle,* ed. Elise Marienstras, Marie-Jeanne Rossignol (Paris: Berg), 23–33; Kent Gardien, "The Dominguan Kettle: Philadelphian-Emigré Planters in Alabama," *National Genealogical Society Quarterly* 76 (1988): 173–83; Jacques de Cauna-Ladevie, "La diaspora des colons de Saint-Domingue et le monde créole: le cas de la Jamaïque," *Revue Française d'Histoire d'Outre-Mer* 81 (1994): 333–59.

21. De Caradeuc, *Memoirs,* 8, 15, 20.

22. De Caradeuc, *Memoirs,* 18–19. Some domestic servants had avoided leaving with the family but soon (as local conditions worsened) agreed to join them. See Boissonière Desuré to Caradeux, 13 Nov. 1792, UNC, folder 3

23. The name changes can be deduced from Achille's notes in item 1, vol. 2, GHS.

24. Marie Augustine "Maxine" Rossignol de La Chicotte, (1789–1870). The Rossignols were a very extensive planter family long established in Saint-Domingue. See Elizabeth Sullivan-Holleman, Isabel Hillery Cobb, *The Saint-Domingue Epic: The de Rossignol des Dunes and Family Alliances* (Bay St. Louis, Miss.: Nightingale Press, 1995).

25. De Caradeuc, *Memoirs,* 34–44.

26. Ibid., 39. Following an agreement reached between the Haitian and French governments in 1825 former colonists or their heirs were awarded 10 percent of the value of real

estate and related moveable property they lost in the revolution. Though the amount payable was reduced by 40 percent in 1838, the periodic repayments continued until 1887.

27. She was a woman of mixed racial descent, who had been freed seventy years before. She was rediscovered in Charleston living in poverty, cared for by a black woman also "French." See GHS, item 1, vol. 2.

28. De Caradeuc, *Memoir,* 34–36.

29. Chapman Milling, "The Acadian and San Domingan French," *Transactions of the Huguenot Society of South Carolina* 62 (1957): 25, 28, 30. "It was as if Judge Waring were today to be appointed to be Superintendent of Education for the Sovereign State of Mississippi," he wrote of the sending to Saint-Domingue of Commissioner Sonthonax, "the spiritual brother of . . . John Brown."

30. Carole Ione, *Pride of Family: Four Generations of American Women of Color* (New York: Summit Books, 1991), esp.127–29, 134–48. Ione speculated that Rollin was either the half-brother of Achille's mother or his great-uncle but neither case is possible. I agree with descendant Patwin Lawrence (personal communication) the men were half-brothers. The migration to Charleston of two men with the same name (father and son) clearly confused family memories.

31. Larry Koger, *Black Slaveowners: Free Black Slave Masters in South Carolina, 1790–1860* (Jefferson, N.C.: Macfarland, 1985); Marina Wikramanayake, *A World in Shadow: The Free Black in Antebellum South Carolina* (Columbia: University of South Carolina Press, 1973).

32. Willard Gatewood, "The Remarkable Misses Rollin," *SCHM* 92 (1991): 172–88.

33. Ione, *Pride of Family,* 127, 134–35, 175. It is not clear whether the "colored family" began in South Carolina or they were also immigrants. They may have included one of the Caradeux domestics, as Ione suggests. There had been Caradeux of mixed racial descent in Saint-Domingue since the mid-eighteenth century but none is known to have gone to the United States. However, Marianne Caradeux (1766–1826), conceivably an illegitimate daughter of Jean-Baptiste or Laurent, had children by Laurent's brother-in-law, Jean-Baptiste Ledoux, and eventually married him. The family settled in Puerto Rico in the late 1790s. See Archives Nationales, Section d'Outre-Mer, Aix-en-Provence, parish records of Croix des Bouquets and Port-au-Prince; personal communication, Diana M. García.

34. Ione, *Pride of Family,* 142.

35. *Mémoire pour les sieurs et dames Caradeux habitants au Cul-de-Sac contre les sieurs et dame Aubry de Tours* (Port-au-Prince,1789).

36. Commission, GHS, folder 2. "Lieutenant of the marshals," the post was not quite as glamorous as it sounds; the *maréchaussée* was the rural mounted police. Its officer corps seems to have functioned as a club for minor aristocrats.

37. Contract, 22 Jan. 1785, UNC, folder 2. Agathe Louise Jeanne "Rochette" de Latoison Rocheblanche (?1765–1791), daughter of Louis, marquis de Latoison Rocheblanche (1726–1790) and Ursule de Caradeux (1744–1809), both Saint-Domingue creoles. Papal dispensation was purchased for 1,162 livres.

38. Sources give conflicting figures, mix up the two men's estates, and may not distinguish rented slaves from those owned. See, however, *État détaillé des liquidations opérées par la commission...de l'indemnité,* 6 vols. (Paris: Imprimerie Royale, 1828–33).

39. 4 Fm 5261, 4 Fn 3295, 4 Fn 3296, BN, Imprimés, Factums.

40. UNC, folder 6.

41. Malenfant, *Des colonies,* 183, 195–97; Maurice Begouen Demeaux, *Jacques François Begouen* (Le Havre: Étaix, 1957), 169; Jacques Cauna, *Au temps des isles à sucre* (Paris: Karthala, 1987), 77, 142–49.

42. GHS, folder 2. This was not quite his first taste of anti-ministerial politics. He had

been in France when his distant and famous cousin, Caradeuc de La Chalotais, president of the parlement de Bretagne, was jailed for his opposition to Louis XV.

43. David Geggus, *Slavery, War and Revolution: The British Occupation of Saint Domingue, 1793–1798* (Oxford: Clarendon Press, 1982), 34, 37; Julien Raimond, *Correspondance de Julien Raimond avec ses frères, de Saint-Domingue, et les pièces qui ont été adressées par eux* (Paris, 1794), 37.

44. See ? to Caradeux *aîné,* 11 Mar. 1790, GHS, folder 3.

45. Jean Philippe Garran Coulon, *Rapport sur les troubles de Saint-Domingue,* 4 vols. (Paris: Imprimerie Nationale,1797–99), 1: 308.

46. *Journal Général de Saint-Domingue* (Port-au-Prince) 26 and 29 Mar. 1791.

47. It seems they just tested official opinion on their first visit, in August. On 10 September, after the slave revolt began, they requested a British takeover. See Geggus, *Slavery, War and Revolution,* 51–53.

48. Guitton to Billard, 18 July 1791, Archives Nationales, Paris (hereafter: AN), Section Moderne, DXXV 78/772; Lacroix, *Mémoires,* 1: 88–89. Lacroix interpreted this as a referring to an incident during the revolution, but it seems to relate to an earlier period. Victor Hugo, using Lacroix as his point of departure, introduced into his first novel the extravagant character of Citoyen-Général C, who suggested surrounding the whole of Cap-Français with impaled heads and offered up five hundred of his own slaves. See Victor Hugo, *Bug-Jargal ou la Révolution haïtienne,* ed. R. Toumson (Paris: Désormeaux, 1979), 225–26.

49. "Journal inédit tenu par le colon Gamot," *Le Document* (Port-au-Prince) 1 (1940): 181–84; Garran Coulon, *Rapport,* 2: 146–57.

50. The words in italics are his interpolations. See De Caradeuc, *Memoir,* 13; Juré to Caradeux, 22 Oct. 1796, UNC, folder 3.

51. Deposition by Félix Ouvière, 14 Mar. 1793, Jamaica Archives, Spanish Town, Council Minutes.

52. Ibid.; Henri de Grimouärd, *L'Amiral de Grimouärd au Port-au-Prince* (Paris: Larose, 1937), 67. His "African Company" supposedly contained twelve hundred (mainly town) slaves by March 1792. As early as mid-October 1791, he was rumored to have armed his own plantation slaves to ambush a free colored/planter expedition. See Jumécourt to Pinchinat, 13 Oct. 1791, AN, CC9A/5.

53. Learning of the October concordat, a northern colonist wrote that Caradeux had marched against the mulattoes and "made them change, with a knife at their throats, almost all the articles" agreed to in earlier negotiations. See Marc Favre, "Le début de la révolte de Saint-Domingue ," *Généalogie et Histoire de la Caraïbe* 48 (1993): 778. Though completely untrue, it suggests the light in which some colonists saw him.

54. BN, Nouv. Acq. Fr. 14878, f. 76; above, note 51; "Journal inédit," 177.

55. Thomas Madiou, *Histoire d'Haïti,* 8 vols. (Port-au-Prince: Deschamps, 1989–1991 [1847–1848]), 1: 107–9; Ardouin, *Études,* 1: 48, 56–57

56. Grimouärd, *L'Amiral de Grimouärd,* 38–70, esp. 43; Garran Coulon, *Rapport,* 2: 474–506.

57. Letters of Feb./Mar. 1792, GHS, folder 3; De Caradeuc, *Memoirs,* 13.

58. Desridellières Leroulx to Caradeux, 5 May 1785, 31 July 1786 (folder 2), 8 Nov. 1792, (folder 3), UNC. Now that the slave insurrection had sent sugar prices through the roof, Caradeux's merchant creditors claimed he could easily pay off his debts by sending just half his sugar to them. They reproached him, referring to his "immense fortune," his "enormous borrowing" from them, and the intact state of his "large and fine plantation."

59. Sasportas to Caradeux, 5 July 1792, UNC, folder 3; above, note 3. Sasportas suggested investing his proceeds in the Bank of South Carolina for a return of at least 10 percent. French-born but resident in Charleston from 1778 to about 1818, Sasportas (1751–1823)

belonged to a Sephardic Jewish family of merchants and money-changers found in many parts of the Caribbean and Europe. They are best known because of Abraham's nephew, Isaac, who, acting as a French agent, sought to organize a slave rebellion in Jamaica in 1799 and was hanged by the British. See Isaac and Susan Emmanuel, *History of the Jews of the Netherlands Antilles* (Cincinnati: American Jewish Archives, 1970), 284–85; Zvi Loker, "An Eighteenth-Century Plan to Invade Jamaica," *Transactions of the Jewish Historical Society of England* 28 (1984): 132–44; Archives Municipales de Bordeaux, 3 E 121/1039.

60. Even so, one of his first house guests, in spring 1793, was the chevalier de Borel, his successor as commander of the West Province National Guard and a fellow planter whose stormy political career very much paralleled his own. Forced to flee Saint-Domingue, Borel traveled via Jamaica to Charleston, whence he sent back his cook to try to bring out the rest of his slaves in an American ship. See interrogation of Toussaint, 8 Sept. 1793, AN, Section Moderne, D XXV 7/31/317; Geggus, *Slavery, War and Revolution*, 61, 421.

61. J. L. Vastey, *Le système colonial dévoilé* (Cap-Henry: 1814), 51–52.

62. See David Geggus, "Haiti and the Abolitionists: Opinion, Propaganda and International Politics in Britain and France, 1804–1838," in *Abolition and its Aftermath: The Historical Context, 1790–1916,* ed. D. Richardson (London: Cass, 1985), 121.

63. Malenfant, *Des colonies,* 172, 195–99. He was known to fling slaves into furnaces and boiling cauldrons.

64. Madiou, *Histoire,* 1: 39–40

65. Madiou *Histoire,* 1: 40, 63–64.

66. Eugène Aubin [Léon Descos], *En Haïti* (Paris: Armand Colin, 1910), 25.

67. Jacques Cauna, "Vestiges de sucreries dans la plaine du Cul-de-Sac," *Conjonction* (Port-au-Prince) 165 (1985): 80–83.

Epilogue

FROM THE MISSISSIPPI VALLEY TO the streets of Rio and the council chambers of the European capitals, the Haitian Revolution had a multifarious impact. The fifteen-year struggle for racial equality, slave emancipation, and colonial independence alarmed and excited public opinion on both sides of the Atlantic. It shaped great power politics, generated migration movements, and opened new economic frontiers. It stimulated slave resistance and new expansions of slavery, while embittering the debates developing about race and abolition. The revolution also inspired one of William Wordsworth's greatest sonnets, Victor Hugo's first novel, works by Heinrich von Kleist, Alphonse de Lamartine, and John Greenleaf Whittier, and in the twentieth century, the new literary genre of marvelous realism. It made an imprint, too, on the philosophy of Georg Wilhelm Hegel.[1]

The repercussions of the revolution were not only diverse but ambiguous and contradictory. An assessment of its international impact, therefore, necessitates weighing its "positive" and "negative" influences, while avoiding the temptation to claim for it a romantically sweeping significance of unjustified proportions. An event of unique significance does not necessarily have uniquely significant repercussions. Bearing in mind Seymour Drescher's distinction between symbol and substance (chapter 2), we need to ask: How much of a difference did the revolution really make? This epilogue is intended, in conjunction with the preface, to sketch a brief balance sheet of the influence of the Haitian Revolution beyond its frontiers. In the spirit of the devil's advocate, it seeks to suggest limits as well as strengths.

The interrelationship of the Haitian and French Revolutions now seems well established (chapters 1 and 3). Traditional interpretations of *La Grande Révolution* that gave scant regard to its colonial dimension or accorded little weight to colonial agency have yielded to the perspective championed by C. L. R. James of mutually intertwined metropolitan and colonial revolutions. Few historians of the metropolitan revolution would now disagree that France's adoption of antislavery and antiracism was primarily a pragmatic response to events in Saint-Domingue, or that these feature among the milestones of the revolution in France. It is nonetheless noteworthy that the historians who have done most to integrate domestic and overseas narratives, Yves Bénot and Robin Blackburn, have both reemphasized the importance of metropolitan idealist and political influences on France's colonial policy and thus shifted the balance within Haitian Revolution historiography somewhat away from a Caribbean-driven perspective.[2]

As regards slave resistance in the Age of Revolution, it is clear that the black struggle in Saint-Domingue served quite frequently as an example and inspiration.

Historians have sometimes assumed rather than proven such a connection, but it doubtless was present more often than the documentary record reveals.[3] The black revolutionaries and the state they created served occasionally as a promised, if bogus, source of support for slave uprisings, though very rarely as an actual source of aid. The Maracaibo plot studied by Aline Helg (chapter 11) was almost unique in this respect, and the Aponte conspiracy explored by Matt Childs (chapter 10) was unusual in its variety of connections with Haiti. The Haitian Revolution acted as one among several causal influences on contemporary resistance but was not the most important. More salient, I would argue, were rebellions sparked by rumors of emancipation that were linked to abolitionism. Eugene Genovese's argument that the Haitian Revolution marked a turning-point toward a new type of resistance remains, in my view, unconvincing.[4] There is no doubt that, after the unprecedented successes of Saint-Domingue's insurgents, all subsequent rebels must have gained courage from contemplating their example, but slaves had always rebelled ever since there was slavery, and they did so with no greater success after the Haitian Revolution than before.

The contribution of slave resistance to the overall progress of slave emancipation is controversial and, as the opening chapters of this book suggest, there is no consensus on the Haitian Revolution's role in ending slavery elsewhere. A major case in point is the British emancipation act of 1833 and its links to the great Jamaican rebellion of 1831, which some have claimed, but not proved, to have been inspired by Haiti. While most historians have usually seen British abolition as an essentially metropolitan phenomenon, Caribbean historians like Eric Williams and Richard Hart have argued the 1831 rebellion made emancipation urgent and inevitable. Mary Turner points out that initial reports of the rebellion sent the resurgent abolitionists into retreat, and that it was only later news of the Jamaican plantocracy's vindictive response to the uprising that catalyzed the final emancipation process. Seymour Drescher depicts the initial negative reaction in Britain to the rebellion as lasting even longer. Thomas Holt, on the other hand, stresses the Christmas Rebellion's early and salutary impact on government officials. Opinions are thus divided as to whether the passage of the 1833 act received a decisive boost from a mounting dread of further slave resistance (on which a Haitian influence can be postulated but not demonstrated), or contrarily was initially hindered by it until propelled forward by sudden disgust with the Jamaican plantocracy, or whether the Jamaican revolt (and the "specter of Haiti") played any causal role at all in ending British colonial slavery.[5]

The Haitian Revolution had a profoundly ambiguous impact, too, on ideas about racial difference and the reform of race relations. In the half-century following the revolution, the legal position of free people of color improved in the British, French, Dutch, and Danish colonies and the Spanish American republics, but tended to worsen in the remaining Spanish colonies and United States. Demographic growth, metropolitan reformism, wars of independence, and the expansion of slavery were seemingly the major influences on these trends, but the creation of Haiti could not be left out of the debate about white racial domination. As it provided arguments, generally based on fear, both for and against extending racial equality, its impact was contradictory and therefore inconclusive, but it certainly served to intensify the conflict.[6]

Particularly interesting is the revolution's contribution to stimulating political activism among free people of color in the nineteenth century. The fascinating glimpses of pro-Haitian sentiment uncovered by Marixa Lasso in Gran Colombia (chapter 12), and those detailed by David Davis (chapter 1) for the United States, join the work of Mott in Brazil, Sheller for Jamaica, and Paquette and Ferrer for Cuba, which similarly hint at the importance of Haiti and its revolution for the development of black politics across the Americas.[7] However, as these scholars show, Haiti's influence in this sphere was no more straightforward than in other domains. Non-white politicians from Antonio Rebouças in Brazil to George William Gordon in Jamaica and Antonio Maceo in Cuba had their careers hampered by charges of seeking to emulate or being in league with the state born of black revolution. Future research will need to separate the smear tactics of white opponents from evidence of genuine admiration. Although perceptions of Haiti varied radically according to race, they were not racially monolithic, and the new state's flirtations with both monarchy and republicanism naturally complicated matters, as did its progressive economic decline.[8] We still lack a clear answer to Mimi Sheller's question: Did black Jamaicans [or blacks elsewhere] see Haiti as an example to follow or avoid?[9]

In the realm of great power politics, the Haitian Revolution represented a costly military disaster for each of the three main colonial powers. The French, Spanish, and British lost astonishing quantities of money and manpower, not to mention prestige, in seeking to conquer or retain the colony. But even within the narrow compass of Caribbean wartime strategy, it would be wrong to assume that Saint-Domingue held center stage. Britain made the east Caribbean its regional priority in the 1790s and lost more troops there than in Saint-Domingue. The old shibboleth publicized by C. L. R. James that Britain's weakness in the French Revolutionary War was due to its occupation of Saint-Domingue is no longer tenable.[10] For France, Saint-Domingue was its most grievous colonial loss but only one of a series it experienced throughout the eighteenth century. Moreover, whatever happened in the colony, the maritime war that began in 1793 would anyway have deprived France temporarily of its commerce, as had previous conflicts. British naval supremacy and the war's resumption in 1803 probably also guaranteed the loss of Louisiana, whatever happened to Saint-Domingue. Finally, the French death toll in the colony, certainly staggering, formed only a small part of France's military losses in these years of constant warfare. As for Spain, the fiasco of its invasion of Saint-Domingue, which precipitated its surrender of Santo Domingo, proved merely the prelude to the collapse of its American empire during the next quarter century.

Because of the destruction it wrought and the refugees it displaced, the revolution played a significant role in shaping the expansion of plantation production at turn of the nineteenth century. It was the main cause of revival of sugar production in Brazil and Jamaica in the 1790s and of the spread of coffee cultivation.[11] Even so, Jamaican coffee production was already expanding before the Domingan refugees arrived, and even if Saint-Domingue's slaves had not rebelled, it seems highly likely Cuba, the Guianas, and Trinidad (though perhaps not Louisiana) would still have had their sugar revolution. David Eltis points out that the shortfall in global production of tropical produce caused by the Haitian Revolution was made up in about a decade (more quickly for sugar, longer for coffee), and that thereafter expansion was driven by increasing demand.[12]

Similarly, the Saint-Domingue diaspora did help change the cultural landscape in the Greater Caribbean but its main impact was confined to Louisiana (chapter 14). The gallicization of Trinidad had begun a decade before the Haitian Revolution and continued to depend mainly on migrants from the eastern Caribbean. In eastern Cuba, the chronology of French/Creole influence remains uncertain; heavy migration from Bordeaux in the 1830s complicates the picture, and formerly supposed links between Haiti and Cuban maroons no longer seem very likely.[13] Perhaps the most interesting migrants from Saint-Domingue were those of the original slave insurgents who, as pensioned soldiers of Spain, were relocated in 1796 to different part of the Spanish empire. Jane Landers's engaging portrait of Georges Biassou in Florida whets the appetite to know more about his counterparts who settled in Central and Meso-America and Cádiz, forerunners of later Haitian exiles like Soulouque and the African monarchs Ja Ja and Behanzin.[14]

Lastly, one might ask in what measure Haitian independence influenced the process of decolonization elsewhere in the Americas. As with Haiti's contribution to slave emancipation and racial equality, the record is complicated. On the one hand, the Haitian Revolution indirectly contributed to keeping Cuba a colony through the nineteenth century in that memories of the revolution reinforced the fears of slave rebellion and race war which deterred and divided Creole resistance. The revolution's example was also used as an excuse in Spain not to extend political liberties to the island.[15] On the other hand, Haitian statesmen assisted several expeditions intended to overthrow Spanish power in the Americas, including Francisco Miranda's 1806 invasion of Venezuela, Francisco Mina's expedition to Mexico in 1816, and (some think) Santiago Mariño's aborted attack on Puerto Rico in 1837. By far the most important were Simón Bolívar's two expeditions to Venezuela in 1816, supported by Alexandre Pétion. Pétion's help may not have been indispensable to winning Spanish America's independence, since Bolívar already had ships at his disposal, but it clearly was a critical catalyst at a time when the Creole revolutionaries could no longer look to British colonies for a base.[16] President Geffrard also assisted the Dominican Republic win its independence war of 1863–1865, although, ironically, it was the Haitian annexation of forty years earlier that had extinguished the Dominicans' first brief experience of independence, as well as their far longer experience of slavery.

The repercussions of Haiti's revolution were thus richly complex and varied. Its international impact bears comparison with that of most other "world" revolutions, though it was less aggressively exported and originated in a society of infinitely humbler dimensions and resources.

NOTES

1. Wordsworth, "To Toussaint L'Ouverture" (1802); Hugo, *Bug-Jargal* (1818); Kleist, *Die Verlobung in St. Domingo* (1811); Lamartine, *Toussaint Louverture* (1840); Whittier, "Toussaint L'Ouverture" (1833). On the origins of marvelous realism, see the prologue to Alejo Carpentier, *El reino de este mundo* (1949); and on Hegel, Susan Buck-Morss, "Hegel and Haiti," *Critical Inquiry* 26 (2000): 821–65.

2. Yves Bénot, *La Révolution française et la fin des colonies* (Paris: Editions La Découverte, 1989); Robin Blackburn, *The Overthrow of Colonial Slavery* (London: Verso, 1988), ch. 5 and 6.

3. I have seen no evidence to suggest the Haitian Revolution was invoked by leaders in the Malé Revolt (Bahia, 1835), as stated in Lester Langley, *The Americas in the Age of Revolution, 1750–1850* (New Haven, Conn.: Yale University Press, 1996), 141. Supposition rather than fact, moreover, appears to underlie the claims, found in Douglas Egerton, *Gabriel's Rebellion: The Virginia Slave Conspiracies of 1800 and 1802* (Chapel Hill: University of North Carolina Press, 1993), 45–48, 168–69, and Richard D. E. Burton, *Afro-Creole: Power, Opposition, and Play in the Caribbean* (Ithaca, N.Y.: Cornell University Press, 1997), 85, that Gabriel's Conspiracy and Jamaica's Christmas Rebellion were Haitian-inspired.

4. Eugene Genovese, *From Rebellion to Revolution: Afro-American Slave Revolts in the Making of the Modern World* (Baton Rouge: Louisiana State University Press, 1979); David Geggus, "Slavery, War, and Revolution in the Greater Caribbean, 1789–1815," in *A Turbulent Time: The French Revolution and the Greater Caribbean,* ed. D. B. Gaspar and D. P. Geggus, (Bloomington: Indiana University Press), 5–18; David Geggus, "The French and Haitian Revolutions and Resistance to Slavery in the Americas," *Revue Française d'Histoire d'Outre-Mer* 282–83 (1989): 107–124.

5. Eric Williams, *Capitalism and Slavery* (London: Andre Deutsch, 1964 [1944]), 206–208; Richard Hart, *Slaves Who Abolished Slavery* (Kingston: ISER, 1985); Mary Turner, "The Baptist War and Abolition," *Jamaican Historical Review* 13 (1982): 31–41; Seymour Drescher, *Capitalism and Antislavery: British Mobilization in Comparative Perspective* (New York: Oxford University Press, 1986), 108–9; Thomas C. Holt, *The Problem of Freedom: Race, Labor, and Politics in Jamaica and Britain, 1832–1938* (Baltimore: Johns Hopkins University Press, 1992), 17–21; above, note 3.

6. David Geggus, "The Influence of the Haitian Revolution on Blacks in Latin America and the Caribbean," forthcoming in *Blacks and National Identity in Nineteenth-Century Latin America,* ed. Nancy Naro (London: University of London).

7. Luiz Mott, "A revolução dos negros do Haiti e do Brasil," *Mensario do Arquivo Nacional* (Rio de Janeiro) 13 (1982): 3–10; Mimi B. Sheller, "Democracy After Slavery: Black Publics and Peasant Rebellion in Postemancipation Haiti and Jamaica" (Ph.D. diss., New School for Social Research, 1996); Ada Ferrer, *Insurgent Cuba: Race, Nation, and Revolution, 1868–1898* (Chapel Hill: University of North Carolina Press, 1999); Robert Paquette, *Sugar is Made With Blood: The Conspiracy of La Escalera and the Conflict Between Empires over Slavery in Cuba* (Middletown, Conn., 1988).

8. Thus the radical Robert Wedderburn, son of a Jamaican slave woman, warned in his London-based newspaper in 1817 that a black king could be as tyrannous as a white: Iain McCalman, ed., *The Horrors of Slavery and Other Writings by Robert Wedderburn* (Edinburgh: Edinburgh University Press, 1991), 87.

9. Sheller, "Democracy After Slavery," 26.

10. C. L. R. James, *The Black Jacobins: Toussaint L'Ouverture and the San Domingo Revolution* (New York: Vintage Books, 1963 [1938]), 214; David Patrick Geggus, *Slavery, War and Revolution: The British Occupation of Saint Domingue, 1793–1798* (Oxford: Clarendon

Press, 1982); Michael Duffy, *Soldiers, Sugar, and Seapower: The British Expeditions to the West Indies and the War against Revolutionary France* (Oxford: Clarendon Press, 1987).

11. Stuart B. Schwartz, *Sugar Plantations in the Formation of Brazilian Society: Bahia, 1550–1835* (Cambridge: Cambridge University Press, 1985), 423; Seymour Drescher, *Econocide: British Slavery in the Era of Abolition* (Pittsburgh: University of Pittsburgh Press, 1977), 76–91, 125; Francisco Pérez de la Riva, *El Café: Historia de su cultivo y explotación en Cuba* (Havana: Jesús Montero, 1944), 51.

12. David Eltis, *Economic Growth and the Ending of the Transatlantic Slave Trade* (New York: Oxford University Press, 1987), 37–39.

13. Gabino La Rosa Corzo, *Los palenques del Oriente de Cuba: resistencia y acoso* (Havana: Editorial Academia, 1991), 115–18.

14. Jane Landers, "Rebellion and Royalism in Spanish Florida: The French Revolution on Spain's Northern Colonial Frontier," in Gaspar and Geggus, *Turbulent Time,* 156–77. On other parts of this particular diaspora, see Jacques Houdaille, "Negros franceses en América Central a fines del siglo XVIII," *El Imparcial* (Guatemala) 13 Mar. 1954, p. 11; and Jorge Victoria Ojeda and Jorge Canto Alcocer, "Impulso y dispersión de los negros auxiliadores: El caso de San Fernando Aké, Yucatán," *Por Eso! Suplemento Cultural* (Mérida) 26 July 1998, p. 3–9.

15. Ferrer, *Insurgent Cuba,* 8, 94, 112; Christopher Schmidt-Nowara, *Empire and Antislavery: Spain, Cuba, and Puerto Rico, 1833–1874* (Pittsburgh: Pittsburgh University Press, 1999), 25.

16. Paul Verna, *Petión y Bolívar: Cuarenta años de relaciones haitiano-venezolanas* (Caracas: Oficina Central de Información, 1969), 87–298; Paquette, *Sugar is Made With Blood,* 171; Jaime E. Rodríguez O., *The Independence of Spanish America* (Cambridge: Cambridge University Press, 1998), 185–87.

CONTRIBUTORS

ROBERT ALDERSON, a Ph.D. candidate at the University of South Carolina, Columbia, is currently finishing his dissertation, "'This Bright Era of Happy Revolutions': Michel-Ange-Bernard de Mangourit in Charleston, S.C., 1792–1794."

ROBIN BLACKBURN is professor of social history in the Department of Sociology at the University of Essex, England. He is author of *The Overthrow of Colonial Slavery* (Verso, 1988) and *The Making of New World Slavery* (Verso, 1997).

OLWYN M. BLOUET teaches history at Virginia State University in Petersburg. She has published on Caribbean topics, and co-edited with her husband *Latin America and the Caribbean: A Systematic and Regional Survey,* 3rd ed. (John Wiley, 1997).

SUSAN BRANSON teaches American Women's History at the University of Texas at Dallas. She is author of a forthcoming book, *Gender, Politics, and American Culture in the Age of Revolution, 1775–1800* (University of Pennsylvania Press).

MATT D. CHILDS is assistant professor of history at Florida State University in Tallahassee. He has published in the *Journal of Latin American Studies, The Americas,* and *The Historian.* He has been awarded fellowships from the Conference of Latin American History, the Social Science Research Council, and the Fulbright-Hays Commission.

DAVID BRION DAVIS is Sterling Professor of History at Yale University and director of Yale's Gilder Lehrman Center for the Study of Slavery, Resistance, and Abolition. His books have won many awards including the Pulitzer Prize for nonfiction, the National Book Award for History and Biography, the American Historical Association's Beveridge Prize, and the Bancroft Prize. Professor Davis was also president of the Organization of American Historians and is a fellow of the British Academy, the American Philosophical Society, and the American Academy of Arts and Sciences.

SEYMOUR DRESCHER is University Professor of History and professor of sociology at the University of Pittsburgh. Among his works on slavery are *Econocide: British Slavery in the Era of Abolition* (1977), *Capitalism and Antislavery: British*

Mobilization in Comparative Perspective (1987), and *From Slavery to Freedom: Comparative Studies in the Rise and Fall of Atlantic Slavery* (1999). He is also co-editor (with Stanley Engerman) of *A Historical Guide to World Slavery* (Oxford University Press, 1998).

LAURENT DUBOIS is assistant professor of history at Michigan State University, where he teaches Early American History, Caribbean History, and Comparative Black History. In 1998 he published *Les Esclaves de la République* (Calmann-Lévy).

DAVID P. GEGGUS is professor of history at the University of Florida, Gainesville. He is the author of *Slavery, War and Revolution: The British Occupation of Saint Domingue, 1793–1798* (Oxford University Press, 1982), of more than seventy articles, and co-editor (with D. B. Gaspar) of *A Turbulent Time: The French Revolution and the Greater Caribbean* (Indiana University Press, 1997). His *Haitian Revolutionary Studies* (Indiana University Press) is forthcoming.

JUAN R. GONZÁLEZ MENDOZA is associate professor of history at Universidad Interamericana de Puerto Rico, San Germán Campus. He has published several articles on Puerto Rican demographic and social history in the late eighteenth and early nineteenth centuries. He was director-editor of *Revista/Review Interamericana* and is past president of the Associación Puertorriqueña de Historiadores and secretary-treasurer of the Association of Caribbean Historians, of which he was also vice president.

ALINE HELG is associate professor in the Department of History, University of Texas at Austin. She has published *Our Rightful Share: The Afro-Cuban Struggle for Equality, 1886–1912* (University of North Carolina Press, 1995), which won awards from the American Historical Association, the Association of Caribbean Historians, and the Caribbean Studies Association. She is also author of *Civilizing the People and Forming the Elite: Education in Colombia, 1918–1957* (1984, Spanish transl. 1987) and of several articles on comparative racial systems in the Americas, Cuba, and Colombia. She is currently working on *Liberty and Equality: Free People of Color, Elite Whites, and Slaves in Caribbean Colombia, 1770–1851*.

PAUL LACHANCE is a professor of history at the University of Ottawa. He has written chapters in scholarly works and published articles in *Plantation Society in the Americas, Histoire Sociale-Social History,* the *Revue d'Histoire de l'Amérique Française, Louisiana History, Social Science History,* and *Slavery & Abolition.*

MARIXA LASSO is completing a doctoral dissertation at the University of Florida on Black Republicanism in Caribbean Colombia, 1791–1830. She is the recipient of awards from the Tinker and Wenner-Gren Foundations and has authored several articles.

SIMON P. NEWMAN is a senior lecturer in history and director of the Andrew Hook Centre for American Studies, University of Glasgow, Scotland. He has taught at Northern Illinois University, and been a Mellon fellow in the humanities at the University of Pennsylvania. His most recent book is *Parades and the Pol-*

itics of the Street: Festive Culture in the Early American Republic (University of Pennsylvania Press, 1997).

LESLIE PATRICK is an associate professor of history at Bucknell University. She is working on a manuscript accounting for the origins of black imprisonment in the United States and editing the *Narrative of Patrick Lyon.*

KARIN SCHÜLLER is assistant professor of Iberian and Latin American History at the University of Cologne, Germany. Her publications include *Die deutsche Rezeption haitianischer Geschichte in der ersten Hälfte des 19. Jahrhunderts: Ein Beitrag zum deutschen Bild vom Schwarzen* (Böhlau, 1992).

Index